ONLINE WORLD LANGUAGE INSTRUCTION TRAINING AND ASSESSMENT

ONLINE WORLD LANGUAGE INSTRUCTION TRAINING AND ASSESSMENT

AN ECOLOGICAL APPROACH

Carmen King Ramírez,
Barbara A. Lafford,
and James E. Wermers

GEORGETOWN UNIVERSITY PRESS / WASHINGTON, DC

© 2021 Georgetown University Press. All rights reserved. No part of this book may be reproduced or utilized in any form or by any means, electronic or mechanical, including photocopying and recording, or by any information storage and retrieval system, without permission in writing from the publisher.

The publisher is not responsible for third-party websites or their content. URL links were active at time of publication.

Library of Congress Cataloging-in-Publication Data

Names: King Ramírez, Carmen, author. | Lafford, Barbara Armstrong, author. | Wermers, James E., author.
Title: Online world language instruction training and assessment : an ecological approach / Carmen King Ramírez, Barbara A. Lafford, James E. Wermers.
Description: Washington, DC : Georgetown University Press, 2021. | Includes bibliographical references.
Identifiers: LCCN 2020045980 (print) | LCCN 2020045981 (ebook) | ISBN 9781647121044 (hardcover) | ISBN 9781647121051 (paperback) | ISBN 9781647121068 (ebook)
Subjects: LCSH: Language and languages—Computer-assisted instruction. | Language and languages—Study and teaching—Computer-assisted instruction. | Language and languages—Study and teaching—Computer network resources. | Language teachers—Training of. | Language acquisition—Ability testing—Evaluation.
Classification: LCC P53.28 .K56 2021 (print) | LCC P53.28 (ebook) | DDC 418.0078/5—dc23
LC record available at https://lccn.loc.gov/2020045980
LC ebook record available at https://lccn.loc.gov/2020045981

22 21   9 8 7 6 5 4 3 2   First printing

Printed in the United States of America

Cover design by Trudi Gershenov
Interior design by BookComp, Inc.

*Para mis hijos, quienes le dan sentido a mi vida,
y mi esposo, cuyo apoyo es incondicional* —CKR

*To my husband, Peter A. Lafford,
for his constant support of my endeavors* —BAL

To my three Es with all my love —JEW

CONTENTS

List of Illustrations   ix

Acknowledgments   xi

Introduction: An Ecological Approach to Online Language Instructor Training and Assessment   1

1 The Challenges of Moving Online   9

2 CALL Teacher Education for Online Environments   21

3 Online Language Instructor Training Challenges and Strategies   45

4 Core Competencies for Online Language Instructors   71

5 Online Language Instructor Assessment   93

6 Instruments for the Assessment of Online Language Instructors   121

7 Self-Evaluation Practices in Formative Assessment   137

8 The Mentoring Relationship in Formative Assessment Processes   151

9 Debriefing and Goal Setting in Instructor Assessment   171

10 An Ecological Approach to the Normalization of a Critical CTE   187

Appendix A: Checklists for Online Language Instructor Training and Assessment   199

Appendix B: Rubrics for Evaluation of Online Language Instructor Training and Assessment   215

Appendix C: Online Language Instructor Performance Rubrics   233

Glossary   251

References   255

Index   287

About the Authors   297

Online resources related to book CTE/CALL Resources are available at www.press.georgetown.edu

ILLUSTRATIONS

FIGURES

3.1 The Online Teaching Evaluation Life Cycle   69
4.1 Technological Pedagogical Content Knowledge (TPACK)   74
5.1 Online Language Instructor Skills Pyramid   101
5.2 Reenvisioned Online Language Instructor Skills Pyramid   104
5.3 Proposed Framework for Online Language Teaching Skills   106
8.1 Stages of Instructor Development: Critical Reflection   157
10.1 Modified Version of Palloff and Pratt's Model for "Best System" for Professional Development of Online Instructors   193

TABLES

4.1 Technical and Pedagogical Knowledge and Skills   75
9.1 Stages and Strategies for Debriefing Conferences   173

ACKNOWLEDGMENTS

We want to express our appreciation to the following Languages and Cultures faculty (College of Integrative Sciences and Arts, Arizona State University) for their input into the OLIMR rubric and the online instructor evaluation process: Margarita Ballentine, Eduardo Caro, Lorena Cuya Gavilano, Olivia Elias Nichols, Andrés Jiménez Rodríguez, Bélgica Quirós-Winemiller, Michelle Petersen, and Olga Sigüenza-Ponce.

Our sincerest thanks to the language faculty who have helped to grow and support the University of Arizona online Spanish program, especially Adriana Betancur, Heidi Coronado, and Brenda Lara. We also acknowledge and appreciate the instructors and mentors from the Department of Spanish and Portuguese (College of Humanities, University of Arizona) who provided insights into their mentoring experiences in chapters 8 and 9 of this volume.

Our sincerest thanks go to Hope LeGro and Elizabeth Crowley Webber (Georgetown University Press) for patience and guidance during various phases of this book project. Much appreciation also goes to Gail Grella, former acquisitions editor at Georgetown, for her encouragement and support on prior book projects.

We also owe a debt of gratitude to Peter A. Lafford for his help with manuscript mechanics and the re-creation of figures and tables.

Introduction

An Ecological Approach to Online Language Instructor Training and Assessment

The following quote from Charles Dickens's introduction to his *A Tale of Two Cities* perfectly captures the ethos of what educational institutions and our global society as a whole have been experiencing since the spring of 2020: "It was the best of times, it was the worst of times, it was the age of wisdom, it was the age of foolishness, it was the epoch of belief, it was the epoch of incredulity, it was the season of light, it was the season of darkness, it was the spring of hope, it was the winter of despair" (1859/1999, 1). Not so long ago our classrooms were filled with students, our professional conferences overflowed with academics networking to find partners for new research endeavors or to find new teaching and research positions in academe, and the simple act of attending a movie or other social gatherings was not considered a life-threatening challenge.

Indeed, we are in the throes of the coronavirus pandemic and its aftermath, a crisis that has called for us to cover our faces, distance ourselves from friends and family, and reconceive education as we know it. In addition, newly imposed travel restrictions pose a real challenge to institutions in their ability to meet the needs of students from various countries who have relied upon international education opportunities to develop their professional skills (Fischer 2020). We dare say not even Thomas Kuhn (1962) could have predicted the enormity of the challenges that this particular paradigm shift would impose on the educational systems we have used in the past to prepare our youth for confronting the future demands of society—which now seem ill-defined and uncertain. Almost overnight, educational institutions had to switch their face-to-face (F2F) instruction into digital pedagogical spaces, the affordances and constraints of which may have been completely unknown to many instructors forced to make this shift.

Although this sudden move to online education could be disturbing for traditional teachers of any discipline, it poses unique challenges for instructors of second languages, who need to ensure that their students have enough interaction with other students, the professor, and native speakers of the target language to build their cognitive structures of knowledge of the target world language (WL) and culture and to develop their psychomotor language-production skills for the purpose of communicating their ideas to other speakers of that language. For many decades language professionals have called on technological resources to aid in this process, from reel-to-reel tape recorders, cassette tapes, video resources, and CDs and DVDs to computer-assisted language learning (CALL) and the use of internet resources and social media to provide authentic input and learner interaction. Thus, in order for instructors to take advantage of current technological affordances to teach languages, theoretically and empirically grounded CALL teacher education (CTE) training is needed to help language instructors develop the skills they need to teach with technology effectively in online environments (Healey et al. 2011; Hubbard and Levy 2006b; Kessler and Hubbard 2017). Moreover, in the spirit of being good *for something* instead of just being good *at something*, we need to develop online content that addresses the issues of unequal access to technology and other resources across demographic groups and the social justice challenges that our society faces. We also need to create equitable assessment paradigms to measure the progress of online language instructors from diverse backgrounds toward their acquisition of online teaching skills.

To that end, this volume provides a critical pedagogical approach to CTE training and assessment of online language instructors. We do this by providing an overview of CTE training and assessment in the field of CALL teacher education for online language teaching, proposing new solutions to training challenges, and creating new rubrics that can be used by various stakeholders to fairly assess online language instructor skills, the training they receive, the assessment process they undergo, and the instruments used for instructor assessment. In the process, it is hoped that as we journey from F2F instruction to teaching in digital environments, we can be inspired by the Dickens quote to orient ourselves toward making the best of our "worst of times," creating groups of educators who use wisdom to confront uninformed foolish online pedagogical practices and online teacher training programs thrown together in haste, making believers of incredulous colleagues, shining a light on the new pedagogical practices to bring us together (virtually), to wake us from the darkness of our social isolation, and, in our despair, to use a critical pedagogy to rekindle our hope in human ingenuity and our ability to remake ourselves, improve our world, and adapt our educational systems to our ever-changing circumstances.

THE MOVE TO ONLINE LANGUAGE EDUCATION

Even before the current crisis, educators had been gradually moving into online teaching spaces. In fact, the *Faculty Survey of Student Engagement* reported that 15 percent of faculty teaching lower-division courses and 22 percent of faculty teaching upper-division courses in the United States impart their classes partly or exclusively online (NSSE Institute 2019). However, this also means that the vast majority of faculty do not regularly teach in online formats, which can prove to be a great challenge when an institution is forced to suddenly move most or all of its teaching to digital formats. Audrey Williams June (2020) notes that a sudden move to online teaching environments is also complicated by the fact that most students strongly prefer taking all or at least some classes in person and that "federal data show that most students at public and private nonprofit colleges aren't enrolled in any distance-education courses at all" (11). She also notes that even with smartphones and laptops, students may not have access to reliable technologies that hold a charge, sufficient and affordable cell phone data plans, or reliable internet access off campus.

Another major obstacle to the move to online instruction is created when F2F faculty resist the move to digital teaching spaces. Faculty who have developed their own established F2F teaching styles and competencies over time may feel that their identity, experience, and worth are threatened by having to completely rethink their pedagogical practices. Thus, a major element of this paradigmatic shift to online teaching spaces is the need to develop strategies in CTE training and assessment to help current faculty feel valued and be willing to embrace this change. In order to set the stage for the rest of this monograph, below we address issues related to the reasons that language teachers should embrace technology, the integration of CALL into the language curriculum, and the need to use an ecological framework to create a reiterative cycle of training them to teach online and assessing their performance.

THE NEED TO EMBRACE CALL/ONLINE TECHNOLOGIES

In Claire Kramsch's (2013) foreword to Robert Blake's second edition of his book *Brave New Digital Classroom: Technology and Foreign Language Learning*, she outlines reasons that language instructors need to embrace the affordances of technological tools and integrate their use into their teaching: "Either teachers embrace the new language learning technologies and integrate them in a new pedagogy or they will not only deprive themselves of the enormous benefits afford by CALL, CMC [computer-mediated communication], distance learning, social networking, and language games, but they will be increasingly out of touch with their own students, who are by now wired, networked, and computer savvy" (xi). Mark Warschauer (2002a) echoes this view in his assertion that the computer is now an essential tool to assist the language learning process, not an optional one.

Robert Blake and Gabriel Guillén (2020) also note that CALL technologies can help teachers and their students to develop six inherent qualities that all humans possess and that help maximize human communicative potential: "We are (1) speakers of tongues, *homo loquens*; (2) both conscious and intuitive analyzers, *homo analyticus*; (3) social beings, *homo socius*; (4) tool users, *homo faber*; (5) game players, *homo ludens*; and, above all else, (6) storytellers, *homo fabulans*" (1). The affordances of CALL technologies, which can be enhanced in online environments, can help maximize the maturation of these human traits and facilitate teachers' and students' professional and personal development. Thus, CALL can help develop all of these facets of human socialization and communication; in other words, it can help make us more human—especially in an age where human contact has been reduced to viewing others within the confines of computer screens within digital spaces. The ability of CTE training and assessment to help develop these human traits is acknowledged throughout the volume.

In addition to helping us become more human, CALL technologies can also support language pedagogy in online learning environments in very specific ways. According to Steve Thorne and Bryan Smith (2011), these technologies increase access to oral and written input in the target language (e.g., internet sites with authentic discourse), broaden opportunities for personal expression with Web 2.0 technologies (e.g., blogs, wikis), extend opportunities for synchronous and asynchronous interaction (e.g., discussion boards, audio and video conferencing), and make use of new platforms for community building through mobile-assisted language learning (MALL) technologies (e.g., phones, tablets) and social networking (e.g., Facebook, Twitter).

THE INTEGRATION OF CALL TECHNOLOGIES FOR ONLINE LANGUAGE TEACHING

In order for students to benefit from the affordances of CALL technologies, online language instructors need to be trained how to integrate them into language learning curricula in a pedagogically sound manner. Kwang Hee Hong (2010) considers that instructor training in this type of integration should be "the ultimate goal of CALL teacher education" (53). The current volume focuses on the creation of quality CALL teacher education programs and assessment instruments to measure the success of the online instructor's integration of technology into their curricula.

In spite of the benefits of language technology integration, several factors influence the extent to which this integration of CALL technologies takes place; these factors can be socioeconomic, geopolitical, institutional, linguistic, logistic and contextual, and human in nature (Torsani 2016). These factors are discussed throughout the volume and are related to issues of the *normalization* of this integration, discussed extensively in chapter 10. As mentioned earlier, one of the most significant barriers to the integration of CALL technologies (especially for the purpose of teaching online) is instructor resistance to changes that would put their established reputations as quality language teachers in doubt. Thus, Levy and Stockwell (2006) note that true integration of CALL into language curricula calls for an ecological change that would require a seismic paradigmatic shift in departmental cultural values and practices, which would necessitate the rethinking of the social contract between faculty and students (Torsani 2016). This paradigmatic shift would also be reflected in the establishment of a continuous cycle of training and evaluation for language instructors who teach online (Tobin, Mandernach, and Taylor 2015), as envisioned in an ecological approach to CTE.

AN ECOLOGICAL VIEW OF CTE ONLINE TRAINING AND ASSESSMENT CYCLE

In her introduction to the 2009 *Modern Language Journal* Focus Issue, Barbara Lafford supports an ecological approach to the study of CALL in which the study of the uses of technologies for language learning would be understood within the particular rhetorical and physical environments in which they were implemented (Van Lier 2004). Such an approach (with tenets similar to those found in sociocultural theoretical frameworks [Lantolf 2000; Vygotsky 1978]) would focus on the following: the study of language use in its social context, an *-emic* analytical approach in which individual differences and views are recognized and respected, the effects of socialization on language learning and building community, recognition and utilization of the affordances of the environment in which the participants operate, the co-construction of meaning that is contingent and dynamic and sensitive to contextual issues, the construction of tasks with ecological validity, and a critical, interventionist view of the role of language educators in working toward a better society for all its members. Throughout this volume, we discuss the need to apply these principles to the tailoring of online language instructor training programs and assessment instruments in order to effect fair and equitable training and evaluation procedures for faculty moving into digital pedagogical spaces. We also discuss the implications of an ecological approach for promoting a critical pedagogy to foster instructor and student social engagement with members of diverse linguistic and cultural communities in order to work with them to address the challenges they face.

VOLUME OVERVIEW

The chapters in this volume explore the use of an ecological approach to CTE in order to ensure appropriate, fair, and equitable trainings and assessments of a diverse group of online language faculty:

- Chapter 1 articulates the significant differences between F2F and online teaching environments and explores the need to more intentionally train and assess faculty for both the transition to online teaching and the critical pedagogy challenges that attend it.
- Chapter 2 provides an overview of CTE literature on current training for online language teaching, the inadequacies of that training, and alternatives to that formal training. A checklist of essential elements for online language instructor training is provided in appendix A-1.
- Chapter 3 uses the investment model proposed by Anthony Muhammad and Luis F. Cruz (2019) to propose strategies to address CTE training challenges and focuses on the cognitive, emotional, and functional investments that administrators need to make in order to ensure quality CTE training for online language instructors. A checklist summarizing these challenges and strategies to address them is found in appendix A-2.
- Chapter 4 draws on the CTE literature to identify the essential core competencies needed by online language instructors. A checklist of these skills is provided in appendix A-3.
- Chapter 5 discusses current assessment frameworks in the CTE literature used to evaluate online language instructor skills, the inadequacies of those frameworks, and the need for new flexible and equitable modular instruments to evaluate instructor performance.
- Chapter 6 discusses rubrics used to assess the performance of online language instructors by students, supervisors, and departmental administrators. Samples of such instructor assessment instruments are

provided in appendix C-1 through C-4. As the results of these instructor evaluations should be triangulated with other stakeholder assessments of the effectiveness of the online instructor training, the instructor assessment process, and the rubrics used to evaluate instructors, sample instruments to assess those elements are provided in appendixes B-1 through B-3.

In addition to appropriate online language instructor training and assessment, we also look at mentoring, a process that facilitates the transition of faculty from trainees into self-directed online learners and teachers. Chapters 7, 8, and 9 describe aspects of this intensive mentoring process and use case study data to illustrate instructor and mentor reactions to the process itself:

- Chapter 7 provides an overview of relevant literature regarding self-assessment and discusses how supervisors can encourage instructors to reflect on their performance. The chapter concludes with a case study that was carried out among language instructors who participated in a formative assessment process based on the Online Language Instructor Modular Rubric (OLIMR) rubric outlined in chapter 6. A set of sample online instructor self-assessment reflection questions is found in appendix C-5.
- Chapter 8 explores the role of mentorship throughout the formative assessment process. Attention is given to peer mentorship versus supervisor oversight. The chapter presents a case study that explores new online language instructors' experiences with a peer mentorship process piloted at their university.
- Chapter 9 outlines best practices for postevaluation debriefing sessions between supervisors and instructors. Special attention is given to how cultural differences can influence the feedback and goal-setting activities. The chapter concludes with a case study that provides examples of online language instructors' perceptions of a debriefing session in which they participated as well as examples of the goals that they set for themselves.
- Chapter 10 discusses issues of the normalization of a Critical CALL approach to ensure appropriate online language instructor training and assessment within an ecological framework and proposes future research on these topics.

Special features of this volume include an appendix with checklists of elements and strategies used to create training programs and identify instructor skills as well as examples of new rubrics for various stakeholders to evaluate online language instructor performance, training, the assessment process, and the rubrics used to evaluate faculty. In addition, the materials that accompany this volume on the publisher's website (found at www.press.georgetown.edu) contain a list of CTE/CALL resources and videos that illustrate the application of the OLIMR instructor evaluation rubric and the assessment process.

In sum, this volume views the move from F2F to online language teaching as an ecological paradigm shift that requires rethinking teaching practices, making strategic investments in CALL/Online teacher training, implementing a critical approach to best practices in teacher training and mentoring to acquire essential online teaching skills, equitably assessing the attainment of those skills within a given institutional context, and recognizing training and assessment as two interrelated processes that require investments by administrators and mentors to ensure instructor sustained success. Although the volume is focused on training faculty to teach languages online, many of the elements and strategies proposed for online instructor training and assessment could also be applied to the professional development of faculty from a variety of disciplines who are moving into digital pedagogical spaces.

1

The Challenges of Moving Online

Online teaching and learning have played an increasingly important role in colleges and universities in recent years. Where online teaching and learning were once the exception to the rule in a landscape dominated by F2F classes, it is more and more common for students and teachers to move into online pedagogical spaces. Furthermore, while the movement online has been under way for quite some time, the COVID-19 pandemic has forced change to happen at a much quicker pace since the first half of 2020. During the past year online teaching and learning became, at least for a time, the primary way in which we teach and learn. While the near universal use of online education may well change as F2F classes resume at institutions of higher learning around the world, it seems clear that online learning will continue to play an essential role moving forward (Alexander 2020; Gardner 2020).

This recent explosion in online teaching and learning has presented numerous challenges, many of them unarticulated, to students, faculty, and administrators. F2F learning has been the primary modus operandi of the vast majority of teachers and learners alike. Learning has tended to happen in physical classrooms, in churches, and around kitchen tables far more often than in digital spaces. While engaging in online environments now is a part of everyday life for many, this does not mean that we are prepared to engage in the complexities of online learning. In this chapter, we begin to unpack what moving education online really means and why the shift from F2F to online learning is one that requires that we think very carefully about teaching and learning and, more pointedly, why it means that we might need to rethink how we evaluate online teaching and learning. Although the rest of this volume focuses on the training and evaluation of online language teachers, this opening chapter explores the ecological shift from physical to digital spaces that faculty in all disciplines are now facing.

THE ECOLOGICAL SHIFT FROM PHYSICAL TO DIGITAL SPACES

The movement from physical to digital teaching contexts requires a major expansion of our understanding of the behavioral norms, cultural values, and the types of spaces that can characterize a "teaching/learning environment" and that can underlie two very different pedagogical ecologies. In order to appreciate just how different online education is from the kinds of F2F teaching and learning that have been going on in higher education for more than a century, it is helpful to briefly consider how and why online education became so important in higher education. These reasons range from increased technological possibilities, to financial pressures facing universities who do not have the resources to build more brick-and-mortar structures, to the desire to reach more students (Turoff 2006). The 2019 survey of faculty attitudes toward technology jointly conducted by Inside Higher Ed and Gallup revealed that "a new high of 46 percent of faculty members, up from 39 percent in 2016 and 30 percent in 2013" reported they had taught a credit-bearing online course at some point in their career (Jaschik and Lederman 2019, 7). Furthermore, a 2018 report by the National Center for Education Statistics (NCES 2018) revealed that, despite recent decreases in overall student enrollment at universities in the United States, there has been a steady increase in the number of students taking online classes, with only 15.6 percent of postsecondary students engaging in any kind of distance or online learning in 2003 and 43.1 percent taking such courses in 2016. This growth in online teaching and learning is both rich with possibilities and challenges.

The consistent growth in online learning in recent years has disrupted education in significant, if sometimes underappreciated, ways. Online teaching and learning have become increasingly ubiquitous as the twenty-first century unfolds, but the foundations of online learning can be traced back as far as the development of text-based correspondence learning in the nineteenth century (Kentnor 2015). Written correspondence courses eventually gave way to new methods of distance learning with the rise of televisual technologies in the middle of the twentieth century (Perry and Pilati 2011) that allowed for courses to be delivered to students' homes. Then, starting in the mid-1990s, the development of internet-based distance education led educators and learners to Web-based technologies. Moreover, in the last two decades, the rise in the public use of digital platforms like social media and learning management systems have offered further opportunities for expanding (and complicating) online learning.

Despite seemingly constant growth and change in distance education, there has not always been a demonstrated interest in exploring in depth the ways in which these changes might, or should, affect pedagogy (Conover and Miller 2014; Major 2015; Montelongo 2019; Montelongo and Eaton 2019; Westbrook 2014). Many early conversations about online learning failed to recognize the unique pedagogical demands of online classes and seemingly assumed that the pedagogical practices of the traditional brick-and-mortar classroom could simply be moved into online spaces (Kentnor 2015). Faculty who had been trained to teach in F2F environments and who had themselves grown up as students in those physical educational environments tended to operate on the belief that they could reproduce what they were already doing in their F2F classes, making small tweaks where necessary.

This ethos of simply moving F2F courses and practices into online spaces, sometimes referred to as "porting," might at first appear to make some sense. On the surface, online teaching and learning might not seem all that different from the kinds of teaching and learning we have done in brick-and-mortar classrooms for at least a century. We are, after all, teaching in the same disciplines and covering much of the same material that we always have. There are, to be sure, some similarities between F2F and online education. Ideally, in both platforms, students and teachers work together toward educational ends that include passing on information, challenging assumptions, developing new knowledge, and eliciting teacher-student and student-student interaction. Also, in both F2F classrooms and online education, such ends are approached through a combination of reading, lectures, discussions, and the submission and assessment of assignments. However, when we look a little bit closer, these similarities end up being only superficial, and there are, in fact, significant differences between F2F and online education.

One way to think about the differences between the F2F and online modalities is to compare them to the differences between American football and *fútbol* (soccer). To the casual observer, football and *fútbol* might appear quite similar. Both games involve two teams of eleven players each pitted against one another and attempting to move a ball toward a goal at either end of a large, lined grass pitch. However, any fan of football or *fútbol* is likely to tell you that despite the similar sounding names and seeming commonalities, the two games are ecologically quite different. Football is a sport of stops and starts, of quick and explosive bursts of energy punctuating relatively long periods of inactivity. *Fútbol*, on the other hand, is a flowing and continuous game of endurance. The unique nature of each of these sports also means that athletes with different kinds of characteristics are required to build effective football and *fútbol* teams. A three-hundred-pound lineman might be essential in the violent starts and stops of football, but they would be significantly less so in a game that required them to run thirteen miles in a single outing. Likewise, the endurance athletes that excel in *fútbol* might find themselves badly out of place in a game that required bulk and mass to slow movement at a point of attack.

As with football and *fútbol*, the apparent similarities between online and face-to-face learning are often superficial. While we are ostensibly teaching the same content in the way that both football and *fútbol* see eleven-person teams moving with purpose toward an opponents' goal, online and F2F teaching actually require very different skill sets and, often, very different teachers as the practices and skills that make a teacher excel in one modality are often a liability in the other. In turn, this means that the skills and tools we have developed for evaluating teaching need to be updated to reflect the significant differences between F2F and online teaching and learning. Many instructional strategies that worked in the past likely will not work now, so the tools we used in the past to assess our accomplishments need to change as well.

Some examples to illustrate the difference in skills needed to teach in F2F and online contexts are in order. Perhaps the clearest example of the gap between F2F and online teaching is how one cultivates a teaching style and persona. It is not uncommon to see faculty who learned through F2F methods and who became themselves practiced and accomplished teachers in physical classroom environments almost naturally employ a wide array of behaviors that correspond to successful F2F teaching. Experienced faculty often know how to make use of the physical space of the classroom to craft and break down barriers. They understand how to modulate their voices for dramatic effect, how to read curiosity and confusion on students faces, and more. These are skills, some of them so subtle as to be almost imperceptible and immeasurable, that are cultivated over a lifetime. They are also skills that likely do not transfer effectively to online learning—that is, learning that takes place in digital spaces and through technologies that can confound even the most seasoned F2F teacher.

It is not only teaching styles that may not easily translate into online spaces from F2F spaces—assessment has to be rethought as well. This includes both the kinds of work that students are assigned and the various modes of feedback provided by faculty in response to that work. We likely all either teach or know faculty who teach online classes that employ many of the same quizzes, writing assignments, and projects that one might find in an F2F class. It is also not uncommon to see faculty employ things like cameras and LockDown Browsers, Web browsers that seek to limit student Web use during a given online course activity. While rarely articulated this way, the logic at work here seems to be that whatever differences exist between online and F2F courses do not necessitate that we recreate our assignments to take advantage of the affordances of new digital spaces. This logic also seems to extend to the manner in which feedback is provided on student work in online classes, with many faculty opting to provide the same kind of written (or typed) feedback that they had been providing in F2F classes instead of taking advantage of feedback digital channels with more teacher presence (e.g., audio or video commentary).

In part, the failure to make the necessary adjustments for the new realities of an online world stems from faculty resistance to online learning. As Robert Ubell (2017) notes, there are a number of factors that lead to faculty resistance to teaching online, including concerns about efficacy, autonomy, and recognition. Such concerns are well captured in the 2019 Inside Higher Ed survey (Jaschik and Lederman 2019) on faculty attitudes toward technology. This survey reveals a common opinion among faculty that online learning is necessarily inferior to face-to-face learning. Only 33 percent faculty surveyed agreed that "for-credit online courses can achieve student learning outcomes equivalent to those of in-person courses" (25). Absent a belief in the efficacy of online learning and its value for students, it makes sense that faculty might be reticent to invest significant time and energy in developing the necessary skill sets to make a change from what they have always done. The same survey also shows skepticism among faculty that the move online will benefit students financially, a key argument of many administrators, with only 37 percent of faculty agreeing that online education is likely to lower the cost of education for students moving forward. There are also persistent concerns about labor in online spaces. Faculty have expressed concerns about how their labor is valued and supported. Only 36 percent of faculty believe their intellectual property is adequately protected when it comes to digital work, and only 35 percent of faculty agree that they are fairly compensated for such work. Further, only 25 percent of faculty believe that administrators fully understand the demands of teaching online, and only 22 percent believe there are appropriate awards in place for contributions to digital pedagogy. Given both the complexity of the move online and faculty perceptions about doing so, it is perhaps unsurprising that we find ourselves in the midst of a major ongoing pedagogical challenge that we are not yet taking the necessary steps to overcome.

In sum, it has become increasingly clear in recent years that online teaching requires that we rethink staid assumptions and practices related to online learners, instructors, and content development (Kebritchi, Lipschuetz, and Santiague 2017; Major 2015). We can see this more clearly if we take a moment to tease out the teaching and assessment issues discussed above. If we are to train instructors in best pedagogical practice, we need to evaluate skills necessary for their success in whatever teaching environment they inhabit.

TRAINING FOR ONLINE INSTRUCTORS

Critics and practitioners have become more and more aware that teaching and learning in online environments are markedly different than they are in F2F environments, and there has been a growing push to begin to think in more robust ways about how we might prepare teachers to meet the challenge. While in the earliest years of online teaching there was little and often no support for teachers moving from F2F to digital environments, there is now a growing body of research on best practices for teaching in this new pedagogical context (Kentnor 2015; Major 2015; Montelongo and Eaton 2019). While there are a variety of online teacher-training programs ranging from preservice programs, to online webinars, to asynchronous online courses, there is a coalescing conversation about what the best of those include. While a more in-depth look at online teacher training in language-learning environments is taken up in chapters 2 and 3, here it is useful to look more broadly at trends in online training and assessment across disciplines.

Rena Palloff and Keith Pratt (2011) have developed an excellent framework for understanding what quality online instruction looks like and for thinking about what training looks like for instructors who need to learn to teach in digital spaces. Building on a body of critical work focused on online instruction (Chickering and Gamson 1987; Graham et al. 2001; Palloff and Pratt 2011; Weimer 2002), Palloff and Pratt (2011) argue that the excellent online instructor is one who

> understands the differences between face-to-face and online teaching... is committed to [online teaching]... is able to establish presence early in the course and encourages students to do the same... is highly motivated and in turn is a good motivator for students... [and] understands the importance of community building and devotes time at the start of the class to this function. (13)

Some of the characteristics listed above undoubtedly overlap with those of the excellent F2F instructor. For example, an instructor's motivation and their ability to motivate students are essential in any learning environment. However, the bulk of what Palloff and Pratt identify here are characteristics that are unique to the challenges of the online environment.

More recently, Florence Martin, Kiran Budhrani, Swapna Kumar, and Albert Ritzhaupt (2019) have identified five different roles that they see as being occupied by the excellent online instructor: facilitator, course designer, content manager, subject matter expert, and mentor. As in Palloff and Pratt's (2011) model, the competencies of an excellent online instructor identified by Martin and colleagues are very often unique to the online teaching environment. The extent to which the excellent online teacher must have a unique set of carefully cultivated characteristics not necessarily present in the excellent F2F instructor has been echoed by numerous other scholars (Chatham-Carpenter and Spadaro 2019; Major 2015; Montelongo 2019; Morris 2018; Shackelford and Maxwell 2012). This has led to a consensus that focused training is required to aid faculty striving for excellence in online environments.

Extant forms of training for online teachers take a variety of forms including, but certainly not limited to, preservice trainings, massive open online courses (MOOCs), focused online modules, and even fully online classes (see chapter 2 for more details on online training formats). At present, there is no systematic or codified standard for how to best train online faculty (McGee, Windes, and Torres 2017). However, it is clear that any quality online training must begin with a frank assessment of the extant competencies of a given faculty member (a needs assessment). While we may live in a world immersed in digital technologies, this does not mean that all, most, or even many faculty will be prepared to immediately and effectively make the move to online teaching. This is particularly important to bear in mind in the present pandemic moment where exigency has forced many faculty to teach online, whether they were prepared to or not.

As Palloff and Pratt (2011) note, the cultivation of the skills and traits required for excellent online teaching can take a number of years and can be productively imagined as proceeding in phases. Many, if not most, faculty make their first moves toward online teaching through the use of some limited deployment of online tools in an F2F classroom (e.g., learning management systems). These faculty members, whom Palloff and Pratt label "visitors," are just beginning down a long path toward the cultivation of skills and traits that will make them excellent online educators. From here, faculty can, with guidance and support, develop the skill sets that enable them to become what Palloff and Pratt label "novices," "apprentices," "insiders," and eventually "masters."

Movement from "visitor" to "master" is not something that happens accidentally; it is the result of effective training programs that clearly understand how complex such progress is. Here again, Palloff and Pratt (2011) provide a valuable framework. Drawing on Caffarella (2002), Palloff and Pratt identify a handful of key elements of effective online training:

- Don't use cookie-cutter approaches.
- Use approaches based on adult learning theory.
- Honor experience!
- Model best practices.
- Incorporate cycles of learning, do, and reflect into training. (43–44)

The focus here on adult learners and honoring experience are particularly important, as faculty resistance can play a central role in challenging the training of online teachers (see chapter 3). It is important to bear in mind that many teachers making the transition to online spaces are master practitioners in the F2F context, and this can help to incubate resistance to embracing new pedagogical contexts in which that sense mastery is challenged (Ubell 2017).

Embracing an adult learner-focused understanding of online training and preparing for inevitable resistance means crafting training programs that draw upon and promote both intrinsic and extrinsic motivations. This is best accomplished through a phased approach to online teacher training and the creation of communities of teacher-learners, also known as communities of practice (Lave and Wenger 1991; Palloff and Pratt 2011). As Palloff and Pratt (2011) note, in a phased approach, a teacher can gradually move from a learner role, to an adopter role, to a co-learner role, to a reaffirmed or rejector role, and finally to a leadership role. Respecting this progression, which builds on the movement from "visitor" to "master," takes a great deal of time and cost, requiring appropriate investments, something to which we return later. Participating in communities of practice allows faculty to develop their skills among supportive colleagues who share their passion (Wenger, McDermott, and Snyder 2002).

EVALUATION OF ONLINE INSTRUCTORS

Together with the need to deploy effective training for online teachers is the need to develop an effective evaluation protocol and appropriate rubrics for assessing their performance. While general online teacher training and, to a lesser extent, evaluation have received growing critical attention in recent years, less attention has been paid to issues related to training faculty to teach online and to evaluating faculty teaching in digital environments (Downing and Dyment 2013; Wolf 2006). Thus, despite the growing recognition of the fact that teaching and learning online require us to rethink our beliefs and practices, we have not yet connected this with an implementation of significant changes in our training and assessment practices. This will be an essential next step if we are to effectively develop online teaching and learning to reach its potential. Further, as the recent crisis in education caused by the COVID-19 pandemic has made clear, online teacher training needs to move from considering online teaching skills to be elective enhancements toward that of requiring basic online teaching competency from all teachers.

It is standard practice at institutions of higher learning to evaluate faculty through a number of mechanisms, including, but not limited to, student evaluations, peer and supervisor observations, and various kinds of administrative oversight. However, despite the significant differences between F2F and online instruction, it is still a common practice to employ the same evaluation tools and rubrics for online and F2F courses (Tobin, Mandernach, and Taylor 2015). Furthermore, as Thomas Tobin, B. Jean Mandernach, and Ann Taylor observe, even when there are tools and rubrics that are designed specifically for online learning, evaluating faculty who are teaching online still often falls on faculty and administrators without significant online teaching experiences themselves. Finally, as has become clear with the hasty transition to online classes at many institutions in the face of the COVID-19 pandemic, there is often simply insufficient time or incentive to develop evaluations specific to the online environment.

The lack of evaluations specifically designed for online teaching is a major issue on at least two fronts. The use of F2F evaluations for online teaching leads to something of an apples-to-oranges comparison. The differences between face-to-face and online learning explored earlier in this chapter should make it clear that the ways in which teachers engage students online are—and should be—radically different than the ways teachers engage students in F2F classrooms. The lack of evaluations specific to online teaching and evaluators experienced in online education means that online teachers may in effect be punished for not using, or even being able to use, practices that work in F2F classrooms. This means that online teachers might be effectively penalized for employing practices that are different than their F2F peers but that are more appropriate for online environments. For example, faculty who move away from or significantly modify traditional summative assessments like quizzes and tests run the risk of being deemed less rigorous than their peers. It is also the case that many aspects of excellent online teaching might not be recognized, as F2F evaluation rubrics may well miss key things going on in the online classroom. For example, faculty efforts to be present in the digital classroom through a variety of planned and just-in-time teaching moves are unlikely to be captured. In short, while there is some progress being made in terms of why and how to evaluate online teaching, there are nonetheless persistent issues.

CRITICAL PEDAGOGY

Part of the needed expansion on best practices in teacher training and assessment includes the dire need for more research that explores the extent to which online pedagogy is often, and wrongly, imagined as a space uninfluenced by issues of race and gender (Killion, Gallagher-Lepak, and Reilly 2015). There is a well-established and decades-old body of scholarship on critical pedagogies rooted in the work of luminaries like Henry Giroux (2011), bell hooks (1994), and Ira Shor (2012, 2014) that interrogates questions of race, gender, and justice in education writ large and with a tacit focus on F2F instruction. There is also some good research that explores the extent to which online learning systems and even the internet itself are marked and marred by inequities and have been this way from their very beginnings (Daniels 2015; Nakamura and Chow-White 2012; Wong 2007). However, there is not yet a sufficient body of literature that brings these two conversations together. While, according to Ricardo Montelongo (2019), "an increasing group of online educators recognizes the importance of developing a critical online pedagogy to reassess how online education questions equity, social justice, and transformative learning experiences in virtual learning space" (68), such voices remain in the minority.

Numerous scholars have pointed out that race and gender can be significant factors in education, and for a variety of reasons. Some have observed that students' perceptions of teachers and teacher effectiveness, as well as teachers' perceptions of students, are highly correlated with race and gender (Cherng and Halpin 2016; Downey and Pribesh 2004). Others have pointed out the need for teachers to think about their own racial identity and the racial makeup of their students if they want to be effective in the classroom (Emdin 2016). Still others have explored how understanding the racial dynamics of the classroom can provide new and engaging pedagogical pathways that might not otherwise exist (Gay 2018).

Despite the rhetoric that abounds about the potential for Web-based technologies at the heart of online learning to be a great equalizer, the available evidence suggests that this is not the case (Daniels 2015). Access to digital classrooms is deeply unequal when examined across racial lines, and students of color are less likely to have consistent and high-speed internet access, making it more difficult for them to engage with online learning (Killion,

Gallagher-Lepak, and Reilly 2015). Further, some critics have argued that the very technologies we use are embedded in structures of racial inequity (Daniels 2015). Persistent stereotypes that see people of color as necessarily less adept on a variety of fronts when compared to their white peers, an issue compounded for women of color who face a double issue on this front, also mean that many educators find themselves negatively impacted by these characterizations (Alexander 2018; Brown, Cevero, and Johnson-Bailey 2000). Finally, the failure to recognize the important roles played by race and gender in digital spaces means that educators often fail to develop pedagogical practices that can both embrace and overcome potential challenges.

These things have the potential to present serious challenges to students and educators alike. There have long been gaps in access and achievement across racial lines in education. If we move into online spaces without a clear understanding of those gaps and how they can be perpetuated or even exacerbated in digital contexts, we run the very real risk of doing immense harm where we intend to do good. Further, given that we know that faculty of color face an uphill battle when it comes to evaluation processes, we must also be cognizant of this reality. Both training and evaluation of online teachers must take into account the need to develop practices to engage students across the demographic spectrum while at the same time understanding that students' and administrators' perceptions of faculty expertise can have a significant impact on how their work is evaluated. Throughout the rest of this volume we discuss ways in which the training and practice of online faculty needs to be informed by critical pedagogical approaches that view both online instructors and students as both inhabitants of new ecological digital teaching spaces as well as members of larger, very diverse societies with whom they can work creatively to address the challenges they face.

PUTTING IT ALL TOGETHER

We are, to put it simply, at a precarious moment in education. An accelerating move toward online education coupled with an all-too-common failure to recognize the challenges that such a move presents means students and educators alike face challenges we may not be ready to meet without serious changes. To meet these challenges, we need to implement the following action items:

- Recognize that there is a clear need for better training and evaluation of online instructors.

- Begin to make a more conscious and conscientious turn toward online teaching and learning built on a recognition that we live in a different world ecology than the one in which we were educated.
- Rethink the things we thought we knew in service to a better future in which we are helping to address and remedy inequities of access and issues of marginalization in online education.
- Be willing to make substantial changes in how we train and evaluate faculty working in online environments.

In chapter 2 we focus on the training of online instructors who will be teaching languages in digital environments.

2

CALL Teacher Education for Online Environments

This chapter provides an overview of CALL teacher education (CTE), which includes a focus on training given to world-language teachers imparting instruction in online environments. Although much of the CTE literature speaks to instruction imparted in both blended (a combination of F2F and online elements; Girons and Swinehart 2020) or completely online pedagogical settings, in this chapter we focus mostly on programs that train teachers to teach completely online. After a brief overview of the CTE field, we review theoretical frameworks prevalent in CTE literature, essential design elements and frameworks for CTE online training, current formats of instructor training to teach in digital online environments, the effectiveness of that training, and formal training alternatives, such as self-directed learning and mentoring.

OVERVIEW AND THEORETICAL BASE OF CTE

Publications focusing on CTE began in earnest with Phil Hubbard and Mike Levy's (2006b) volume. Although Hubbard and Levy (2006a) noted that much of the growth in this training had been "bottom-up and for the most part *ad hoc*" (3), CALL teacher preparation has expanded and can range from workshops, a teaching methods course unit on technology, graduate courses, and certificates dedicated to CALL, to CALL-focused graduate degrees. However, the growth of the CTE field faces many challenges that are explored in detail later in chapter 3. Hubbard (2008) states that the greatest of these is the "lack of qualified personnel able to integrate technology into language education effectively" (185). Without institutional instructors and staff with experience and knowledge of the options and advantages of technology integration into language courses, there is effectively no good way to provide

CTE pre- and in-service training for world-language instructors or to "train the trainers,"—that is, to train language program directors who, in turn, would provide pre- and in-service professional development opportunities to incoming teaching assistants and new language instructors. Therefore, the provision of CTE training for all language instructors needs to be a paramount concern of all world-language department administrators.

Consonant with the social turn taken by the field of second language acquisition (Block 2003), most of the published CTE research has used socially oriented theoretical frameworks. More specifically, this research relies on the tenets of sociocultural theory (SCT) (Lantolf 2000; Vygotsky 1978), which inspired social constructivism (Hickey 1997). These theories propose that learning is first and foremost an interpersonal process and that learners draw on current and past experiences to construct new knowledge through collaborative interaction with other individuals. SCT proposes that learning occurs when learners interact in various contexts with more expert interlocutors who can scaffold their development. More learning occurs when their zone of proximal development, the distance between what learners can do alone and with help, decreases over time. For instance, in CTE a solid mentoring program would have as its goal the production of mentees who have acquired their knowledge through scaffolded interaction with their mentor (perhaps via collaboration in communities of practice, or CoPs) but who are then able to stand on their own as autonomous (self-directed) learners and become mentors to others.

Building on constructivist theories (Bruner 1966; Piaget 1971), which assumed that human beings use their individual experiences to construct their own understanding of the world, socioconstructivist models added a social focus by emphasizing "the impact of collaboration, social context, and negotiation on thinking and learning" (Hickey 1997, 175). Thus, one's language and knowledge of the world are co-constructed through social discourse with others instead of being the result of an individual's processing of information from the world around them. In the discussion that follows, we show that several CTE frameworks emphasize many of these socially focused theoretical tenets—that is, the importance of the role of collaboration, CoPs, scaffolded learning (mentoring), and situated learning in CALL teacher education. Depending on the audience for CTE professional development sessions, trainers should decide how much focus on the theoretical bases of CALL should be included in that training.

The ecological frame we are using to discuss CTE training is discussed throughout this chapter, most importantly in the sections on situated learning, using technology to teach technology, and the importance of consideration of the audience in planning CTE training. The implications of an ecological approach to CTE for promoting a critical pedagogy is discussed in chapter 3 on CTE challenges and strategies to assess them.

ESSENTIAL ELEMENTS OF CTE TRAINING FOR TEACHING LANGUAGES ONLINE

As noted in chapter 1, institutional pressures and advances in technology have created incentives and opportunities for faculty to teach in virtual environments (Duensing et al., 2006). However, teaching languages in an online environment demands a critical rethinking of the use of pedagogical spaces. In fact, the type of reimagining of the pedagogical context necessary for the creation of effective online educational programs constitutes a paradigm shift (Kuhn 1962) in the way we conceive of teaching and learning. Our job as applied linguists is to figure out the best ways to teach and engage students in active learning as they pass from physical to virtual learning spaces.

As Annette Duensing and colleagues (2006) and Susan Yue Hua Sun (2011) note, to teach effectively online, one does not simply port materials and teaching techniques developed for face-to-face instruction into a virtual environment. Instead, Susan Easton (2003) suggests that instructors entering online teaching spaces for the first time needed to shift the way they perceive instructional time and space, develop management techniques for virtual environments, and create ways to engage students in completely virtual communication. This can be accomplished by incorporating all of the training elements described above for general CALL training and by focusing especially on those elements that are crucial to the development of online teaching expertise—that is, situated and project-based learning, collaboration and the creation of CoPs, and the creation of reflective, autonomous teacher-learners—throughout their training program.

Regine Hampel and Ursula Stickler (2005) propose that in addition to acquiring different skills than those needed by face-to-face language instructors, faculty teaching languages online also need to develop abilities distinct from those of online teachers in other disciplines, whose subject matter may not require as much synchronous interaction among students (e.g., history, natural sciences). For instance, Hampel and Stickler (2005) state that "the asynchronicity of communication in written conferencing and the lack of non-verbal cues in audio-conferencing are examples of new challenges for online language tutors" (Hampel and Stickler 2005, 312). Moreover, Hampel (2009) notes that "although some of the skills and knowledge that an online language teacher should possess are similar to those of online teachers generally, language teaching does pose specific challenges, as an area where the message (i.e., the second language [L2] that is taught) is also the medium used to teach it" (7). In addition, Barbara Lafford, Carmen King Ramírez, and James Wermers (2018) point out that, in contrast with online courses from other disciplines that may have larger numbers of students and less mandatory student-student interaction, online language classes require instructors to spend time interacting with their students, especially in lower-division courses that require the formation of basic L2 language skills.

Online language instructors also have to be trained to acquire specialized lexical items that are commonly used in virtual environments in the target culture; these would include target language terms related to online environments (e.g., "social media," "course site," "browser"). In addition, these instructors need to understand and acquire cultural and pragmatic norms that determine netiquette rules in target culture social media environments that may differ from those of the native language and culture. As a result of the need for language faculty to acquire distinctively new skills to teach online, Hampel and Stickler (2005) state that "institutions offering online courses would be in serious error if they underestimated the investment that needs to be made into training and continuing development as well as research into online teaching" (323).

In the next section we review the essential elements of current CTE language instructor training. As several detailed volumes (e.g., Goertler and Winke 2008; Hampel and Stickler 2015; Hubbard 2009; Hubbard and Levy 2006b; Kassen et al. 2007; Son and Windeatt 2017a; Torsani 2016) and several key articles (e.g., Arnold 2017; Hanson-Smith 2016; Hubbard 2008; Kessler and Hubbard 2017; Torsani 2015) have been written on CTE training, we will only highlight salient themes of those training models here.

Over the past two decades, CTE training has evolved from inserting isolated technology training elements into larger language-teacher training programs (e.g., *ACTFL/CAEP Program Standards for the Preparation of Foreign Language Teachers* [ACTFL/CAEP 2013]; *European Profile for Language Teacher Education* [Kelly et al. 2004]) to creating CTE training that is focused primarily on the acquisition of CALL competencies in the context of blended/online language learning. In this section we focus on essential design elements of CTE programs that focus on training language teachers to teach with CALL technologies in online pedagogical contexts.

Elements that are essential for the effective training of language teachers in online environments include the following:

- Considering the audience for CTE training
- Conducting a needs analysis
- Taking a breadth-first versus depth-first approach
- Including situated learning
- Using technology to teach technology
- Developing project-based learning
- Including reflective learning
- Implementing collaborative learning and communities of practice
- Integrating teacher technology standards into CTE

Considering the Audience for CTE Training

In an ecological approach to CTE planning, there is a need to keep one's audience in mind when creating tasks to be performed in a given rhetorical situation (Lafford 2015a; Sproat, Driscoll, and Brizee 2012). For instance, when planning a CTE training program, the teacher trainers must take into account the roles and responsibilities of the instructors to be trained and their prior experience teaching languages with technology or in completely online environments.

The audience for formal CTE training normally consists of pre- and in-service teachers (e.g., track faculty, contract faculty, teaching assistants, adjunct faculty) working as full- or part-time language instructors. Hubbard and Levy (2006a) classified these faculty members by their roles as a member of an educational institution (pre- and in-service classroom teachers, and expert and adjunct CALL specialists and professionals) and by the functions they perform (practitioner, developer, researcher, and trainer).

Michael Moore and Greg Kearsley (1996) also identified and defined functional roles for stakeholders in a distance education system, that is, students, course developer, site coordinator, tutor, proctor, student support services, management/administration, and teacher. When creating, reviewing and evaluating CTE training programs and proposed skill sets for online language teachers, it is imperative to keep in mind the role of the person being trained. For instance, a tutor with no control over course design or content does not have the same training needs as course designers and teachers, who are responsible for designing and creating modules for online courses.

In addition to the roles and responsibilities of instructor trainees, their teaching experience with technology and current skill levels are also relevant in the planning of CTE training for specific audiences. For instance, as noted in chapter 1, Rena Palloff and Keith Pratt (2011) propose a classification system for practitioners in any field who teach online (visitor, novice, apprentice, insider, and master); these levels are defined by the extent to which these individuals increase their integration of technology into their classes, the amount of time they have taught online, their comfort level in an online teaching environment, and their technological understanding and skills.

Skills relating to these technological, pedagogical, and content areas are discussed in more detail in chapter 4, in which we identify core competencies, skills, and standards needed by effective online language instructors.

Conducting a Needs Analysis

Before creating CTE training session, several CTE scholars have suggested conducting a needs analysis on the instructors' current level of technological and pedagogical skills, their frequency of use of certain basic technologies and applications, and their comfort level with them (Palloff and Pratt 2011; Reinders 2009).

A survey of the technological abilities of several language faculty was conducted in Europe in 2008 and updated in 2011 and 2013 by the Council of Europe's European Centre for Modern Languages as part of the DOTS (Developing Online Teaching Skills) project (2008–11) and the More DOTS Project (2011–13) (Germain-Rutherford and Ernest 2015; Stanojevic 2015). The primary objective of the 2008 survey was diagnostic, to understand the technological tools teachers used, the objectives they reached through the use of those tools, and their training needs. The 2011 and 2013 surveys focused on reflecting technological changes that were taking place and how the use of technological tools had affected their teaching practice. Surveys such as these need to be given regularly in order for CTE training to keep up with teachers' demands for timely and relevant professional development.

Various types of needs assessment instruments have been proposed to gather information that is useful to the creation of language instructor CTE training programs as well as general online educational programs. Examples of needs assessment questionnaires used for preparing trainings for in-service language instructors wanting to use technology in their teaching can be found in Hoven (2007, 157–61) and in Palloff and Pratt (2011, 149–58).

Taking a Breadth-First versus Depth-First Approach

As acknowledged by Deborah Healey and colleagues (2011), CTE training courses can take either a breadth-first or a depth-first approach. Training that focuses first on breadth is likely to provide trainees with information about a wide variety of technological tools from which they choose to reach their pedagogical goals. Although this approach provides teachers with a wide range of technological options, trainees may spend hours learning technologies that will not be relevant to them in their teaching situations. Training that focuses first on depth is more focused on providing information about a narrower range of options that they can explore in a detailed fashion (e.g., short courses on the use of Twitter or certain augmented reality applications [e.g., "Aris," Wisconsin Center for Education Research n.d.]). However, by definition, these short courses may not provide all the training needed by faculty to meet performance indicators in the standards (see chapters 4 [core competencies], 5 [instructor assessment], and 6 [assessment instruments] for a more in-depth explanation of these performance indicators). In addition, Martine Peters (2006) suggests integrating CTE skill-building activities throughout courses in the instructor degree program instead of confining this training to stand-alone modules at the beginning or end of their course of study.

Including Situated Learning

In order for learning activities to have ecological validity, the training of online language teachers should include a situated learning experience to prepare them to teach their own courses in online environments. Situated learning is a construct associated with the work of John Seeley Brown, Allan Collins, and Paul Duguid (1989) and Jean Lave and Etienne Wenger (1991). According to this concept, knowledge and skills are best acquired by learners in contexts that resemble those in which they will use those abilities. However, sometimes language instructors do not always understand how to apply what they learn in technology trainings to their own pedagogical context. Therefore, CTE training should provide ongoing opportunities for teachers to be able to immediately apply their new digital skills to the language courses they are teaching. Joy Egbert (2006) discusses an example of how teachers can effect a direct application of their online technology training into their classroom activities during the semester in which they teach their language courses. In situations where this type of immediate integration of teaching into practice is not possible, teachers can discuss how they would accomplish such integration through the use of case studies. In addition, Egbert, Trena Paulus, and Yoko Nakamichi (2002), propose anchoring teacher training and technological experimentation in a specific pedagogical context so that trainees can develop a better understanding of the constraints of their institutional setting.

Using Technology to Teach Technology

In order to provide trainees with ecologically valid, situated training experiences, Healey and colleagues (2011) propose using technology to teach about its use so that instructors gain an online student's perspective as they take an online course as part of their training program (using technology to teach technology). Diane Slaouti and Gary Motteram (2006) note that "teachers need to learn *about* online learning *through* online learning" (89). This practical experience with technologies will give future teachers more confidence in their technological abilities, make them more comfortable with the technological devices and infrastructure, and allow them "to experience the use of technology firsthand as they discuss its potential in the language classroom" (147).

Developing Project-Based Learning

Another example of situated learning can be seen in project-based CALL learning, in which current or future language teachers collaborate to create a digital product that resembles those that would be created by them or their students in the technology-mediated courses they teach. Christine Bauer-Ramazani (2006) proposes that the CTE teacher trainer can model "effective incorporation of technology into the classroom through hands-on, task- and *project-based experiences* that follow a constructivist, inquiry-based approach" (186). In addition, Robert Debski (2006) describes a project-based activity in a CALL course for language teachers in which they collaboratively created a Web portal containing cultural information. This example of "learning by doing" prepared teachers for the task of creating informational Web sites and for guiding students to work collaboratively to create other digital objects. Simone Torsani (2015) also shows that the completion of complex projects is superior to tutorials and guided design in developing a teacher's ability to integrate technologies into their curricula.

Including Reflective Learning

As a reflection of the general sociocultural approach to CTE research and the framework of situated learning, CTE teacher training has focused on the topics of reflection, collaboration, and community. The importance of reflective learning has been noted by several education scholars (Dewey 1938/1988; Knutson 2003; Schön 1983, 1987) who understand that reflection is a key element in experiential learning. CTE scholars who have promoted self-reflection as a tool for language teacher professional development include Nicolas Guichon (2009), Healey and colleagues (2011), Slaouti and Motteram (2006), and Torsani (2015). As the theme of self-reflection in the professional development of online language teachers is explored in depth in chapter 7, we do not discuss it further here. The other two tenets of SCT reflected in CTE training, collaboration and community building, are discussed just below.

Implementing Collaborative Learning and Communities of Practice

In this section we explore the concepts of collaboration and community as manifested in the literature on communities of practice and communities of inquiry. Lave and Wenger (1991) coined the term "community of practice" (CoP) as a mechanism for facilitating learning by belonging (Wenger 1998). Wenger, Richard McDermott, and William Snyder (2002) define CoPs as "groups of people who share a concern, a set of problems or a passion about a topic, and who deepen their knowledge and expertise in this area by interacting on an ongoing basis" (4). Elizabeth Hanson-Smith (2006, 2016) proposes the following elements for a CoP: a domain or purpose, a collaborative practice ("hands-on work with technology in a collaborative educational environment" [2016, 279]), tools for collaboration at a distance, social support, and peer mentoring.

The opportunity for future CALL educators to connect in CoPs can be crucial to their success as educators. For instance, Hanson-Smith (2006) notes that soon after their training is over, CALL teachers may find that the technologies that they are expected to use have evolved from the ones on which they were trained. Those newly minted CALL instructors can benefit from joining CoPs in which they can learn about these new technologies from more-experienced CALL educators and avoid feeling isolated in departments where they are trying to lead or follow the charge to integrate technology into the language curriculum. CoPs can afford these teachers an ongoing opportunity to maintain and update their knowledge and skills as well as improve their confidence and comfort in using technology.

Another construct dealing with collaboration and community is a "community of inquiry" (CoI), a term coined by D. Randy Garrison, Terry Anderson, and Walter Archer (2000). This framework, specifically designed to understand text-based online learning, focuses on three types of teacher presence (cognitive, social, and teaching) that are necessary for successful online interaction. CTE studies focused on the use of CoIs include Arnold, Ducate, and Lomicka (2007); Belz and Müller-Hartmann (2003); Grosbois (2011);

Arnold and colleagues (2005); Ernest and colleagues (2013); Germain-Rutherford and Ernest (2015); and Meskill and colleagues (2006).

Integrating Teacher Technology Standards into CTE

The last major category of elements to be integrated into CTE curricula is that of teacher technology standards. Referring to the standards proposed by Healey and colleagues (2011), those authors propose that Goal 1 of the teacher technology standards (Language teachers acquire and maintain foundational knowledge and skills in technology for professional purposes) should be attained by the trainees in a preservice training program. The authors also suggest that preservice training include integration of the other three teacher technology goals: Language teachers integrate pedagogical knowledge and skills with technology to enhance language teaching and learning; language teachers apply technology in record keeping, feedback, and assessment; and language teachers use technology to improve communication, collaboration, and efficiency. Healey and colleagues (2011) also propose integrating knowledge of student technology standards (discussed in that same volume) into CTE programs and for trainees to teach each other technology skills in order to prepare them to help their students attain those standards.

While the CTE literature on essential training elements reviewed here is useful in training language instructors to integrate technology into their F2F, blended, or online courses, several training models have been developed specifically to prepare instructors for teaching fully online language courses. In the next section, we briefly describe these frameworks by Hampel and Stickler (2005), Hampel (2009), and Lily Compton (2009).

CTE TRAINING FRAMEWORKS TO TEACH LANGUAGES ONLINE

Several frameworks for training language instructors to teach in online environments have been proposed within the past two decades. We briefly discuss three of those models here, the frameworks proposed by Hampel and Stickler (2005), Hampel (2009), and Compton (2009). While Hampel and Stickler's (2005) and Hampel's (2009) training models and instructor skill sets focus on training online tutors in the Open University setting, Compton's (2009) framework is more comprehensive and focuses on developing several areas of expertise for language faculty who are teaching online and may have the responsibility of creating or modifying the language courses they teach. Therefore, we focus more deeply on Compton's model.

Training for Online Language Tutors

Both Hampel and Stickler (2005) and Hampel (2009) describe training programs and skill sets proposed for tutors in the Open University (OU) in the United Kingdom. In order for these proposed programs and skills to be reviewed appropriately, the role of tutors in the OU online educational system must be understood.

The OU distance learning system uses tutors to interact with and offer support to language students. Tutor responsibilities are described as follows: "Tutors mark assignments, provide detailed written feedback, and offer support to students by telephone, e-mail, or computer conferencing. They also run group or online tutorials and day schools. Some are full-time members of staff, but most are associate lecturers: experts in their subject who combine their work as tutors with other academic or industry jobs" (Open University, n.d.). However, OU tutors are not responsible for the design and creation of course modules. Instead, the course content and technological framework is created by "multi-disciplinary course teams comprising: academics, educational technologists and media specialists contributing pedagogic and technical expertise, respected academics from other universities working alongside OU colleagues, external examiners" (Open University, n.d.). In other words, the OU tutors are given a ready-made language course, and their role is to understand the affordances and constraints of the technologies used and to use their creativity and personal teaching style to facilitate student interaction and collaboration, which helps students develop their communicative competence and a sense of community. It is in this context that Hampel and Stickler's (2005) and Hampel's (2009) proposed online training program and skill sets for OU tutors should be understood.

In order for trainees to sustain and develop their skills past the training period, Hampel and Stickler's (2005) online language tutor training program identifies three main sources of self-directed, follow-up support, and continuing development beyond the initial course training: "1. research in online education and technology-enhanced second language teaching; 2. the exchange of experience, ideas, and opinions with their peers who are using the same or comparable software; and 3. Their own reflective practice in online tuition" (322). The first source (research in CALL and online teaching) provides a valuable base for a tutor's general knowledge of the field and for those doing action research. The second source of support consists of peer exchange and peer mentoring to encourage new and continuing online tutors to form vital CoPs to continue their learning about online environments. The third source lies in online tutors' reflective practice, continuous self-observation and self-evaluation to promote self-directed learning so that they can become autonomous learners and acquire more understanding of their progress toward attaining crucial online language teaching skills and their need for more training.

Compared with Hampel and Stickler's (2005) generalized training framework, Hampel (2009) provides a more detailed model of the structure of the training program itself. This model includes the following stages: tutor selections, initial tutor training, support through course design, and continuing support and staff development. Hampel (2009) provides a detailed outline of this training program and extended explanations of each step of the training process. Most notable are the provision of in-house developed material for self-directed learning (support through course design) as well as post-training regional professional development events and peer mentoring with oversight (continuing support and staff development). Hampel (2009) also identifies several institutional support elements that need to be in place to facilitate tutors' support of learner interaction and collaboration, for example, tailoring training to institutional needs and circumstances, and regulating and monitoring tutor workload. Without this kind of ongoing institutional support of the training of online language tutors, a successful online language program cannot be sustained.

Training for Online Language Faculty

Instead of focusing on the training of language tutors, Compton's (2009) model of online teacher training assumes more responsibility on the part of the language instructor, that is, the ability to create and modify courses in the online program. Including a review of Hampel and Stickler's (2005) European model for OU tutors, Compton (2009) states that "the term 'tutors' will be used interchangeably with the United States (US) equivalent, 'teachers' or 'instructors'" (Compton 2009, 76). However, as will be pointed out later in the discussion, this conflation of terms is somewhat problematic as the roles and expectations of OU tutors differ in significant ways from those of teachers and instructors who may have more control over the curriculum.

Compton (2009) provides several general recommendations in the following areas for language-teacher education programs that train language faculty to teach online:

- Developing online language teaching skills through existing courses
- Developing online teaching skills at different levels of expertise and responsibilities for different roles
- Revamping existing technology training
- Implementing early virtual field experiences and virtual practicum

In her discussion of the first recommendation, Compton (2009) states that, ideally, language-teacher education would include separate courses focused on developing the three areas in her skills model: technology in online language teaching, pedagogy of online language teaching, and evaluation of online language teaching. However, due to logistical reasons, she understands that online teaching skills would probably need to be imparted throughout the teacher-training curriculum (e.g., as units within methodology and pedagogy courses), as suggested by Egbert, Paulus, and Nakamichi (2002); Guichon and Mirjam Hauck (2011); Kessler (2006); and Peters (2006).

Compton's (2009) second recommendation for CTE training programs that focus on developing online language teaching skills includes the levels of expertise (novice, proficient, expert) proposed for Compton's (2009) three skill set areas (technology, pedagogy, evaluation) as well as the roles and responsibilities of members of a CTE program proposed in Moore and Kearsley (1996) (student, course developer, site coordinator, tutor, proctor, student support services, management/administration, teacher). Compton (2009) proposes that training programs teach novice skills in all three skill areas early in the program and then help teachers acquire the abilities of a proficient teacher in later program coursework. In addition, the author stated that expert-level skills can be acquired during the latter part of the training program and also gained in the field and through practical experience.

Compton (2009) also recommends that all teacher candidates (even those who have no plans to teach online) acquire basic technological competence in language teaching online (Guichon and Hauck 2011; Kessler 2006) as they may change roles from a face-to-face instructor to a site coordinator in charge of online programs as their career develops. Therefore, it is incumbent upon all future language teachers to "know what roles and responsibilities exist in online learning systems and how the different components work together as a system" (Compton 2009, 93).

Compton's (2009) third recommendation for revamping existing technology training brings up the question of when to offer technology training in a language-teacher education program. On the one hand, she notes that Volker Hegelheimer (2006) had proposed a mandatory technology course early in a language-teacher training program to serve as a foundation for teachers to integrate technology more fully into the courses they teach. However, as noted earlier, Hubbard (2008), Peters (2006), and François Desjardins and Peters (2007) propose that CALL technology training be started early in their training regime and also be integrated into existing methodology and other educational program courses that teacher candidates take as they progress through the program. Desjardins and Peters (2007) also warn against having the technology course be too focused on the practical use of particular technologies and treating the technology course as an elective "add on" to enhance the program.

In order to avoid the view of technology training as an optional "add on," Compton (2009) proposes that trainees should be taught to put pedagogical objectives before technological ones (Fuchs 2006; Guichon and Hauck 2011). For instance, she proposes adding a critical element to courses with technology components (e.g., discussion of the affordances and constraints of using a particular technology in a specific teaching context) and encouraging discussions of how the principles of language learning theories can inform the choice of pedagogical assignments and tasks in a given pedagogical environment.

In order to provide teacher candidates with a deeper understanding of online teaching environments, Compton (2009) proposes that early in the program they should take part in virtual field experiences, that is, carefully guided observations of online teaching in which the teacher candidates could work with online teachers, students, and curricula to build the cognitive structures they need to carry out various roles in online teaching environments (teachers, tutors, or site coordinators). In fact, Compton and Niki Davis (2010) found that "the virtual field experience helped to clarify misconceptions, preconceptions, and concerns and led to a better understanding of Virtual School teaching skills and teacher's role as well as the supportive role of technology" (309). Later on in their training program the candidates could take part in a virtual practicum (similar to student teaching in an F2F course) in which instructors at the proficient teacher level take on more responsibility in an online teaching environment. Although not specifically mentioned by Compton (2009), these situated online learning experiences (virtual field experiences and virtual practicums) could provide teacher candidates with an opportunity to reflect on and share their practical experiences by collaborating and forming CoPs with practitioners in the field as they go through their training program.

Compton's (2009) framework for CTE training differs in significant ways from those of Hampel and Stickler (2005) and Hampel (2009). For instance, Compton does not specifically discuss several key elements needed in such training to prepare teacher candidates for lifelong learning. Although Compton mentions the fact that teacher candidates can still learn on the job after their training is over and take professional development courses offered by professional organizations, in her framework there is no specific mention of training teachers to be self-directed learners, capable of seeking out on their own the professional development sources to teach online. There is also no focus on the need for ongoing mentoring after the training session is over. In addition, in Compton's model no mention is made of training teachers for reflective learning, which would allow them to self-evaluate their technical, pedagogical, and evaluative skills throughout their career. In contrast, Hampel and Stickler (2005) and Hampel (2009) focus on the availability of resources for online teachers to update and develop further skills for online teaching through self-directed reading of CALL and online education literature in the field, forming mentoring relationships with more experienced faculty in the field, and participating in self-reflection activities to focus on their areas in need of improvement.

In addition, in contrast to Hampel and Stickler's (2005) and Hampel's (2009) training models for online tutors, Compton's list of pedagogical skills to be acquired by online language faculty imply that they have control over course content and possess the knowledge and ability to apply theories of language learning to the choice and modification of course materials and to online teaching practice. Because the OU tutors described in Hampel and Stickler (2005) and Hampel (2009) are not expected to create or significantly modify their language courses, knowledge of language learning theories and their application to course design and teaching may not be considered a core skill for their role and responsibilities. However, we believe such training in language-learning theories would benefit any language instructor's teaching practice.

Compton's (2009) model also lacks mention of an important core skill needed by faculty who create course content, that is, the ability to carry out a needs assessment before creating the course. Faculty in charge of content need to be able to carry out such an assessment so that their course meets the needs of its future audience (e.g., general language students, future members of the medical and legal professions).

FORMAL AND ALTERNATIVE MODES OF CTE TEACHER TRAINING

As resources available for training language teachers to teach with technology or completely online vary among institutions, this training can take place in formal, alternative, and informal settings. In this section we review selected studies that focus on each of these contexts.

Formal CTE Language-Teacher Training

Professional preparation programs that train teachers to teach languages with technology in blended or in completely online formats can take the form of graduate CALL certificates, applied linguistics PhD tracks in CALL, pre- and in-service workshops, symposia, and talks. In the United States, graduate CALL offerings mostly take the form of graduate certificates (e.g., Arizona State University, Boise State University, Ohio University, University of Arizona, University of Colorado, Boulder), but PhD concentrations in CALL are offered at Iowa State University and the University of South Florida. In Europe and Asia, graduate offerings in CALL often take the form of master's degrees (e.g., University of Manchester [UK]; University of Essex [UK], Cyprus University of Technology, University of Canterbury [NZ]) and PhD programs (e.g., University of York [UK]). (See CTE/CALL Resource list on this book's Web page at www.press.georgetown.edu.) Other formal CTE training can take the form of pre- and in-service training programs.

Preservice training and CTE course design. Preservice CALL training often takes place in departmental units, where new teaching assistants and other new instructors are introduced to CALL through short "just-in-time" training modules as part of their orientation to prepare them for their first teaching assignments. Often, however, these training programs focus mostly on understanding the affordances and constraints of the learning management system used at that institution (e.g., how to record grades, how to set up interaction among students via discussion boards or Zoom, how to access or upload content). In addition, current language faculty need to advise teacher candidates of CALL professional development opportunities sponsored by language teaching organizations in which they can participate at the local, regional, national, and international levels before they begin to teach.

Examples of research on preservice CTE training include five chapters in the Hubbard and Levy (2006b) volume (Part 3: CALL Pre-Service Courses): Hegelheimer (2006), on students' reactions to a required first-semester technology course in an MA program at Iowa State; Eskenazi and Brown (2006), on teaching how to create software that uses speech recognition; Egbert (2006), on situated language-teacher learning; Bauer-Ramazani (2006), on training CALL instructors to teach online; and Peters (2006), on the need to spread technology training throughout a curriculum instead of limiting that training to a preservice contest. Other studies on preservice CALL training include Başöz and Çubukçu (2014), on attitudes of preservice English as a foreign language teachers toward CALL, and Samani, Baki, and Razali (2014), on preservice English as a second language teachers' perceptions of the use of CALL programs and their views on factors that inhibit the success of these programs.

Torsani (2016) notes that the design of preservice courses often takes a breadth-first approach (Healey et al. 2011), that is, "a course aimed at providing a general introduction to the field and a basic and extensive training" (169). However, Torsani also takes into account the need to keep one's audience in mind when creating tasks to be performed in a given rhetorical situation (Lafford 2015a; Sproat, Driscoll, and Brizee 2012). Consequently, she provides two different models for preservice CALL training courses, a course aimed at providing professional preparation for future teachers and a different model for trainees who wish to pursue a different career track (e.g., working for publishing houses that produce CALL materials).

Despite challenges that these preservice programs face, Hubbard (2008) notes that they are manageable because they can determine the learning objectives and course design of the training (depth first or breadth first) regardless of the teaching and computer experience teacher candidates may have. In-service programs, however, serve a population that may have specific needs and established pedagogical practices that need to be taken into consideration in their training.

In-service training and CTE course design. After their preservice training ends, more in-depth CTE training would take place after language instructors have acquired some experience teaching in the field. Tita Beaven and colleagues (2010) note that in-service teachers need training that is of high quality, appropriate, and ongoing. In addition, Egbert (2006) states that effective in-service training should be mandated or rewarded and should be made relevant to the teachers by linking it to or situating it in the teachers' own instructional settings.

These in-service CALL trainings on uses of technology could be taken by teaching assistants as CALL courses that form part of their graduate program (e.g., graduate CALL certificates) or by other faculty as workshops given by departments, institutions, or professional organizations (e.g., state, regional, national, and international language teaching CoPs). In-service training sessions should focus on ways to enhance their language teaching through the use of cutting-edge technologies (e.g., mobile-assisted language learning [MALL] [smartphones, tablets], gaming, telecollaboration / virtual exchanges) and ways to teach languages completely online. Often institutions require faculty to take specific training courses regarding how to teach online before they are allowed to teach in virtual environments. However, as pointed out in chapter 1, institutional-level training to teach online does not specifically focus on how to teach languages in that context. Therefore, specific in-service training on teaching languages in virtual environments should be offered by units focused on language instruction or by language resource centers and must be required of all language faculty asked to teach online.

Examples of research on providing in-service CTE training include five chapters in the Hubbard and Levy (2006b) volume (Part 4: CALL In-Service Projects, Courses, and Workshops): Rickard, Blin, and Appel (2006), on training for trainers in the Irish education system; Chao (2006), on the affordances of WebQuests; Olesova and Meloni (2006), on designing and implementing collaborative internet projects; Jones and Youngs (2006), on teacher preparation for online instruction; and Wong and Benson (2006), on the factors behind two teachers' successful or unsuccessful integration of technology skills acquired in an in-service course into the language courses they taught. Other studies on in-service CALL training include Levy, Wang, and Chen (2009), which combines online practice teaching with self-reflection and self-monitoring, and Ernest et al. (2013), which focuses on fostering collaboration among the teacher candidates through a hands-on approach. As mentioned earlier, the DOTS project (2008–11) gathered data on the needs of in-service language instructors to inform the design and content of the training and the materials used in order to ensure that the training remained relevant to the needs of the trainees (Germain-Rutherford and Ernest 2015; Stanojevic 2015).

Torsani (2016) also provides several models of course design for in-service CALL training courses. One of these courses (a general course for practicing language teachers) resembles to a great extent the preservice course for language teacher candidate. Torsani (2016) also provides sample syllabi for more focused in-service short courses on computer-mediated communication and vocabulary as well as goals and syllabi of CALL training courses meant for CALL specialist/developers, CALL professional researchers, and CALL in-service teachers/instructors of CALL courses (training for the CALL trainers). We refer the reader to chapter 9 in Torsani's (2016) volume for further details on the proposed syllabus topics for those courses and to Bauer-Ramazani (2006) and Rickard, Blin, and Appel (2006) for further examples of CALL training course design. In addition, Jeong-Bae Son and Scott Windeatt's (2017a) volume, *Language Teacher Education and Technology: Approaches and Practices,* explores the structure and content of nine CALL courses taken as part of master's degree programs in Australia, the United

Kingdom, and the United States. A valuable resource contained in this book is a table in their appendix A, with an overview of the features of the nine CALL training courses presented in the book (e.g., objectives, contents, text and readings, workload, assessment, and other requirements).

To complement departmental trainings, many universities have established a centralized teaching support center that offers pedagogical trainings and support (Knapper 2010). In online education, there are also teams of course designers and technology experts whose main purpose is to work with faculty. While these efforts provide many important resources for educators, the services they offer are often too general to meet certain departmental and subject-specific needs (Scott 2002).

As it is important to continuously modify CALL training courses to be responsive to the changing needs of their audiences, it is imperative that the trainees provide feedback on their training to the individuals responsible for designing those courses. In the next section we explore several studies that have reported on this type of trainee assessment of the effectiveness of their formal professional development programs.

Effectiveness of CALL Training Programs

Despite the efforts by CALL educators to create timely and relevant CTE training programs, several scholars have noted that CALL teacher education appears to be inadequate and ineffective (Arnold and Ducate 2015; Healey et al. 2011; Hubbard 2008). Son and Windeatt (2017b) point to several factors that can render these programs ineffective and inadequate for the needs of language instructors, that is, a lack of opportunity to attend training, the training that is offered is not appropriate for their needs, and the lack of follow-up training offered to them.

Hubbard (2008) notes that in spite of institutional demands for language teachers who are knowledgeable about technology, CALL education and training for language instructors was lacking in the majority of existing teacher preparation programs at the time. Hubbard offers several reasons for the scarcity of CALL training within these programs: *inertia* on the part of language program administrators of successful programs who want to maintain the status quo; *ignorance* of the affordances of CALL technology to enhance language teaching; *insufficient time* for students to take CALL courses in an already packed graduate curriculum; *insufficient infrastructure* with a lack of up-to-date hardware and software needed for training purposes; *lack of (language technology) standards* (at the time, 2008); *lack of established methodology* that Hubbard addresses in his 2008 article; and a *lack of experienced, knowledgeable educators,* which Hubbard argues is "the single, most critical obstacle for the field as a whole" (178).

Kessler (2006) also addresses the unavailability of sufficient CALL training opportunities in his survey of graduates from North American master's TESOL programs. Specifically, his survey found that at that time (2006) most respondents were not required to take courses focused on technology (79.2 percent), nor did they take such courses (56.7 percent) or any other courses with CALL training in their degree program. Kessler's (2006) survey also found that 84 percent of survey respondents believed that insufficient time was given to learning about CALL in their graduate program and that 87.5 percent said they would have benefited from more CALL-focused training. Both Kessler (2006) and Berber-McNeill (2015) found that the duration of the CALL training offered was too limited to allow faculty the time to effectively use the tools available to them. Healey and colleagues (2011) state (and it is even more true today) that, given the high demand for technology-savvy language instructors, teacher training programs must offer sufficient CALL professional preparation opportunities to their teacher candidates.

In addition to noting teachers' complaints over the lack of availability of CALL training, Son and Windeatt (2017b) also point out that the teachers voiced concerns over the quality of whatever technology training they did receive. Kessler (2006, 2007) notes that a high percentage of MA TESOL program graduates were not satisfied with the professional preparation they received on integrating technology into their language curriculum. These authors note several shortcomings of current teacher training, for example, a focus on technology over pedagogy, a lack of initial technical preparation in language teachers, a lack of expertise on the part of teacher trainers and language program directors, and training programs that were too short to be effective.

Although Hampel and Stickler (2015) note that the literature on CALL teacher training has progressed from a focus on technology to pedagogically driven uses of technology, many CTE training sessions still focus primarily on developing teachers' technological expertise. Several scholars have noted that a focus on technology over pedagogy in CALL training courses can lead to tools being presented without discussing the possibilities, affordances, and appropriate uses of those tools in specific pedagogical contexts (Comas-Quinn 2011; Hanson-Smith 2016; Kessler 2006; Son and Windeatt 2017b).

Several CALL scholars have provided readers with the assessment instruments (e.g., surveys, focus groups, interviews) they used to assess the effectiveness of their CALL training programs. Examples of such instruments are found in Winke and Goertler (2008), Kessler (2006), and Windeatt (2017).

Guichon and Hauck (2011) note a recent trend to move away from traditional surveys, focus groups, and interviews toward the use of action research and reflective learning to inform CALL training and practice and help teachers reach their development goals. For instance, Julie Belz and Andreas Müller-Hartmann (2003) found that teachers' self-reflection on their telecollaborative experiences with educators in other countries promotes instructors' intercultural development. Tim Lewis (2006) used a teaching journal with recorded self-reflections that allowed him to engage in critical analysis and become more aware of his pedagogical practice. He also reported on how the use of observations from a "critical friend" gave him a better understanding of how teachers can use this feedback to enter a phase of "autonomous self-development" (598) to improve their performance. A review of selected works on autonomous self-development and mentoring opportunities are presented in the next section as alternatives to formal CTE training.

Alternatives to Formal CTE Training

The primary forms of alternative CTE training include self-directed learning (SDL) and mentoring. These options are explored in the sections below.

Self-directed learning. Due to teachers' dissatisfaction with the formal CTE training programs in which they have participated and the lack of adequate follow-up to those programs, studies have shown that those trainees seek out other opportunities for more informal, autonomous self-training, especially after they have started their teaching careers. In fact, Kessler's (2006) data shows that 91.7 percent of respondents said they had taken the initiative to go outside their degree program to take courses on teaching with technology, and several of them sought out self-learning resources (e.g., LISTSERVs, professional conferences, colleagues, training websites, CALL CoPs). One reason for these language instructors seeking further CTE training may result from the fact that most respondents said that in their current workplace the use of technology was encouraged and incentives were given to faculty to use and develop technology for teaching. If CALL skills are valued in the workplace, these skills need to be integrated into and valued by the MA training programs that prepare candidates for those employment contexts. However, CTE programs also need to "provide teachers with the tools and experiences to enable continuing professional growth" (Healey et al. 2011, 150). In that way, they become autonomous, self-directed learners who can adapt their skills for use with any new applications that appear in the quiver of tools that can be used to enhance student online learning (Healey et al. 2011; Kessler 2006). This is especially important for teachers who go on to teach in programs that lack sufficient professional development opportunities for online instructors.

Studies that discuss the need for instructor SDL include Hampel and Stickler (2005), Hampel (2009), Kolaitis et al. (2006), Hubbard (2020), Hanson-Smith (2016), and Meskill and Anthony (2015). As discussed above, Hampel and Stickler (2005) propose that specific resources (access to CALL research, CoPs of online instructors, their own reflective practice) be available to and used by instructors for SDL after their training course ends. Moreover, Hampel (2009) incorporates continuing support and staff development to prepare trainees to become self-directed learners as a required element of the OU's tutor training program for language teachers. Marinna Kolaitis and colleagues (2006) report on a project in which teachers engaged in SDL when they collaborated to focus on strategies for training their language students in CALL technologies. According to the authors, this collaborative group training approach was the most effective of the CALL training models at their institution. In that vein, Hubbard (2020) promotes the use of collaborative debriefing on collaborators' experiences, successes, and failures with CALL tasks and software in order to consolidate their learning and dispel the sense of isolation that may come from working on computer tasks on their own.

Although several lists of SDL resources may exist, two resources in particular (Hanson-Smith 2016; Meskill and Anthony 2015) provide specific information on materials, internet sources, CoPs, and teaching strategies that can be used by autonomous learners. Hanson-Smith (2016) suggests that teachers set up personal learning environments by immersing themselves in technology education materials (e.g., Web sites to explore tools, prerecorded training webinars, teacher technology blogs, educational technology MOOCs) and create personal learning networks that can be formed by participating in CoPs with other language teachers interested in technology. While Hanson-Smith provides critical reviews of the affordances and constraints of selected resources for teaching with technology, Carla Meskill and Natasha Anthony (2015) specifically focus on providing teachers with information about strategies for teaching languages in digital environments. This last resource is especially appropriate for teachers new to online language teaching as it also contains glossary of key terms and introductions to different teaching methods.

Finally, Stockwell (2009) sums up the most important strategies that teachers can use for effective SDL about CALL technologies: critically examine the environment, seek sources of information, keep up with technological development, set and adhere to learning goals, and track their own progress though reflection. Thus, autonomous, self-directed teacher-learners must be taught how to reflect on their own learning and where to seek out future training resources to help them improve their online language teaching. (See the CTE/CALL Resource List on this book's Web page for CALL resources for SDL.)

Mentoring. The need for ongoing professional development after initial training sessions has been noted by several CALL scholars (Comas-Quinn 2011; Eib and Miller 2006; Hampel 2009; Hampel and Stickler 2005; Kelly et al. 2004; Kolaitis et al. 2006; Meskill et al. 2006). After instructors take formal training programs offered at the departmental level for all trainees, faculty mentorship programs can be established at the individual level in order to promote continuous faculty interest and expertise in teaching online. Such programs pair an experienced online instructor with a teacher new to digital instructional platforms in order to address apprehensions associated with online language instruction, to share best practices (Gabriel and Kaufield 2008; Zhao and Cziko 2001), to establish good communication models of a professional relationship, and to model professional behavior expected of online language instructors. As Comas-Quinn (2011) states, "Since a 'one size fits all' approach to professional development is unlikely to succeed when teachers' backgrounds in online learning range from experts to novices, personalized support from a mentor often works better than general training sessions" (221). A more in-depth discussion of mentoring processes as a follow-up to initial training is found in chapter 8 of this volume.

This chapter has reviewed the CTE literature focused on identifying essential elements of the "best practices" of CTE teacher training. In order to facilitate the creation of training programs that adhere to these best practices, we have created a checklist of those "essential elements" so that both pre- and in-service language instructors and teacher trainers can understand what design principles and content should be included in various types of CTE training. That checklist (appendix A-1) can be used in CALL graduate courses or for teacher training courses and workshops as a tool for promoting collaborative discussions on the creation of effective CTE training for specific purposes to a particular audience within the logistical constraints imposed by their institutions.

PUTTING IT ALL TOGETHER

This chapter on CTE training for online language instruction has inspired the following ideas for implementation:

- In light of the growing demand for online language teaching, administrators need to support faculty and teacher trainers to facilitate this transition.
- When creating online training for language instructors, teacher trainers must consider the essential elements of CTE training that need to be included to meet the needs of their particular pedagogical context.
- In order to determine best CTE practices, teacher trainers need to familiarize themselves with CTE literature and frameworks focused on preparing language teachers to teach in online environments.
- Language programs should offer a variety of pre- and in-service formal CTE online training opportunities and assess the effectiveness of that training in facilitating the integration of technology into the language curriculum.
- To prepare language instructors for continuing education in online teaching, language programs should train instructors to become autonomous, self-directed learners and provide them with mentoring opportunities.

Despite the best efforts of CTE training programs, several factors pose challenges to the ultimate success of these initiatives; in general, these challenges relate to faculty not understanding what is expected of them, faculty feeling undervalued and overwhelmed by technology, faculty and faculty trainers lacking the necessary skills to implement technology into the language curriculum, and faculty assessment issues. In chapter 3 we briefly discuss each of these types of challenges and propose strategies to address them.

3

Online Language Instructor Training Challenges and Strategies

Many of the factors that have posed challenges to CTE online training, resulting in a lack of teacher technological expertise and teacher readiness for such training, stem from the fear many instructors have not only of technology but of change itself. Forms of this change can include the rate of technological change and its role in a given institution, changes in the way experienced instructors perceive their value in institutions that demand they teach in new virtual environments, changes in the way they view their teaching role, changes in the way they conceptualize teaching within the affordances and constraints of digital ecological spaces and within the technological environments provided by their teaching institutions, and changes in expectations regarding their technopedagogical skill levels.

Echoing these themes, Deborah Healey and colleagues (2011) propose that faculty resistance and the lack of language teacher readiness for technology integration into their courses results from teachers' lack of "an understanding of the role of technology, a will to change, and the necessary expertise" (144). These three factors that hinder teacher readiness for CALL integration can be addressed with strategies inspired (in part) by Anthony Muhammad and Luis Cruz (2019), whose book focused on the challenges faced by educational leaders who need to deal successfully with faculty resistance to change.

According to Muhammad and Cruz (2019), resistance to change in an organization arises because individual or collective needs have not been met. They proposed that these needs emerge from negative professional and personal experience on the part of the resisters and can be resolved only by the administration understanding the dynamics of employee (faculty) motivation and their resistance to change. Thus, in order to ensure effective leadership, educational institutions must focus on creating transformational leaders, that is, "leaders who understand that their behavior significantly contributes to their schools, districts, families, communities, and the world" (Muhammad and Cruz 2019, 5).

To successfully address faculty resistance to change, the educational institution needs their transformational leaders to "strike a balance between the important elements of focusing on the task and focusing on relationships and between providing support and requiring accountability" (Muhammad and Cruz 2019, 16). In the context of CTE training, a focus on task (Bass 1981) would manifest as a focus on setting up the training structure, providing information, and setting up rules and a system of rewards and punishments for faculty compliance. A focus on relationships (Bass 1981) would entail recognizing and acknowledging prior accomplishments of faculty and finding ways to lower their level of anxiety about learning new skills. An institution or program that is providing support for technological integration by its language faculty would provide training opportunities, lists of resources for self-directed learning, and ongoing mentoring. Finally, requiring accountability would entail appropriately assessing the attainment of the skills taught in the CTE training by faculty participants and evaluating the extent to which that training has been integrated into pedagogical practice and the selection and creation of materials for digital spaces.

Regarding these last two points, Muhammad and Cruz (2019) describe support as a kind of investment, and the return on that investment would be faculty accountability for the training they have received. Extending this investment metaphor, the authors state the following:

> Most resistance to change manifests a need that a leader has not met, or a critical investment that a leader has neglected. Before a leader can criticize a follower for not embracing a vision or a directive, he or she has to first assess whether he or she has made all the necessary investments to warrant a return on investment. Leaders have to make three non-negotiable investments to create the right conditions for intrinsic motivation for change: (1) cognitive investment, (2) emotional investment, and (3) functional investment. (19)

These three investments can be rephrased (respectively) as ones of establishing communication (cognitive investments), trust (emotional investments), and capacity building (functional investments), with faculty accountability (getting results) needed to demonstrate a return on that investment. Thus, in order for these investment strategies to be effective, all of them must be seen as necessary for the professional development of online instructors as they interact with individuals within a specific ecological context.

In the discussion that follows, we use this investment / return on investment metaphor to frame our proposal of cognitive, emotional, and functional strategies that can be employed within an ecological framework to meet specific challenges to CTE training and that require faculty to demonstrate accountability for that training.

COGNITIVELY BASED CHALLENGES AND INVESTMENT STRATEGIES

To make cognitive investments in CTE training programs, administrators and supervisors need to clearly explain to language faculty why technological integration or teaching in online digital formats for all teachers is important to the success of all their students, many of whom may have to balance their studies with work or have familial obligations. Muhammad and Cruz (2019) propose that in order to attain this understanding and to reach a conclusion that this change to digital environments is beneficial, faculty and other stakeholders must be allowed to examine evidence, weigh options, and engage in dialogues about these issues both with individuals within the department or institution and those located in other (external) venues. These authors believe that when educators are denied the opportunity to engage in such dialogues, they become frustrated and pessimistic and resist this type of institutional change. This type of resistance leads to several (cognitively based) challenges to CTE online training discussed below. After each cognitively based challenge (e.g., C-1, C-2), investment strategies to address those issues are proposed.

CALL scholars note that faculty do not always understand their unit's vision for the role of technology in the department and how it can be used effectively in an online pedagogical context. Faculty may also not understand their roles and responsibilities relative to those of other stakeholders in their online instructional system, or what specific skills they need to acquire to succeed in online pedagogical environments.

- Challenge C-1: Faculty do not understand the unit's vision of the role of technology and how it can be used effectively in their online pedagogical context (Comas-Quinn 2011).

Transformational leaders can address the first issue by inviting faculty to collaborate and explore barriers that arise to successful technology integration and online pedagogical training and to propose viable solutions to those challenges. This solicitation of instructor input generates a sense of faculty empowerment and ownership of their department's move to online teaching spaces and their own professional development. Greg Kessler (2006) also suggests involving all stakeholders in this decision to move to online language-teaching spaces and to provide a list of resources (e.g., Web sites, webinars, empirical research) to do so. This list should also include resources that address the affordances and constraints of various forms of online technological innovation.

Administrators and supervisors calling this meeting can explain the need to embrace online language teaching to meet student needs. These needs can be ongoing (e.g., striking a work/family/school balance) or situational (e.g., the sudden need to put courses online due to the COVID-19 pandemic). Muhammad and Cruz (2019) also suggest that the dialogue focus on a vision of the organization after having met the challenges it currently faces and that administrators and supervisors solicit faculty ideas for creating such a vision and ask for their assistance and leadership to make this move toward technological integration. The assumption behind these proposed dialogues among all stakeholders is that involvement of all interested parties in the visioning process would promote buy-in to this vision by current language faculty.

- Challenge C-2: Faculty may not understand their role and responsibilities relative to those of other stakeholders in their online system for language instruction.

In order for instructors to understand program expectations for their new roles, trainers should provide faculty with information on how the responsibilities of their online instructor role compares with the duties of various other members of an online educational system (e.g., students, course developers, site coordinators, tutors, proctors, student support services, management/administration, teachers, researchers, trainers [Hubbard and Levy 2006a; Moore and Kearsley 1996]). By doing so, all stakeholders can be confident in their understanding of the expectations their academic unit has for them and for which they will be held accountable.

In addition, instructors must take into account how student learning styles and behaviors may manifest in digital spaces and understand how interaction in digital spaces may reshape student and teacher roles and relationships. Teacher trainers should clearly articulate online instructor roles (e.g., facilitator of knowledge acquisition by students) and how they might differ from traditional classroom roles (e.g., imparter of knowledge) in a student-centered pedagogy (chapter 4).

- Challenge C-3: Administrators and faculty may hold naive beliefs that there is no need for technology training among younger scholars (digital natives [Egbert, Paulus, and Nakamichi 2002; Healey et al. 2011; Prensky 2001; Winke and Goertler 2008]).

The third challenge to online training involves departmental naivete regarding the ease that scholars who have been exposed to technology from a young age (digital natives) will be able to integrate technology training into their courses without difficulty (Healey et al. 2011). Administrator and faculty assumptions that digital natives do not need CTE training (Prensky 2001) have been proven false by Paula Winke and Senta Goertler (2008). That is, their students could easily work with applications they already used in their personal lives (e.g., navigating and copying internet files, playing video and audio files); however, they had a harder time working with applications with which they were unfamiliar (e.g., working with multimedia graphics, creating video and audio files). Therefore, faculty need access to sources of research that challenge the assumption that digital natives need little to no CTE training.

Moreover, CTE training involves much more than a focus on technical skills; that is, it also involves facilitating knowledge and understanding of possible pedagogical uses of those applications in digital spaces. Therefore, as all faculty need these skills, all should be involved in CTE training. In addition, teacher trainers must carry out a needs analysis so that they are aware of the skill levels and needs of the particular audience they will be addressing in their training sessions.

- Challenge C-4: Faculty may not understand what skills they need to acquire to succeed as language instructors in online pedagogical environments (Compton 2009; Hampel and Stickler 2005; Healey et al. 2011).

In order for faculty to know what skills they need to teach online, trainers must make sure faculty are aware of the technological, pedagogical, and evaluative skills they need to acquire to be successful online language instructors. (See chapter 4 for a detailed discussion of these core competencies.) Knowing their current skill level and what skills they will need to acquire will help faculty set reasonable goals for their improvement in these areas (chapter 9) and will allow them to reflect in a more in-depth and critical manner on the progress they make toward those attaining those goals.

As a result of the need for clear messaging among all stakeholders to address cognitive challenges, emotional strategies are needed to establish effective communication and rapport between faculty trainees and their teacher trainers and mentors.

EMOTIONALLY BASED CHALLENGES AND INVESTMENT STRATEGIES

Muhammad and Cruz (2019) propose that transformational leaders create "organizational environments that are motivating, inclusive, organized, and focused on outcomes" (17) by developing human relationships between leaders and followers that are connected to a moral purpose (Kouzes and Posner 2003). Both of those groups must connect with each other's values and with those of the institution they serve. Muhammad and Cruz state that these connections can start at the intellectual or cognitive level, but deep connections occur at the emotional level only when educational leaders recognize and respond to their instructors' emotions and life experiences so that faculty feel valued and believe their concerns are understood.

When this emotional connection is lacking, trust between leaders and followers is also lacking, and this can lead to a fear of and resistance to change. This resistance leads to language faculty's lack of "a will to change" (Healey et al. 2011, 144), which is also brought about in part by emotionally based challenges. Below we discuss these emotional challenges to CTE online training (e.g., E-1, E-2) and propose strategies to address them.

In the CTE literature, emotionally based faculty resistance to online training has been tied to issues of time availability and time management, lack of appreciation and rewards for the extra time faculty spend preparing and teaching online language courses, faculty resentment of unit expectations for them to reinvent themselves as pedagogues, and a lack of critical cultural awareness among stakeholders.

- Challenge E-1: Faculty feel overwhelmed by time availability and time management issues (Bauer-Ramazani 2017; Comas-Quinn 2011; Egbert, Paulus, and Nakamichi 2002; Hanson-Smith 2006; Hubbard 2008; Lafford, King de Ramírez, and Wermers 2018; Son and Windeatt 2017b).

Many faculty members feel overwhelmed by the number of hours needed to get online instructor training, to implement skills learned in their courses, and to actually teach languages online with many hours of interaction among participants in the course. Moreover, Elizabeth Hanson-Smith (2006) notes that teachers with technical preparation spend much of their time helping more novice teachers and have little time for developing their own skills and interest in integrating technology.

Transformational leaders can address this first challenge by initiating changes in institutional structures and policies to support time availability and time management issues. For instance, supervisors can encourage faculty to use internet-based activities to automatically grade selected homework assignments (e.g., Pearson n.d.) and use specialized rubrics to grade essay drafts holistically (Michieka 2010) so the instructor can spend more time interacting with students or setting up and assessing their interactions. In addition, faculty need access to information on resources on best practices regarding the efficient creation and evaluation of online interaction (e.g., via professional development training, CoPs with more experienced online faculty). Moreover, no-cost graders (e.g., undergraduate preservice language teacher candidates needing internship credit) with a high level of target language proficiency could be assigned to classes to help ease the instructor's workload.

Christine Bauer-Ramazani (2017) notes that time management issues also occur when requiring synchronous communication among online students coming from different time zones. In some cases, only asynchronous online communication platforms may be feasible due to lack of internet or Wi-Fi access in certain parts of the globe. Nevertheless, Bauer-Ramazani notes the value of working through the challenges of synchronous communication across distances, as this ability "constitutes twenty-first century digital citizenship and is expected in the global economy, thus providing authenticity to such tasks and contexts" (146).

- Challenge E-2: Faculty feel underappreciated due to a lack of rewards for the time and effort they spend integrating technologies into their online language curriculum and maintaining effective communication with their online students (Lafford, King de Ramírez, and Wermers 2018; Son and Windeatt 2017b; Wolcott and Betts 1999).

Administrators and supervisors should also address the issue of faculty feeling underappreciated due to a lack of rewards and incentives for the large number of hours they spend training themselves for teaching in online environments, selecting or creating appropriate digital materials, and fostering quality interaction with and among students online.

Perhaps the most common solution to motivating faculty to teach online is found in extrinsic motivators, or those that elicit a particular behavior/task in exchange for a tangible incentive (McKeachie 1961). While money is the most common extrinsic motivator in the workplace, funding is usually limited or reserved for a specific group of actors. In the case of online education, economic incentives are often limited to start-up funds and special projects (EdSurge 2014; US Department of Education n.d.). Furthermore, administrations may be reticent to provide funding for the development of online courses as instructional designers and other technical personal dedicated to online education are becoming commonplace at most institutions (Irani and Telg 2001, 2002; Lee 2001; Pan and Thompson 2009).

Kessler (2006) notes the need to provide language faculty with incentives for time spent on technology integration in the form of heightened employment prospects (for preservice teachers) and release time, recognition, and financial compensation (for in-service teachers). More specifically, recognition of faculty efforts to take on the challenges of online teaching could include payment for online course development, release time for faculty teams to work on creating a series of online language courses for their units, awards for excellence in teaching online, digital badges for attaining certain levels of technological expertise, travel money for teachers to present their original ideas at language-teaching conferences, and the inclusion of recognition of online teaching expertise in annual reviews that determine merit pay and in promotion and tenure cases. In addition, tenure-track and tenured faculty coming up for tenure or promotion may be reticent to take on the task of teaching online, especially if there are few or no institutional rewards or recognition for the time it takes them to be trained and the extra preparation time that they need to teach in a new (digital) environment (Wolcott 1997; Wolcott and Betts 1999). Other possible rewards and incentives for this work are discussed in the "return on investment" section (challenge FA-5).

- Challenge E-3: Faculty resent institutional pressure for them to reinvent themselves as pedagogues and change their pedagogical practice to teach in digital spaces (Comas-Quinn 2011; Cutrim and Whyte 2012; Drewelow 2013; Lafford, King de Ramírez, and Wermers 2018; Peters 2006; Strambi and Bouvet 2003).
    - Faculty asked to teach online do not feel respected and valued for their prior pedagogical knowledge and experience in nondigital spaces.
    - Faculty perceive institutional pressure to have them teach in digital spaces as a face-threatening experience that challenges their perceptions of their autonomy and control over their teaching, their roles, and their identities.

CTE scholars have noted that one of the factors contributing to faculty resistance to online teaching was their reluctance to reinvent themselves as pedagogues and potentially lose face. Teachers who have been successful in face-to-face classroom environments could feel disrespected and not valued for their prior experience. In addition, they could perceive a threat to their identity and self-image "when told that they must substantially rethink and revise much of what they do in order to reflect best practices in online pedagogy" (Lafford, King de Ramírez and Wermers 2018, 99). Moreover, in Isabelle Drewelow's (2013) study, teaching assistants failed to understand that their role was one of moderator of communication (rather than to serve in a more traditional role as a conduit of knowledge) in online environments. As a result, they perceived that the online component of the course "reduced their roles and presence in the classroom, becoming even an impediment to their teaching" (Drewelow 2013, 1015).

The face-threatening process of moving from a comfortable classroom ecological environment to a virtual ecological educational context requires a tremendous amount of change in the way language teachers perceive their roles and their control over their own pedagogy. Lafford, King de Ramírez, and Wermers (2018) note that "language teachers above the level of Graduate Teaching Assistants (TAs) are usually accustomed to some degree of autonomy over curricular issues and the design/format of the course they teach, and may resist giving up that control" (97). Moreover, the expectation that one would have a significant degree of pedagogical autonomy and control becomes part of language instructors' disciplinary culture from the beginning of their teaching careers. Thus, when forced to teach in unfamiliar digital spaces, language teachers may feel that this autonomy and control is being taken away from them, which could cast doubts on the way they perceive their status, worth, and identity in their departmental culture. Anna Comas-Quinn (2011) notes that the magnitude of this change may feel overwhelming to instructors, who then exhibit negative attitudes toward teaching with technology or imparting an entire course online. As a result of these attitudes, many teachers may decide to just keep their old teaching frameworks and techniques and attempt to adapt the technology to their "tried and true" pedagogical practices (Cutrim and Whyte 2012).

The challenge of the institution is to create faculty buy-in to this move to online teaching, so administrators must come up with strategies to create an environment in which faculty learn to accept and help promote this new way of conceiving pedagogical spaces for world language education. The first step in the process of countering faculty's emotional resistance to change is for administrators and supervisors to meet with resisting faculty and intentionally acknowledge those faculty members' pedagogical success as experienced world language professionals in nondigital spaces. Respect for these faculty members can also be shown by soliciting their faculty's collective advice, collaborative problem-solving, and input into online program goal-setting, the creation of the online training itself, the assessment process, and the rubrics that will be used to evaluate faculty's implementation of the training in their own pedagogical practice. As noted earlier, bringing resistant faculty into the planning process for effecting institutional change creates in them "a sense of empowerment and ownership" (Muhammad and Cruz 2019, 82) of the process, which will make them a stakeholder in the success of the initiative.

Administrators and supervisors can prepare faculty to accept their new roles and identities in a new digital environment by building their confidence and encouraging them to seek out advice from more experienced online faculty mentors who belong to CoPs (Arnold 2017; Comas-Quinn 2011). Faculty confidence can be built by having them teach each other in online environments about the use of technological applications or digital teaching techniques, encouraging them to establish ongoing mentoring relationships with more experienced online faculty via participation in CoPs, and making them feel like a valued member of a unit culture that appreciates pedagogical uses of technology and the time and effort faculty invest in learning about technological integration and online teaching. After preparing their faculty emotionally for the change to digital teaching spaces, administrators should encourage faculty to reinvent themselves and their pedagogical practice so they can serve as role models for other online faculty to help students succeed in new digital environments (Sun 2011). In addition, administrators can encourage trained faculty with the proper level of expertise to take a leadership role in helping to facilitate and shape the unit's movement into online teaching spaces.

- Challenge E-4: The administrative unit lacks critical cultural awareness to recognize and address issues of technology access, training, and usage among marginalized social groups and to include in the language curricula social justice issues to meet the needs of marginalized students, faculty, and communities (Byram 1997, 2012; Lafford 2019).

The fourth emotional challenge stems from the fact that departmental administrators, supervisors, and faculty lack critical cultural awareness (CCA) to recognize and address issues of technology access, training, and usage among marginalized social groups and to include in the language curricula social justice issues to meet the needs of marginalized students, faculty, and communities. Michael Byram (1997) defines the CCA construct, part of his model of intercultural communicative competence, as the "ability to evaluate critically and on the basis of explicit criteria, perspectives, practices and products in one's own and other cultures and countries" (63). In 2012 Byram added to this construct the importance of reflecting critically on "personal and social identities and their relationships to culture" (9). The following strategies for incorporating CCA into CTE online instructor training within an ecological framework were inspired by those proposed by Barbara Lafford (2019).

In an ecological approach to CTE, training instructors need to see themselves not just as a member of a language department but as a fully functioning member of the society at large who are aware of issues of access and marginalization affecting their students and members of the target culture. As part of their CTE training, instructors should be provided with information about the technological access and training that students from marginalized and multicultural communities may lack that would compromise their success in their language courses (Clark and Gorski 2001; Winke and Goertler 2008). For example, Pew Research Center (2019) provides a general overview of technological access and use by these communities, while other authors explore this issue among specific marginalized groups, for example, Aaron Smith (2014) on African Americans and Gretchen Livingston (2011) on Latinx community members in the United States. In addition, students who live at home with multiple school-age siblings may face the challenge of having to share scarce computer resources with others at different times throughout the day. Some students may also suffer from a lack of a stable internet connection, which also compromises their ability to learn in an online environment (Anderson and Perrin 2018). Andrew Perrin (2017) also notes the digital gap that still persists between rural and nonrural residents in the United States.

Language teachers should also be aware of access, training, and usage issues for students living with disabilities (Fox 2011; Greene 2013; Moore 1995), and they should make sure that their internet sources and Web pages meet the compliance standards of the Americans with Disabilities Act (1990/2008) and follow the Web Content Accessibility Guidelines developed by the WC3 Web Accessibility Initiative (W3C WAI 2019).

Teachers should also be given information on another valuable technological resources for meeting the needs of marginalized students and those living with a disability, for example, using mobile-assisted language learning (MALL) such as phones and tablets to access course-related materials. The Pew Research Center (2018) has shown that although 23 percent of African American and 25 percent of Hispanic adults do not use broadband at home or may not have personal computers, they do tend to own smartphones with which they can access materials and communicate with teachers, other students, and target language communities.

In addition to including information on technology access issues, a Critical CALL approach within an ecological framework would also incorporate opportunities for teachers to understand that they are part of a larger social ecology and, consequently, that language programs need to meet the needs of diverse faculty, students, and communities who have been marginalized in their society. Much has been written on how we need to bring in more teachers from minority backgrounds into the classroom (Berchini 2015; Strauss 2015) so they can serve as role models for minority students. In this regard, special efforts should be made by administrators and university professors to recruit more faculty of color (e.g., African Americans, Latinx, or Asian American heritage language speakers as well as international faculty of color) with a willingness to acquire more technological skills as they enter into the language-teaching profession.

Following ideas proposed by Morva McDonald (2005) and George Theoharis and Joanne O'Toole (2011) on the incorporation of social justice issues into teacher training, Lafford (2019) proposes that these critical pedagogical issues could be addressed by including units/modules on CCA as part of the pre- and in-service CTE training. This Critical CALL training would help language teachers meet social justice standards, similar to those proposed by the Teaching Tolerance (2016) initiative in their antibias K–12 pedagogical model. In addition, online language teachers should be aware of excellent sources on teaching languages through the lens of social justice (Glynn, Wesely, and Wassell 2018) and cultural diversity (Hannon and D'Netto 2007) and should be informed that ACTFL (2019) has set up a Critical and Social Justice Approaches special interest group that sends out information and encourages online discussions of incorporating these topics into language teaching.

In addition, teachers of online courses on language, literature, culture, and linguistics can be encouraged to incorporate textbook readings and internet sources that look at Latin American, European, and US history with a critical lens and include social justice topics (e.g., Leeman and Rabin 2007; Martínez-Arboleda 2013; Mojica-Díaz and Sánchez-López 2016). Students can then be asked to participate in discussion boards and video-based telecollaboration projects with other students or with community members in which they can use these readings as a basis for an exchange of ideas on the analysis of social justice issues of power, ideologies, and positionality (Vollmer Rivera 2018) that are expressed in podcasts and social media. As language students perceive the communities standard as the most important of the five world readiness standards (Magnan, Murphy, and Sahakyan 2014), many of them would welcome the chance to interact with target-culture community members via technology (and via F2F meetings when possible).

In addition, a Critical CALL approach with a social justice turn would focus on "engagement with issues of power and inequity and an understanding of how our classrooms and conversations are related to broader social, cultural and political relations" (Helm 2015, 4). One way of trying to effect this kind of engagement would be through the use of telecollaboration / virtual exchanges among students from different socioeconomic backgrounds or cultures so they might directly engage with other language learners to learn more about each other's cultural perspectives, practices, and products (ACTFL 2015; Lewis and O'Dowd 2016a, 2016b). However, Robert O'Dowd (2018) notes that critical cultural reflection in online international (telecollaborative) exchanges does not necessarily lead to action in learners' worlds or communities. María Ocando Finol (2019) states, "By neglecting to address the real-life implications of intercultural learning, educators are renouncing their most significant contribution to society, which is to be facilitators of learning that can drive social change" (28–29).

Just as online teachers need to be aware of issues of inequitable access to technology and social marginalization affecting their students, teacher trainers also must be cognizant of those same issues affecting the language instructors they need to train. If these issues are not addressed in the CTE programs, teachers from marginalized groups may feel that their identities, cultural backgrounds, and life experiences are not being respected and recognized in the training and assessment activities (see chapter 9). Thus, in order for pre- and in-service language instructors to understand how technology can be used to discuss and act on social justice and technology access issues, teacher trainers must normalize a critical approach to online language instructor training. The issue of the normalization of a Critical CALL into the culture of teacher training and evaluation is explored in the concluding chapter of this volume (chapter 10).

In sum, emotional resistance to change may cause faculty to resist training, resulting in their technological inadequacy to handle the institutional changes that lie before them. Thus, in addition to following the suggested strategies for addressing the emotional issues identified above, teacher trainers also need to realize that they must provide faculty with the tools they need to build their technological skills and understanding of online language pedagogy through functional investment strategies.

FUNCTIONALLY BASED CHALLENGES AND INVESTMENT STRATEGIES

According to Muhammad and Cruz (2019), functional investment strategies are those that build capacity among members of an organization. Healey et al. (2011) point out that one of the major factors leading to language faculty's resistance to online training is that they believe that they lack the necessary expertise to carry out the institution's vision for technological integration. Because it would not be fair for administrators to hold faculty accountable for teaching in online environments without providing the training necessary for them to do so, "transformational leaders must fuel their followers with the capacity to confidently perform the task at hand, because failure to do so will result in frustration that, over time, will produce resistance to change" (Muhammad and Cruz 2019, 64).

In addition, departmental leaders must be aware of the knowledge and skills their language faculty will require to teach successfully in virtual environments (discussed in chapter 4), and they must be willing to make functional investments to address the challenges to online training arising from faculty's lack of expertise in technological integration. Below we explore functionally based challenges to CTE online training (e.g., F-1, F-2) and strategies to address them.

This category of challenges is related to many faculty lacking the necessary skills to integrate technology into the online language curriculum and many of them believing they have received insufficient and inadequate CTE training to meet workplace needs. Moreover, faculty and CTE scholars have voiced concerns over a lack of sufficient infrastructure, a prioritization of technology over pedagogy, a lack of qualified online faculty trainers, a lack of access to current and reliable equipment and technical support, faculty technophobia, a lack of sufficient online instructor presence, and insufficient follow-up to their initial training, for example, a lack of information on resources for self-directed learning and opportunities for ongoing mentoring.

- Challenge F-1: In-service faculty believe that they have received insufficient and inadequate online training for them to meet their workplace needs (Comas-Quinn 2011; Healey et al. 2011; Kessler 2006, 2007; Son and Windeatt 2017b).

Language faculty dissatisfaction with their CTE training is discussed extensively in chapter 2. This first functional challenge can be met by providing frequent and ongoing hands-on training focused on both breadth-first and depth-first approaches for faculty at different levels of expertise (Beaven et al. 2010; Compton 2009; Healey et al. 2011; Torsani 2016; Son and Windeatt 2017b). Tita Beaven and colleagues (2010) argue that teacher training must take these disparate levels of trainee expertise into account as the needs of novice teachers are different from those of in-service instructors who are reassessing their roles and pedagogical practices to include technology integration.

As a matter of course, this training would allow teachers to be given hands-on practice with the technologies they will be asked to use and to be given sufficient time to learn and implement technology integration into their online curriculum. In order for faculty to have sufficient time to explore the affordances and constraints of new technologies in different contexts, administrators need to start online training early and integrate it into existing methodology and other educational program courses that teacher candidates take as they progress through the program (Desjardins and Peters 2007; Hubbard 2008; Peters 2006).

Supervisors also need to provide training that respects faculty time and types of preferred learning experiences (Germain-Rutherford and Ernest 2015; Tobin, Mandernach, and Taylor 2015). Amber Dailey-Hebert and colleagues (2014) carried out a survey of adjunct instructors that showed a preference for mostly static and asynchronous online faculty development initiatives over those that were synchronous (e.g., video conferencing, peer review, or live chats). The flexibility provided by asynchronous online training would be an advantage to adjunct and full-time instructors who need to adjust their training time to their busy schedules. However, when feasible, hands-on F2F or one-on-one synchronous online training may be preferred by some instructors new to technology integration. In addition, research should be conducted into the effectiveness of CTE training (Kessler 2006) for meeting current technological needs of in-service teachers in the workplace in order to inform future training for pre- and in-service teachers.

- Challenge F-2: Faculty have voiced concerns over a lack of reliable infrastructure, lack of access to current and reliable equipment and applications, and lack of technical support (Bauer-Ramazani 2006; Hubbard 2008; Peters 2006).

In order to address faculty concerns over a lack of a reliable infrastructure and a lack of opportunity to explore current software applications, administrators need to provide teacher trainers and instructors with state-of-the-art technological equipment and training materials that will allow them to explore cutting-edge applications for online teaching (Son and Windeatt 2017b). Administrators and supervisors should also investigate whether a lack of technological infrastructure hinders the abilities of teachers and students to meet language technology standards (Healey et al. 2011), and they should provide online language faculty with the hardware and software they need to function efficiently in online environments in order to meet those standards. Finally, CTE trainings should also include information of where faculty and students can access 24/7 technology support from their educational institution or technology providers (e.g., for teleconferencing tools [Zoom, Skype] or course management systems [Canvas, Blackboard]).

- Challenge F-3: A focus on technology over pedagogy in CTE training courses can lead to tools being presented without discussing the possibilities and appropriate uses of those tools in specific pedagogical contexts (Comas-Quinn 2011; Compton 2009; Hanson-Smith 2016; Kessler 2006, 2007; Son and Windeatt 2017b).

A major area of concern by CALL scholars relates to the fact that CTE training courses often focus more on teachers learning to use technologies than on pedagogically sound ways of implementing those tools into the language curriculum. A focus on technology over pedagogy in CTE training courses can lead to tools being presented in a pedagogical vacuum with a lack of discussion on the affordances and appropriate uses of those tools in specific pedagogical contexts.

In order for the teachers' use of technologies to facilitate the attainment of pedagogical objectives, language instructors must understand the affordances and constraints of the technologies presented to them during the training. They also need to be aware of what technologies lend themselves more easily for use in their particular educational contexts and must be able to "adjust the potential of any tool to their pedagogical objectives" (Guichon and Hauck 2011, 191). Therefore, CTE training must involve a discussion of the affordances and constraints of tools used in online teaching contexts and how to implement technological tools effectively to help students meet their learning objectives.

- Challenge F-4: There is a lack of CALL expertise on the part of teacher trainers and supervisors, who believe a CALL specialist should be hired to train them (Beaven et al. 2010; Hubbard 2008; Healey et al. 2011; Kessler 2006).

The lack of CALL expertise on the part of teacher trainers and supervisors leads to their reluctance to be labeled as a CALL specialist in their administrative unit. Kessler (2006) and Beaven and colleagues (2010) note that many language faculty felt that CALL was beyond their grasp and that language programs really needed to hire a CALL specialist to train faculty.

In response to the need for a CALL specialist to lead online language instructor training, administrators should invest in hiring a trainer who uses an approach that prioritizes pedagogy over technology and is grounded in relevant theoretical frameworks and empirical CALL research (Compton 2009; Fuchs 2006; Guichon and Hauck 2011; Healey et al. 2011; Kessler 2006; Lafford, King de Ramírez, and Wermers 2018; Son and Windeatt 2017b; Stockwell 2009). No matter the job title this CALL specialist carries, supports should be put in place to ensure that this person has ample time to pursue activities that meet the expectations of their job description. Thus, assistant professors still in their probationary period should not be expected to direct an online language program in addition to carrying out heavy research and teaching commitments.

Call specialists should use the CTE training they provide in situated, online environments as a model for training faculty to acquire relevant skills to use in those same digital contexts (Compton 2009; Gleason and Schmitt 2018; Slaouti and Motteram 2006), including technological skills for teaching (to improve their own communication, collaboration, and efficiency), record keeping, feedback, and assessment. Relevant faculty skills also include the ability to carry out needs analyses and create effective tasks and course designs; to facilitate student interaction and collaboration and student acquisition of communicative and intercultural communicative competence; to critically reflect on their own and others' teaching performance via self-evaluation or use of a critical friend; and to evaluate student outcomes and the effectiveness and quality of tasks, courses, programs, training, assessment processes, and rubrics (Compton 2009; Egbert 2006; Hampel and Stickler 2005; Healey et al. 2011). In addition, CALL specialists should work with departmental administrators and supervisors to set up virtual field experiences and virtual practicums for preservice teachers to build their confidence before they take responsibility for an online class (ACTFL/CAEP 2013; Compton 2009).

- Challenge F-5: As a result of these functional challenges, faculty can develop a discomfort with technology (technophobia), which diminishes their willingness to integrate technology into their language curricula (Bauer-Ramazani 2006; Healey et al. 2011; Kessler 2006; Robb 2006).

Faculty who feel frustrated by the lack of current and reliable infrastructure at their institution and overwhelmed by their need to keep up with the pace of technological change without proper support and a sustainable infrastructure may develop a fear of having to integrate new technologies into their language curriculum (technophobia). Kessler (2006) notes that this discomfort with technology on the part of many language teachers affects the quality of their teaching. However, comfort with these materials is something that develops over time as a function of their understanding of the value of technological integration, their buy-in to technological integration, and their opportunities to explore new technologies and receive guidance over how they can ready themselves to incorporate technology into a language curriculum.

To begin, Lafford, Carmen King de Ramírez, and James Wermers (2018) suggest that faculty explore to a greater degree the affordances and constraints of their course management system to see what tools and applications are already included in that environment. Kessler and Phil Hubbard (2017) proposes addressing this resistance by preparing teachers for changes in technologies, interactive materials, and a social future. Trainers need to prepare faculty for changes in technologies, for developing basic information and communications technologies competence, specific technical competence of the software, and for dealing with constraints and possibilities of the medium and affordances and constraints of their institutional environment (Hampel and Stickler 2005; Kessler 2006; Kessler and Hubbard 2017; Lafford, King de Ramírez, and Wermers 2018; Major 2015; see also the CTE/CALL Resources on this book's Web page, www.press.georgetown.edu).

These authors note the need for teachers to receive training on new technologies and to leverage students' interest in interactive materials via preferred platforms already used for personal communication (e.g., Twitter, Instagram, Snapchat, Facebook, gaming, natural language processing) for the purpose of language learning. In addition, new MALL technologies enable students to use applications on their own mobile devices (e.g., cell phones, tablets) to learn languages (see CTE/CALL Resource List on this book's Web page, www.press.georgetown.edu) for references on these technologies). As long as instructors can match student interest to tools taught in the training, the use of technology will be relevant and fresh for the student (Kessler 2006). If students react positively to the teacher's efforts to include their preferred technologies in the online language curriculum, instructors may feel more comfortable integrating those applications into their teaching.

In order for faculty to be prepared for a social future in which they are adept at being active members of online communities, they need to be comfortable using the tools that are available for participating in and creating new CoPs and CoIs (see Major 2015, 250–52) with other online language teachers. To facilitate faculty participation in CoPs, trainers can encourage teachers to join already established professional CoPs to increase their knowledge of the use of these tools in specific educational contexts (e.g., Webheads in Action). (See CTE/CALL Resource List on this book's Web page for more information on these CoPs, www.press.georgetown.edu.)

Thus, trainers should help prepare teachers for a social future and participation (with teacher cognitive, social, and teaching presence) in postcourse discussion lists, CoPs and CoIs, and MOOCs; involve them in project-based collaborative tasks (e.g., wikis); encourage them to develop their creativity and own personal style in these spaces; and give them a target language lexicon for working in digital spaces and target-culture netiquette norms (Arnold, Ducate, and Lomicka 2007; Arnold, Ducate, Lomicka, and Lord 2005; Debski 2006; Hampel and Stickler 2005; Hanson-Smith 2006, 2016; Kessler and Hubbard 2017; Robb 2006; Son and Windeatt 2017b).

- Challenge F-6: Discomfort may also arise when language teachers ("students") do not feel connected to language teacher trainers ("faculty") when using technology to communicate and interact in digital spaces (Hampel 2009; Lamy and Hampel 2007).

Faculty discomfort may also arise when they do not feel connected to their teacher trainers when using technology to communicate and interact. For instance, Regine Hampel (2009) proposes that a lack of instructor social presence can cause a number of socioaffective challenges to arise—namely, difficulties in building a sense of community, anxiety, and lack of motivation. Research has shown that all these factors impede interaction and successful communication (Lamy and Hampel 2007).

D. Randy Garrison, Terry Anderson, and Walter Archer (2001) propose that teachers need to establish cognitive, social, and teaching presence in their digital classroom spaces in order to connect with students and establish a rapport that will help them overcome their anxiety about the technologies they are required to use and the acculturation process they go through while learning to communicate and learn in digital spaces. Although mention of this anxiety challenge first arose in the CALL literature when discussing the anxiety students felt about their connections to their language instructors (Chametzky 2019; Horwitz, Horwitz, and Cole 1986; Martin and Álvarez Valdivia

2017), faculty trainees ("students") may also experience this type of anxiety in online sessions with teacher trainers ("instructors"). Leading by example, teacher trainers need to instill in language teachers the need to establish cognitive, social, and teaching presence in virtual teaching environments.

- Challenge F-7: Faculty have noted insufficient follow-up (resources or ongoing mentoring) to their initial training (Bauer-Ramazani 2006; Kessler 2006; Son and Windeatt 2017b).

The need for follow-up to initial training and mentoring is explored in chapter 2. This challenge can be met by providing faculty with a list of online resources for self-directed learning (Davies 2012; Hanson-Smith 2016; Hubbard 2020; Kessler 2006; Major 2015; Meskill and Anthony 2015; Son and Windeatt 2017b) and by providing faculty with opportunities for ongoing mentoring as pre- and in-service teachers with mentoring oversight (Eib and Miller 2006; Hampel 2009; Hampel and Stickler 2005; Kolaitis et al. 2006; Palloff and Pratt 2011).

As noted in chapter 2, Hanson-Smith (2016) coined the term "personal learning environments" to refer to the milieus in which online faculty immerse themselves, which they have created by exploring, collecting, and curating the knowledge they acquire about specific topics. During their training, language teachers should be provided with a list of resources for online teaching so that they can continue their professional development as self-directed learners and practitioners after their initial training comes to an end. A detailed list of CTE and CALL online resources is found in the CTE/CALL Resource List on this book's Web page, at www.press.georgetown.edu.

In addition, language teachers need to have opportunities for ongoing mentoring throughout their training program, and administrative units need to provide mentoring oversight to ensure that best mentoring practices are being followed. They can do this through a formal one-on-one mentoring program (pairing new faculty and teaching assistants with established online teachers, chapter 8) or they can seek out peer mentors in the CoPs / personal learning networks in which they participate (Hanson-Smith 2006, 2016). Robert Marzano, Timothy Waters, and Brian McNulty (2005) propose that students can also serve as mentors to faculty. In this reverse mentoring process (Chaudhuri and Ghosh 2012; McCanney 2018), senior faculty are assigned young mentors to facilitate their engagement with millennials.

Faculty who have been mentored successfully can develop confidence in their skills and a sense of empowerment, which will fuel their desire to "make change happen—not because the leader tells them to do so, but because they understand why the change is needed and they feel equipped to successfully accomplish the task" (Muhammad and Cruz 2019, 65). Thus, high-quality training and mentoring play a key role in making it possible for administrators to get a return on their investment. However, in order to demonstrate this return, faculty have to be held accountable for their training.

FACULTY ACCOUNTABILITY CHALLENGES AND STRATEGIES

Muhammad and Cruz (2019) propose that leaders have the right to collect a return on their investments, but it is illogical to expect that return without them having made the appropriate cognitive, emotional, and functional investments in faculty development described above. Thus, during their training and after their initial training has ended and teachers have had the chance to explore the uses of new technologies and ways of thinking about digital spaces, they must be held accountable (through formative and summative evaluations) for being able to integrate technology into their online pedagogical practice. In this section we discuss challenges to effecting this sort of faculty accountability and strategies for addressing them.

Challenges to faculty accountability for their online training include the need for consistent and grounded assessment practices, fair and contextualized faculty evaluations, ongoing assessment of CTE training, assessment processes and rubrics, and recognition of the value of online language teaching by traditional institutional cultures.

- Challenge FA-1: A consistent, theoretically and empirically grounded method of holding faculty accountable for their technological, pedagogical, and evaluative training may be lacking in academic units (Lafford, King de Ramírez, and Wermers 2018).

Even though academic units may be imparting CTE online training that is theoretically and empirically based, administrative units may not always have a plan to consistently hold their language faculty accountable for the training they receive. In recognition of the fact that CTE faculty development is an ongoing need, trainers could assign a mentor to monitor and assess faculty integration of technological, pedagogical, and evaluative skills into their language curricula (during and after their training) using formative and summative assessments (Eib and Miller 2006; Kolaitis et al. 2006; Meskill et al. 2006; Son and Windeatt 2017b).

- Challenge FA-2: Faculty need to be assessed fairly on their integration of technology into their pedagogical practice, according to their individual circumstances (Lafford, King de Ramírez, and Wermers 2018).

Online language faculty may feel that their individual circumstances (e.g., access to and experience with teaching with technology, expectations for feedback that are culturally based [see chapter 9]) are not being taken into account when they are assessed on their integration of technology into their online pedagogical practice (Lafford, King de Ramírez, and Wermers 2018). However, an ecological approach to assessment (chapters 6 through 9) would consider all of these factors when assessing online faculty and would tailor appropriate assessments for faculty.

Just as CTE trainings need to take participants' prior experience and skill levels, roles, and institutional circumstances into account for structuring particular types of CTE training, assessments of faculty's implementation of technology into their online curricula also need to address those same factors. Therefore, faculty assessment rubrics need to fairly assess faculty expertise in online language teaching according to their level of pedagogical, technological, and evaluation skills; their roles; their cultural expectations for types of feedback; and the affordances and constraints of their workplace environment. Lafford, King de Ramírez, and Wermers (2018) suggest the creation of a flexible, modular rubric from which appropriate assessment modules would be chosen according to the circumstances and roles of the person being evaluated. We propose such a rubric in chapter 6 and appendix C-2 of the current volume.

- Challenge FA-3: The conclusions of faculty self-assessments may vary widely from those of supervisor assessments, even when the same rubric is used (Lafford, King de Ramírez, and Wermers 2018).

The conclusions of faculty self-assessments and the evaluations of their teaching carried out by their supervisors may differ considerably, even when the same rubric is used (Lafford, King de Ramírez, and Wermers 2018). These problems may be addressed by inviting instructor input into the creation of the faculty assessment rubrics and having them participate in norming sessions so that there is agreement on the manner in which the rubrics are to be applied. In these norming sessions, "terms are defined and operationalized, and evaluations of online teaching would be carried out individually (and then compared) to see where discrepancies occur in the application of the rubric" (Lafford, King de Ramírez, and Wermers 2018, 109). Chapter 9 of this volume provides more detailed discussion of the issue of discrepancies between instructor and supervisor evaluations.

- Challenge FA-4: The quality and usefulness of training programs, assessment processes, and rubrics need to be evaluated by all stakeholders, and those results should inform future iterations of training and assessment instruments (Kessler 2006; Winke and Goertler 2008).

In addition to assessments of language faculty, the CTE training programs, assessment process, and the rubrics used to assess online instructor performance need to be evaluated by users, and those results must inform future professional development programs and the ongoing adjustment of assessment instruments (Kessler 2006; Winke and Goertler 2008). To address this challenge, all stakeholders need to provide feedback on the unit's CTE training, the assessment process, and assessment rubrics, and administrators and trainers must incorporate that feedback into improving the quality of their training programs and assessment instruments. One way of facilitating this process is to include goals for incorporating stakeholder feedback on CTE training and assessments into criteria established for departmental program assessments required annually by university administrations. Sample rubrics for evaluating of CTE training programs, the assessment process, and assessment instruments can be found in appendices B-1, B-2, and B-3, respectively.

- Challenge FA-5: Traditional institutional culture may not recognize and appreciate the value of digital teaching spaces and the time and expertise it takes to integrate technology successfully into a language curriculum and to maintain a quality online language program (Hubbard 2008; Lafford, King de Ramírez, and Wermers 2018; Modern Language Association 2007).

Another challenge to effecting results and faculty accountability may be due to the inertia of a traditional institutional culture steeped in decades of F2F teaching assumptions; such a culture does not necessarily recognize and appreciate the value of digital teaching spaces and the time and expertise it takes to integrate technology successfully into a language curriculum and to maintain a quality online language program. We propose that there is a need to change institutional cultures to value and reward technological integration into the language curriculum, and to do so using a student-centered, constructivist approach within a normalized Critical CALL cultural ecological framework.

Just as the Modern Language Association (2007) urges language departments to create new structures for a globalized, changed world (post 9/11) that expands language curricula to include a more interdisciplinary focus and breaks down walls between the study of language and literature and between faculty ranks, these administrative units are now being required to create new, innovative departmental cultural structures that value digital teaching spaces in our post-COVID19 world (June 2020; McMurtrie 2020). Faculty's willingness to make an ecological cultural paradigm shift into digital learning spaces will also allow their students to become more comfortable with technology and develop the technological expertise they will need to succeed in a twenty-first-century skills-based job market.

As this type of ecological cultural change has to come from the top, an institution's transformational leaders need to make the aforementioned three types of investments to get the results they want. By attending to the cognitive, emotional, and functional needs of language faculty, these leaders help to prepare faculty to transition to a place and time in a new departmental culture where they can be held accountable for their performance in a new digital workplace environment. This process of cultural transformation involves the creation of a "third place" (Kramsch 1999, 2009) between the home (C1) and target (C2) cultures for students to inhabit as they negotiate new understandings of how these home and target cultures function and intersect. Although this third place metaphor originally meant to focus on the acquisition of intercultural competence as one transitions from the sole use of the cultural lens of the home culture to the incorporation of target culture perceptual lenses, we believe that it aptly describes the processes involved in effecting the intellectual shifts necessary for language faculty from a traditional F2F teaching culture (C1) to acquire the perspectives and skills needed to navigate new digital teaching environments (C2). Thus, as language teachers become more comfortable in new digital environments, they can start constructing their understandings of what it means to teach and interact in those new ecological spaces.

Following what CTE literature has proposed, the collective norms, values, and beliefs of this new departmental culture could include an implementation of a student-centered approach grounded in a constructivist pedagogy. Supporting this point is Lillian Wong and Phil Benson's (2006) case study that shows that the teacher who is more comfortable with a student-centered approach is able to more effectively integrate technology into the language curriculum than the instructor favoring a teacher-centered approach.

A digital-friendly departmental culture would also value and reward faculty who integrate technology into their language teaching. For instance, university faculty who bring new ideas about online teaching could be recognized as leaders (e.g., provost or university/department teaching fellows) in online instruction initiatives and be invited to share those ideas in institutional professional symposia or in virtual forums. In addition, administrators could encourage both new and experienced online teachers to share digital

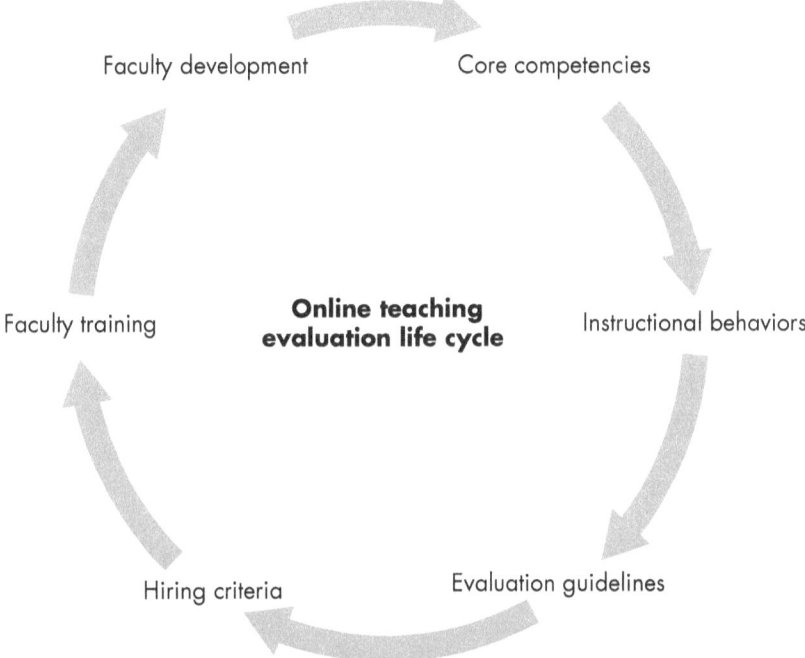

FIGURE 3.1 The Online Teaching Evaluation Life Cycle (Tobin, Mandernach, and Taylor 2015, 242)

stories on their third place experiences as they transition from traditional to digital teaching cultures. If faculty are openly invited to join the new digital culture and are supported and incentivized to do so, perhaps they will feel less resistant to the journey they are being asked to take.

An integral part of this new departmental culture would be the establishment of an online teaching evaluation life cycle, such as that proposed in Tobin, Mandernach, and Taylor (2015). As figure 3.1 shows, in this life cycle, faculty training leads to faculty development of core competencies. These abilities are demonstrated in certain faculty behaviors, which are then assessed according to established *evaluation guidelines*. The establishment of core competencies and desired faculty pedagogical practices (behaviors) would then be included in the hiring criteria for faculty expected to teach in online environments. The recursivity of this life-cycle system is seen when faculty hired to teach in digital environments arrive on campus and continue to undergo further faculty training to increase their skill capacities and perhaps participate in training new faculty to teach in online spaces.

Tobin and colleagues' (2015) training/evaluation life cycle shows how these two processes are inexorably linked. Explaining the value of such an integrated system to all language faculty would constitute one of the cognitive investments that administrators need to make to support and recruit language faculty who teach in online environments. Functional faculty investments throughout this cycle could be made through assigning a mentor to carry out formative and summative assessments, meet with faculty to go over their self-assessments, help faculty set goals for improvement, and determine future faculty training needs. In order to foster online language teacher success, mentors must keep in mind the importance of the emotional investment of establishing and maintaining a supportive teacher-mentor relationship throughout the iterations of this recursive cycle.

In sum, we are calling for a fundamental cultural change in which transformational educational leaders motivate language departments to create a set of values and norms that promote technology integration, support teaching languages in online environments with pedagogical practices grounded in student-centered learning and Critical CALL approaches, and demonstrate a willingness to not only reward these activities but to welcome and support new faculty members during their cultural journey from more traditional F2F teaching environments into new ecological teaching spaces constructed in a digital world.

To prepare teachers for this cultural journey, they need to receive training based on best practices of online teaching that highlights the skills they need to acquire and on which they will be assessed (Palloff and Pratt 2011). In chapter 4 we explore the skills that CTE scholars have identified as crucial to the success of online language instructors.

PUTTING IT ALL TOGETHER

Throughout this chapter, challenges to CTE online training are followed directly with strategies to address them, based on Muhammad and Cruz's (2019) investment model. For each set of challenges, specific ideas are proposed for the implementation of cognitive, emotional, and functional administrative investments to facilitate language faculty's transition to digital pedagogical spaces. A summary of these challenges and strategies to meet them is found in appendix A-2. This checklist can be used by language programs to choose strategies needed for a given training program for online instructors.

4

Core Competencies for Online Language Instructors

Core competencies for language instructors who integrate technology or teach blended and online environments need to be established in order to set instructional goals, provide them with relevant training, and inform stakeholder assessments of their abilities. Thomas Tobin, B. Jean Mandernach, and Ann Taylor (2015) note the need for institutional expectations of those competencies to be "current, relevant, and aligned with research findings" (242).

As is the case for CTE training models, the identification of skills and standards necessary for language instructors to teach with technology has evolved from its ancillary status in more general world language professional development models (e.g., the *ACTFL/CAEP Program Standards for the Preparation of Foreign Language Teachers* [ACTFL/CAEP 2013]; and the *European Profile for Language Teacher Education* [Kelly et al. 2004]) to occupy a more central place in departmental curricula. This chapter explores CTE literature devoted to the identification and development of CALL skills and standards needed to teach languages successfully by integrating technology or teaching in online environments.

DEVELOPMENT OF CALL LITERACIES

CALL scholars have proposed several different types of computer literacies needed by language instructors. Going beyond the International Technology Education Association's definition of technological literacy as "the ability to use, manage, assess, and understand technology" (ITEA 2003, 9), Jesse Gleason and Elena Schmitt (2018) followed the lead of William Cope and Mary Kalantzis (2015) and New London Group (1996) in their preference for the terms "new literacies" or "multiliteracies," which highlight "the multitude of multi-modal, technology-mediated spaces and environments in which we live and learn today" (Gleason and Schmitt 2018, 117). Gleason and Schmitt (2018) propose that language instructors should develop these technology-specific literacies by taking graduate courses in which the use of various technological tools is required. By having to learn how to use these tools as students in their own graduate courses (a situated learning environment), future language instructors will be better able to train their future students on the best ways to take advantages of the affordances of these tools. However, they also note that the ever-changing technological landscape requires teachers to learn to use new tools that emerge after their initial training.

In addition, Mark Warschauer (2002a) proposes four electronic literacies that language teachers need to develop for CALL instruction: "computer literacy (i.e., comfort and fluency in keyboarding and using computers), information literacy (i.e., the ability to find and critically evaluate online information), multimedia literacy (i.e., the ability to produce and interpret complex documents, comprising texts, images and sounds), and computer-mediated communication literacy (i.e., knowledge of the pragmatics of individual and group online interaction)" (455). Christine Bauer-Ramazani (2006) made these four literacies into goals for her online CALL course, noting that participants in the course were expected to engage in certain behaviors to satisfy these literacies proposed by Warschauer (2002a), that is, to create vibrant learning communities to share knowledge and build competence; learn how to use various technologies, applications, and resources to author multimedia materials and activities; use discussions, peer reviews, and critical reviews to evaluate tools, media, and resources for their pedagogical effectiveness; and review literature on CALL research and the influence of theories and practices in related fields (e.g., second-language acquisition, applied linguistics, educational fields) on the development of the field. The importance of these particular skills for online language instructors has been noted by several CALL scholars, which is evident in the sections that follow.

These literacies are related to the more inclusive construct of digital literacy, defined by Colin Lankshear and Michele Knobel (2008) as "a shorthand for the myriad social practices and conceptions of engaging in meaning making mediated by texts that are produced, received, distributed, exchanged, etc., via digital codification" (5). Christoph Hafner, Alice Chik, and Rodney Jones (2015) note that CALL research on this topic includes a focus on the idea that "new modes of reading, writing, and communication create new learning needs that can be addressed in second and foreign language education" (3) and that "globalized, online spaces create new, multilingual contexts, within which second and foreign language learners can autonomously capitalize on learning opportunities" (3).

Aside from these general literacy frameworks, CALL scholars have also proposed certain sets of skills necessary for the success of language teachers integrating technologies into their curriculum and teaching online. A discussion of these skill sets constitutes the focus of the next section.

INSTRUCTOR SKILLS NEEDED TO INTEGRATE TECHNOLOGY INTO WORLD LANGUAGE CURRICULA

The CTE literature abounds with studies that identify the skills that language instructors should possess in order to facilitate their integration of technology into their curricula. A discussion of selected key studies on this topic follows below.

Building on Lee Shulman's (1986) identification of pedagogical content knowledge (PCK) skills as those needed by instructors in educational technologies, Punyashloke Mishra and Mathew Koehler (2006) add technological knowledge to this model to create the concept of technological pedagogical content knowledge (TPACK). This model focuses on the interaction and integration among all three components and highlights new types of knowledge needed where these fields intersect (see figure 4.1). For instance, the intersection of technological knowledge and the other two components produces technological content knowledge (TCK) and technological pedagogical knowledge (TPK). TCK can inform a teacher's use of technology to enhance or modify content and can also help students create digital products to evidence their own understanding of the content, for example, a Web site comparing the intersection of the work of poets and artists from a given era, such as those living in Paris in the 1920s. On the other hand, TPK could inform a teacher's decision to use a particular type of tool to foster specific forms of discussion (e.g., an asynchronous tool like a discussion board or blog to elicit carefully thought-out arguments on a given topic in written form, or a synchronous tool like Zoom or Skype to foster informal discussions or debates, where students have to think on their feet to defend their points of view). In this TPACK model, the knowledge integration that results from the intersection of all three elements forms the ideal knowledge base for teachers integrating technology into their classes.

To illustrate how these types of knowledge can be applied to pedagogical practice, Shu-Ju Diana Tai (2015) moved this TPACK construct into a model focused on experiential learning called the TPACK-in-Action model. This model, based on a learning-by-doing approach, is carried out in a five-step integrated process: modelization, analysis, and demonstration of a linguistic activity executed with a given technology by the teacher, followed by the

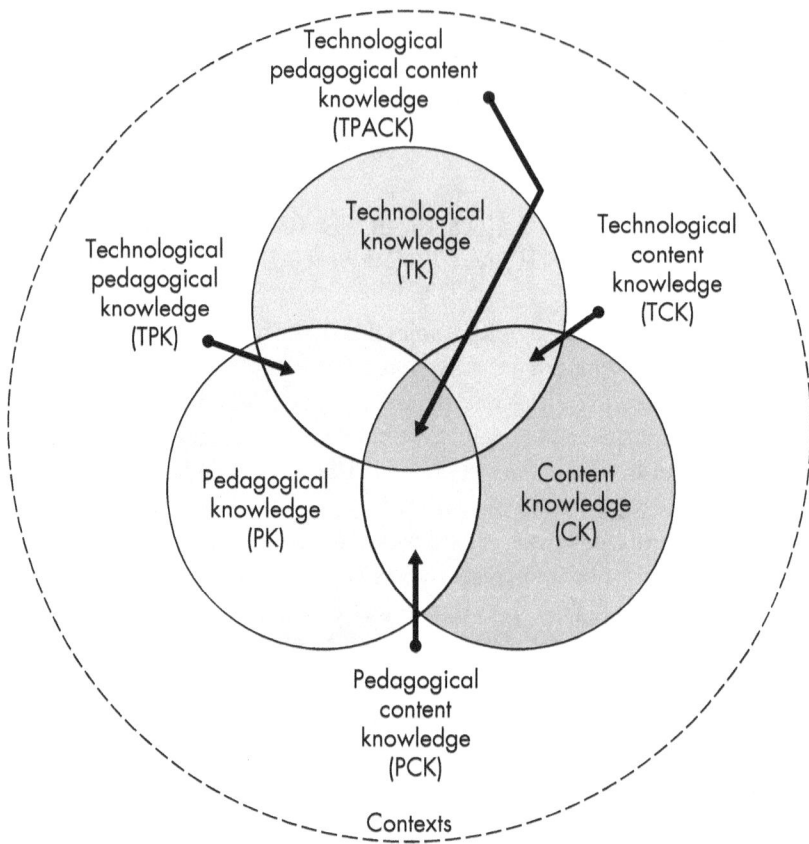

FIGURE 4.1 Technological Pedagogical Content Knowledge (TPACK) (Mishra and Koehler 2006; courtesy of Media Wiki)

students' application of this knowledge to the realization of the activity and, finally, by students' reflection on their CALL activity.

In Phil Hubbard and Mike Levy's (2006a) CALL teacher education model, a distinction is made by the authors between an instructor's mere knowledge of technological and pedagogical competencies and their ability to put that knowledge into practice through the possession of actual skills in these areas (see table 4.1). The authors also note that these competencies (knowledge and skills) will need to be interpreted and honed within the context of the particular functional roles played by pre-and in-service classroom teachers, CALL specialists, and CALL professionals, that is, practitioner, developer, researcher, and trainer.

TABLE 4.1 Technical and Pedagogical Knowledge and Skills

	Technical	Pedagogical
CALL Knowledge	Systematic and incidental understanding of the computer system, including peripheral devices, in terms of hardware, software, and networking.	Systematic and incidental understanding of ways of effectively using the computer in language teaching.
CALL Skill	Ability to use technical knowledge and experience both for the operation of the computer system and relevant applications and in dealing with various problems.	Ability to use knowledge and experience to determine effective materials, content, and tasks, and to monitor and assess results appropriately.

Source: Hubbard and Levy 2006a, 16.

Scholars based in Europe have also proposed a set of technopedagogical general competencies for CALL teachers. For instance, Nicolas Guichon and Mirjam Hauck (2011) identify a list of the types of abilities required of language teachers who wish to integrate technology into their curriculum; these skills are incorporated into the thematic discussion below. However, these authors also stated that in order to carry out these tasks effectively, online instructors need to possess critical semiotic awareness, "i.e., teachers' capacity to adjust the potential of any tool to their pedagogical objectives and to the relation they wish to establish with their (distant) students, so that pedagogical skills gradually become semio-pedagogical ones and thus reflect the demands made on language professionals" (191).

In addition to identifying general TPACK and technopedagogical skills for all language teachers, some studies have specifically looked at competencies and skills that language instructors must have when they teach online. Because the skills needed to integrate CALL technologies into blended language courses overlap to a great deal with those needed to teach completely online, we review CTE studies that focus on language instructor skills and standards needed in digital pedagogical environments.

In the CTE literature, studies identifying technopedagogical skills needed by language instructors present those abilities as either skill lists or standards. Lists of skills proposed by Lily Compton (2009), Regine Hampel and Ursula Stickler (2005), and Susan Yue Hua Sun (2011) are characterized by short phrases (e.g., "Emphasise learner cooperation and collaboration"; Sun 2011, 444), while standards proposed by Graham Davies (2012) and Deborah Healey and colleagues (2011) consist of declarative sentences that create clear expectations for the instructor (e.g., "GOAL 4: Language teachers use technology to improve communication, collaboration, and efficiency"; Healey et al. 2011, vii).

The wisdom of creating such standards for online language instructors in lieu of just listing technological skills that they should possess is characterized by Simone Torsani (2016) in the following manner: "Standards... constitute an obvious benchmark, as they provide a shared and thorough body of assumptions about what a teacher needs to be able to do in order to successful integrate technology" (182). Greg Kessler (2016) believes that standards "can be used in objective evaluation of teacher abilities" (79), and Elizabeth Hanson-Smith (2016) proposes that "a set of standards demonstrates to teachers, teacher educators, administrators, curriculum writers, publishers and students what is meant by competency in the pedagogical uses of current technologies" (219).

Hubbard and Levy (2006b), writing in their preface to *Teacher Education in CALL* about Kathryn Murphy-Judy and Bonnie Youngs's (2006) chapter on the establishment of technology standards for language teacher education, credentialing, and certification and the implementation of those standards in three different geographic regions, concur with Kathleen Graves (2009) and Torsani (2016) that the establishment of standards is a double-edged sword: "Standards may suffer from being too prescriptive and narrowly defined, or alternatively, they may be too general and vague. Overly prescriptive standards can have a strong and detrimental impact on creativity in CALL and provoke a negative reaction because teachers and students feel their hands are tied whenever they want to try something new; on the other hand, standards that are too general and vague may provide so little direction that they are of no practical value" (Hubbard and Levy 2006b, 44). Thus, the creation of technology standards for online language instructors must strive to find the "golden mean" between being overly prescriptive and unnecessarily vague.

Complementing studies of instructor technopedagogical skills and standards, Chun Lai, Yong Zhao, and Ning Li's (2008) study proposes design principles for distance foreign language environments that language teachers should follow when creating online language courses. These principles are written with imperative verb forms as "action items" to guide instructors in their online course design: "Facilitate high-quality interactions with multiple opportunities for negotiation of meaning and cultural understanding" (85).

In the following discussion we focus on the thematic categories that identify language instructor technopedagogical skills identified in key works in the CTE literature (i.e., general CALL skills [Davies 2012; Guichon and Hauck 2011; Healey et al. 2011] and online skills [Compton 2009; Hampel and Stickler 2005; Lai, Zhao, and Li 2008; Sun 2011]). The three thematic categories were inspired (in part) by those used by Compton (2009), that is, technological skills, pedagogical skills (course design, student-centered learning, interaction and socialization), assessment skills, and professional development. Although we review the core competencies below as sets of skills, in the new, modular online language instructor evaluation rubric that we propose in chapter 6, the skill expectations are written as standards to set out explicit expectations for faculty attainment of those competencies.

In the sections below we identify general skill types without reference to levels of ability within each skill. The question of expertise levels are explored in chapter 5 on assessment and chapter 6 on the rubrics we propose to assess various aspects of online language instruction.

Technological Skills

The CTE literature has advocated for online language teachers to develop basic technological skills that meet or exceed the technology standards for students in their unit and ensure that students meet those standards (Compton 2009; Guichon and Hauck 2011; Hampel and Stickler 2005; Healey et al. 2011). Instructors can start by exploring the use of features within their learning management system (e.g., Blackboard, Canvas) and technologies required for the course so they can use and modify them; they should also be able to identify and understand the affordances and constraints of these technologies within the unit's pedagogical context (Compton 2009; Guichon and Hauck 2011; Hampel and Stickler 2005). Language faculty also need to make the unit aware of technological infrastructure insufficiencies (e.g., lack of equipment able to accommodate current technological demands) or course-related issues that would hinder pedagogical progress. They also need to know what kind of 24/7 technical support to deal with software applications or hardware problems is available to them and to their students (Lai, Zhao, and Li 2008) and to make students aware of these resources.

As noted in this book's introduction, instead of merely adding on technologically based activities to a traditional curriculum, CTE scholars call for faculty to integrate technology coherently into their pedagogical approaches (Gruba 2004; Healey et al. 2011; Hong 2010; Levy and Stockwell 2006). In order to effect this integration, language faculty must choose suitable technology and software to match online tasks and facilitate online language learning (Compton 2009; TESOL International Association 2010; Healey et al. 2011); develop critical semiotic awareness (Guichon and Hauck 2011) to use, troubleshoot, adapt, and create technology applications for online tasks (ACTFL/CAEP 2013; Compton 2009; Guichon and Hauck 2011;

Hampel and Stickler 2005; Warschauer 2002a); and apply technology appropriately in record keeping and feedback (Healey et al. 2011; Kessler 2016; Lai, Zhao, and Li 2008).

To ensure that the technological choices they have made are beneficial to the language program, language teachers must be able to reflect on the pedagogical effectiveness of their use of technology (Guichon and Hauck 2011; Hubbard 2008; Healey et al. 2011; Warschauer 2002a) and student engagement with it. To engage students in their roles as *homo faber* (tool user) and *homo ludens* (game player), faculty must leverage students' interest in personal uses of technology (e.g., Twitter, Instagram, Snapchat, Facebook, AR, gaming, multimedia resources, podcasts, internet) to provide authentic input and interactional opportunities to engage students for language learning (ACTFL/CAEP 2013; Kessler 2006; Sun 2011). After their training is over, online language faculty must demonstrate an understanding of where to find CALL resources to catch and maintain students' interest (ACTFL/CAEP 2013). In addition, they must strive to expand their skill and knowledge base to evaluate, adopt, and adapt emerging technologies in their program and throughout their careers (Gleason and Schmitt 2018; Healey et al. 2011).

CALL scholars have offered checklists of technologies for language learning and skills associated with them ("can-do" lists) for language teachers to determine their own skill levels on applications they need for their professional use. However, if not kept up to date, these lists soon become outdated as newer technologies emerge (e.g., Davies 2012). Thus, instead of focusing CTE training on teachers becoming proficient in the use of specific software applications, pre- and in-service professional preparation should focus on encouraging online language instructors to be flexible and open to learning new, cutting-edge technologies (state-of-the-art hardware and software applications, e.g., gaming, augmented and virtual reality, MALL). (A list of CTE/CALL resources for identifying and exploring new technologies is found on this book's Web page, at www.press.georgetown.edu.)

Pedagogical Skills

Even though integrating technology into a language curriculum by definition requires attention paid to the use of those technologies, the use of technology should always be contingent upon the pedagogical goals it is meant to facilitate. As discussed in chapter 2, teacher training programs need to make sure that trainees (faculty) apply their knowledge of the development of the field of CALL, relevant learning theories, and CALL empirical research to prioritize pedagogical objectives over technological ones and make sure that their choices of technological resources help to facilitate the attainment of student linguistic and intercultural learning outcomes (ACTFL/CAEP 2013; Compton 2009; Fuchs 2006; Guichon and Hauck 2011; Healey et al. 2011; Kessler 2006; Lafford, King de Ramírez, and Wermers 2018; Son and Windeatt 2017b; Stockwell 2009; Warschauer 2002a). The pedagogical skills required to effect this prioritization of pedagogy over technology involve the ability to create effective course designs for teaching languages online, to implement a student-centered pedagogy, and to foster interaction, collaboration, and socialization.

Course design. The design of online language courses should be grounded in curriculum design frameworks, relevant linguistic and educational theories, and empirical research for acquiring communicative, intercultural, and technological competencies (Compton 2009). It is important that faculty integrate relevant linguistic, cultural, technological, and professional standards into the language curriculum to set course goals and objectives (ACTFL 2012, 2015, 2017; ACTFL/CAEP 2013; Armstrong 2019; Bennett 1986, 1993; Byram 1997; Council of Europe 2001; Healey et al. 2011; Lafford and King de Ramírez 2018; NACE 2017; P21 2019; TESOL International Association 2010). Instructors should make sure that students are prepared to meet the ACTFL World Readiness Standards (ACTFL 2015)—communities, communication [interpretive, presentational, and interpersonal modes], culture [perspectives, practices, products], comparisons, and connections—as well as the proficiency standards set by the administrative unit (ACTFL 2012; Council of Europe 2001).

Just as a needs analysis is essential for the creation of CTE training, language faculty teaching online also need to be able to carry out such an analysis to meet the needs of their particular online students, who may vary in their access to and their experience with various technologies (Guichon and Hauck 2011; Healey et al. 2011). Results from these analyses inform instructors regarding the types of course objectives that need to be set to meet students' linguistic, cultural, technological, and professional needs as well as the types of tasks and materials that would be most useful for their student audience. For instance, the creation of an online language course focusing on the use of the target language in professional settings (e.g., Spanish for Healthcare, Chinese for Business) should be informed by the results of a needs analysis that investigates the linguistic tasks students need to carry out in those settings as well as the cultural and technological competencies needed for them to be successful communicators in workplace venues (Torres and Serafini 2015).

Online language instructors also need to incorporate digital materials that provide authentic input to students; Compton (2009) also notes that online instructors need to be able to choose materials that are suitable to the online language learning task at hand. The positive aspects of using learning materials that provide authentic input to students and group- or project-based work that allows for student interaction in low-risk environments (ACTFL/CAEP 2013; Healey et al. 2011; Hubbard 2008; Sun 2011) have been reviewed in language teaching literature for several decades (authentic materials: Mishan 2005; group work: Bejarano et al. 1997; Pica and Doughty 1985). The rewards of project-based learning (Debski 2006; Healey et al. 2011) are discussed in chapter 3.

Online language courses also need to be designed with a focus on form and use of task-based instruction (Compton 2009; Ellis, Basturkmen, and Loewen 2002; Guichon and Hauck 2011; Lai and Li 2011; Lai, Zhao, and Li 2008; Sun 2011). Rod Ellis and colleagues (2002) define focus on form as "a particular type of form-focused instruction—the treatment of linguistic form in the context of performing a communicative task" (419). The importance of task-based instruction has been noted by second-language-learning scholars for decades (González-Lloret 2016; Long 1985; Skehan 1998). Lai and Guofang Li (2011) propose that a task-based activity is one that contains a connectedness and resemblance to real-world activities, with a primacy of meaning and nonlinguistic goals. Such activities provide a form of situated learning with ecological validity in which learners can practice their linguistic abilities and apply their intercultural competence to the execution of meaningful activities that they might have to perform outside their language classrooms. The challenge to online language instructors is their need to use technological tools to create task-based activities in digital spaces that resemble the tasks they will need to perform in either digital or F2F contexts and that reflect the needs and interests of their students. A student-centered pedagogical approach can facilitate the creation of appropriate tasks and activities for language students. (See González-Lloret 2016 for an excellent practical guide to integrating technology into task-based teaching.)

To ensure a high-quality online course product, the online language instructor can also follow Universal Design for Learning (Hall, Meyer, and Rose 2012) and Quality Matters (2018) standards for course design (course overview and introduction, learning objectives [competencies], assessment and measurement, instructional materials, learning activities and learner interaction, course technology, learner support, accessibility, and usability), which are often required at the institutional level for any online course.

Focus on student-centered learning. Online language instructors need to use a pedagogical approach that focuses on student-centered learning, in which learning is seen as a process and student agency is promoted in order to create a supportive learning environment that meets individual students' needs (ACTFL/CAEP 2013; Sun 2011; Tobin, Mandernach, and Taylor 2015). In this framework instructors must use clear communication to clarify instructions and course expectations (Ernest et al. 2013; Lai, Zhao, and Li 2008; Tobin, Mandernach, and Taylor 2015), provide quality and timely written/oral feedback for individuals or the class as a whole, and encourage students to provide feedback to their peers (Lai, Zhao, and Li 2008; Tobin, Mandernach, and Taylor 2015). In this approach, language faculty also need to vary the course structure to cater to various student learning needs, learning styles, access to technology, and disabilities (Lafford 2019; Lai, Zhao, and Li 2008; Tobin, Mandernach, and Taylor 2015; Wong and Nunan 2011). Instructors also need to ensure that their Web pages and other internet sources comply with the standards of the Americans with Disabilities Act (1990/2008) and follow Web content accessibility guidelines (W3C WAI 2019). In addition, in a student-centered framework, language instructors must promote student efficacy by encouraging self-directed, self-regulated, individualized, and personalized learning (Lai, Zhao, and Li 2008; Sun 2011).

Online language instructors also must develop creativity and personal style in using, adapting, and creating technological applications and culturally appropriate materials to meet student needs (Compton 2009; Hampel and Stickler 2005; Guichon and Hauck 2011; Sun 2011; TESOL International Association 2010). In turn, they must also encourage learners to be creative in telling their stories and to co-construct their own understandings, and co-create new learning and knowledge (Lai, Zhao, and Li 2008; Sun 2011) to serve as class resources in their learning environment. This can be facilitated by teachers and teacher trainers being taught to encourage students and faculty trainees (in their *homo fabulans* [storyteller] role) to apply their knowledge and skills to create new digital products to express their identity and their ideas (e.g., creating digital stories [Alexander 2015; Oskoz and Elola 2016]; creating and posting study guides [Tobin, Mandernach, and Taylor 2015]).

In order for students and faculty to develop their potential as *homo analyticus* (analyzers), online instructors also need to be taught (in situated contexts) to foster real-life problem solving, critical thinking, and reflective skills among students (Selber 2004; Sun 2011; Tai 2015). These skills can be developed using student-centered active learning techniques to promote self-efficacy, in which online students are required to participate in situated learning activities in their communities (e.g., shadowing and interviewing professionals) and to take leadership roles by summarizing and proposing new steps when tackling a problem-solving activity (Tobin, Mandernach, and Taylor 2015). Students can also be encouraged to keep reflective learning journals or portfolios that chronicle their challenges and successes at meeting goals in online language learning environments (e.g., LinguaFolio [CASLS 2020]).

Finally, in line with the implications of an ecological approach to CTE training discussed in chapter 3, online language instructors must be able to create learning activities that are focused on student interests and that allow them the opportunity to make a difference in their community. According to Barbara Lafford (2019), this can be accomplished, in part, by having online faculty develop critical cultural awareness (CCA), the "ability to evaluate critically and on the basis of explicit criteria, perspectives, practices and products in one's own and other cultures and countries" (Byram 1997, 63). For instance, this ability would be honed by having teachers learn how to decode visual elements in target-language newscasts (Gruba 2007) to help them (and their students) understand the entirety of the intended message in its social context. In addition, Kristen Nugent and Theresa Catalano (2015) propose that CCA "encourages language educators to craft learning opportunities that guide learners in observing clear connections between classroom lessons and real-world issues which exercising critical thinking skills throughout the process" (15). This move toward the use of technology to facilitate the use of a critical pedagogical approach is also reflected in the TESOL Technology Standards for teachers: "Language teachers use technology in socially and culturally appropriate, legal, and ethical ways" (Healey et al. 2011, 191).

As discussed in chapter 3, Lafford (2019) calls for the development of CCA as part of the ecology of a Critical CALL approach to teaching languages with technology. Such an approach would require online language instructors and students to acknowledge and embrace the social justice turn in second-language acquisition and applied linguistics that would focus on "the goal to decease human suffering and to promote human values of equity and dignity" (Ortega 2018). Topics included in this social justice approach include the issue of the digital divide, a term that has traditionally referred to "the difference between the low level of physical access to computers and connectivity experienced by marginalized groups and the high level of such access that is typical of more privileged (white) US communities" (Lafford 2019, 135). However, Warschauer (2002b) points out the inadequacy of this construct to capture the reality of technology access and use by different social groups, and proposes instead a "technology for social inclusion," a construct that "reflects particularly well the imperatives of the current information era, in which issues of identity, language, social participation, community, and civil society have taken central stage." Language instructors also need to be aware of digital gaps and student technology use around the globe (e.g., reliable access to computers, social media used by different demographic groups and countries) in order to set up viable social media groups and intercultural telecollaboration / virtual exchange projects (Lafford 2019).

To address the real-life implications of intercultural learning, online language instructors can lead students to develop their own CCA by setting up situated or experiential learning opportunities (community service learning or internships, either in person or virtual [Bosch and Creus 2013]) for students as part of required coursework so they can increase their sense of self-efficacy and make a difference in the lives of residents in their home communities or abroad, in countries where the target language is spoken. Instructors can then require students involved in community service learning or internships to share ideas about access, diversity, and social justice issues in their communities via telecollaboration (virtual exchanges using discussion boards, blogs, wikis, video chats, or social media [Reinhardt 2020]). Students at home can communicate with their peers who are involved in similar experiences in domestic or international settings in order to learn more about the cultures and the workplaces in which they or their colleagues are placed and in which they develop their communicative and intercultural competencies. In addition, language learners can deepen their understanding of the target language culture and their own native culture through collaborating on international education projects with native speakers of their target language through Collaborative Online International Learning (COIL) experiences (King de Ramírez 2019; King Ramírez 2020).

Student-centered pedagogy can lead to student engagement when students feel comfortable with their teacher due to the instructor's socioaffective skills, the instructor's creativity and clear communication, the instructor's focus on encouraging student creativity and on developing students' critical thinking and problem-solving skills, and students' CCA (involving interaction with local or global communities). Student engagement is also fostered by the ability of the online instructor to build community among online class members.

Interaction, Collaboration, and Socialization Skills

Several CALL scholars have noted the importance of an online language teacher's ability to promote interaction, collaboration, and socialization in digital ecological spaces.

Interaction. In order for students to develop their *homo loquens* (speakers) role, language teachers must be able to facilitate student oral and written interaction and stimulate active student participation in discussion boards and various communication tools (e.g., social media platforms), in paired and group discussions for different interaction purposes (ACTFL/CAEP 2013; Compton 2009; Guichon and Hauck 2011; Lai, Zhao, and Li 2008; Meskill and Anthony 2007; Stickler and Hampel 2015; Sun 2011). These high-quality student interactions should take place with different interlocutors (including target-language community members) and with multiple opportunities for negotiation of meaning and cultural understanding so students can develop their communicative, intercultural communicative, and technological competencies (ACTFL/CAEP 2013; Compton 2009; Guichon and Hauck 2011; Hampel and Stickler 2005; Lai, Zhao, and Li 2011; Tobin, Mandernach, and Taylor 2015). Instructors must also provide students with information on the target-language lexicon and behaviors (netiquette) appropriate for target culture online interaction (Hampel 2009).

Collaboration. Online language faculty must implement practices to allow students to progress from interaction to actual collaboration with a goal in mind. Instructors can use technology to facilitate and maintain effective student-instructor communication and collaboration among stakeholders to work together on a project, solve a problem, advocate for language and culture learning, and address social justice issues that affect target culture communities (ACTFL/CAEP 2013; Healey et al. 2011). Online language teachers must also promote, plan, and manage student collaboration; design appropriate activities; moderate appropriately; choose appropriate environments and tools; and get students to negotiate ground rules for collaboration (Ernest et al. 2013; Sun 2011). In addition, instructors must also promote reciprocity and cooperation among students (Sun 2011; Tobin, Mandernach, and Taylor 2015) and encourage student collaborative tasks (e.g., wikis, telecollaboration / virtual exchanges) (ACTFL/CAEP 2013; Lewis and O'Dowd 2016a, 2016b; O'Dowd 2015a, 2015b; Sun 2011) and project-based activities (Debski 2006) (discussed in chapters 2 and 3).

Socialization. Several CALL scholars have noted the importance of a teacher's ability to facilitate the development of socialization (social cohesion among teachers and learners) in a community of online language practice (Compton 2009; Guichon 2009; Hampel and Stickler 2005; Jones and Youngs 2006; Murphy 2015; Stickler and Hampel 2015). The sense of community created in an online language class by the socialization process can help develop students' and instructors' roles as *homo socius* (social beings) and increase their motivation toward interaction with peers and other interlocutors that can facilitate language acquisition and community building. However, in order to be an effective facilitator of online interaction and socialization, the online language teacher must possess the skill of socioaffective regulation (Guichon 2009) in order to build rapport and a sense of community.

Guichon (2009) defines socioaffective regulation as "the capacity to establish a relationship with a learner or a group of learners, to maintain it despite distance, and to eventually build a learning community" (169). Indeed, the ability of online language instructors to establish good rapport with students who are physically distant from the instructor by being approachable and committed is one of the desired teacher qualities most highly rated by students (Murphy 2015). Linda Murphy states that the results of her study of online language teaching in the United Kingdom's Open University from the learners' perspective "clearly shows that teachers need to transform existing teaching skills in order to create the kind of structured, non-threatening, inclusive online learning space which learners need in order to explore, exchange information, connect and apply ideas and successfully develop their language skills" (2015, 61).

To serve as effective mentors within this inclusive online space, instructors need to be aware of and to address the anxiety issues of online language students (Chametzky 2019; Horwitz, Horwitz, and Cope 1986; Hurd 2007; Martin and Álvarez Valdivia 2017). Elaine Horwitz and colleagues (1986) define foreign language anxiety as "a distinct complex construct of self-perceptions, beliefs, feelings, and behaviours related to classroom language learning arising from the uniqueness of language learning process" (128). Since Horwitz, Horwitz, and Cope (1986) introduced a Foreign Language Classroom Anxiety Scale, CALL scholars have used it or modified it to diagnose factors that cause anxiety in language learners.

In recent years, research on factors that cause anxiety in language students learning in online pedagogical environments has been specifically addressed. For instance, Stella Hurd (2007) found that the factors that induced anxiety in online learners included lack of instant feedback on their production, difficulty assessing their own progress compared with that of other students, a feeling of isolation, reduced opportunities for speaking, and a lack of confidence when working autonomously.

In addition, Barry Chametzky (2019) found that online students feel anxious when the instructor is no longer the "sage on the stage" (teacher-centered approaches) and instead takes on the role of facilitator and guide for student interaction (student-centered learning). In addition, anxiety may be present if online learners are asked to understand an authentic oral text from a native who speaks at a faster rate than the instructor if the text of the native speaker's output is not readily visible. Chametzky (2019) also found that although some learners are comfortable using online technology, they prefer writing in the target language to speaking it. Their discomfort with speaking in online classes causes them to prefer asking an instructor a question privately in an e-mail rather than voicing that question in front of online classmates. Sidney Martin and Ibis Álvarez Valdivia's (2017) work focuses on speaking anxiety in online language classes and the relationship between anxiety levels and students' preferred form of teacher feedback. They found that students with high levels of anxiety prefer recasts and metalinguistic feedback from the instructor over other forms of feedback and feedback from peers.

Despite the anxiety caused by learning in online contexts, Hurd (2007) also found that certain factors alleviate anxiety for some students in online environments, for example, age [older students are less anxious than younger ones], competence in another language, not having to perform in front of other students, the ability to practice on their own, and flexible scheduling of online sessions that allows students to fit their learning around work and family responsibilities. In addition, François Pichette (2009) and Xiuyuan Zhang and Gang Cui (2010) found that foreign language anxiety in online spaces seems to decrease with more experience online. Moreover, Junhong Xiao (2012) notes that successful online second-language learners show initiative in dealing with the anxieties of the distance learning experience. Finally, Volkan Yuzer, Belgin Aydin, and S. Ipek Kuru Gonen (2009) propose that the creation of interactive spaces for online students to practice speaking and writing the target language can also alleviate anxiety.

Under normal circumstances, learners generally make a conscious choice to take online courses, which can mitigate their stress in their new digital environment. However, the recent COVID-19 pandemic has forced many students to study online even though their preferred method of learning is in F2F environments. Action research on student anxiety caused by this sudden change and ways to mitigate it to allow quality language learning to occur in digital spaces should be foremost on the minds of applied linguists and practitioners.

To alleviate student anxiety, mediate interaction, and foster socialization in an online language course, teachers must develop a strong cognitive, social, and teaching presence (Garrison, Anderson, and Archer 2001; Lucas 2015). This idea is also supported by Hampel (2009), who notes that individuals communicating at a distance "can develop group cohesion and identity without having met in person, and teachers play a crucial role in this by, for example, integrating community building into online activities and helping to develop an online netiquette in the group" (8).

Finally, using their experiences in CoPs and CoIs during their own online training, language teachers must foster the creation of online learning communities among students in order to provide them an opportunity to create their own personal learning networks (PLNs) to support them in their online learning endeavors (Compton 2009; Hanson-Smith 2016; Hampel and Stickler 2005; Hampel 2009; Sun 2011; Warschauer 2002a).

Evaluation Skills

In this section we discuss the types of evaluations that language instructors must be able to carry out to be effective online teachers. Discussion of the models of evaluation of actual levels of expertise for a given skill and what abilities characterize instructors at those levels (e.g., basic skills [locate, evaluate, select, distribute, integrate] versus advanced skills [create, customize, convert, repurpose], Kessler 2016) can be found in chapter 5 of this volume.

Compton (2009) notes the need for language faculty to develop evaluation skills to teach online courses effectively. Although not mentioned specifically by Compton, teachers must carry out thoughtful self-assessments to critically reflect on their own performance and their pedagogical choices (Hampel and Stickler 2005; Hampel 2009; Healey et al. 2011; Selber 2004) or must request feedback from a "critical friend" (Lewis 2006) in order to identify what they do well and areas in which they need improvement. This type of self-assessment should be both formative and summative in nature and needs to guide the creation of goals for future self-attainment. The current volume provides in-depth discussions of the processes involved in self-assessments and goal setting in chapters 7 and 9, respectfully, and a rubric for faculty self-assessment can be found in appendix C-5.

Instructors also need to require that learners measure their own linguistic, cultural, and professional competencies within the context of the ACTFL World Readiness Standards and the NACE and P21 career-readiness standards (ACTFL 2015; ACTFL 2017; ACTFL/CAEP 2013; Healey et al. 2011; Lafford and King de Ramírez 2018; NACE 2017; P21 2019; TESOL International Association 2010). Online faculty also need to facilitate students' acquisition of these competencies so that they can transfer these skills to their own professional contexts, for example, critical thinking, adaptability, intercultural competence, and collaboration skills (King Ramírez and Lafford 2018).

In addition to assessing their own performance online, language teachers need to be able to use technology to critically review the online teaching performance of others via peer evaluations (chapter 8) and carry out appropriate, systematic, and reliable assessments of student performance.

Scholars have proposed that faculty evaluate student performance via both formative and summative assessments and a standardized grading system (ACTFL/CAEP 2013; Compton 2009; Healey et al. 2011; Lai, Zhao, and Li 2008; Quality Matters 2018). The student performance to be assessed should not only include evaluations of their communicative and intercultural communicative competencies (ACTFL/CAEP 2013; Compton 2009; Healey et al. 2011) but should also entail assessing the effectiveness of specific student uses of technology to enhance teaching and learning (Healey et al. 2011).

Language faculty also need to evaluate and select materials for suitability and effectiveness (Compton 2009; Hampel and Stickler 2005; Healey et al. 2011; Warschauer 2002a). Resources to assess the quality and appropriateness of CALL materials include guidelines to evaluate software, courseware and tutorial applications, websites, and MALL applications; resources for those evaluations are found in the CTE/CALL Resource List on this book's Web page (www.press.georgetown.edu). Before purchasing software, Healey and Johnson (2009) propose doing a needs analysis that takes into account the audience, student goals, settings in which the software will be used, teacher CALL expertise, available hardware and technical assistance, and financial resources to spend on these purchases.

Online teachers must also have the ability to evaluate tasks for suitability and effectiveness in supporting language acquisition in their pedagogical context (Chapelle 2001; Compton 2009; Jamieson, Chapelle, and Preiss 2005). The following criteria for CALL task evaluation were proposed by Chapelle (2001) and reiterated in a study by Jamieson, Chapelle, and Preiss (2005):

> *Language learning potential:* The degree of opportunity present for beneficial focus on form; *Meaning focus:* The extent to which learners' attention is directed toward the meaning of the language; *Learner fit:* The amount of opportunity for engagement with language under appropriate conditions given learner characteristics; *Authenticity:* The degree of correspondence between the learning activity and target language activities of interest to learners out of the classroom; *Positive Impact*: The positive effects of the CALL activity on those who participate in it; and *Practicality:* The adequacy of resources to support the use of the CALL activity. (94)

In addition, language teachers also must be able to provide constructive commentary when asked to evaluate their own CTE courses/training for suitability and effectiveness (ACTFL/CAEP 2013; Goertler and Winke 2008; Kessler 2006; Windeatt 2017) and to evaluate the assessment process, as well as the rubrics used to assess instructor performance (Lafford, King de Ramírez, and Wermers 2018) (see appendix B-1, B-2, and B-3, respectively). The results of all this evaluative research would then serve to improve online teaching, the selection of materials, and the planning of future iterations of tasks, courses, training modules, assessment procedures, and rubrics.

Language faculty and administrators can also gather data and interpret the results of these evaluations via theoretically and empirically grounded action research that collects information from their online language courses on the effectiveness of the use of certain types of technologies, materials, and tasks to increase student engagement and outcomes (Healey et al. 2011). Faculty evaluation of CALL courses/training, assessment procedures, and rubrics would entail all of these task evaluation skills and could also include elements of program assessment discussed in chapter 6.

PROFESSIONAL DEVELOPMENT AND PROFESSIONALISM

In order for faculty to keep honing their communicative, intercultural communicative, and technological competencies, they must seek out and participate in professional development opportunities at the department level and beyond and must use professional development resources to improve teaching (ACTFL/CAEP 2013; Healey et al. 2011). This ongoing training can help teachers create effective personal learning environments (e.g., lists of resources for online language teaching most relevant for their teaching environment, see CTE/CALL resources found on this book's Web page, at www.press.georgetown.edu.) and PLNs (e.g., CoPs with other online teachers in different university environments) to facilitate ongoing self-directed professional development (ACTFL/CAEP 2013; Hanson-Smith 2016). Most important, they should seek to work with a mentor to receive personal feedback and set goals for improvement (Eib and Miller 2006; Hampel 2009; Hampel and Stickler 2005; Hanson-Smith 2006, 2016; Kolaitis et al. 2006; Meskill et al. 2006; Palloff and Pratt 2011). Chapters 8 and 9 of this volume provide in-depth discussions on mentoring and goal setting.

In addition to these professional development activities, language faculty need to hone their own professional skills as well as instill a sense of professionalism in their students (Lafford, Abbott, and Lear 2014). Faculty can develop foundational professional skills by establishing good communication with people to whom they report or supervise and by modeling professional behavior for students.

PUTTING IT ALL TOGETHER: IDEAS FOR IMPLEMENTATION

This chapter on core competencies and skills for language instructors teaching with technology and online within an ecological framework demonstrates the need for instructors to

- develop CALL literacies as a core competence;
- develop TPACK and critical semiotic awareness to effectively integrate technology into their teaching;
- develop basic technological skills, integrate and reflect on the pedagogical effectiveness of their use of technology, and be open to learning new technologies;
- apply their knowledge of the development of the field of CALL, relevant learning theories, and CALL empirical research to prioritize pedagogical objectives over technological ones;
- follow established principles of good course design when creating curricula; these principles must be grounded in curriculum design frameworks, relevant linguistic and educational theories, and empirical research;
- be able to carry out a needs analysis to meet the needs of their students;
- incorporate task-based group and project-based activities that are based on authentic materials and a focus on form;
- focus on student-centered learning, develop creativity and personal style, and foster real-life problem solving, critical thinking, and reflective skills in their students;
- develop critical cultural awareness as part of a Critical CALL approach to teaching languages with technology and need to lead their students to develop their own CCA by setting up situated/experiential learning opportunities (community service learning or internships);
- use technology to facilitate effective student oral and written interaction and stimulate active student participation and collaboration in digital environments;
- facilitate the development of socialization (social cohesion among teachers and learners) and socioaffective regulation in order to build rapport and a sense of community in digital spaces;
- be aware of and address the anxiety issues of students using language learning technologies or taking online language courses;
- develop a strong cognitive, social, and teaching presence in digital teaching spaces and foster the creation of CoPs and online PLNs;

- carry out thoughtful self-assessments to critically reflect on their own performance and their pedagogical choices, critically review the online teaching performance of others via peer evaluations, and carry out appropriate, systematic, and reliable assessments of student performance with a variety of formative and summative assessments and a standardized grading system;
- evaluate and select digital teaching materials for suitability and effectiveness;
- assess their own CTE courses/training, the assessment process, the rubrics used to evaluate them for suitability and effectiveness, and the evaluation process;
- seek out and participate in professional development opportunities at the department level and beyond;
- work with a mentor to receive personal feedback and set goals for improvement; and
- hone their professionalism by establishing good communication with supervisors and students, modeling professional behavior and facilitating their students' acquisition of transferable skills.

Language instructors with a departmental research expectation should

- carry out theoretically and empirically grounded action research on various aspects of the move to digital pedagogical spaces, for example, the effect of student and teacher anxiety on their performance in digital instructional spaces and the effectiveness of various teaching strategies, materials, and tools for teaching in digital environments.

In addition, supervisors must set clear standards for language instructors to attain core technopedagogical competencies. Appendix A-3 offers a checklist of the core competencies of online language instructors as a way for training/course designers to indicate whether a given skill is needed at a particular time, not expected at that time, or not applicable to program needs or to particular online instructors' roles.

As discussed at the end of chapter 3, the online teaching evaluation life cycle proposes that faculty training and professional development leads to the development of core competencies, which produce instructional behaviors that must be assessed in order to hold faculty accountable. Chapter 5 reviews the CTE literature on assessing the behaviors associated with the acquisition of core competencies and skills (presented in this chapter) that language teachers need to be successful pedagogues in online spaces. These core competencies and skills also form the basis of the rubrics we propose in chapter 6 for evaluation of online instructors by students, supervisors, administrators, and peers and in chapter 7 for instructor self-evaluations. In addition to these rubrics for instructor evaluation, instruments for assessing the quality of training programs, the assessment process, and the instructor evaluation rubrics are found in appendix B-1, B-2, and B-3, respectively, of this volume. Videos on how to apply those rubrics accompany the current volume and are available at www.press.georgetown.edu.

5

Online Language Instructor Assessment

As discussed in prior chapters, the CTE training of online language instructors to develop core competencies is inextricably linked to appropriate assessments of their abilities through the online teaching evaluation life cycle (Tobin, Mandernach, and Taylor 2015). In this recursive cycle, ongoing faculty training (chapters 2 and 3) helps faculty to develop teacher core competencies (chapter 4) that are manifested in instructional behaviors, which can be evaluated through formative and summative assessments (see chapter 6). The guidelines established for that evaluation are used to create criteria for hiring faculty to teach online, and the faculty are then trained and given further professional development opportunities—and the cycle continues. In addition, the assessments of faculty skills, their training programs, the evaluation process, and the evaluative rubrics used to assess them provide valuable feedback to administrators and faculty in charge of continuously improving elements of this training assessment cycle.

As the evaluation of online language faculty should ideally form part of an overall assessment of the online language program in which they teach, we briefly discuss the evaluation of language programs in order to contextualize our discussion of assessing online language instruction.

LANGUAGE PROGRAM ASSESSMENT

There is a substantial and ever-growing body of work on developing and assessing the quality of online university language-education programs. However, to date most of this work focuses on program design (Bustamante and Moeller 2013; Lai, Zhao, and Li 2008; Meskill and Anthony 2007), teacher training (Ernest et al. 2013; Hubbard and Levy 2006a, 2006b; Kessler 2006), and the identification of skill sets for teachers (Comas-Quinn 2011; Compton 2009; Hampel and Stickler 2005; Healey et al. 2011; Lai, Zhao, and Li 2008) instead of carrying out empirical assessments of training and faculty performance (Lafford, King de Ramírez, and Wermers 2018). Also lacking in the language program evaluation literature is research on the gaps between administrator, peer, and self-assessment of online language faculty performance. Our case studies, described in chapters 7–9, will help fill these gaps in the literature on the assessment of online instruction.

Recently three major works have explored the evaluation of language programs (Davis and McKay 2018; Gruba et al. 2016; Healey et al. 2011). For instance, the TESOL Technology Standards volume (Healey et al. 2011) dedicates a chapter for administrator use that provides them with a rationale for using the standards to help evaluate online teaching. In addition, the volume contains a program assessment checklist rubric (211–17) containing declarative statements that help to evaluate administrative support given to instructors (Goal 1, Standard 1: "Administrators ensure that teachers are either hired with the requisite level of technological competence or provided with training to bring them to that level of skill. Just having technical support available for teachers in their classes is not enough" [211]), and administrative practices to build a sustainable CALL/online language program (e.g., Goal 2, Standard 2: "Administrators recognize and compensate expert-level teachers who support or train their peers in technology use" [213]). However, these references to evaluating administrative support are simply incorporated into relevant sections of the goals and standards that were originally set up just to evaluate technology expertise in language instructors.

As in the case of the self-assessment checklist instrument proposed by TESOL Technology Standards (Healey et al. 2011), the standards program assessment checklist is accompanied by a Likert-type evaluation scale. While the self-assessment instrument uses the terms to determine how well the practitioners view their ability to perform the functions listed in the rubric ("Very well," "Adequately," "Not so well," "Not at all," and "N/A"), the program assessment instrument indicates the degree to which the actions mentioned in the declarative statements are being carried out in the program ("Very much so," "Adequately," "Not so much," "Not at all," "N/A"). This type of fine-grained scale is very helpful to gauge progress in an individual area, but not all areas of program administration are taken into account in these standards checklists (e.g., there is no mention of taking student evaluations of instructors into account, no results of needs analyses to inform curriculum development, and no assessment of student learning outcomes). These issues are, however, treated in more recent models of language program evaluation models (Davis and McKay 2018; Gruba et al. 2016).

John Davis and Todd McKay (2018) provide an invaluable guide to the evaluation of language programs without focusing specifically on online language instruction. However, their edited volume as a whole is a model for administrators who need to create an evaluative infrastructure to measure the efficacy of their language program. Chapters by different authors focus on best practices for language program evaluation success, planning for useful evaluation, identifying indicators for evaluation data collection, selecting methods and collecting data for evaluation, conducting focus groups for evaluation, conducting evaluation interviews, forming questionnaires for evaluation, analyzing evaluation data, and providing a sample evaluation plan. This practical resource (with samples of several program assessment instruments) would help administrators through each step of the process of language program evaluation.

Paul Gruba and colleagues (2016) provide a useful resource for the evaluation of blended language programs. The authors summarize their approach as follows: "Building upon the work of [Carol] Chapelle..., we propose adopting an argument-based approach for evaluating blended language programs with a focus on the four considerations about blended learning (i.e., purpose, appropriateness, multimodality, and sustainability) and three levels (i.e., micro, meso, and macro) at which blended language program evaluation can occur" (33). Their argument-based approach to program evaluation was inspired by the research of Kane (2006) and Chapelle, Enright, and Jamieson (2008). In their two-stage evaluation framework, the first (developmental) stage creates an interpretive argument, while the second (appraisal) stage requires the creation of a validity argument. Michael Kane (2012) proposes that an interpretive argument "specifies the proposed interpretations and uses of assessment results by laying out a network of inferences and assumptions leading from the observed performances to the conclusions and decisions based on the assessment scores" (8). In contrast, a validity argument "provides an evaluation of the interpretive argument's coherence and the plausibility of its inferences and assumptions" (Kane 2012, 8). Paul Gruba and colleagues (2016) provide several case studies that illustrate this argument-based approach to the assessment of blended language programs.

Due to the complexity of blended language programs, Gruba and colleagues (2016) also propose that the integration of technology into a language program be discussed at three different levels in an educational institution: the micro level (classroom level involving teachers and students), the meso level (departmental level dealing with work cultures and division of labor), and the macro level (institutional level bringing into consideration how policies and initiatives influence the implementation of blended pedagogical approaches). Then, drawing on the work of Gruba and Don Hinkelman (2012), the authors propose four program considerations to set boundaries for program design and to encourage further debate and research on blended programs, that is, the purpose of the program (reasons for integrating technology into the language curriculum); the appropriateness of blended approaches for the resources, abilities, and linguistic proficiency of students in that institutional context; the multimodality of resources to foster multiliteracy development for instructors and students; and the sustainability of the program through the reuse and repurposing of materials, lessons, and technology.

Gruba and colleagues (2016) also recognize that evaluation processes need to be open to modification so that the evaluation can remain relevant by evolving and adapting to a changing educational landscape. Thus, the dynamic nature of an argument-based framework does not view evaluation as a "static, one-time endeavor" but rather as a "series of negotiated, participatory and cyclical activities" (36). Gruba and colleagues (2016) also state that their argument-based approach to evaluating blended language programs "departs from earlier perspectives of language program evaluation that were based primarily on pre-determined criteria and, instead, offers a framework that is flexible in response to local needs and can allow for a complex evaluation project to be broken down into components that can be addressed one at a time" (33). This flexible, argument-based approach informs our ecological stance on the recursive cycle of the training and assessment of online language instructors in which the circumstances, role, and experience of instructors are taken into account in the preparation of their training, in the rubrics chosen to evaluate them (requiring evidence to back up their arguments relating to their attainment of the proposed standards), and in their goal-setting process.

As noted above, a pivotal component of online language program evaluation is the assessment of the online language instructors who teach in the program. In the rest of this chapter we briefly review the importance of teacher assessment and the context of online language teaching assessment, we critically review selected extant evaluation rubrics for online language teachers, and we suggest areas for evaluation not contained in those rubrics.

EVALUATION OF ONLINE LANGUAGE INSTRUCTORS

Language faculty who teach in F2F and in blended or online environments receive feedback on their teaching as part of an annual evaluation process (Watanabe, Norris, and González-Lloret 2009). Information gathered from rubrics used to assess F2F teaching as part of formative (peer mentor) and summative (student evaluations and classroom/course site observations by supervisors) at the micro level often play a large role in meso-level departmental administrative summative assessments of a faculty member's teaching ability. Gillian Lord (2014) notes that these rubrics need to be continuously updated to keep up with changes in technology and pedagogical practice.

Challenges involved in the move from F2F to online language teaching, which would also affect how instructors are assessed, have been explored by David Donnarumma and Sarah Hamilton (2018). These challenges include the fact that this move puts into question established pedagogical practice, traditional instructor behavior, and the effectiveness of established teaching approaches (Redmond 2011). The switch to an online environment not only mandates adjustments to one's teaching style; it also requires that the instructors rethink the use of ecological spaces to take advantages on the affordances offered by an online environment. For instance, teachers new to the online environment should go beyond simply using course management systems as document repositories for students and should explore the judicious use of the internet for informational sources and communication. Moreover, online teaching that is student-centered changes the instructor's role from "information provider" to "guide on the side" to facilitate student learning via the exploration of online content and tools. In addition, the reduction in F2F interaction with students in an online environment forces instructors to spend time planning ways to foster interaction, socialization, and the building of online communities.

As the purpose of the Donnarumma and Hamilton (2018) study was to assess instructor readiness to develop online materials for teaching, the authors worked with five participants with master's degrees and some experience developing materials online. The participants worked with an instructional designer to create different learning units and the questionnaires and focus group instruments used in their study. Questionnaires based on Liz Bennett's (2014) framework for developing online materials were administered to the participants before and after their training. A focus group was held after the posttest questionnaire to discern the participants' perceptions of changes to their skills, challenges they faced and how they overcame those difficulties, and lessons learned to pass on to other developers. These instruments are included in the appendix of Donnarumma and Hamilton's (2018) chapter. The results of the study show that the assessment of language instructor readiness to develop materials for online environments is related to the ability of developers to communicate and collaborate with each other, to know their student audience and their needs, and to manage their time well. Other necessary attributes that indicate readiness for online language teaching involve the instructor's willingness to take a class online in a student role, to engage in critical reflection, and to participate in peer reviews.

Issues and challenges in the assessment of online language teacher performance are explored by Barbara Lafford and colleagues (2018), in a book chapter in which they address four issues that can complicate the evaluation of online language teaching: (1) uneven training, uneven institutional expectations; (2) faculty resistance to online teaching and to their assessment as online instructors; (3) training instructor populations with diverse experiences; and (4) instruments used to assess online language faculty. While the first three of these issues are explored in other chapters of the current book, the fourth issue (insufficiencies in the instruments currently used to assess online language faculty) are explored in depth in the rest of this chapter.

ASSESSMENT OF FACULTY ONLINE COMPETENCIES AND SKILLS

In this section we critically evaluate extant frameworks for evaluating the competencies and skills needed by online faculty. Specifically, we look at frameworks proposed by Rena Palloff and Keith Pratt (2011) for general online instructors, and by Regine Hampel and Ursula Stickler (2005), Stickler and Hampel (2015), Lily Compton (2009), and Deborah Healey and colleagues (2011) for faculty teaching languages online.

Thomas Tobin and colleagues (2015) declare that rubrics used to evaluate F2F teaching are not adequate for the assessment of the skills needed by online instructors. For instance, assessing teacher facilitation of interaction in an F2F classroom would use different metrics than those needed for evaluating how the instructor fosters interactivity in an online class (see discussion of Palloff and Pratt 2011, below). In addition, the rubrics and assessment models that currently exist to evaluate online instructors vary substantially in what they assess (e.g., course organization, pedagogical skills, technological knowledge, evaluative skills, the use of technology for feedback and record keeping, ability to foster socialization and a sense of community).

In the sections that follow we critically review selected extant rubrics and other instruments that have been proposed for the assessment of online language instructors. These rubrics can be used by institutional evaluators (peers, administrative supervisors, and department administrators) in formative and summative assessments of online faculty. Descriptions of each instrument discuss the skills assessed and the evaluation format of the instrument; these descriptions are followed by a discussion of the challenges each presents and how subsequent rubrics developed to meet those challenges. We begin with the discussion of a rubric designed to evaluate one important aspect of any online course, that is, its level of interactivity; this is followed by a discussion of three more extensive online language teacher evaluation models and their accompanying rubrics.

Palloff and Pratt (2011)

In their book on training and assessing online instructors, Palloff and Pratt (2011) reintroduced their (2009) rubric for the evaluation of the level of interactivity that an instructor needs to build into any online course. This instrument can be used to evaluate the design of the online course as well as faculty performance. The four metrics to be evaluated are the following: development of social presence, instructional design for interaction, evidence of learner engagement, and evidence of instructor engagement. Within each of these areas, the instructor is evaluated on a five-point scale (low, minimum, average, above average, high) according to the instructor's performance carrying out various tasks. For example, within the category development of social presence, the differences in descriptors for the above average and high level are listed below (differences between the descriptors at the two levels are noted in italic):

> ABOVE AVERAGE: Intros and bios are required. Instructor responds to intros and bios as a model for students. An ice-breaker activity is included at the start of a course and a café area is included in the course. (157)

> HIGH: Intros and bios are required. Instructor responds to intros and bios as a model for students *and may use audio or video as part of the instructor intro.* An ice-breaker activity is included at the start of a course. A café area is included in the course *and students are encouraged to engage with one another and the instructor in the café through informal discussion.* (158)

There are both positive affordances and drawbacks to this model. One of the positive aspects is that each skill level builds and expands upon the one that immediately precedes it. For instance, the descriptions of the two levels (above average and high) for development of social presence show that the skill sets are very similar but that the higher level requires the instructor to seek out multimedia solutions to enhance the instructor's introduction (e.g., by using audio and video files). In addition, at the higher level, the instructor goes beyond setting up a café section to actively encouraging its use among students and between students and the instructor. This structure allows the students to see immediately what they would need to improve in order to receive a higher-level evaluation.

The drawback to this rubric, however, also lies in the fact that this is an additive model—that is, progress is made on the scale only by adding or expanding upon skills proposed in the level beneath it. Thus, within a given category (above average or high), there are four different criteria grouped together (requiring intros and bios, instructor response to intros and bios, ice breakers, and a café area). This would seem to imply that in order for an instructor to be evaluated at the high level, the instructor would need to demonstrate fulfillment of all the criteria listed at that level within that category area. What if the instructor uses audio or video for the introductory video and yet fails to encourage students to use the café? Does this instructor receive a full high (5) rating anyway? Or only a 4.5? There is no indication of how this issue would be addressed. It would be more fair to assess online instructors on each of these submetrics using a more fine-grained rubric that could judge the quality of the attainment of each subskill separately (e.g., allow the evaluator to use a 1–5 scale for judging the level of encouragement for café use evidenced by the teacher separately from assessing the quality and content of the audio/video used for the instructor's intro video).

The next three instruments described go beyond the evaluation of just one important aspect of any online course (level of interactivity) and form part of three different models of assessment specifically for online language instructors. Frameworks for the assessment of online language instructors discussed in this section include Hampel and Stickler (2005), Stickler and Hampel (2015), Compton (2009), and Healey and colleagues (2011).

Hampel and Stickler (2005) and Stickler and Hampel (2015)

Compton (2009) notes that Hampel and Stickler's (2005) article is "the first clear effort on the topic of teacher training for online language learning" (76). Although (as explained in chapter 2) their article specifically focuses on skills needed by language tutors in the Open University environment of the United Kingdom, the skills they identify are also those needed by any language instructor teaching online. Basing their work on the tenets of the communicative approach to language teaching, grounded in interaction and the construct of communicative competence (Canale and Swain 1980), Hampel and Stickler

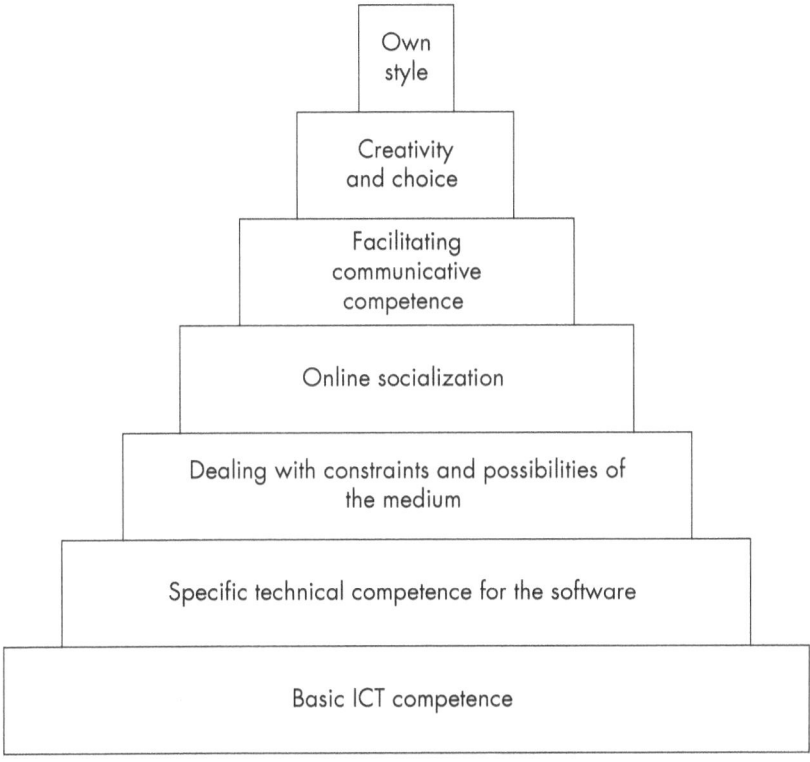

FIGURE 5.1 Online Language Instructor Skills Pyramid (Hampel and Stickler 2005, 317)

(2005) created a pyramid-shaped model of instructor skills that are necessary to teach languages online (see figure 5.1).

The first three levels of the pyramid focus on the instructor's knowledge and use of technology for online language teaching: (1) basic information and communications technology (ICT) competence, (2) specific technical competence for the software, and (3) dealing with constraints and possibilities of the medium. The first level pertains to the instructor's ability to use basic technology hardware (networked computers, keyboard, mouse) as well as basic programs and applications (word processing, internet). The second level of the pyramid involves the instructor's ability to use specific software applications that their institution provides to teach online (e-mail, course management systems to deliver courses such as the commercially available Blackboard or a custom-made conferencing software like Lyceum, used by the Open University). The third level refers to the instructor's ability to understand and deal with the constraints and possibilities of the particular software they need to use to teach at their institution (e.g., being able to adapt appropriately their F2F materials to an online format).

In the top four levels of the skills pyramid, Hampel and Stickler (2005) further develop an idea originally proposed by Shirley Bennett and Debra Marsh (2002), which says that, in addition to technical skills, online language instructors also need to be able to acknowledge the differences between F2F and online teaching and to facilitate interaction with identified strategies and techniques. The influence of Vygotskian-based sociocultural theory (Lantolf 2000; Vygotsky 1978) on Hampel and Stickler's model can be seen by their focus on the socially based and creative skills that require expertise beyond technical knowledge and abilities: (4) online socialization, (5) facilitating communicative competence, (6) creativity and choice, and (7) own style.

Level 4 (online socialization) refers to the instructor's ability to create a sense of community online and to adhere to certain rules of social interaction (netiquette); creating an atmosphere of respect, trust, and social cohesion among students in the class is necessary for the successful enactment of tasks based on interpersonal communication and meaningful interaction (role plays, dialogues, etc.). The fifth level, focusing on instructor facilitation of the development of students' communicative competence, takes for granted the creation of a community of learners in level 4; such facilitation would entail task design and tutor intervention to promote communication among learners to develop the components of communicative competence (grammatical, sociolinguistic, discourse, and strategic competencies; Canale and Swain 1980). The sixth level (creativity and choice) refers to the instructor's ability to demonstrate their creativity in their adaptation of F2F tasks to an online environment and in their design of new online activities based on the principles of communicative language learning. When instructors' abilities reach the top level of the pyramid and the instructors have mastered all six levels beneath, they are able to develop their *own* teaching style, "using the media and materials to their best advantage, forming a rapport with [their] students and using the resources creatively to promote active and communicative language learning" (Hampel and Stickler 2005, 319).

Criticisms of Hampel and Stickler's (2005) model include the following:

- The model's implication that a mastery of each skill level is needed before proceeding to the next highest level is not necessary as instructors can learn different skills simultaneously (e.g., online socialization and the facilitation of communicative competence) (Compton 2009).

- The pyramid provides no indication of criteria used to determine when a language instructor is ready to teach online (Compton 2009).
- Despite the fact that Hampel and Stickler (2005) emphasize that the skill sets of online language teachers differ from those needed by online teachers in other disciplines, only one or two skills on the pyramid are specifically related to online language learning (online socialization and facilitating communicative competence), and most of that communication is assumed to take place via computer-mediated communication (CMC; e.g., chat function) (Compton 2009; Sun 2011).

In addition, the creation of a sense of community "is not a universally attainable goal and success in this sense cannot be guaranteed by any endeavor" (Torsani 2015, 130)—indeed, it is a skill that "may be taught but not necessarily learnt" (Torsani 2015, 130).

In 2015 Stickler and Hampel reenvisioned their original 2005 skills pyramid (see figure 5.2). In Stickler and Hampel's (2015) reenvisioning of their original 2005 pyramid model, they grouped the original seven levels into three categories above the first level (Basic ICT competence, Level 0) as negotiating online teaching spaces. The emphasis placed on negotiating social interaction in levels above Basic ICT competence can be traced to the theoretical framework on which this model is based, that is, a combination of sociocultural and socioconstructivist approaches to language acquisition.

Original levels 2 and 3 were combined into one category, "matching pedagogies and technology" (1), original levels 4 and 5 were fused into the new category "developing social cohesion and fostering communication" (2), and the top two original levels (6 and 7) formed the new category "enhancing creativity online" (3).

By fusing levels 2 and 3 (technical competence and dealing with constraints and possibilities of the medium) into matching pedagogies and technology, Stickler and Hampel (2015) demonstrate in more detail the need to prioritize pedagogical concerns and make sure that the technologies chosen serve to facilitate the attainment of pedagogical goals. In their discussion of developing social cohesion and fostering communication, they provide concrete examples of engaging students in online interaction (e.g., guiding students on how to join authentic online communities; preparing students to acquire intercultural literacy for their telecollaborative sessions to record, reflect, and rerecord messages before posting them to an online forum) and call upon suggestions from Pauline Ernest and colleagues (2013) to suggest ways in which instructors can facilitate online interaction and a sense of

	Level 3: Enhancing creativity online
	Own style
	Creativity and choice
Negotiating online teaching spaces	**Level 2: Developing social cohesion and fostering communication**
	Facilitating communicative competence
	Online socialization
	Level 1: Matching pedagogies and technologies
	Dealing with constraints and possibilities of the medium
	Specific technical competence for the software
Basic ICT competence	

FIGURE 5.2 Reenvisioned Online Language Instructor Skills Pyramid (Stickler and Hampel 2015, 66)

community, for example, close monitoring of student interaction (especially at the beginning of the course), moderating online communication, providing regular feedback, and encouraging student reflection on their online interaction experiences. The authors propose that online language instructors can foster enhancing creativity online for themselves and their students in specific ways (e.g., "selecting creativity-enhancing online tools . . . , explaining the pedagogical value of creativity in language learning, providing supportive evaluation and positive feedback and furthering critical self-evaluative skills in learners"; Stickler and Hampel 2015, 73).

In addition to providing more insight into the relationships among the skills mentioned in their 2005 model, Stickler and Hampel's 2015 framework provides additional affordances for the framework. For instance, although Hampel and Stickler (2005) emphasize the importance of reflective practice by online language instructors, their original article did not contain an instrument to facilitate this process. In 2015, however, they did provide a self-reflective instrument (2015, 76–77; see chapter 7 of this volume for more on online instructor self-assessment). Stickler and Hampel (2015) also addressed Compton's (2009) criticism of their 2005 model—that it implies that one level of skills has to be acquired before those at the next level—by saying, "The pyramid model indicates that skills build on each other, not in a successive time sequence of training events but as increasing competence, with the lower levels forming a solid, reliable foundation" (65). Stickler and Hampel (2015) do point to the intended recursive nature of their model by noting that technological changes may require a revisiting of Basic ICT skills even after instructors are functioning at higher levels of the pyramid. In addition, Stickler and Hampel (2015) go beyond Hampel and Stickler's (2005) assumption of reliance on CMC for interpersonal communication among students, and they mention many forms of interpersonal communication that instructors could have students use to develop their communicative competence (e.g., asynchronous tools such as discussion forums, blogs, and social media; chatbots; and synchronous tools, such as audio conferencing with Skype).

Compton (2009)

Compton (2009) proposed the next major framework to assess the expertise of online language instructors. Compton's model is designed for the evaluation of language teachers with control over the curriculum, as opposed to Hampel and Stickler's (2005) framework to evaluate OU tutors without such purview.

Compton's (2009) evaluation framework substantially expands the Hampel and Stickler (2005) pyramid of skills and reorganizes it into three competence areas (technology, pedagogy, and evaluation) and three skill levels (novice, proficient, and expert teachers) (see figure 5.3). Compton's (2009) detailed model of online language teaching skills represents an expansion of Hampel and Stickler's (2005) model in that it incorporates elements similar to those of the 2005 model and to the TPACK model (technology in online language teaching, pedagogy of online language teaching); however, it also goes a step further by adding evaluation of online language teaching as a major element of the framework. The ability of online CALL instructors to use evaluative frameworks to critically reflect on, analyze, and modify CALL language tasks and courses is crucial to their success as a pedagogue in new digital environments. Compton's (2009) framework also distinguishes what abilities instructors at the novice, proficient, and expert levels should be able to demonstrate in each of these three skill areas (technology, pedagogy, and evaluation).

In Compton's (2009) framework, within a given column (skill area), instructors could be determined to be at the novice, proficient, or expert level,

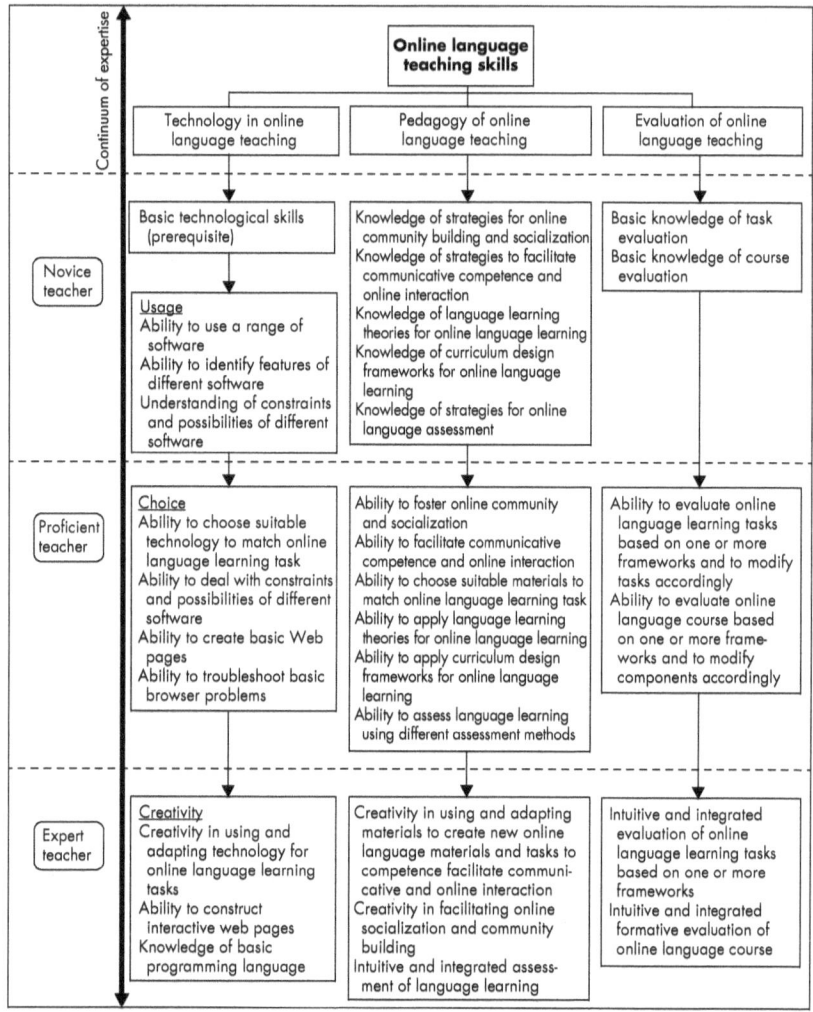

FIGURE 5.3 Proposed Framework for Online Language Teaching Skills
(Compton 2009, 82)

depending on the type of subskill that has been acquired. For instance, in the "Technology in online language teaching" column, at the novice level the instructors would have acquired basic technological skills as a prerequisite for advancing within the technology category (but not necessarily before advancing in the pedagogical or evaluation columns). At the novice level, the instructors would also have the ability to use a range of existing technologies, identify their features, and understand their constraints and possibilities.

When the instructors reach the proficient level in the area of technology, they possess enough efficacy to be able to choose appropriate software, to recognize and be able to deal with its constraints and affordances, to create basic Web pages, and to troubleshoot basic browser issues. At the expert level, the instructors can use their creativity to use and adapt technology for online tasks, create interactive Web pages, and possess knowledge of basic programming language. Although these skills may be implied in Hampel and Stickler's (2005) model (Basic ICT competence, specific technical competence for the software, and dealing with constraints and possibilities of the medium), those authors do not provide mention of specific technological skills needed by online language teachers, as Compton (2009) does in her framework.

In the center column of figure 5.3, the instructors are judged on their abilities regarding the pedagogy of online language teaching. At the novice level, the instructors possess knowledge of strategies for online socialization and community building, facilitating online interaction and communicative competence, and online language assessment as well as knowledge of language learning theories and curriculum design for online language learning. At the proficient level, the online language instructor evidences more self-efficacy by being able to foster a sense of community and facilitate online interaction, socialization, and the acquisition of communicative abilities; these skills correspond to Hampel and Stickler's (2005) skills of online socialization and facilitating communicative competence. Compton's (2009) proficient instructors can also choose suitable materials that match the online learning task, apply language learning theories and curriculum design frameworks for online language learning, and assess student language learning in an online environment. At the expert level the instructors display creativity in using and adapting materials and in facilitating online socialization and community building; these qualities correspond to Hampel and Stickler's (2005) skills regarding creativity and choice and own style. The inclusion of the ability to apply language learning theories for online language learning and the ability to assess language learning using different assessment methods (pedagogical proficient level) and intuitive and integrated assessment of language learning (pedagogical expert level) in this skills framework demonstrates Compton's commitment to grounding pedagogical practice in current research on language learning and using a variety of tools and intuitive and integrated methods to assess student progress, abilities not mentioned in Hampel and Stickler's (2005) model.

Finally, the last column in Compton's (2009) framework focuses on the evaluation of elements of online language teaching. At the novice level, the instructors possess basic knowledge of task and course evaluation. At the proficient level, they expand their abilities in this area and are able to evaluate and modify online tasks and course components based on one or more frameworks. These assessment skills are further developed at the expert level, in which the instructors are able to perform intuitive and integrated evaluations of online language learning tasks and courses based on one or more frameworks and formative evaluations of online language courses. Thus, with a focus on instructor assessment of tasks and courses, Compton again assumes more agency on the part of online language teachers than do Hampel and Stickler (2005) and Stickler and Hampel (2015) in their frameworks focused on OU language tutors.

In addition, Compton's (2009) framework for assessing online language teachers proposes a different perspective than that of Hampel and Stickler (2005) on the process of attainment of the skills necessary to teach languages online. For instance, while in Hampel and Stickler's (2005) model, pedagogical skills build upon the mastery of the basic technology skills (a vertical, progressive approach), Compton's model acknowledges more clearly that the acquisition of pedagogical and technological skills can happen simultaneously and more independently, with instructors possibly demonstrating the ability to be creative in facilitating online socialization and community building (pedagogical expert level) before they can create a basic Web page (technology proficient level). Thus, instructors could acquire technological, pedagogical, and evaluation skills (the three columns in figure 5.3) simultaneously and be judged to be at different skill levels in these three areas at any one time. In addition, Compton does not assume that online learning can only be identified with interaction and CMC (as Hampel and Stickler's [2005] model does). Drawing on work by Chapelle (2005), Compton also acknowledges that her 2009 model tries to encompass the entire experience of learning language online (e.g., interactions between the learner and course content-bearing oral and written texts [interpretive mode of the communication standard] as well as between learners [interpersonal mode of the communication standard; ACTFL 2015]). In addition, due to the fact that Compton's (2009) framework assumes more instructor agency than that of Hampel and Stickler (2005), Compton's model adds an entire column of evaluative skills necessary for online language teachers, for example, the ability to evaluate tasks and courses.

Even though Compton's (2009) model presents a more developed framework for evaluating online language teachers than Hampel and Stickler's (2005) skills pyramid, Susan Yue Hua Sun (2011) criticizes both models for their lack of details on what actions teachers can take to meet their proposed skills criteria, for example, teachers need practical suggestions on what to do (or not do) and how to accomplish what they need to do in order to teach successfully in an online environment. Sun (2011) notes, "What is most needed by online teachers is advice and guidance with sound theoretical basis for everyday teaching practice but they are largely missing from the research literature. It seems that online teachers are, by and large, left to do their own experiments and perhaps learn from their own mistakes" (431).

In addition, in both these models, instructor abilities are conceived as phrases that describe abilities (Hampel and Stickler [2005]: online socialization→ Compton [2009] ability to foster online community and socialization) instead of as standards (using declarative sentences), which would more clearly illustrate what the instructor is expected to do. Also, in the Compton (2009) model the author astutely recognizes that instructors improve in a given area (technology, pedagogy, and evaluation) when they build on one skill to acquire one that represents a higher order of cognition than the level below it (e.g., novice instructors begin with "knowledge of strategies for online community building and socialization," which they use to develop the "Ability to foster online community and socialization" as proficient teachers). They become expert teachers when they demonstrate "creativity in facilitating online socialization and community building." However, Compton's model provides no guidance as to how instructors should be judged regarding their progress toward mastering a given subskill within a larger skill level category, for example, ability to foster online community and socialization (proficient teacher).

Compton's (2009) model also shares the same drawback as Palloff and Pratt's (2009) rubric that gauges interaction, for example, various skills are grouped together within each level of expertise (novice, proficiency, expert) with no indication of how to designate the level of an instructor that is functioning well in some (but not all) of the skill abilities listed for that level. To avoid this problem, each skill or subskill needs to be scaled and evaluated on its own. To gauge progress toward the attainment of this ability, a more fine-grained assessment instrument is needed, that is, one that provides a graded scale for each ability at each level. For instance, a Likert-type scale could be based on an instructor's gradation of agreement with a statement about his or her online teaching ability: "Instructor is able to foster socialization among his or her students." (Strongly disagree→ Disagree→ Somewhat disagree→ Somewhat agree→ Agree→ Strongly agree). However, in order for the evaluators to be able to gauge the instructor's progress in this area, departments will have to operationalize all constructs related to assessment (i.e., define terms being used [e.g., "socialization"] and indicate how progress toward the attainment of that construct is to be measured in their particular pedagogical context [e.g., students seek out opportunities to chat/discuss with other students regarding personal information (hobbies) or on issues brought up in class outside of assigned interactive tasks]).

Finally, although Compton's (2009) model provides an excellent outline for the evaluation of online language teachers, it does not mention the need for rubrics for self-evaluation. Models of assessment for online language teachers should include self-assessments as well as institutional evaluation instruments to be used by peers, administrative supervisors, and departmental administrators. Ideally, rubrics for program assessment would also be a part of one large set of cogent, evaluative instruments for online language instructor and program evaluation. The rubrics created by the TESOL Technology Standards Project (Healey et al. 2011) come close to meeting this goal.

Healey and Colleagues (2011)

In 2008 the professional organization Teachers of English to Speakers of Other Languages (TESOL) published the TESOL Technology Standards framework (Healey et al. 2008) to provide guidance to language programs regarding the level of skills that students and instructors of English (and, by extension, world languages) should possess to integrate technology into the language curriculum in order to benefit language learners and teachers. In 2011 this framework document was expanded by Healey and colleagues to include more vignettes to contextualize each standard, a more in-depth explanation of the theoretical and empirical bases for the standards, a chapter that compares TESOL standards with other standards created by the International Society for Technology in Education's National Educational Technology Standards (ISTE 2000, 2007, 2020) and the UN Education, Scientific, and Cultural Organization's Information and Communication Technologies Competency Standards for Teachers (UNESCO 2008a, 2008b, 2008c), and chapters targeted toward teacher trainers, administrators, and instructors who teach language online. In addition, checklists for self-evaluation and program assessment are included in the 2011 TESOL Technology Standards framework.

Healey and colleagues (2011) provide a detailed justification for the need to establish technology standards for language students and instructors and to identify content for those standards. They cite research showing the benefits of using CALL technologies in terms of improved learning outcomes (Brandl 2002; Grgurovic and Chapelle 2007), motivation and development of positive attitudes toward second language learning (e.g., Meunier 1998; Pennington 1996; Warschauer 1996), and improvement of retention rates (e.g., Ioannou-Georgiou and Michaelides 2001). Referring to Yong Zhao's (2003) literature review and metanalysis of CALL literature, Healey and colleagues also note the need for further research on CALL curriculum development and empirical studies on uses of technology in the classroom. In addition, Healey and colleagues (2011) point out that the incorporation of technology into language curricula can help students develop electronic literacy skills ("accessing, evaluating and utilizing information" [9] as well as second language proficiency (Lightbown and Spada 2006).

Finally, Healey and colleagues (2011) note that inadequate teacher and learner training result in CALL technology not being used to its full potential to facilitate language learning. The authors provide evidence for this assertion by referring to Greg Kessler's (2006) acknowledgment of the need for language teachers to increase their understanding of and ability to use CALL technologies, and to Chapelle and Volker Hegelheimer's (2004) statement that CALL resources could "provide a valuable opportunity to rethink and perhaps reinvent what constitutes the knowledge base for L2 teachers" (314). Healey and colleagues (2011) believe that part of this new knowledge base would consist of a set of technology standards that could be used to gauge the technological expertise of language instructors and their progress in various technology areas. Although not focused specifically on setting goals for online language teachers, their technology standards for language teachers can certainly serve as indicators of basic technopedagogical knowledge that all language instructors should have, including those who teach entirely online.

Although the Healey and colleagues (2011) volume contains technology standards for both students and instructors, we discuss only the technology standards for language teachers here. The four technology standards goals, along with three to four standards for each, consist of the following:

- Goal 1: Language teachers acquire and maintain foundational knowledge and skills in technology for professional purposes.
    - Standard 1: Language teachers demonstrate knowledge and skills in basic technological concepts and operational competence, meeting or exceeding TESOL Technology Standards for students in whatever situation in which they teach.
    - Standard 2: Language teachers demonstrate an understanding of a wide range of technology supports for language learning and options for using them in a given setting.
    - Standard 3: Language teachers actively strive to expand their skill and knowledge base to evaluate, adopt, and adapt emerging technologies throughout their careers.
    - Standard 4: Language teachers use technology in socially and culturally appropriate, legal, and ethical ways.

- Goal 2: Language teachers integrate pedagogical knowledge and skills with technology to enhance language teaching and learning.
    - Standard 1: Language teachers identify and evaluate technological resources and environments for suitability to their teaching context.
    - Standard 2: Language teachers coherently integrate technology into their pedagogical approaches.
    - Standard 3: Language teachers design and manage language learning activities and tasks using technology appropriately to meet curricular goals and objectives.
    - Standard 4: Language teachers use relevant research findings to inform the planning of language learning activities and tasks that involve technology.
- Goal 3: Language teachers apply technology in record keeping, feedback, and assessment.
    - Standard 1: Language teachers evaluate and implement relevant technology to aid in effective learner assessment.
    - Standard 2: Language teachers use technological resources to collect and analyze information in order to enhance language instruction and learning.
    - Standard 3: Language teachers evaluate the effectiveness of specific student uses of technology to enhance teaching and learning.
- Goal 4: Language teachers use technology to improve communication, collaboration, and efficiency.
    - Standard 1: Language teachers use communication technologies to maintain effective contact and collaboration with peers, students, administration, and other stakeholders.
    - Standard 2: Language teachers regularly reflect on the intersection of professional practice and technological developments so they can make informed decisions regarding the use of technology to support language learning and communication.
    - Standard 3: Language teachers apply technology to improve efficiency in preparing for class, grading, and maintaining records. (Healey et al. 2011, vii)

Each of these goals is also accompanied by five to eleven performance indicators for each standard. An example of a goal with a corresponding standard and performance indicators is demonstrated below (Healey et al. 2011, 169):

Goal 1: Language teachers acquire and maintain foundational knowledge and skills in technology for professional purposes.

Standard 1: Language teachers demonstrate knowledge and skills in basic technological concepts and operational competence, meeting or exceeding TESOL Technology Standards for students in whatever situation they teach.

Performance indicators: Language teachers have the ability to perform basic functions with digital devices; prepare instructional material for students using basic technological tools, such as a word processor and presentation software; and exercize appropriate caution when using online sources and communicating online.

In addition to the list of standards, Healey and colleagues (2011) expanded the number of vignettes (roleplays to illustrate how standards are applied) and included the following information to contextualize each vignette: teacher profile role and student profile type, age range, proficiency level; context of the roleplay (EFL/ESL, classroom, blended, online); focus of the roleplay (language skills practices, approach, and tools). One of the affordances of the vignettes is that they demonstrate Critical CALL awareness by rating a vignette (e.g., low, medium, high) according to the level of resources and accessibility available to students in a particular teaching environment.

Even though these standards provide guidelines for gauging the technology expertise in language instructors (perhaps teaching a technologically enhanced or hybrid language course), several factors need to be taken into account when those instructors teach a course completely online. Healey and colleagues (2011) discuss in detail four of those factors: technology infrastructure (ensuring instructor and learner expertise with course tools), learning environment (creating a learning community through collaboration and supportive asynchronous and synchronous interaction), time (establishing clear time lines so students can plan time for course assignments and avoid conflict with personal demands), and teacher and learner presence (social, teaching, and cognitive presence to create a community of inquiry; Garrison, Anderson, and Archer 2001). At the end of their chapter (8) dedicated to online teaching, Healey and colleagues (2011, 169) propose implications of each standard for online language learning environments. For example:

Goal 1: Language teachers acquire and maintain foundational knowledge and skills in technology for professional purposes.

Standard 1: Language teachers demonstrate knowledge and skills in basic technological concepts and operational competence, meeting or exceeding TESOL Technology Standards for students in whatever situation they teach.

Performance indicators: Language teachers have the ability to perform basic functions with digital devices; prepare instructional material for students using basic technological tools such as a word processor and presentation software; and exercize appropriate caution when using online sources and communicating online.

Implications for online teaching: More technical competence is generally required in an online course than in a face-to-face course with occasional use of technology. Teachers should be able to respond to basic technical questions, including frequently asked questions about hardware and course tools, and recognize which questions need to be forwarded to technical support staff.

The ability of the online language instructor to discern when they or their students could benefit from advice and assistance from technical support staff is crucial to the success of their students, especially those who are novice technology users.

The TESOL Technology Standards for teachers share some similarities with the models already discussed (Hampel and Stickler 2005; Stickler and Hampel 2015; Compton 2009), such as measuring progress by adding on more complex skills and abilities in higher levels of expertise. Another similarity between the TESOL standards (Healey et al. 2011) and Compton's (2009) is the fact that the different domains of expertise in both models (e.g., technology, pedagogy, and evaluation; Compton 2009) and the four goals of the technology standards (i.e., foundational knowledge of technology, integration of pedagogical skills and technology; application of technology in record keeping, feedback, and assessment; use of technology to improve communication, collaboration, and efficiency; Healey et al. 2011) can be evaluated independently. Expertise in one domain does not necessarily assume accomplished expertise in the other domains (as in Hampel and Stickler 2005; Stickler and Hampel 2015).

Despite some similarities with prior models, there are also distinct differences between the standards model and those that preceded it. For instance, the TESOL standards constitute the most developed framework of the three models of skill sets. First, instead of using phrases such as "online socialization" (Hampel and Stickler 2005) and "ability to foster online community and socialization" (Compton 2009), the TESOL standards are stated as full, declarative sentences in goals and standards that state more clearly what is expected of teachers—for example, Goal 4: Language teachers use technology to improve communication, collaboration, and efficiency. Goal 4, Standard 1: Language teachers use communication technologies to maintain effective contact and collaboration with peers, students, administration, and other stakeholders.

Another difference to be highlighted between the TESOL standards and prior frameworks is the way in which they indicate distinct levels of expertise. For example, Compton's (2009) model creates three levels of teacher competence (novice, proficient, and expert teacher), while the TESOL standards only distinguish between levels of ability that should be required of all language teachers using CALL technologies from those that are needed by expert instructors who serve as technology specialists in "settings that rely heavily on technology" (Healey et al. 2008, 4). Unlike Compton (2009), who distinguishes three levels of expertise (novice, proficient, and expert) within each area (technology, pedagogy, and evaluation), the TESOL standards distinguish an expert level only in certain goals and standards (Goal 2, Standards 2, 3, and 4; all standards in Goals 3 and 4).

There are also limitations of all of the rubrics discussed so far. For instance, in all models, progress in instructor technological abilities is defined by reaching a higher level that involves a more complex skill than the one below it. As discussed above, the Hampel and Stickler (2005) and Stickler and Hampel (2015) models assume that each level of the pyramid takes for granted the acquisition of the skills below it, and in Compton's (2009) model the expert teacher's ability to demonstrate "creativity in facilitating online socialization and community building" illustrates a more complex ability than simply possessing the "ability to foster online community and socialization" (at the proficient teacher level). This assessment of increasing level of skill complexity in more advanced instructors is also illustrated in the TESOL standards for language teachers when they compare performance indicators for the basic versus expert level of abilities:

Goal 4: Language teachers use technology to improve communication, collaboration, and efficiency.
   Standard 1: Language teachers use communication technologies to maintain effective contact and collaboration with peers, students, administration, and other stakeholders.
   Performance indicator: Teachers belong to online communities (e.g., mailing lists, blogs, wikis, podcasts) with other language teachers.
   Performance indicator (expert level of technology): Language teachers advise administration on the use of online technology to improve communication. (Healey et al. 2011, 119)

In this example, the difference between the basic and the expert level of technological ability involves going from a state of belonging or experiencing forums in which language teachers can communicate to being able to advise administration about online technologies that can improve communication. Although these abilities are related, they involve different skill sets. Thus, moving from a basic to an expert level of expertise in the TESOL standards involves adding on a more complex skill (evaluating communication technologies) to a skill already achieved (experiencing online communication technologies). Although this aspect of the TESOL evaluation metric (higher levels of expertise require more complex skills) resembles those of the other models discussed here (Compton 2009; Hampel and Stickler 2005; Stickler and Hampel 2015), there is one major difference. In contrast to the other "additive" models, the TESOL standards (Healey et al. 2011) do include some metrics for individual skills to be assessed at each level.

For instance, as illustrated just above, the performance criteria for meeting Goal 4, Standard 1 provides descriptors for different individual skills at the basic and expert level. The same wording is used to describe the performance indicators at each of those levels in the self-assessment rubric (Healey et al. 2011, 202), which contains Likert-scale assessments of each skill at each level.

Although the essence of these same abilities is reflected in the program assessment rubrics provided in the TESOL standards volume (Healey et al. 2011), the wording differs from the original Goal 4, Standard 1, and some basic and expert level skills are all contained in one complex description (to be evaluated as a whole) with no way to factor out and evaluate each of the skills separately: "Teachers interact with students electronically and share material with each other electronically.... Expert-level teachers set up methods to communicate with students, have their students create and submit work electronically, advise administrators about digital communication methods, and digitally share material" (216).

Thus, although the TESOL Technology Standards program evaluation rubric (Healey et al. 2011, 211–17) does include several measures to evaluate instructors that generally correlate with the description goals, standards, and performance indicators for teachers (71–127) and with the teacher self-assessment rubrics (189–205), there is no separate rubric for evaluating online instructor performance; for example, several of the performance indicator metrics in the program assessment rubrics are geared toward evaluating the affordances that administrators provide for teachers rather than the abilities of the instructors:

> Goal 1: Language teachers acquire and maintain foundational knowledge and skills in technology for professional purposes.
> Standard 4: Language teachers use technology in socially and culturally appropriate, legal, and ethical ways.

Performance indicator (Instructors): Online teachers are vigilant in protecting learner privacy in online courses (e.g., using BCC as appropriate to address e-mail to everyone in the group).

Performance indicator (Administrators): Administrators provide opportunities for teacher development related to legal and ethical use of electronic information and media. (Healey et al. 2011, 212)

In sum, even though Healey and colleagues (2011) do provide fine-grained self-assessment and program evaluation rubrics that correlate with the TESOL standards for teachers, what is still missing from the TESOL Technological Standards are fine-grained rubrics to be used by various institutional evaluators (e.g., students, peers, administrative supervisors, department administrators) who assess instructor skills at each level of expertise (basic and expert) in an evaluation instrument dedicated solely to the evaluation of online language instructors as well as rubrics to assess CTE training, the online instructor evaluation process, and the quality and applicability of the rubrics themselves.

In addition, lacking an ecological approach to assessment, all of these models are rather inflexible in their application. The metrics are often general and not applicable or relevant in certain educational environments. For instance, no questions are asked about the instructor's prior experience teaching with technology so that evaluators can make contextualized assessments of instructors' abilities to use technology effectively. In addition, some of the evaluative criteria assume that the instructor teaching the course has also created the course and has the authority to choose materials and technology environments for the class (e.g., "Ability to choose suitable materials to match online language learning task" [Compton 2009, 82]; "Language teachers choose a technology environment that is aligned with the goals of the class" [TESOL standards, Healey et al. 2011, 97]), which may not be the case in many contexts (e.g., Hampel and Stickler [2005, 2015]). What is needed is a flexible, perhaps modular, rubric that has components designed to be applied only when the instructor has the authority and ability to make curricular choices; those sections would not be chosen to appear in the rubric used to gauge the performance of online instructors who are teaching a course created by others and may have no authority to modify course elements (e.g., teaching assistants, instructors, lecturers, and adjunct faculty).

Another element lacking in all rubrics evaluated here is any kind of in-depth self-reflection. Although the TESOL standards do provide self-assessment checklists for the online language instructor, and some of those checklists mention the need for self-reflection on their own teaching styles and pedagogical approaches, no self-reflection questions are provided by the framework to accomplish that task. The value of in-depth self-reflection to foster continuous improvement in online language teaching performance makes it imperative to include this type of assessment in instructor evaluation procedures (see chapter 7).

Other necessary online language instructor abilities include the ability to carry out a needs assessment and to focus on issues related to CCA in instructors or students (mentioned in the TESOL Technology Standards [Healey et al. 2011]). Although the ability to conduct needs analyses may only be needed by instructors with curricular control, the ability to deal with issues related to CCA should be assessed in all online language instructors. The TESOL Technology Standards contain two notable recognitions of access issues, that is, the rating of vignettes (e.g., low, medium, high) according to the level of resources and accessibility available to students in a particular teaching environment, and the mention of access issues in Goal 2, Standard 1, Performance Objective 2 of the TESOL Technology Standards: "If students in online courses have poor connectivity, the teacher adapts the material used (e.g., video may not be usable in low-bandwidth areas)" (Healey et al. 2011, 213). Instruments used to measure intercultural sensitivity, an element of CCA, include Milton Bennett's (1986, 1993, 2004) Developmental Model of Intercultural Sensitivity, which measures attitudes toward other cultures on a scale from ethnocentrism to ethnorelativism, and Guo-Ming Chen and William Starosta's (2000) Intercultural Sensitivity Scale, which measures five factors of intercultural sensitivity: intercultural engagement, respect for cultural differences, interaction confidence, interaction enjoyment, and interaction attentiveness. Another rubric informed by Bennett's model was created by the Association of American Colleges and Universities to measure intercultural knowledge and competence (AACU n.d.).

PUTTING IT ALL TOGETHER

This chapter on the assessment of online language instructors has inspired the following ideas for implementation:
- The training/assessment cycle for online language instructors should take place within the larger context of ongoing language program evaluation.
- Evaluations of online language instructors can take place formatively with peer mentors and supervisors at the micro level and summatively at the micro (students, supervisors) or meso levels (departmental administrators).

- Extant models of assessment have several shortcomings that need to be remedied:
  - Extant models of assessment for online language faculty do not take an ecological approach to assessment in that evaluations are not normally contextualized to take an instructor's context into account (e.g., instructor's experience teaching online, their roles and responsibilities, their preferred way of receiving feedback, their technological challenges or lack of access) when evaluating those instructors.
  - Extant models of assessment for online language faculty do not require intensive and ongoing self-reflection activities.
  - Extant models of assessment of online language instructors do not focus on the development of critical cultural awareness to recognize access and social justice issues that may challenge their students and their community.
- In order to address these issues, the following steps can be taken:
  - A needs analysis should be done by the online language teacher in order to uncover challenges that their students may be having trying to access technology to complete their assignments.
  - Critical cultural awareness should be added as an evaluation component in the assessment of online language instructors so they become aware of access and social justice challenges faced by the target culture.
- Adopting an ecological approach to the assessment of online language teachers would help to contextualize instructor assessments and have faculty use a critical lens to investigate access and social justice concerns of their students, the target culture community, and the community at large.

Chapter 6 builds upon the excellent base provided by the evaluation models discussed above (Compton 2009; Hampel and Stickler 2005; Stickler and Hampel 2015; Healey et al. 2011) by proposing new modular rubrics that can be used as part of a contextualized evaluation process to assess the performance and progress of online instructors after a training program and during mentoring and debriefing sessions. Appendixes B-1, B-2, and B-3, respectively, also contain rubrics for evaluating the CTE training, the assessment process, and the rubrics used for instructor assessment.

6

Instruments for the Assessment of Online Language Instructors

In this chapter we discuss the assessments of online language instructors that are performed by students, faculty supervisors, and departmental administrators, and we provide concrete examples of instruments to facilitate those assessments. Chapter 5 discusses resources for language program evaluation (provided by Gruba et al. 2016; Davis and McKay 2018; and Healey et al. 2011, 211–17), and instructor self-assessments are discussed in detail in chapter 7 (with a sample self-assessment rubric in appendix C-5), so these two types of assessments are not discussed here.

THE IMPORTANCE OF TEACHER ASSESSMENT

The twenty-first century has seen sweeping changes in educational policies that aim to make schools increasingly accountable for students' academic success and retention (Faubert 2009; Looney 2011). Measures to increase teacher accountability are due to a variety of factors, including government initiatives, the competitiveness wrought by internationalization, and the rising cost of tuition (Marginson 2006; Ramsden 1995). Furthermore, university students increasingly view their education from a consumer perspective, demanding measurable outcomes and skills in exchange for the time and money they have invested (Lao and Gonzales 2005; Pyszczynski et al. 2004).

In the United States, improving the quality of education has been synonymous with nationally mandated student and teacher assessments. K–12 instructors have borne the brunt of government-led educational reform under campaigns such as No Child Left Behind (Abedi 2004; US Department of Education 2001). Educational accountability for instructors at institutions of higher education pale in comparison to the scrutiny that state and federal government agencies give to primary and secondary educators (Taubman 2010). In recent years there have been efforts to improve the standards, training, and assessment of higher education on a global scale. However, while countries such as Australia, England, and China have established standards of quality for their institutions of higher education, the US movement for universal standards in higher education is still in its infancy.

THE CONTEXT OF FACULTY ASSESSMENT

The need for more oversight of university professors has been a topic of discussion for several decades. However, this question is complicated by the fact that teaching is only one facet of professors' workloads as they also hold time-consuming commitments to institutional committees and academic research. While the popular "publish or perish" adage may be losing some traction, it is still common that promotion and tenure evaluations tend to prioritize research over teaching (Dewar and Bennett 2014).

Although teaching quality has traditionally not been as valued as research at institutions of higher education, surveys carried out among faculty prove that professors value teaching just as much, if not more, than their research responsibilities (Scott and Scott 2016). These findings negate the notion that university professors are not invested in teaching and point to other factors responsible for shortcomings in the quality of higher education.

Historically, institutions of higher education have created a culture of practice whereby attaining an advanced degree in an area of study automatically qualifies an individual to teach in that area (Marincovich, Prostko, and Stout 1998; Ramsden 2003). While the idea that an active researcher equals a good teacher has been thoroughly refuted (Hughes 2003), this long-held practice has created a population of college professors who have little to no formal teacher training (Aylett and Gregory 2012; Ellis 1993). In fact, recent evaluations of academics' pedagogical training have confirmed that professors' teaching preparation is limited primarily to the completion of an obligatory methods course during graduate school (Lafford 2017; Lord 2014). Even in these cases, the scope and quality of methods courses greatly vary and most only provide training for lower-division course development (Lafford 2017). Given the lack of in-depth and continued teacher training, instructors commonly teach how they were taught (Scott and Scott 2016). Instructors' reliance on teaching methods that mirror their own student experiences often results in outdated pedagogical approaches, a lack of alignment between teaching materials and course objectives, and inappropriate assessment methods (Allen et al. 2010; Scott and Dixon 2008; Scott and Issa 2006).

INITIATIVES FOR INCREASED FACULTY ASSESSMENT

Issues related to instructor training and assessment have not gone unnoticed in postsecondary education as there are increased efforts to help faculty cultivate effective teaching skills (Prosser and Trigwell 1999). Many universities have established a centralized teaching support center that offers pedagogical training and support (Knapper 2010). In online education, there are also teams of course designers and technology experts whose main purpose is to work with faculty. While these efforts provide many important resources for educators, the services they offer are often too general to meet certain departmental and subject-specific needs (Scott 2002).

Issues related to centralized teacher trainings are also present in university-wide assessment tools used to measure faculty teaching effectiveness. The most frequent type of feedback that postsecondary instructors receive comes from course evaluations that students complete at the end of the semester (Cohen 1981). While student evaluations can be helpful in highlighting underlying issues with the course content and instruction, this type of assessment does not automatically trigger a debriefing session or the reflection exercises that the instructor would need to make significant changes to the course (Centra 1976, 1993). Furthermore, as discussed in chapter 1 of this book, the bias that many students show in their assessment of their instructor has led faculty members to advocate for less weight to be placed on student teaching evaluations (Aylett and Gregory 2012; Barnett 1992; Pennie 2001).

In the absence of formative teaching evaluations, academic departments must respond to the need to design and implement their own faculty teaching assessments. In his book *Quality Assurance for University Teaching*, Roger Ellis (1993) emphasizes the importance of implementing assessment measures for professors. Ellis outlines the following process for improving teaching methods and outcomes:

- Establish clear standards for quality teaching.
- Create a system that ensures that professors follow the established standards.
- Request student feedback regarding the instructors' effectiveness.
- Implement an instructor improvement plan.

In keeping with the multistep assessments, Shelleyann Scott and Kathryn Dixon (2008) advocate for evaluation processes, adding that it is important to provide professional development that is "psychologically safe." In this model, academics create a space in which they can share ideas, collaborate to solve problems, and gain a sense of empowerment. One way of gaining a sense of self-efficacy is through the process of evaluating one's own work (self-assessment), discussed in chapter 7.

In the rest of this chapter and in the three chapters that follow, we explore the assessment of online language instructors using an ecological framework to allow for evaluations that are fair assessments of an online language instructor's skills within the context of their particular pedagogical environment.

AN ECOLOGICAL APPROACH TO ASSESSMENT

As we note in chapter 5, an ecological approach to online instructor assessment takes into account the circumstances, role, and experience of instructors in the selection of rubrics chosen to evaluate them. This holistic approach to instructor assessment helps to ensure that individual teachers are being evaluated fairly within their particular pedagogical context, instead of having their performance assessed in a reductionist manner through the use of rubrics that are applied to all online language instructors regardless of their background and current job responsibilities. In this chapter, more in-depth discussions of the application of this ecological approach to instructor assessment can be found in the section "Importance of Audience in Instructor Assessment."

The sections below contain a discussion of various types of assessments (e.g., formative, summative, and high and low stakes), the importance of considering audience and context in instructor evaluations, and samples of rubrics that could be used by online language students and other institutional stakeholders (peer mentors, faculty supervisors, departmental administrators) to assess online language instructor performance.

Summative and Formative Assessments

Thomas Tobin, B. Jean Mandernach, and Ann Taylor (2015) identify two primary goals in evaluation of online teaching: "(1) to gauge instructors' overall effectiveness or skill in an online classroom in order to inform their subsequent teaching experience (summative evaluation) and (2) to gain feedback during a course to improve the ongoing teaching and learning process (formative evaluation)" (76). These summative and formative assessments

(Scriven 1967), carried out at the micro, meso, and macro levels (Gruba et al. 2016), need to become part of the departmental culture of a training/assessment life cycle. Some assessments that are commonly implemented in institutional settings (e.g., student and supervisor evaluations at the micro level and departmental program audits at the meso or macro level) can be summative, providing an overview of compliance with program and departmental standards and policies to provide accountability at the end of a given period of time. On the other hand, formative assessments of language faculty are carried out over time at the micro level between instructors and mentors so that detailed feedback can be given along the way to help improve instructor performance.

A summative assessment measures learners' performance through exams and certifications and is often used by state and national organizations to illustrate a panorama of how specific learner populations meet educational standards. While summative assessment is widely used in education, there are several problematic issues related with this type of measurement (Looney 2011; Taras 2008). Unlike formative assessment, summative assessment does not provide details needed to design interventions for individual learners. Furthermore, the timing of summative assessment is often delayed, given the large quantity of data that must be processed at the end of a semester. Other challenges presented by summative evaluations include their general lack of ability to measure high-order cognitive skills such as problem-solving and collaboration (Taras 2005). While summative assessment can offer a general overview of a given context, it does not normally capture the nuances of faculty performance, growth, and opportunities for improvement that formative assessments are able to examine.

In contrast to summative assessment, formative assessment measures learner progress in order to identify areas of strengths and weaknesses; this information can help inform the teacher of how they can modify their teaching style and content to better serve the class. Research has proven that the frequent use of formative assessments helps learners to improve their academic performance and thus are commonly used as a teaching tool that enhances the learning process (Black and Wiliam 1998).

Approaches to formative assessments may take many forms such as peer-to-peer discussions, question-and-answer sessions, and self-reflection (Sadler 1989). In order for formative assessment to be an effective learning tool, instructors must dedicate time to changing their pedagogical approaches (Smith et al. 2005). Furthermore, learners must understand how formative assessment will be used to aid them in their own learning process. When learners conceive of a formative assessment as a learning tool, they show increased intrinsic motivation, self-concept, and performance (Harrison 2009; OECD 2001; Sebba 2006).

High- versus Low-Stakes Assessment

Many of the complaints associated with formal assessments are that the outcomes are often linked to high stakes. In education, high-stakes assessments are increasingly common as state and national initiatives reward high-scoring schools while threatening low-scoring schools with the possibility of reformation or closing (Abedi 2004; Black and Wiliam 2005; Jennings and Rentner 2006). In this way teachers focus their attention on meeting the state and nationally mandated benchmarks and are encouraged to teach to the test.

As a result of high-stakes assessment, teachers often feel that they cannot implement teaching styles and content that are not highlighted in the mandated external assessments (Looney 2011). Furthermore, the focus on student assessment has excluded teachers from major discussions about the assessment of pedagogical approaches and implementation. Therefore, scholars have called for more studies that evaluate and reward teachers, for example, providing them with formative feedback on their performance and rewarding innovative practices (Centra 1993; Herman, Osmundson, and Silver 2010).

As research has shown that student achievement is most influenced by the perceived quality of one's teacher (Fullan 2005; Hamre and Pianta 2005), high-quality professional development for educators is the key to achieving student success. E. Caroline Wylie and colleagues (2008) suggest that in order to improve the quality of our teachers, we must identify effectives practices, consider current practices that can be improved, and engage teachers in modifying their teaching style. In order for teachers to take the risks necessary to incorporate changes in their teaching style, there must be a low-stakes, formative assessment process that allows for gradual yet permanent change to occur. Chapters 7–9 provide in-depth discussions on possibilities for implementing this type of formative assessment for online language instructors.

Importance of Audience in Instructor Assessment

Just as effective training programs must take into account the prior experiences of a particular audience for their online instructor preparation (e.g., teaching assistants versus in-service instructors), fair assessments must also take into consideration the current skill level and past experiences of the audience (person) being evaluated. For instance, an ecological approach to assessment demands that when assessing online language faculty, it is necessary to contextualize those evaluations with information on the teachers' background in teaching languages, teaching with technology, and teaching an online language course. In addition, information must be gathered on the instructor's access to required technology and applications in order to evaluate fairly their use of those technologies and software programs.

Other important factors that need to be considered in instructor assessment concern the cultural background of the person being evaluated to understand the best way to provide constructive feedback to them (see chapter 9), their control over the curriculum, and the role the instructor will play in the online learning system (Hubbard and Levy 2006a). For instance, a person with the role of tutor, with no control over course design or content, should not be judged on ability to design and create modules for online courses (the domain of course designers and teachers). The Online Language Instructor Modular Rubric (OLIMR) presented in this chapter facilitates this tailored evaluation process.

STUDENT EVALUATION OF ONLINE LANGUAGE INSTRUCTORS

As seen in chapter 5, the evaluation of online instructors is a relatively new area of assessment research. While some institutions implement assessments of online courses via external or internal reviews based on preestablished Quality Matters (2018) criteria, and many institutions use the same instructor assessment forms for F2F, blended, and online courses, online courses at a great number of institutions may go unregulated and unassessed by appropriate formal evaluation procedures created within a particular departmental context.

When assessments of online courses are carried out, there is more opportunity to scrutinize online instructors as their course materials, lessons, and student interactions are accessible via learning management systems. The relatively easy accessibility and high visibility of online courses have resulted in higher expectations for instructors to deliver quality teaching and measurable learning outcomes (Price and Kirkwood 2014). The heightened expectations for online courses make instructors especially vulnerable in both student and peer assessment, especially when the assessment instruments used do not capture specific online instructor skills (e.g., effective use of technology to facilitate online student interaction).

The most frequent type of feedback that postsecondary instructors receive comes from summative student course evaluations (SCEs) that they complete at the end of the semester (Cohen 1981). While SCEs were originally intended to help instructors improve pedagogical areas identified by students, there is little evidence that teachers use SCEs to inform their teaching or that their mentors follow up on those assessment results to help instructors improve their teaching formatively over time (Nasser and Fresko 2002). As a result, SCEs are most commonly used as summative assessments for accountability and auditing (Galbraith 2012).

As discussed in chapter 1, it is clear that online courses are markedly different from courses in face-to-face and hybrid teaching formats, and assessment instruments need to reflect those differences. A major concern for online instructors is that many universities do not have SCEs that have been specifically designed to reflect the online teaching environment, and the evaluation criteria may not reflect theories on effective online teaching (Ory and Ryan 2001). Aside from a lack of valid criteria on which online SCE items are based, instructors also struggle with the opinions of students who may lack experience with online courses. As research has shown that SCE results are greatly influenced by students' opinion of good teaching (Goldstein and Benassi 2006; Kember, Jenkins, and Ng 2004), this is problematic if their previous learning experiences have been solely based on F2F methodological approaches. Furthermore, as discussed in chapter 1 of this book, the gender and racial bias that many students show in their assessment of their instructor has led faculty members to advocate for less weight to be placed on student teaching evaluations (Aylett and Gregory 2012; Barnett 1992; Pennie 2001).

Another challenge associated with online course evaluations results from the manner in which students respond. When compared to paper evaluations filled out in the classroom, digital SCEs have lower response rates (Sorenson and Reiner 2003), which can skew the data and diminish the validity of the results.

Some scholars have argued for improving SCEs through the establishment of interinstitutional standards for evaluation, while others support the formation of departmental support structures to improve formative assessment models via mentoring and administrative workshops (Sorenson and Reiner 2003). Regardless of the path chosen, it is important that all instructors are trained to reflect on and respond to the student assessment responses that they receive.

Appendix C-1 presents a rubric that can be used by students to evaluate online language instructors. The items in this evaluative instrument were inspired by the CTE literature reviewed in chapter 4 on essential online instructor skills and questions contained in assessment rubrics from Arizona State University (2019a, 2019b, 2019c) and Quality Matters (2018). This rubric to evaluate the quality of teaching by online language instructors can be given to students at the end of their online course as a summative assessment of the faculty member. This evaluation provides feedback that can facilitate the comparison of instructor performance over time and in relation to that of other instructors.

The rubric in appendix C-1 only provides suggestions for items that could be included in these student evaluations; the list of metrics is not meant to be used in its entirety as an appropriate rubric for every language program. Administrators and supervisors are encouraged to create their own student rubrics by choosing the evaluation questions that are most relevant to their particular teaching context. Questions pertinent only to a given department or language section may also be added to the rubric being created (e.g., questions on the use of a certain technological application to assist students with the understanding and production of non-roman alphabets or writing systems). Once those student instructor evaluation rubrics are produced, they can be tested for reliability and validity in the context of that department and institution. In addition, it can also be useful to modify the list of questions so that they can be administered to students taking online courses in any subject in order for institutions to comparatively evaluate the quality of their online instruction across disciplines.

INSTITUTIONAL EVALUATIONS OF ONLINE LANGUAGE INSTRUCTORS

In addition to student evaluations (and self-assessments), departmental units need to effect assessments of the performance of online language instructors administered by peer mentors, supervisors (e.g., teacher trainers), and departmental administrators. In this way the voices of all these stakeholder groups can be triangulated to create a nuanced understanding of faculty strengths and areas for improvement for attaining the departmental standards contained in the OLIMR rubric.

Peer Mentors

As part of ongoing merit evaluations, language instructors are often asked to evaluate their colleagues' teaching by observing a class and giving feedback on that observation to the practitioners and their supervisors. Robert Menges (1985) proposes a formative evaluation approach to collaborative peer review to allow instructors to develop their skills by getting ongoing feedback on their teaching and coaching from fellow faculty members. Martin Tobin (2004) proposes the establishment of a peer mentoring program in which a newly trained online teacher is paired with a more experienced colleague. Through this program the mentor shadows the online courses of the new instructor, provides ongoing feedback (using appropriate departmental rubrics), and meets regularly with the new online faculty member for support and encouragement. These informal reviews by colleagues should take place in a collaborative learning environment and can take the form of unstructured observations or more focused feedback on specific issues that instructors have identified as challenges for them. The sustainability of this type of mentoring program would be ensured if the new language instructors eventually became mentors of new language faculty asked to teach in online environments. (See chapter 8 for an in-depth discussion of peer mentoring.)

Although John Ross and Catherine Bruce (2007) note the positive impact that peer reviews can have on teacher self-assessments and performance, challenges arise to the establishment of peer mentoring relationships among online faculty. Ernest and Hopkins (2006) note that many faculty who teach online may work part time at several institutions, which means they would have no official service commitment to give them credit for volunteering to mentor their peers. In addition, Ernest and Hopkins state that faculty do not want to impose or "spy" on their colleagues' teaching practices unless peer observations are required of them. To address these challenges, supervisors and departmental administrators should brainstorm solutions to reward participation in mentoring processes in which seeking constructive peer feedback is considered a core value of departmental culture.

Supervisors

In addition to receiving feedback on their online teaching from students and peer mentors, language instructors should be regularly evaluated by their supervisors. These supervisors may also be in charge of a department's entire language program (face-to-face, blended, and online courses). Although these administrators may have a great deal of practical experience training F2F language instructors, Tobin and colleagues (2015) note that "many administrators who are called upon to evaluate online instructors have never taught online themselves" (98).

In these cases, supervisors would be wise to set up the peer mentoring program described above (and in chapter 8) and rely heavily on peer evaluations when evaluating new online faculty. In addition, in order for supervisors to gain a greater understanding of the rewards, demands, and challenges of teaching online courses, they should seek out training for themselves on best practices of online teaching and teach an online course themselves. These experiences will give supervisors a better idea of how to support online faculty (Tobin, Mandernach, and Taylor 2015).

Supervisors should also set up initial and ongoing online training for online language instructors and implement formative and summative assessments that are appropriate to their particular instructional context. To carry out these assessments, they could use questions from the OLIMR rubric and appendix C-4, conduct post-observation debriefing sessions with online faculty to provide constructive feedback, and engage focus groups in which faculty provide these supervisors and administrators with background information about the online context in which they work and the challenges they face.

Having both peer mentors and supervisors use the same (OLIMR) rubric helps to facilitate a common understanding of the assessment process and the use of a common language in their discussions of instructor performance to attain the standards evaluated by the OLIMR rubric. Before the mentor and supervisor evaluator groups apply the rubric to online instructor evaluations, they should meet in a norming session to assess online instructor performance using data from a contrived course shell so that personal data from actual instructors and students are not inappropriately shared. This way peer mentors will become more familiar with the instruments that those supervisors will be using to assess their performance as well.

Departmental Administrators

It is often the case that the ultimate head of the departmental unit (chair, faculty head) is required to evaluate online language instructors. These departmental administrators (DAs) may not only lack online teaching experience, but in smaller institutions they may even be experts in a different language from the one the instructor teaches or even hold a professorship in another humanities-related discipline (history, communication, philosophy, women's studies). The further the distance between the academic background and the online experience of the department administrator and the instructor being evaluated, the more difficult it will be for the administrator to provide expert assessment of the online instructor's abilities.

In cases where the academic experience of the DA and the online instructor differ greatly, it would be beneficial for the DA to rely heavily on faculty self-assessments and peer mentor / supervisor evaluations when assessing the capabilities of the online instructor. Tobin and colleagues (2015) suggested concrete steps DAs can take to understand the quality of the teaching of the online language faculty: "phone or e-mail current students to follow up on the observation, look up past performance data on current students' previous courses, compare observation data from the instructor's previous classroom and online course visits, recommend (and often enforce) instructor remediation actions for noted challenges, provide incentives for improved teaching practices, retention and student satisfaction" (127).

Another way for DAs and supervisors to understand and track the developmental trajectory of the online instructor's skills is for them to require online faculty to create and continuously update a digital teaching portfolio that would provide evidence of the attainment of departmental online teaching standards and expectations (CASLS 2020; Cummins 2007; Tochon and Black 2007; Van Olphen 2007). These portfolios would also include peer mentor observations and supervisor evaluations regarding the online instructor's progress toward meeting these goals.

Because DAs are not directly supervising or mentoring the online language instructor to provide them feedback on an ongoing basis, most DA meso-level assessments of online faculty are normally summative in nature and are carried out in the context of formal instructor annual reviews and evaluations for faculty to obtain promotions or tenure. As noted earlier, DAs may not be experts in the instructor's field, so they need to rely heavily on the results of micro-level student evaluations, instructor self-assessments, and peer mentor / supervisor evaluations of the online language instructor. Of course, if DAs have some experience teaching languages online, they may also wish to use the OLIMR rubric to evaluate the online instructor, in addition to answering reflection questions similar to those found in appendix C-4.

THE ONLINE LANGUAGE INSTRUCTOR MODULAR RUBRIC (OLIMR)

The evaluation rubric presented in appendix C-2 on the quality of teaching by the online language instructor can be administered by institutional stakeholders (e.g., instructors [self-evaluations], peer mentors, supervisors, DAs). The evaluation can be formative in nature when it is meant to provide micro-level feedback to instructors on their pedagogical practices as they teach. The rubric can also be used summatively at the meso and macro levels by DAs for online instructor evaluations for annual reviews, promotion/tenure evaluations, and program assessments. Evaluators can also use information from the instructor's self-evaluations, teaching statements, or interviews to make these assessments.

To ensure a fair assessment of the instructor's work, questions on the prior experience, responsibilities (curricular control), and the role of the faculty member being evaluated are included in the OLIMR rubric. The answers to these questions provide the evaluator with background information that will help to contextualize the findings and assist the instructor in setting appropriate goals for professional development with the guidance of their supervisors. The questions provide feedback that can facilitate the comparison of an individual instructor's performance over time or in relation to that of other instructors.

The items included in the OLIMR rubric provide suggestions for items that could be included in formative or summative evaluations of online language instructors by their supervisors. It is not meant to be used in its entirety as an appropriate rubric for every language program. Supervisors are encouraged to create their unit's instructor evaluation rubrics by choosing the evaluation standards and reflection questions that are most relevant to assessing online instructor performance in relation to their departmental standards, to the curricular control and role of the instructor, and to their particular teaching context. In that sense, the OLIMR rubric is modular—that is, only those skills expected by a certain type of instructor would be contained in that teacher's OLIMR modified rubric (e.g., standards related to curriculum design may be relevant for full-time faculty but not for teaching assistants or adjunct faculty without curricular control).

In addition, departments can modify these evaluation standards and add others (e.g., items from the questionnaire used by students to evaluate online language instructors; see appendix C-1) to meet their program evaluation needs (see appendix A-3 for a checklist of essential online instructor core competencies that can be used to inform the creation of assessment rubrics). Once departmental rubrics are created for supervisors to evaluate distinct groups of online language faculty (e.g., those with and without curricular control), they can be tested for reliability and validity in the context of that unit.

The items in the OLIMR were inspired by the CTE literature on online instructor skills (reviewed in chapter 4) and assessment frameworks found in Compton (2009), Hampel and Stickler (2005), Stickler and Hampel (2015), Healey and colleagues (2011), and Quality Matters (2018).

Instructions for Application of the OLIMR Rubric

The rubric presented in appendix C-2 covers the six modules that can be modified to meet the different needs/circumstances of language programs and instructors.

I. Course Design
II. Online World Language Teaching
III. Feedback and Assessment
IV. Technology in Online Language Teaching
V. Professional Development
VI. Self-Reflection Questions

For example, if the instructor did not design the course content, the evaluator may wish to forgo Module I: Course Design but use the other modules.

In order to use the OLIMR for Formative Assessment, the following procedures need to be followed:

- The course instructor and supervisor review the evaluation rubric together to choose applicable criteria and clarify any questions.
- The course instructor completes a self-evaluation using the rubric for the online course being evaluated. The instructor must include evidence for this evaluation (see below).
- After completing the self-evaluation, the instructor e-mails the completed rubric to the supervisor.
- The supervisor carries out an evaluation of the instructor using the same rubric as well as the evidence provided by the course instructor.
- The supervisor schedules a follow-up meeting with the instructor to discuss the evaluations and set teaching goals.

Determining Criteria for Online Instructor Evaluation

In this chapter we have presented a sample evaluation rubric that contains selections from the instructor skills checklist (appendix A-3) and were modified to fit the needs of the program described in the case studies in chapters 7, 8, and 9. The ecological approach we take to training and evaluation of online language faculty demands that departments customize instructor evaluation rubrics to reflect the experiences, roles, and responsibilities of teachers within the unique culture of one's academic institution. The OLIMR modular rubric presented in appendix C-2 is designed to serve as a base for the customization process so that language departments can conduct fair and appropriate faculty assessments and bring about optimal job satisfaction (Galbraith 1977).

Evaluations used for a department's online faculty should be as unique as the faculty is. In creating customized rubrics, supervisors should consider what aspects of the rubric will most appropriately assess what their faculty actually do. We believe that this ecological approach to faculty assessment will create an academic culture in which faculty are treated fairly and in which their experiences are valued.

PUTTING IT ALL TOGETHER

This review of online instructor assessment has inspired the following ideas for implementation:

- Before an assessment is conducted, the evaluation criteria should be determined and thoroughly reviewed within a personal learning network for online education.
- Evaluation criteria should represent a broad scope of one's experience with online teaching including professional development and participation in personal learning network activities.
- Evaluations must be collaborative, allowing for the supervisor and instructor to conduct assessments with the same criteria.
- Instructors should be invited to formally reflect on their experiences and the overall online program.
- The supervisor must provide a space to address the feedback that the instructors provided about their experiences with an online program as well as issues they have identified and suggestions for future modification.
- Supervisor feedback must include detailed information about the instructors' online performance with specific examples based on their course sites and other personal documentation.

This discussion of the assessment of online language instructors has centered on the types of evaluation carried out by various institutional stakeholders (students, supervisors, DAs). To gain a deep understanding of the abilities of a language instructor for teaching in an online environment, these institutional stakeholder evaluation results need to be triangulated with self-assessment data (chapter 7) within the context of an ongoing mentoring program that provides constructive feedback to teachers for improving their instruction (chapters 8 and 9).

7

Self-Evaluation Practices in Formative Assessment

In our ecological approach to self-assessment, the instructors see themselves as part of a larger unit with values (standards) they must strive to achieve and as individuals striving to improve their knowledge and practice of online language teaching to connect more effectively with their students and with members of the target language community. Rena Palloff and Keith Pratt (2011) discuss the need for faculty to regularly assess their own training needs and devise strategies to meet them so they can take responsibility for their own learning. The authors also note that self-assessments by truly novice faculty should first determine their readiness to teach online, while more experienced faculty should seek out training to improve and perfect the skills they already have. Palloff and Pratt also suggest conducting a needs analysis on the instructors' use of certain basic technologies and applications as well as their frequency of use and comfort level with them. Then practitioners can create their own ongoing training plan and seek out professional resources at their institutions and professional conferences or via online training to improve their knowledge of and skill levels regarding teaching technologies.

CHECKLISTS FOR SELF-EVALUATION BY ONLINE PRACTITIONERS

Thomas Tobin, B. Jean Mandernach, and Ann Taylor (2015) discuss ways of having practitioners generate self-evaluative feedback. For instance, faculty can use a checklist of skills to assess the quality of how they performed as a teacher in the online class. This checklist can take the form of "How well did I..." statements on a checklist of online teaching skills (Tobin, Mandernach, and Taylor 2015, 93); for example, "How well did I handle student questions and responses in the online forum," or "integrate multimedia to foster learning for a range of student learning styles." Next to each skill on this checklist, teachers use a Likert-type scale to indicate how well they carried out those activities: "Very well, Satisfactory, Not very well, Poorly, Does not apply."

Palloff and Pratt (2011) provide a more detailed self-assessment checklist, dividing the skills into technical skills, experience with online teaching and learning, attitudes toward online learning, and time management / time commitment. The statements in this rubric are declarative statements in the present tense, such as "I support learner-to-learner interaction and collaborative activity as a central means of teaching" and "I have received training in online instruction." Practitioners then use a Likert-type scale to indicate their agreement/disagreement with these declarative statements: "Strongly disagree, Disagree, Neither agree nor disagree, Agree, Strongly agree."

Another format that is used for self-assessment checklists to gauge WL instructors' technology skills are the "rate my ability" or "can do" lists for language teachers who want to evaluate their expertise in integrating technology into their teaching. Examples of two such lists can be found on the Information and Communications Technology website for language teachers (ICT4LT; Davies 2012) and in Deborah Healey and colleagues' (2011) TESOL Technology Standards. The ICT4LT ability lists (Davies 2012) allow practitioners to gauge their knowledge of basic technology skills (e.g., how to use Windows, Word, Excel, PowerPoint, e-mail, video recording and editing software; virtual worlds [*Second Life*]) and to evaluate their expertise in those areas, for example, "I would describe my ability to use *Video Recording and Editing Software* as (1–3)" (Davies 2012, 18), with 1 ranked as basic, 2 as intermediate, and 3 as advanced. This list could still be valuable to some learning contexts even though it has not been updated since 2012 to include more modern applications and social media sites like Facebook, Instagram, and Twitter; ARIS (augmented reality for interactive storytelling) games; and the use of MALL (mobile-assisted language learning) technologies such as accessing CALL applications and social media via mobile devices like phones, and iPads (for a more updated list of CALL resources, see the CTE/CALL Resource list on this book's Web page at www.press.georgetown.edu). In addition, there are a number of essential "I understand" statements pertaining to specific applications or actions that are still very relevant and valid; for example, "I understand the implications of copyright and plagiarism when using materials downloaded from the Web" (Davies 2012, 5).

Another self-evaluation checklist format—"Can do statements"—was proposed in the TESOL Technology Standards volume (Healey et al. 2011) for both WL students and instructors to evaluate their own technology skills.

The TESOL Technology Standards for Language Teachers rubric (described in chapter 5), consists of four goals with three to four standards for each goal and several performance indicators for each standard. Teachers are asked to evaluate their abilities at the performance indicator level using a Likert-type scale: "Very well, Adequately, Not so well, Not at all, Not applicable (N/A)." An example of a goal, standard, and performance indicator follows:

> Teacher Goal 1: Language teachers acquire and maintain foundational knowledge and skills in technology for professional purposes.
> Goal 1 Standard 1: Language teachers demonstrate knowledge and skills in basic technological concepts and operational competence, meeting or exceeding TESOL technology standards for students in whatever situation they teach.
> Performance Indicator (can-do statements): "I can perform basic functions with available digital devices in order to accomplish instruction and organizational goals." E.g., "I can launch and exit software applications." (Healey et al. 2011, 189)

These performance indicators often indicate two levels of expertise ("standards that all teachers should meet" versus "additional performance indicators for technology experts"; Healey et al. 2011, 71) and include mention of more modern technologies (e.g., podcasts, wikis, blogs). However, they also leave open the possibility of new technologies that should be evaluated for feasible use in a CALL-mediated or online course; for example, "I learn about and try new technologies as they become available and determine whether or not they would be appropriate in my teaching" (Healey et al. 2011, 204). Although these types of "can do" checklists are a valuable self-assessment resource for language teachers, in-depth self-reflection is needed to raise teacher awareness about the technological knowledge and abilities they currently possess and what they need to improve.

ONLINE PRACTITIONERS USING REFLECTIONS FOR SELF-EVALUATION

John Dewey (1938/1988) believed that all genuine education comes about through experiences that engage learners and have continuity with their future experiences. David Kolb (1984) describes "the process whereby knowledge is created through the transformation of experience" (41) as experiential learning. Sonja Knutson (2003) argues that "experiential learning as a philosophy is based on the ideals of active and *reflective* learning, building on previous learning experiences and requiring the personal involvement of the learner" (53). Therefore, ongoing reflection on one's own learning or teaching practices is essential to the continuous improvement of the learner's (or, in this case, the developing language practitioner's) knowledge and skills.

Donald Schön (1983, 1987) noted that traditional teaching models do not help students to link the learning of new material with a meaningful understanding of that same material. He posited that, through reflection, one could reach a level of understanding that encouraged changes in one's behavior or thought pattern. Schön found that the process of reflection led students to question whether their actions were appropriate and what they needed to change to improve their professional skills. Moreover, Diane Slaouti and Gary Motteram (2006) note that teachers need to reflect on their firsthand experience with teaching tools and their own situated learning in pedagogical environments in order to facilitate and reveal cognitive processes that facilitate the transformation of competencies. Nicolas Guichon's (2009) study demonstrates the advantages of having teacher candidates in France reflect on, critique, and receive peer feedback on a video-recorded planning activity they had carried out with another candidate during their training session to teach intermediate French online to North American students. Finally, Simone Torsani (2015) proposes that reflective processes would undoubtedly be "an advantage for the development of the ability to integrate technology into language education" (119).

Several second language and CALL scholars have written extensively on the use of self-evaluation via the use of self-reflection exercises. Consonant with Dick Allwright's (2003) discussion of the use of instructor self-reflection in exploratory practice, Robert Blake (2013) notes the need for teachers to develop critical literacy skills by reflecting on their own pedagogical practices. In addition, Tim Lewis's (2006) study supports the use of critical analysis and reflection in a teaching journal combined with feedback from a "critical friend" on pedagogical decisions to promote autonomous learning within the context of an informal, nondirective approach to teacher training.

Although the TESOL Technology Standards for Language Teachers (Healey et al. 2011) reference the need for instructors to engage in self-reflection, saying, "Language teachers demonstrate understanding of their own teaching style" (94) and "Language teachers review personal pedagogical approaches in order to use technology to support current teaching styles" (32), the standards framework does not provide any self-assessment questions or instrument designed to carry out these reflections.

On the other hand, Palloff and Pratt (2011) do include self-evaluation and reflection questions for online faculty in their appendix C: Resources for

Administrators of Online Programs. The reflection questions focus on the learning experiences for students ("Were students motivated and involved throughout?") and instructors ("Were there challenges? If so, how did you meet them?" "What worked well?"). However, many of these questions could be answered in a yes/no format without any discussion or evidence of their claims required by the instructions ("Did they [students] meet expected outcomes?" and "Did you feel supported in your teaching experience by staff and colleagues?"). There are also no self-reflection questions on linking their skills to standards set by their department or on identifying areas in which they need to improve (with the exception of a question on what they would do differently next time).

By filling in these gaps, Ursula Stickler and Regine Hampel (2015, 76–77) provide an excellent example of a self-evaluation instrument for online WL instructors. The reflection is divided into three sections: (1) instructors reflect on their strengths, giving concrete examples (evidence) to support those assertions; (2) instructors link those skills to different skill levels/standards defined by the language program; and (3) instructors identify areas in which they need more training, support, or peer advice. The authors also provide sample instructor reflections following this structure to serve as models for faculty reflective assessments. Thus, this instrument demonstrates best practices for self-reflection by WL online language teachers; that is, it requires supporting evidence for claims made by WL online practitioners as they reflect on their skills and practices, and it requires them to link their skills with departmental expectations and to self-identify areas in which they need to improve.

In addition, CTE researchers (Cummins 2007; Tochon and Black 2007; Van Olphen 2007) and CASLS and PEARLL (2020) have proposed the use of digital portfolios as a reflective tool that teacher candidates can use to gauge their progress in acquiring technical, pedagogical, and content knowledge (among the core competency skills) needed for incorporating technology into their language curricula.

Self-Reflection and Formative Evaluation

An individual's ability to reflect on their work can provide meaningful insights into strengths and areas for improvement (Klenowski 1995). However, not all self-evaluation methods render the same results. Researchers have found that without documentation, individuals using self-evaluation tend to overestimate their performance (Andrade and Valtcheva 2009; Chang, Tseng, and Lou 2012; Falchikov and Boud 1989). While overestimation of one's abilities and effectiveness may be due to several factors, including high-stakes evaluation practices or a desire to enhance one's accomplishments (Boud and

Falchikov 1989), it is recommended that self-evaluation not form part of a summative assessment but instead constitute part of formative professional development opportunities (Centra 1993).

Several scholars have discussed how self-assessment may be used in a positive manner that fosters professional growth (Chang, Tseng, and Lou 2012; Fox and Dinur 1988; Pakaslahti and Keltikangas-Jarvinen 2000). Researchers agree that in order to increase validity and user satisfaction, individuals must be trained to apply self-evaluation tools (McDonald and Boud 2003; Ross and Starling 2005). John Ross (2006) recommends the implementation of the following four stages of self-assessment training:

1. Involve individuals in setting evaluation criteria to reflect administrative cognitive and emotional investments (Muhammad and Cruz 2019). This includes using language that is understandable and choosing criteria that is meaningful.
2. Practice applying assessment criteria in low-stakes contexts. The trainer may create a "sample teacher" that all faculty assess with the rubric in a norming session.
3. Compare the practice assessment results with those of the trainer and other faculty. Discuss how their evaluation scores for the "sample teacher" were similar or different.
4. Use the results of the assessment to identify possible programmatic issues as well as personal improvement plans.

The authors of the current book have taken into account aspects of this process in the initial design and launch of the OLIMR evaluation process. The OLIMR process encourages faculty to participate in their own evaluation by applying the same evaluative rubric to assess their performance that the supervisor uses and answer self-reflection questions (at end of OLIMR rubric and in appendix C-5). The completion of the rubric is followed by a debriefing meeting between supervisor and instructor, followed by goal-setting activities (see chapter 9).

Applying Self-Reflection Tools with a Professional Learning Network

Discrepancies between instructor self-evaluations and mentor evaluations of instructor performance may include differences in performance perceptions, the amount of feedback provided, and the extent to which the evaluator understands the course content and classroom culture. For example, an assessment may look for concrete evidence of skills or task achieved but not take into account the effort exerted or progress that is made but does not yet meet the assessment benchmark (Ross 1998). However, assessments carried out within an ecological frame of reference see instructor practice as a reflection of their background knowledge, their experience teaching online, their effort put into their work, and their incorporation of the feedback they receive. In an ecological framework, mentors and supervisors should provide the type of feedback that would be the most appropriate for an instructor from a specific cultural background working within a particular department culture and ecology.

By training individuals how to use self-evaluation tools, it is more likely that they will interpret their assessment as a formative learning opportunity (Bandura 1997). Furthermore, individuals undergoing formative assessments will be more prone to focus on their progress rather than compare themselves to others (Ross, Hogaboam-Gray, and Rolheiser 2002).

SELF-ASSESSMENT IN THE OLIMR EVALUATION PROCESS

Relatively little qualitative or quantitative research has been conducted regarding language teacher self-evaluation practices (Ross 2006). However, researchers have called for more studies that highlight how self-assessment may positively influence course design, pedagogical approaches, and student experiences (Ross and Bruce 2007). The following sections provide information on a case study conducted by King Ramírez regarding online WL instructors' experiences with the OLIMR evaluation process that incorporates the online instructor modular rubric (including self-reflection questions). The aim of this study was to distinguish similarities and differences between their past teaching evaluation experiences and their experience with applying the online instructor modular rubric (see chapter 6).

Methodology

Carmen King Ramírez conducted online instructor trainings for faculty interested in teaching language online for the first time at their university. Between 2017 and 2020, those who enrolled in the training were invited to participate in a post-training survey. In a review of the survey results, King Ramírez found that forty-four out of fifty-seven (77 percent) of these future online instructors had never taken an online course. These findings were important given that, in the absence of online instructor training, it has been observed that some instructors struggle with the shift of teacher-student dynamics in the online classroom, have not been exposed to pedagogical approaches that they could transfer to their own teaching methods, and have not been required to rely solely on technology for instructional purposes (Blake and Guillén 2020).

In order to provide continual training and formative assessment opportunities for online Spanish faculty, at the end of their first semester of teaching in a 100 percent online format, King Ramírez (the online program director) introduced instructors to a modified version of the online instructor modular rubric presented in this book. The instructors were provided an overview of the rubric and asked to evaluate themselves on each portion of the rubric. Given that online courses cannot be observed in the same way as a face-to-face course, the instructors were required to provide a justification for each designation (developing, performing, excelling) that they assigned themselves by providing evidence from their course site. Evidence could be a screenshot, a copy of an e-mail, or other course-related materials.

After completing each area of the rubric, the instructors answered open-ended reflection questions. A copy of the completed rubric and the responses to the reflection questions were sent to the instructors' online program director before their scheduled debriefing meeting. King Ramírez reviewed the instructors' self-assessment, compared the assessment to her own observations, and then met with each instructor individually via Zoom to discuss the findings.

Participants. Fifty-seven language instructors elected to participate in a post-survey administered at the end of the two-week intensive training mentioned previously. The participants were from six different countries and had completed postsecondary coursework in over thirty different institutions. Participants held a variety of academic positions, including graduate students, adjunct faculty, instructors, lecturers, and assistant professors.

King Ramírez chose a sample of twelve instructors who had taught online Spanish for at least one semester and had undergone a formal evaluation process involving the online instructor modular rubric. The sample included three instructors from each faculty rank that participated in the study. Faculty ranks represented in this study included graduate students, adjunct faculty, instructors, and lecturers. No tenured or tenure-track faculty participated in this study. All of the faculty self-identified as Hispanic. The average age of participating faculty was thirty-five.

Instruments. Four sections of the OLIMR rubric presented in this book (see chapter 6) were used as the self-evaluation tool for this case study. The modified rubric consisted of the following modules: Online World Language Teaching, Feedback and Assessment, Technology in Online Language Teaching, and Professional Development. As these instructors did not design the course, the Course Design module of the OLIMR rubric was not used to evaluate their performance. After completing the rubric modules, the instructors provided written responses to the following open-ended reflection questions. The responses to these questions were discussed during the oral interview.

- What were your past evaluation experiences like?
- How did this evaluation process differ from past evaluations?
- In what areas of online instruction do you excel?
- In which areas would you like to improve as an instructor?
- Describe a challenge that you faced with an online learner and how you resolved it.
- What types of technology/assignments would you like to implement in your online course?
- Are there areas for which you would like to be recognized that were not represented in this rubric?

Results

Given the specific self-evaluative focus of this chapter, the following section reviews three of the questions that the instructors responded to in the opened-ended written reflection questions and the oral follow-up interview with the supervisor.

Question 1: What were your past evaluation experiences like? There were some similarities in the answers that the instructors provided regarding their experience with teaching evaluations. For example, the evaluation of F2F classes commonly included a visit (many times unannounced) to the instructor's class by a designated evaluator. Instructor 3 noted that the class visit was followed up by a debriefing session several days later.

> Cuando ella llega yo le entrego a ella mi plan de día para que ella pueda guiarse. Ella toma nota . . . hace apuntes sobre la conexión con el estudiante, los power points, el diseño, a sea todo lo relacionado a la clase. Al final de la clase pues me agradece nada más . . . se va a su oficina. En unos días ella me habla para platicar conmigo sobre la evaluación. (Instructor 3, oral follow-up interview)

> [When she arrived, I gave her my lesson plan for the day so that she could use it as a guide. She took notes . . . about the connection with

students, the power points, the design, you know, everything related to the class. At the end of the class, she just thanked me ... and she went to her office. A few days later she called to talk about the evaluation.]

Similarly, Adjunct Faculty 2 related that when she was a graduate student at another university, someone visited her class to conduct an evaluation and afterward provided a list of areas for improvement.

> Iba a la clase la profesora, me explicaba lo que iba a revisar pero nunca me entregaba a mí nada al final. Nada más platicaba conmigo para ver qué es lo podía mejorar. (Adjunct Faculty 2, oral follow-up interview)

> [The professor would go to the class, she explained to me what she was going to look for but she never gave me anything at the end. She just talked to me about what I could improve.]

This same instructor outlined that she was never provided a rubric and that she felt the online evaluation process in which she was currently participating was the first "real" evaluation she had received during her three years of teaching.

> Es en sí, la primera evaluación que me hacen así, bien. Porque en la Universidad de X como era T.A. y no era evaluación tan grande, era algo muy corto. (Adjunct Faculty 2, oral follow-up interview)

> [Actually, this is the first evaluation that I have had done like that, done well. Because at the University of X since I was a T.A. and the evaluation wasn't very long, it was something really short.]

A common thread that runs through the comments provided by the faculty is that their previous evaluation experiences excluded their voice from the process. This led Graduate Student 1 to view the evaluation process as impersonal and one-sided.

> Previous evaluations are impersonal, and they do not take into account the input of the instructor that is being evaluated. Additionally, those evaluations are usually the only measure against which instructor performance is being measured. I believe this rubric is richer and also gives instructors a chance to reflect on their own practices. (Graduate Student 1, written evaluation response)

Faculty also commented that their past evaluation experiences were infrequent.

> Tiene un par de años que no me evalúan. Esto fue únicamente el primer semestre. Hay muchísimos instructores y graduate students que están enseñando. Entonces se enfocan más en los nuevos. Si estás haciendo un buen trabajo, ya dejan de evaluar tu forma de enseñar en la clase. (Instructor 2, oral follow-up interview)
>
> [It has been a couple of years since I was evaluated. It was just the first semester. There are a ton of instructors and graduate students that are teaching. So they focus more on the new ones. If you are doing a good job, they stop evaluating the way you teach class.]

Instructor 1 had only been given one teaching evaluation in over a decade of working at her institution. This evaluation was not based on a rubric nor was it followed by a debriefing session with the evaluator.

> In the past 11 years, I have only had one evaluation for face-to-face teaching. The only evaluation I had received was one where it was a class visit. She [the observer] used to give us a paper that she would put in our mailbox—it was just notes. It would say like, "you did a really good job engaging the students." It was very specific to that one class. I had not been evaluated using a rubric before. (Instructor 1, oral follow-up interview)

Question 2: How was this evaluation process different from past evaluations? The participants noticed several differences between their past evaluation experiences and their experience with the online evaluation rubric presented in this book. While some of the instructors were provided the rubrics that would be used to evaluate them, none of the instructors had ever been given the opportunity to use that same rubric to self-evaluate. Several instructors commented that the self-assessment portion of the OLIMR evaluation process led them to critically review their progress during the semester.

> Es diferente porque me forza [sic] a regresar a todo lo que hice en el semestre y hacer conexiones sobre lo que creo que hice bien, lo que hice mal, donde necesito mejorar. (Instructor 3, written evaluation response)

[It's different because it forces me to go back to everything I did during the semester and make connections between what I think I did well, what I did poorly, and where I need to improve.]

Similarly, Lecturer 2 stated that through this process she was able to synthesize all of the activities she had completed throughout the semester.

It was helpful in that I am able to see a summary of what I have done. By doing that, I was able to reflect on the areas in which I excel and in the ones I need to improve. (Lecturer 2, written evaluation response)

By requiring a period of self-assessment before the debriefing meeting with the supervisor, the instructor is encouraged to make time for reflection. It was also noted that the OLIMR evaluation process included areas of teaching that are not often highlighted in the evaluation process.

I think this rubric is holistic and it tackles key areas of online instruction that I as an instructor would not normally reflect on during my daily teaching routine. Having a specific rubric helps me to set aside some time to reflect on these important areas. (Graduate Student 1, written evaluation response)

The holistic nature of the rubric was also noted by Graduate Student 2. She stated that the rubric was more inclusive of the instructor and their overall experience with the course.

This evaluation is more holistic. Because you are not only addressing not only the class instruction but also the instructor. It engages the instructor more in the process of online teaching in terms of the questions are not necessarily just about teaching or grading but the feel of the course. (Graduate Student 2, written evaluation response)

Question 3: What would you like to be recognized for that was not part of the rubric? The self-assessment portion of the OLIMR evaluation process not only creates a space for instructors to reflect on their course but can also allow them to provide valuable input about the evaluation process as a whole. In chapter 8 we note that the evaluation process is reiterative; as such, each new iteration should take into account the feedback provided by the most recent cohort of teachers who have completed the process. The modified rubric used for this group of instructors included an open-ended question regarding areas of recognition that were important to the instructors but not represented in the rubric itself. In response to this question, Instructor 2 asked that the rubric include a section regarding nonacademic student-instructor interactions: "I would add an area in how to reflect about problematic students or different types of students and the way an instructor deals with them" (Instructor 2, oral interview response). This suggestion points to an important aspect of teaching (student behavioral issues) that often goes overlooked but frequently impacts the classroom community, student learning outcomes, and the language program's reputation.

Equally difficult to measure in a traditional evaluation rubric is the suggestion made by Lecturer 2. She felt that there needed to be a way to demonstrate her dedication to efficient and empathetic student-instructor communication:

> I always made the effort of being "present." What I mean by that is I always tried to answer their e-mails as soon as I was able to do it. I answered their phone calls and talk to them as long as they needed. Every time we had a video conference (exam, etc.) I asked them about their questions and concerns about the class. Not to mention the amount of time I invested in grading and trying to make the learning material more accessible for them. (Lecturer 2, written evaluation response)

Instructor 1 commented that she was not interested in being evaluated for certain things she does but would like to be recognized for them. She also expressed interest in being involved in developing new teacher training activities with which she has experience.

> Problem resolution with students. Dealing with their emotions. You turn into a therapist, provide guidance, and advising. I would like to be recognized, but not evaluated on this. I don't think it's fair to ask everyone to be an advisor. Maybe including the instructor in brainstorming ideas for trainings on things and asking their opinion. It makes the instructor feel like they are recognized. (Instructor 1, oral interview response)

Upon reviewing instructors' response to the open-ended reflection questions provided at the end of the OLIMR rubric, it is clear that their past evaluations have been mostly summative. The nature of those evaluations left little to no opportunity for follow-up or negotiation of the results. These findings are important given that the OLIMR evaluation process is quite different from the current culture of assessment at many universities. Therefore, the implementation of the OLIMR process will require buy-in by both the administration and faculty.

PUTTING IT ALL TOGETHER

The discussion in this chapter on instructor self-reflection has inspired the following ideas for supervisors to implement:

- Meet with instructors to discuss their past evaluation experiences as well as their feelings about those evaluations.
- Discuss with instructors the differences between formative and summative assessment.
- Be clear about the purpose of the assessment process and how the data gathered will be used (e.g., informal documentation, goal setting, departmental record keeping).
- Let instructors know that their opinions are important in the evaluation process. Explain the instructors' role in post-evaluation debriefing meeting (see chapter 9).
- Administration should understand the nature of the OLIMR formative evaluation process. Support may need to be identified to help the online program director or other supervisors carry out the various steps of the evaluation process.

In chapter 8 we explore how the mentoring process builds on the self-assessment activities described in this chapter.

8

The Mentoring Relationship in Formative Assessment Processes

This chapter discusses the formation of beneficial instructor-mentor relationships both leading up to and during the formal teaching assessment. Given that new and veteran instructors need continual mentorship to hone their craft, an instructor may have several mentors throughout their tenure as an online teacher. This chapter specifically looks at the role of peer mentors (other instructors who also teach online) and supervisors who act as mentors during the formative evaluation process. We also provide qualitative data on this process from our case study and provide implications for the implementation of solid mentoring partnerships between online language faculty and their mentors to facilitate the post-observation debriefing process discussed in chapter 9.

In our use of an ecological framework for understanding mentoring relationships, we propose that supervisors facilitate instructors' and mentors' understanding of the mentoring process as one that unites its stakeholders toward the pursuit of a common ecological goal—to appreciate their roles as complementary members of a learning environment focused on improving the quality of online language instruction in their unit.

In this chapter we use the terms "supervisor" and "mentor." Depending on the administrative support that each institution allots their online instructors, they may have a combination of these two resources or neither. Therefore, the terms may be interpreted by the reader and used independently or interchangeably depending on the teaching context.

MENTORING IN THE CTE LITERATURE

Mentoring can be seen as embodying several theoretical principles that undergird sociocultural theories of learning. For instance, many scholars consider

Lev Vygotsky's (1962, 1978) Zone of Proximal Development (ZPD) as foundational to the notion of mentorship in educational settings. The ZPD is often described as the distance between students' cognitive ability to solve a determined problem alone and the increase in that same problem-solving ability when given guidance by a more expert actor. David Wood, Jerome Bruner, and Gail Ross (1976) built on ZPD in their concept of instructional scaffolding as a process in which a more advanced mentor works with a novice learner to help them recognize solutions to a given problem.

Scaffolding in the form of professional mentorship has been highlighted as a key for ensuring the success of new online instructors as it eases the instructor's transition to online learning and teaching. Wood and colleagues (1976) found that effective mentoring consists of a series of carefully planned and executed steps that include capturing the learner's attention, simplifying or limiting the task(s) at hand, aiding in continual engagement with the task, and encouraging the learner to confront the next task in the learning process. Formal mentorship and scaffolding have been endorsed by organizations to promote excellence in online pedagogies. The Sloan Consortium provides recommendations associated with scaffolding techniques such as sharing experiences, practices, and knowledge among online educators. In the Sloan Consortium's five pillars of quality teaching, mentorship/scaffolding is positively associated with both faculty development and satisfaction (Moore 2005).

As discussed in chapter 2, CTE training program models for language instructors have included mentoring as part of ongoing professional development for trainees. For instance, Regine Hampel and Ursula Stickler (2005) note that one of the options available to OU tutors after their training ended entailed "the exchange of experience, ideas, and opinions with their peers who are using the same or comparable software" (322). This exchange either can occur informally in CoPs with other language educators using technology or it can be incarnated in a more formal official mentoring program. Mentoring also forms an important part of the last stage of Hampel's (2009) OU tutor training program, continuing support and staff development, which includes peer mentoring by more experienced tutors. Oversight of this OU mentoring process is provided by regional academics with experience in online teaching who observe the mentees and give them valuable feedback. However, for this mentoring to succeed, pairings of mentor-mentee need to take into consideration the experience levels of both parties (expert versus novice).

Carla Meskill and colleagues (2006) describe a mentoring project with an "integrated field experience design in which pre-service teachers learn to use technology via mentoring by experienced educators in their classrooms" (284). In their Technology-Assisted Language Learning plan, preservice teachers were mentored by in-service teachers in the working teachers' classrooms to implement technology-based projects in a K–8 English for speakers of other languages setting. While the in-service teachers brought to the table their expert pedagogical experience and expertise, the novice preservice teachers brought fresh ideas and knowledge of new technologies to which they had been exposed during their preservice training. In addition, both the pre- and in-service teachers were mentored by doctoral students with experience in current CALL practices and curriculum development. Reflections from all three groups of participants showed that these mentoring collaborations were mutually beneficial to each group's professional development goals.

The key to success to any mentoring program for pre- and in-service language teachers is its continued availability over time and its ability to form a community of practice (CoP) of expert and novice users of technology to facilitate feedback-driven, formative professional development for all parties. Marinna Kolaitis and colleagues (2006) show the positive effects of continuous formative mentoring and expert feedback on the development of technological skills in post-secondary English as a second language instructors. The formation of these informal and formal expert-novice mentoring relationships facilitates the appropriate integration of pedagogically grounded, technologically based activities into the teaching practices of these in-service teachers and gives them guidance on how to train their students to use that technology. As B. J. Eib and Pamela Miller (2006) state, "When faculty development is viewed as an ongoing need and when we approach faculty development as a long-term, continuous effort, community building becomes a part of the process" (abstract, 1).

Forming Online Mentorship Relationships

Dana Tesone and Peter Ricci (2005) propose three basic means of learning: trial and error, observation, and mentorship. While the formation of excellent online instructors undoubtedly entails all three of the modes, mentorship lessens the frustration associated with the learning curve. Literature on professional mentorship defines it as the relationship between two individuals who are at different stages of their career and/or possess different levels of knowledge about a specific topic (Allen, Eby, and Lentz 2006). Objectives of mentorship may include facilitating motivation, providing information, aiding in the adjustment to a new task, and increasing one's personal and professional development (Bierema and Merriam 2002).

Mentorship can happen in both formal and informal settings. While an instructor may have only one supervisor, they can establish a network (a

CoP) of diverse informal mentors who differ in age, experience, and training (McCann and Johannessen 2004). Diversifying the mentor network ensures that the instructor is exposed to a variety of perspectives, ideas, and resources (Rodesiler and Tripp 2012; Steeples and Jones 2012). While formal mentorships may be set up by the instructor's institution, informal mentorship may take place in a variety of settings including social media platforms. Once a mentoring relationship has been established, sharing course materials, showing empathy and support, and recognizing mentees' ideas and abilities can strengthen the professional relationship as well as increase the mentors' self-confidence (McCann, Johannessen, and Liebenberg 2010).

The setting of formal mentorships is often guided by institutional policies and practices and may take place in person or virtually; however, research pertaining to the development of online instructors recommends carrying out mentorship activities via a virtual format (Vitale 2010; Williams, Layne, and Ice 2014). When online instructors are required to access their professional development activities online, in virtual mentorships they have more opportunities to use interactive technologies, reinforce concepts related to collaborative online learning, and engage in a situated learning experience similar to that of their students (Guasch, Alvarez, and Espasa 2010; Lackey 2011; Terantino and Agbehonou 2012).

Online or e-mentoring has become a popular option for twenty-first-century professional development initiatives as it can mitigate restrictions related to time and space. Communication in a virtual environment can be a challenge due to time zones, cultural backgrounds, and individuals who may have issues regarding technology proficiencies. Jill Nemiro (2004) suggests that "there is an urgent need for virtual team members to learn how to be active and effective communicators, and to design an effective communication plan that supports their creative process" (6). Aside from logistical advantages, psychosocial advantages such as increased self-esteem, confidence, and risk-taking are also associated with virtual mentoring (Single and Single 2005). Some specific examples of the psychosocial benefits of e-mentoring include reports that e-mentoring is less intimidating for the mentee as compared to F2F mentoring (Kasworm and Londoner 2000; Kim and Bonk 2002). In addition, e-mentoring programs connect women and marginalized groups with individuals who can provide professional guidance and support both within and outside of their institutions (Headlam-Wells, Gosland, and Craig 2006; Scandura and Hamilton 2002). Another advantage of e-mentoring is the relative ease with which an interaction can be recorded for administrative purposes and to provide opportunities for reflection for both the mentor and instructor. In fact, using recordings of mentorship interactions for reflection provides the mentor with the rare opportunity to be observed and reflect on their own mentoring practices (O'Donoghue 2015) and allows for administrative oversight of the mentoring process.

For mentoring programs to be successfully implemented and sustainable, the institution must determine the objectives of the mentoring program, how those objectives will be met, who will participate in the mentorship program, and how the realization of the objectives will be measured (Cunningham 2007). After establishing a clear purpose and approach, the mentorship program can move forward with identifying mentorship partners. This step is crucial as the success of the mentorship depends on paired professionals' compatibility, communication, and dedication to the set objectives (Purcell 2004). Roadblocks in mentorships are reported when one or both of the parties fail to communicate in a timely manner, solicit last-minute work, and do not provide supportive/constructive feedback (Butterworth, Henderson, and Minshell 2008).

The complex task of mentorship has been described as a cycle that moves the participants through a series of phases: choosing a mentor, getting acquainted, setting goals, growing the relationship, ending the relationship, and evaluating the relationship's success (Pieper 2004). Following is an outline of the phases and responsibilities of the mentoring process, as modified from Pieper's (2004) multistep mentor process.

- Preparing
    - Determining the format of the mentor program
    - Setting expectations for the mentor-instructor interactions
    - Recruiting participants
- Matching
    - Requesting mentor volunteers
    - Orientation for interested volunteers
    - Matching the mentor-instructor
- Mentoring
    - Carrying out mentoring sessions
    - Check-in sessions with mentor supervisor
    - Setting goals
    - Mentors provide resources for instructor
    - Supervisor provides resources for mentors
- Ending the Mentorship
    - Reflecting on the progress that has been made
    - Discussing future goals and aspirations
    - Providing a report for the program director
    - Celebrating the mentorship, recognizing the participants

Most of the time dedicated to the mentor relationship will be spent in the mentoring step of this system. Arguably, mentors can more effectively accomplish the tasks related to this stage by employing approaches to learning that incorporate best practices of andragogy (instructing adult learners). In his seminal work on adult learning, Malcolm Knowles (1975, 1980) outlines the factors for effectively working with adults as (1) providing a reason for what they are learning, (2) implementing experiential learning, (3) allowing the learners to plan and evaluate their own instruction, and (4) teaching material of immediate relevance. Incorporating these practices into a mentoring relationship facilitates the formation and maintenance of a mentoring mindset among faculty and supervisors / peer mentors.

Mentors' Role in Facilitating Reflection

The mentor's responsibility to respond to the changing needs of the instructor highlights the importance of establishing a mentorship that spans the stages of preparing, matching, mentoring, and ending the relationship. When teaching evaluations are carried out by individuals who have not been involved with the entire mentorship process, they may not appreciate how initial teaching objectives and expectations set out at the beginning of a course have been interrupted and changed throughout the semester (Zeichner and Tabacknick 1982). Long-term mentors are better prepared to aid instructors in redirecting their teaching approaches when required by incorporating frequent opportunities for instructors to reflect throughout the professional development process.

As noted in chapter 7 on self-evaluation, John Dewey (1938/1988) introduced the importance of reflection in his concept of reflective action or the idea that all knowledge should be critically examined regarding its origins and consequences. In the context of teacher education, it is believed that through reflection activities, teachers will become more open-minded, flexible, and willing to acquire new skills (Lackey 2011; Van Manen 1991). Max van Manen (1977) approaches reflection as a developmental continuum measured on a three-point scale (i.e., technical rationality, practical action, and critical rationality), illustrated in figure 8.1. As instructors increase their ability to reflect on their teaching, they move from being concerned with the application of teaching methodologies to considering the impact of what and how they teach. Thus, a reflective teacher is one who considers and addresses all three levels outlined by Van Manen (1977). Often an instructor can move consciously through the stages of reflection with the help of an experienced mentor. The challenges and opportunities for an instructor's

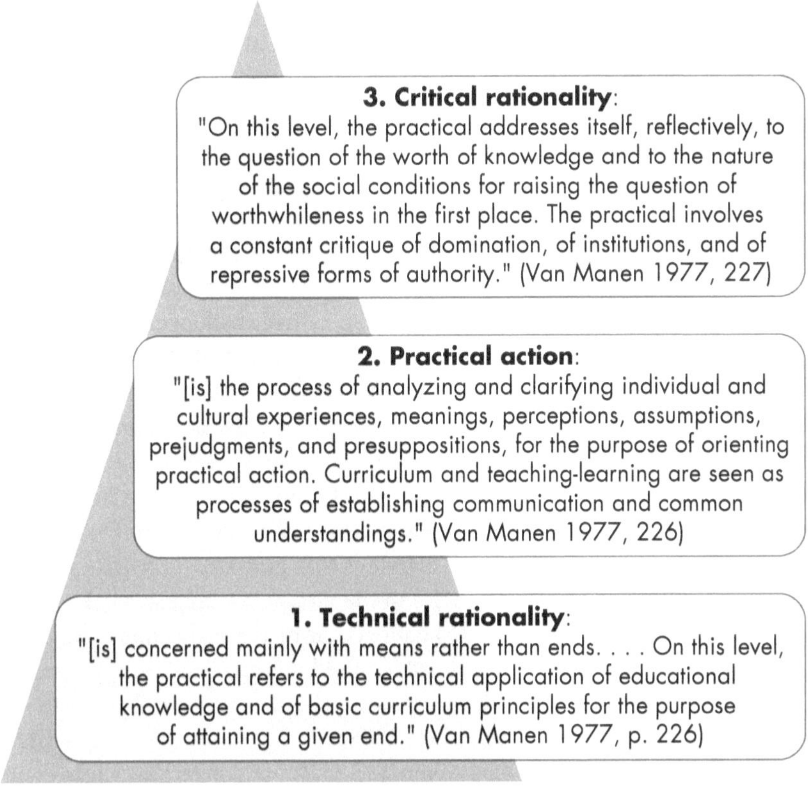

3. Critical rationality:
"On this level, the practical addresses itself, reflectively, to the question of the worth of knowledge and to the nature of the social conditions for raising the question of worthwhileness in the first place. The practical involves a constant critique of domination, of institutions, and of repressive forms of authority." (Van Manen 1977, 227)

2. Practical action:
"[is] the process of analyzing and clarifying individual and cultural experiences, meanings, perceptions, assumptions, prejudgments, and presuppositions, for the purpose of orienting practical action. Curriculum and teaching-learning are seen as processes of establishing communication and common understandings." (Van Manen 1977, 226)

1. Technical rationality:
"[is] concerned mainly with means rather than ends. . . . On this level, the practical refers to the technical application of educational knowledge and of basic curriculum principles for the purpose of attaining a given end." (Van Manen 1977, p. 226)

FIGURE 8.1 Stages of Instructor Development: Critical Reflection (Van Manen 1977)

professional development that arise during the mentoring process are explored in the next section.

Challenges and Opportunities in Mentorship

The challenges to establishing a functional mentoring relationship are similar to those that confront CTE training programs (see chapter 3). For instance, the research has shown that many F2F instructors are initially hesitant to transition to online teaching due to such factors as the need to learn new teaching methodologies, increased workloads, concerns about intellectual ownership of materials created, and the instructors' ability to use educational technologies (Bauer-Ramazani 2006; Comas-Quinn 2011; Healey et al. 2011; Windes and Lesht 2014). The disconnect between the growing demand for online teaching and the reservations that many educators express about it has created a difficult paradox that evaluators must confront when moving through the assessment process. In this sense, one of the most challenging aspects of mentoring is learning how to mitigate the levels of frustration and stress that the learners (instructors) associate with the task at hand (Wood, Bruner, and Ross 1976).

Mentors must take into account that teaching online presents even the most seasoned instructors with a series of new challenges. For instance, teacher identity is often at the heart of issues related to resistance to moving to online platforms (Barkhuizen 2016). Other challenges in moving to online teaching spaces include physical and social separation (Cowan, Neil, and Winter 2013; Mitchell, Parlamis, and Claiborne 2015), reliance on written communication, increased time dedicated to grading and course development (Palloff and Pratt 2011), miscommunication or misinterpretation of course content, and unresponsive students (Petrides 2002).

To prepare online instructors to meet these challenges, mentorship programs can implement self-directed activities that move the instructor toward greater confidence and competencies in the virtual teaching skills (Knowles 1975). Self-directed learning (SDL) has become increasingly important for all twenty-first-century citizens as we are required to access and decipher information on a variety of digital platforms used in both personal and professional life (Lai 2011; Vonderwell and Turner 2005). Philip Candy (1991) describes SDL as the learners' ability to develop and apply new skills that allow them to adapt to specific contexts. According to Candy, the four major constructs of SDL include learner-controlled instruction (autonomy), autodidaxy (self-regulation of learning), self-management, and personal autonomy. Candy emphasizes both institutional responsibility (promoting SDL through activities that allow learners to choose the pace, topics, and means of their instruction) and individual responsibility (taking initiative to use resources and follow-through with the learning process).

Much research on SDL has been published since Candy's (1991) seminal work. Most of these studies are dedicated to exploring cognitive and motivational processes as well as the effect of personal attitudes on the learning process (Brockett and Hiemstra 1991; Kasworm and Londoner 2000). Cognitive and motivational processes associated with SDL can be controlled through the way learning materials are designed and implemented. For example, a mentor may break activities into smaller chunks to decrease the cognitive learning load and provide collaborative opportunities for online instructors (Hill and Hannafin 2001).

While mentors may manipulate processes to facilitate instructors' experiences with SDL activities, online instructors must ultimately take responsibility for their personal attitudes toward online teaching (Hartley and Bendixen 2001; Song and Hill 2007). Personal attitudes toward engaging in SDL activities are related to an instructor's ability and willingness to self-monitor and self-motivate (Garrison 1997). Research has proven that SDL processes and abilities both rely heavily on such factors as the instructor's technological savvy, the perceived difficulty of the task at hand, personal interests, and professional incentives (Quinney, Smith, and Galbraith 2010). Carefully managed mentorships can lessen impediments to the successful completion of SDL activities through addressing common issues such as procrastination, the failure to prepare course materials, and delays in timely grading and feedback (Elvers, Polzella, and Graetz 2003; Song and Hill 2007). When SDL is successfully carried out, it can lead to a transformative experience that changes previously held attitudes or perceptions (Merriam 1998; Mezirow 1991; Pilling-Cormick 1997).

In order for mentorships to produce independent and self-reliant actors who are capable of SDL, a positive mentor-instructor must have been established within the ecology of the mentoring relationship. The next section of this chapter explores strategies to establish those positive relationships.

Establishing a Positive Mentor-Instructor Relationship

Achieving positive relationships between supervisors and instructors is dependent on several factors, including a shared purpose, approach, and consequence associated with the evaluation process (Holland and Gelman 1998). When professional development goals and evaluation criteria are not clear, it is unlikely that critical reflection and transformational learning will take place (Zeichner and Liston 1987). If the supervisor has also served as a mentor to the instructor throughout the semester, it is probable that they are aware of the instructor's progress as well as any changes to the initial learning objectives that have been required.

While supervisors who play a dual role (also serving as mentors) may possess a better understanding of the details related to the instructor's professional journey, there can be complications related to mentorships that involve summative evaluations. For example, instructors may be reluctant to ask for help in fear that it could signal incompetency, an omission that later affects their teaching evaluation at the end of the year (Hollenbeck, Williams, and Klein 1989; Williams and Johnson 2000). In light of the dual role that supervisors often play as both mentors and evaluators, they must find a balance between providing constructive feedback through mentoring via formative evaluations and fulfilling their administrative duty through summative reporting. A solid, ongoing mentoring relationship between supervisors and instructors will help ease tensions that may arise during both types of evaluative processes.

A large body of research has been dedicated to understanding and improving the supervisor-instructor relationship (Benwell and Stokoe 2006; Bucholtz and Hall 2005; Burgoon and Hale 1987; Chamberlin 2000). Many of these studies emphasize the impact of verbal and nonverbal communication styles in establishing trust between the two parties. Supervisor-instructor relationships that lack a sense of mutual trust and respect make it unlikely that the instructor will openly disclose information about their teaching experience, examine personal beliefs, and solicit interventions. In other words, the mentor and the instructor can more easily develop mutual trust if they think of themselves as allies who share core values and who participate together in a larger ecological educational environment with a common purpose—to serve their students by improving the quality of online language instruction that they receive.

To effectively establish relationships with the instructors they oversee, supervisors should be well versed in the understanding of communicative competence and pragmatics, that is, the ability to use appropriate verbal and nonverbal cues to achieve a goal (Spitzberg and Cupach 1984). Studies related to nonverbal cues indicate that body posture, social distance, and eye contact all have bearing on the type of relationship that is built between two individuals (Mehrabian 1971; Schwartz, Tesser, and Powell 1982; Spiegel and Machotka 1974). For example, if the supervisor is too busy taking notes to engage in direct eye contact with the instructor while they speak, this may signal an air of superiority or lack of care (Cappella 1985; Ellyson and Dovidio 1985; Harper 1985). The supervisor will indicate dominance or openness depending on how these nonverbal cues are incorporated. Furthermore, as asynchronous forms of communication (e-mail and messaging) do not provide visual cues and body language, the interlocuters must depend on a preestablished rapport to overcome misunderstanding in light of the power dynamics inherent in the mentor-mentee relationship (Scandura and Hamilton 2002). In addition, miscommunications due to the aforementioned issues may be mitigated through the use of Web cameras that catch body language and voice tone in teleconferencing platforms or emoticons in written messages that provide clues to the intended tone (Kruger et al. 2005; Neumann 2009).

CASE STUDY OF CONTINUING DEVELOPMENT AND SUPPORT IN A MENTORING CONTEXT

Most online instructors receive little to no formal training before teaching their first online course (Allen and Seaman 2011; Herman 2012). Those instructors who do receive training most frequently have done so under the purview of a university digital support department or instructional designers, as few online training programs are carried out by colleagues from the same area of expertise (Palloff and Pratt 2011). In the absence of formal observation and mentorship opportunities in their area of expertise (Bair and Bair 2011; Tesone and Ricci 2005), online instructors disproportionately rely on trial-and-error approaches to learning the craft of online education.

The following case study relates to the other case studies found in this book. The participants in this study participated in the OLIMR self-assessment process reported in chapter 7 and also participated in the formative evaluation process reported in chapter 9. The current study reports the implementation of a peer mentorship program that was created to provide continuing development and support for new online instructors. This study not only illustrates important feedback provided by instructors who participated in the formative process described in this book but also contributes to the research that has been carried out regarding online language instruction mentorship programs.

Methodology

Mentors in this program were chosen based on their excellent performance as online language instructors and their excellent formative evaluation reviews. The supervisor and her assistant compiled a list of possible mentors, and invitations were sent out to those instructors. The faculty from that list who responded positively to the invitation were paired with new online instructors in a mentor-mentee relationship.

All participants in this case study completed a mandatory preservice two-week training led by the supervisor. The workshop was carried out in a completely online format and introduced new online instructors to interactive technologies used for the university's language program, the course learning management system, and best practices in online course design. Upon completing the training, the participants were assigned their first online course. The supervisor and her assistant provided a course-specific orientation before the beginning of the semester as well as monthly instructor meetings. Due to instructors' request for more online teaching support, the supervisor implemented the peer mentorship program described here. The mentorship program sought to offer more individualized attention to each instructor by assigning them an experienced mentor who taught Spanish in the same program.

The program outlined that each mentor-instructor pair must meet at least once per month (either in person or virtually) for one semester. The participants were given guidelines about appropriate uses of the mentorship. For example, the meetings should not be used to obtain technical support but to ask questions about course content, policies, student issues, and so on. These guidelines were set in place in order not to overburden the volunteer mentors, who were teaching a full course load in addition to their mentorship responsibilities.

Participants. The current case study focuses on nine new online instructors and three peer mentors who agreed to have their information shared for research purposes. These instructors taught online for the first time in the spring of 2020 but had previous language teaching experience. The mentors had taught for the online Spanish program for a minimum of three academic semesters and were identified for their excellence in language teaching and their knowledge of the online program content and policies.

All of the new instructors self-identified as Hispanic on the questionnaire (four Mexican, two US Latinx, one Spanish, one Argentinean). The instructors had differing faculty affiliations/roles (one lecturer, two instructors, five graduate students, and two adjunct faculty). Two of the three mentors participating in this study were instructors and one was a lecturer. Two of the mentors identified as Hispanic (Colombian and Mexican) and one identified as Caucasian (United States).

Instruments. After their first semester teaching online with the guidance of a peer mentor, the instructors completed an anonymous online survey via Qualtrics regarding their experience with the mentorship program. The survey consisted of eight (multiple choice and open-ended) questions focused on mentoring logistics, types of help given in a mentoring session, and the instructor's experience with the mentoring program. After reviewing the survey responses from the new online instructors, King Ramírez interviewed the mentors using the same questions as the survey completed by the instructors. A comparative look at the instructor and mentors' answers is provided below. As the answers to this instructor survey were anonymous, instructors in the discussion below have been identified with capital letters (A, B, C) instead of numerals, used when the identities were known to the researcher (as in the case of mentors in this chapter and instructors in chapters 7 and 9).

The following section is divided into thematic sections pertaining to the answers that the new online instructors provided in the survey. These answers are followed by feedback given by the instructors' online mentors.

Results of the Online Instructor Survey

The survey uncovered general tendencies in the online mentorship program. The following section illustrates commonalities found in how and when instructors met with their mentors, the type of assistance and feedback that they sought from their mentors, and their overall experience with the online peer mentor program.

Meeting Logistics. While the mentor-instructor groups were required to meet only once a month, five out of nine instructors met with their mentor four or more times the first two months of the semester. When asked if issues were encountered in setting up the mentorship meetings, Instructor C responded in a written survey, "We haven't met, but she's sent me a Panopto video and responded to several e-mails." This instructor's mentor provided more information about the failure to meet synchronously, stating that the instructor was unresponsive in her various attempts to contact him: "I looked up his office phone, I had his phone number, I sent two e-mails. At that point, I said I need to escalate [contact the online language program director]" (Mentor 1, oral interview). However, issues with establishing communication seemed to be an outlier in this program as other instructors did not report the same. Mentor 2 credited the ease of the meeting logistics to the fact that her team followed the same meeting time every month: "It was a set time—every Friday at 9:30am for a half an hour." No issues were reported by Mentor 3 (oral interview), but that mentoring pair programmed meeting times only on an "as needed" basis: "He would text me if he had questions about his online course. I would just tell him to call me. We met once in Zoom but preferred over the phone."

Most of these mentoring meetings were carried out online (five of nine) with some instructor-mentor groups (three of nine) meeting in an F2F environment (e.g., on campus). One of the instructor-mentor groups did not meet F2F or synchronously online during the first two months and only corresponded via e-mail. Two-thirds of the instructors (six of nine) reported that these meetings lasted for approximately fifteen to twenty minutes each. In contrast, all mentors' responses to this same question (three of three) noted that the meetings were generally forty-five minutes to one hour in length. However, the mentors clarified that the longer meetings were at the beginning of the semester, with the meeting duration decreasing as the semester progressed. Mentor 1 explained the reasons for the longer initial meetings:

> At the beginning I met with both of them for 2 hours each [for coffee]. To get them up and running and answer questions. One of the instructors was coming from Canvas [a different LMS (language management system) from D2L (Desire2Learn)] and didn't know anything about D2L. She knew general things about online teaching but needed specifics about how to set up her course site. As they get more comfortable, they become more independent. On average I met for 1.5 hours per week. Sitting with them, answering e-mails, via phone. And then it got lower, about 30 minutes per week, it was just answering questions. I would just check in with them. (Mentor 1, oral interview)

While Mentor 1 did not describe the frequency with which the meetings were held, Mentor 3 stated that there could be multiple meetings every week: "[We met] between 40 minutes and 1 hour. Towards the first week, it could be two sessions per week but then it goes to once every two-weeks or so" (Mentor 3, oral interview). In sum, mentoring sessions were more frequent and longer in the beginning and were fewer and of a shorter duration later in the semester.

As mentors in this program work on a volunteer basis, time availability and time management issues that confront online instructors (see chapter 3) may pose challenges to the scheduling of mentorship sessions. However, mentors and mentees with a positive view of and commitment to the process will undoubtedly find the time to negotiate reasonable meeting times that meet their individual needs.

Types of Help Given in Mentoring Sessions. The new instructors reported that they often sought out their mentors regarding assignments and grading policies. "My mentor has clarified doubts with grading, inserting links to D2L and has given me tips to organize myself" (Instructor B, written survey). In some cases, the mentor even provided extra how-to videos for the new instructor and shared personal materials from their own online course: "Mentor X [not one of the three mentors mentioned in this section] has made videos (tutorial) to help me understand assignments, has shared her material with me, and answered all my messages" (Instructor F, written survey). The mentors provided similar information regarding the content of the meetings, stating that they spent time clarifying issues related to the personalization of the LMS. "Minor details of D2L set up, how to use the rubrics, how to change the widgets, how to set up oral exam calendars, etc. Minor things that might not be intuitive. It was more about the technical part of D2L" (Mentor 2, oral interview). One mentor noticed that while her assigned instructor navigated the LMS with relative ease, there were many questions about the online program and how its policies and assignments differed from the F2F language program in the same department: "Generally, we would talk about the changes instructors could make to the course and what the program expectations were. He just wanted to verify what he was expected to do. I would always get a phone call when a new assignment came up during the semester such as oral dialogues. Once they get the hang of the assignments, they are good to go" (Mentor 3, oral interview).

Mentors were asked in interviews if they had experienced any communication issues with their assigned instructors. Their responses shed light on the emotional aspect of teaching in a new modality. Mentor 2 explained that in her initial meeting with the instructor, she was already very frustrated: "In our first meeting there was a lot of venting." As Mentor 3 noted, much of the frustration expressed by new online instructors is due to differences between their preconceived ideas of teaching online and the realities they faced: "New instructors often had a different impression of what online courses are. Once they get into the program, they realize that it's a lot of work and go through the emotions of learning everything" (Mentor 3, oral interview). Mentor 1 felt that the emotional response to the feedback she provided instructors was due to the tendency for instructors to associate their personal teaching style with their own identity: "We are in a profession that is considered a vocation. A part of your being. So the criticism feels like you are criticizing the person, not their job. That can be a problem in teaching. It's not just their teaching, but their personal style" (Mentor 1, oral interview). This mentor's observation perfectly reflects the feeling of frustration that new online language instructors feel when they are asked to completely rethink the way they teach. The possible threats to their identity that they may perceive as a result of the requested pedagogical paradigm shift need to be met with emotional investments made by administrators and supervisors (see chapter 3).

Experience with the Mentorship Program. The third portion of the survey was related to the participants' overall perceptions of the mentorship program. When asked if they felt that the mentorship program had been helpful, eight of nine instructors and three of three mentors responded positively. As a follow-up to this question, Instructor D related in a written survey that she had felt a sense of disconnect when transitioning to online teaching: "I was somewhat lost at the beginning. When we teach a face to face class, we see our peers in the main office or in the hallway and we can always ask simple questions." The mentorship program helped her to create important connections with online colleagues.

Mentor 2 added that the mentoring program allowed for less front-loading of information in the orientation, which can create a stressful cognitive overload for new online instructors: "There is less pressure to provide all of the information they might need in a 2-hour orientation. It was overwhelming and not very productive. It relieves the amount of pressure about how much you have to provide at the beginning of the semester. You know you have backup because the mentors answer a lot of the questions that new instructors have at the beginning of the semester" (Mentor 2, written survey). Mentor 3 also commented that the mentorship program relieved a great amount of stress from the instructors and highlighted the socioemotional benefits of the mentorship program: "I feel like it's a way to take the stress off of the instructors. They feel like they are in a safe zone where they are not going to be criticized for not understanding information that was discussed previously in a meeting. Also, they can reach out to the mentor when they need it most and don't have to wait for a scheduled meeting" (Mentor 3, oral interview).

When asked about how helpful the mentorship had been, Mentor 1 replied that the experience varied with each mentor-instructor relationship. "It depended on the mentee. I had one who was absolutely receptive and grateful. Then I had a guy who was too self-assured. He needed to be asking more questions. You have to know what you don't know and be humble enough to ask the questions. Some people don't know they don't know stuff and think they are fine. He was one of those" (Mentor 1, oral interview). While the majority of the participants agreed that the mentorship program was helpful, they provided several ideas for how it could be improved in future iterations. The common thread in their feedback was the desire to have very specific guidance in both the materials they are provided as well as the type of mentorship they receive, "Pair the mentee with a mentor that has EXACTLY the same class. There was a lot of confusion because my mentor had a 7-week course" (Instructor C, written survey). Another instructor requested an activities checklist for new instructors so that she could better gauge her own progress. "I feel I've learned a lot through trial and error. When I'm contacting my mentor, I feel that it is because I'm entirely already overwhelmed or in trouble. Provide the checklist to us new instructors and we could double check if we understand everything" (Instructor E, written survey).

The mentors also noted that by starting the mentorship program the same day that the courses start is problematic because so much of the online course preparation is completed weeks ahead of the first day of classes. However, the mentors felt that this issue was a departmental problem. Given that student enrollment numbers can greatly fluctuate in the weeks leading up to a new semester, instructors are generally not given their specific course assignment until the week before classes begin. "[Working with mentors before the semester begins], it would go back to one thing that is a reoccurring problem. It would be ideal if we could be assigned [new instructors] ahead of time. It would be wonderful if we could have our mentees 1 week or 10 days before the semester began" (Mentor 1, oral interview). Also in alignment with the instructors' feedback was the recommendation to have the mentorship pairs be arranged according to the course levels that they teach. "It would be very good to pair people with someone who is teaching the same level. I don't know how possible that would be. We have the people we have and need to spread them out as best as we can" (Mentor 2, oral interview).

Aside from limiting the ability to arrange mentorship groups from the same course levels, the small number of volunteer mentors also affects the possibility of changing mentor group if a professional or personality conflict arises between the pair. "[I would suggest] having a bigger base of mentors. I think right now there are only 4 or 5 mentors. This would give instructors the option to change mentors if there is a personal issue with their mentorship assignment" (Mentor 3, oral interview). Mentor 1 also mentioned that having a limited number of mentors can be problematic as the same individuals are always asked to volunteer their time. "It becomes kinda a grind on the list of what you have to do. A lot of universities lean on people who are most competent to the point of breaking them. They need to learn how to spread the element of service so you don't burn out your best people" (Mentor 1, oral interview). This mentor's statement reflects the need for administrators and supervisors to respect faculty's time and to recognize and limit their mentoring time to avoid burnout (see chapter 3). Creating a larger pool of possible mentors not only helps to relieve the mentoring service burden but (as mentioned earlier in this chapter) also ensures that the instructor will benefit from advice from a number of expert online instructors (Rodesiler and Tripp 2012; Steeples and Jones 2012).

Mentorship Recognition. Given the considerable amount of time that the mentors spend with the new online instructors, in the oral interview King Ramírez asked them how they would like to be recognized for their contributions. Mentor 1 provided several appealing suggestions: "The university could put in place some kind of recognition that we did service for the university as lecturers or adjuncts and take that into account in our evaluations.... I think there should be a limit on number of times you are asked to do this during a year. Give people a break. Two semesters on and one semester off" (Mentor 1, oral interview). When asked how she would like to be recognized for her efforts, Mentor 3 responded that the payoff was being able to work in a positive, successful program.

> The reward is that everybody learns and is on the same page. You are not alone in this and you have a bigger community. You ensure that there is consistency in the program—it makes it "our" program. We are contributing, there is ownership. If I have a problem I can go to you, and if you have a problem you can go to me. When you are in the right environment, it's rewarding. (Mentor 3, oral interview)

As discussed in chapter 3, for instructors to buy in to moving to digital spaces and to the assessment process, faculty who serve as mentors and mentees need to buy in to the mentoring process itself. Cognitive and emotional investments made by administrators will help increase faculty agency and recognize faculty participation in the mentoring program. When faculty have a voice in the mentorship process, they are more likely to feel as though they are co-owners of the program and feel invested in its success.

PUTTING IT ALL TOGETHER

To ensure continuous improvement of the mentoring process, the CTE literature and the results of the case study just described call for the implementation of the following ideas:

- Supervisors should facilitate instructors' understanding of the mentoring process as one that unites its stakeholders toward a shared ecological goal of improving online instruction in their academic environment.
- Programs should assign mentoring partners and have them communicate as early as possible before the semester begins.
- Online instructors should be assigned a peer mentor from the same language program, ideally teaching the same class or at the same level.
- The mentorship objectives and policies must be established from the beginning and clearly stated in writing.
- Supervisors need to provide both mentors and instructors with the same checklists of instructor expectations at the beginning of the mentoring program.

- Participants in the mentorship program should write a reflection about their experience. This reflection may provide insights for the formal instructor assessment and for improving the mentoring program.
- Mentors should be trained to provide ongoing support and empathy to address online instructor frustrations within the online CoP that they form.
- Administrators need to make cognitive, emotional, and functional investments in the mentoring program, remunerating mentors for their time when possible.
- Administrators need to ensure that a sufficient number of mentors are available to avoid burnout and allow for changes in mentorship partners should the need arise.
- Participation by the mentor and instructor should be recognized as professional development and accounted for in formative and summative evaluations.

Chapter 9 explores mentoring interactions within the context of the postobservation interview and goal-setting sessions.

9

Debriefing and Goal Setting in Instructor Assessment

While peer mentorship (see chapter 8) facilitates the establishment of a CoP among instructors and creates a low-stakes environment in which one may clarify questions and seek help, mentorship programs should work in conjunction with formal supervisor evaluations (Rockoff and Speroni 2010; Sergiovanni and Starratt 2002). The feedback provided by a supervisor proffers programmatic oversight, constructive feedback, and opportunities for professional development (Stronge 2006; Vásquez 2004).

Historically, supervisor evaluations have been described as anxiety-inducing processes in which instructors were critiqued on their ability to impart specialized subject matter within the parameters of specific pedagogical practices (Peterson 2000; Vásquez 2004). However, the twenty-first century has ushered in changes to evaluative practices moving from prescriptive, summative assessments to ones that allow for negotiation and reflection (Chamberlin 2000). Much attention has been given to the reflective supervision model (Centra 1993), which favors a holistic, more ecological approach to assessment and seeks to make the instructor an active participant in their own evaluation (Bell 2001; Britzman 1991). For a reflective supervision model to be successful, the supervisor and instructor must engage in equitable, meaningful dialogue regarding the assessment process and results (Bell and Mladenovic 2008; Grimm, Kaufman, and Doty 2014). The current chapter provides an overview of effective methods for carrying out such dialogues via post-observation meetings and goal-setting sessions and activities.

THE POST-OBSERVATION DEBRIEFING

Post-observation debriefings should be carried out after both the instructor and supervisor have had the opportunity to review and reflect on the instructor's performance using the same evaluative criteria (Chamberlin 2000; Ovando 2005). They can prepare for the debriefing by completing a standard rubric (e.g., a version of the OLIMR rubric presented in chapter 6) and reflecting on discussion points that address strengths and areas for improvement. The systematic use of common evaluation criteria, feedback, and formal debriefing sessions creates a culture of formative evaluation that prioritizes continual professional development (Kochan and Trimble 2000).

The manner in which the post-observation debriefing is carried out can be more important than the evaluation itself, as it will determine who is given a voice, what information is shared, and how that information is internalized. One popular vein of reflective supervision research concerns conversational positioning (Davies and Harré 1990), that is, how power is shared between supervisor and instructor. According to conversational positioning theories, one may be in a reflexive or interactive position at different points in the conversation. Interactive positioning entails how one's comments position the other in the conversation, while reflexive positioning is how one positions oneself (Davies and Harré 1990). Awareness of conversational positioning is important for creating an inclusive dialogue that results in positive identity making (Engin and McKeown 2012; Vásquez and Reppen 2007). For example, if supervisors begin the meeting with a laundry list of recommendations for the teacher, this will most likely place the supervisor in a position of power and the instructor becomes a passive listener. However, if the supervisor strategically positions themself in a way that invites the teacher to be an active participant, a more reflective conversation will result because of this emotional investment (Muhammad and Cruz 2019). Table 9.1 (based on Vásquez and Reppen 2007) illustrates how a mentor may position themself to elicit more inclusive dialogue with the instructor. The ultimate goal of the conversational positioning strategies is to place the instructor and supervisor as equal stakeholders in the evaluation process practiced within the ecology of their departmental culture. For this to be accomplished, the supervisor must also invite the instructor to explain their pedagogical choices and reflect on the effectiveness of these choices in realizing the desired outcomes (Engin and McKeown 2012). When pedagogical choices do not render the desired result, the supervisor may ask the instructor to identify strategies that would render a different outcome in the future.

Recognizing and discussing challenges that the instructor has faced throughout the semester may create tension during the debriefing session. Supervisors should be aware of how their tone and the language can positively or negatively influence the instructor's reception of the critique. Louise Venables and Stephen Fairclough (2009) found that when positive feedback, even when unmerited, is more motivating than is merited negative feedback,

TABLE 9.1 Stages and Strategies for Debriefing Conferences

Debriefing Stage	Mentor Strategy	Sample Language
Start Meeting	Invite the instructor to reflect on the course that was evaluated.	How was your experience with your online course this semester?
Specific Questions	Ask open-ended questions about parts of the evaluation rubric.	How did you promote student-student interactions during the course?
Yes/No Questions	Ask a specific yes/no question that may allude to strengths and weaknesses of the class.	Did all of the students have the opportunity to practice oral dialogues with a partner?
Fill in the Blank Questions	Start a statement and let the instructor finish the sentence.	You allowed for partner online dialogues so that students ...
Expert Insights	Identify a problem noticed during recorded class interactions. Follow this comment by one of the previous prompts.	You did not provide a specific rubric for oral dialogue activities. How did you systematically grade these?

Source: Adapted from Vásquez and Reppen 2007.

the individual will be motivated to meet the standards of the positive opinion that was expressed. Conversely, the same study found that negative feedback often results in the individuals shutting down and not pursuing the goal at hand. Supervisors may signal the delicate nature of certain feedback by using specific speech acts such as pauses in speech, *I*-statements, repetition of key ideas, and acknowledgment tokens (Vásquez 2004).

When an area in need of improvement is identified during the debriefing, the supervisor should be prepared to contextualize critiques and provide specific examples (Mena Marcos, Sánchez, and Tillema 2008). Preparing constructive feedback before the meeting will help guide the critiques as well as ideas for professional development (Gordon 2003; Kersten and Israel 2005). Constructive criticism accompanied by positive feedback is especially important when individuals are struggling with specific aspects of teaching (Planar and Moya 2016). When the feedback received is negative, learners will more than likely try to decipher points of divergence between the goal prompt and their task performance (Dasborough, Harvey, and Martinko 2011). In doing so, they will analyze internal and external factors that may have affected their performance as well as the feedback given by the mentor (Weiner 2008). The conclusions that individuals reach during this phase of reflection will significantly influence their reaction to the feedback as well as their motivation to improve (Lam, Huang, and Snape 2007).

Aside from the strategic use of speech acts that are pragmatically appropriate, supervisors can also draw upon their understanding of the instructors' cultural backgrounds to provide a more positive debriefing experience. Cultural practices and values influence the type of feedback that an individual prefers as well as their reaction to that feedback (Taras, Kirkman, and Steel 2010). For example, people who identify more with an individualist culture tend to prioritize personalized feedback, while those who identify with a collectivist culture often feel more comfortable with implicit feedback (Sully De Luque and Sommer 2000; Taras, Kirkman, and Steel 2010; Van de Vliert et al. 2004). For example, in individualist cultures such as Germany, an employee may be motivated to set personal goals when given individualized feedback (Van Dyck et al. 2005). In collectivist cultures such as China that tend to value high-power distance relationships, individuals may not seek feedback from their superiors but choose to do so with their peers (Erez 2010; Van de Vliert et al. 2004). In contrast, individuals from low-power distance cultures may be comfortable with feedback from their supervisors. Thus, individual feedback is more frequently sought and provided in individualistic cultures with low-power-distance cultures and less sought out in collectivistic, high-power-distance cultures (Morrison, Chen, and Salgado 2004).

Working within an ecological framework with a critical pedagogical approach, supervisors who work with instructors from diverse cultural backgrounds should be aware of these differences and take them into account when giving feedback. They can also set in place a variety of sources of feedback and development opportunities (such as peer mentorship programs) in which these differences are also accounted for. The identification of areas for improvement requires structured follow-up in order for the formative assessment processes to be meaningful and effective (Harris and Ovando 1992; Ovando 1995). To this end, the debriefing meeting should include an invitation for the instructor to identify areas for improvement as well as set goals for personal development in those areas. Goal setting has increasingly become an integral part of the evaluation process because it helps to focus attention on certain aspects of work life. The following section explores the phases of goal setting and factors that influence those phases.

GOAL SETTING IN THE ASSESSMENT PROCESS

Given that evaluation is an ongoing, iterative process, there will be opportunities for both formative and summative assessments. The debriefing session, described above, is an opportunity for the instructor to engage in a negotiable summative assessment process. This means that the debriefing session will result in a formal summary that may be filed and used for departmental record keeping as well as for the instructor's professional portfolio. Appendix C-3 contains a sample instructor evaluation summary document that refers to points on the OLIMR but has been tailored for the needs of a particular institution.

While the debriefing session may allow for the instructor to set a new goal and follow up on previously set goals, the process of achieving a set goal should be part of a formative assessment process. This process may be carried out with the supervisor or online mentor. Literature on goal setting often refers to the goal-performance relationship. In this dichotomy, performance outcomes are directly related to an individual's goal choice as well as their effort, commitment, and strategy related to achieving that goal (Locke and Bryan 1969; Terborg 1976).

Choice

There is a large body of literature that supports providing individuals with opportunities to set their own performance goals as opposed to having those goals set for them by someone else (Latham, Mitchell, and Dossett 1978; Latham and Saari 1979). Individuals who exercise choice in professional goal setting experience multiple benefits, including increased dedication, understanding, and appreciation of the goal at hand (Locke and Latham 1990).

While it is imperative that the instructor be involved in setting personalized goals for themself, the mentor should collaborate in this process in order to ensure the quality of the goal and the feasibility of its attainment by the instructor. In fact, allowing instructors to set low-quality goals can undermine the effectiveness of the formative evaluation process (McGreal 1983). The quality of a goal is related to its specificity and difficulty. Individuals who set more specific goals with higher degrees of difficulty have larger margins of success than those who set easier, more general goals (Locke et al. 1981; Pinder 2014). This may be because more specific and difficult goals require the learner to invest more time and effort in the associated tasks (Bavelas and Lee 1978). The mentor may guide the goal-setting process in order to help the instructor to identify goals with the appropriate scale of difficulty as well as frame the goal within the larger institutional context (Locke and Latham 1990).

While setting a goal that is too difficult can be an issue, so can setting goals at a lower level in order to ensure that the goals are met. In this scenario, a mentor can also intervene by letting the instructor know that they will have to justify and be accountable for choosing a level-appropriate goal (Frink and

Ferris 1998). Mentors may also encourage instructors to personalize the difficulty of their goals according to their experience in their current position, and their prior performance (Webb, Jeffrey, and Schulz 2010). This contextualization of goal setting that takes the instructor's prior experience into account is another reflection of the ecological approach taken to CTE assessment in this volume.

Mentor involvement may also help to lessen an individual's use of goal-setting activities as a form of impression management—that is, an attempt to change another person's perspective about oneself (Goffman 1959; Leary and Kowalski 1990; Schneider, Klemp, and Kastendiek 1981). For example, an instructor may set a lofty goal in order to impress a supervisor or colleague. While impression management can have positive effects if the goal is attained, it can also lead to negative consequences when the goal is not reached, thus causing the individual to "lose face" with their colleagues and supervisors (Crant 1996; Gardner and Martinko 1988; Jones and Pittman 1982).

Some studies on goal management have recommended that mentors can help to guide individuals by offering a menu of goals (Webb, Jeffrey, and Schulz 2010). This approach allows mentors to choose a variety of program-specific goals for the instructor but still allow the instructor some choice in goal selection. When choosing this option, supervisors must consider that achievement rates may suffer if the goals are too difficult, not appealing, or the participants need more guidance in choosing goals that are suitable for them (Webb, Jeffrey, and Schulz 2010). Furthermore, mentors may help the instructor to identify the needs of various stakeholders and set instructor goals that align with individual, student, program, and organizational needs (McGreal 1983).

Effort

The amount of effort that an individual will invest in the goal-setting process is key in effecting the desired outcomes (Fischer and Ford 1998). Effort refers to time spent on task as well as the type of effort exerted by the learner (Paas, Van Merriënboer, and Adam 1994). While two individuals may spend the same amount of time on a given task, the mental effort required to successfully complete the task will vary by individual. Variation in effort exerted on a task depends on the individual's previous knowledge, skills, and abilities related to the task. As the learner gains knowledge, skills, and abilities pertaining to a specific task, they will incur a smaller "mental workload" or cost to perform this task at a satisfactory level in the future (Hart and Staveland 1988; Kanfer and Ackerman 1989).

While it is clear that the amount of effort that a task entails can increase or decrease according to one's experience and knowledge, it is difficult to observe and systematically measure an individual's effort (Ambrose and Kulik 1999; Kanfer 1990). Some researchers have attempted to measure effort by tracking its intensity or the amount of resources that one needs to complete a task (Kanfer 1990; Porter and Lawler 1968). As previously stated, resources may include the time it takes to complete a task; however, they may also refer to professional and personal contacts, research, and experimentation dedicated to solving the task.

Mentors may also be involved in the goal-setting process to ensure that the instructor perceives the goal as attainable. This is particularly important when the instructor has voiced concerns about attaining a goal due to external factors they cannot control (Dieterich et al. 2019). This scenario refers to one's locus of control, which is closely related to self-efficacy beliefs, or the belief that one is able to successfully achieve a task (Bandura 1986; Zimmerman 2000). When instructors believe they can achieve the goal at hand, they are more likely to put more effort into that goal and persist when difficulties are encountered (Bandura 1997; Bandura and Locke 2003).

Commitment

Goal performance is directly associated with one's commitment to the goal. As mentioned above, one factor that increases commitment is the ability to choose and personalize the goal. Instructor participation in goal setting is likely to lead to a clearer understanding of the goal, programmatic expectations, and the benefits of achieving the goal (Drake 1984; Salo et al. 2019). Therefore, participation in the goal-setting process leads to more well-thought-out goals and thus greater commitment to their attainment (Gollwitzer, Heckhausen, and Ratajczak 1990).

Frequently, the initial enthusiasm of setting a new goal wears off with time. Changes in commitment can be observed through the amount of effort that one allocates to achieving the task(s) over time. We often refer to the relationship between commitment and effort as motivation (Blau 1993; Kanfer 1990; Katzell and Thompson 1990). When an individual allocates high effort to attain a goal, they are considered to be highly motivated. In contrast, one who exerts low effort may be viewed as poorly motivated. Motivation itself is affected by many factors (Kanfer and Ackerman 1989). If one feels that they are likely to succeed in the set goal, it is more probable that they will remain committed to the process when confronted with obstacles and setbacks (Ambrose and Kulik 1999; Bandura 1986; Kanfer

1992). Mentors should work with learners to keep them committed to the set goal.

Strategy

In keeping with the collaborative nature of the aforementioned facets of the goal-setting process, it is imperative that the learner be involved in developing strategies for achieving the set goal (Milheim and Martin 1991). Strategy entails how the individual will use their current knowledge and resources to attain a specific purpose (Burton and Weiss 2008; Locke 1968). Effective goal planning must include a clear vision that includes expectations and specific explanations of what evidence will be used to measure its attainment. Based on those expectations, learners can make a more informed decision about how to use their resources. To this end, mentors must play an active role in helping the learners set measurable, observable learning outcomes that will ultimately aide in their attainment of the goal.

The establishment of learning outcomes will undoubtedly be linked to the learner's knowledge and skill set related to the task. The mentor and learner should determine the nature of the learning outcomes to decide if the focus is on attitudes/motivation, skills, or verbal knowledge (Button, Mathieu, and Zajac 1996). Following the establishment of the type of learning outcome desired, a learning strategy must be chosen. Learning strategies include activities such as rehearsing, organizing, and creating (Branch and Kopcha 2014). Educators may be familiar with these strategies as they appear in a continuum in Bloom's Taxonomy, which places memorization (rehearsing) as the first step in learning new material and application (creation) at the most advanced level of knowledge (Anderson and Krathwohl 2001).

Strategy is akin to self-regulation because it refers to the learner's ability to allocate effort to specific tasks (Kanfer and Ackerman 1989). In fact, procrastination, or the lack of effort to initiate and complete tasks in a timely manner, is often due to a lack of strategy and not a lack of knowledge (Klassen, Krawchuk, and Rajani 2008). To avoid pitfalls of self-regulation, many individuals write down and publicly share a goal as a means to officially commence the process of goal strategy, commitment, and self-monitoring (Hollenbeck, Williams, and Klein 1989; Lyman 1984). However, it has been pointed out that writing down and posting goals is a preliminary step in the larger strategic scheme (Weinberg et al. 2019). In fact, written goals must be followed by measurable action items that may take the form of short-term goals that help the learner to incrementally grow as well as have a sense of accomplishment during the goal-setting journey and progress reports (Matthews 2007). Strategies for goal attainment are most successful when a timetable for short- and long-term goals are established and resources are allocated accordingly (Pintrich 2004).

Strategy is not static but requires continual self-management and assessment. For individuals to successfully self-manage, they must develop a set of abilities that includes communication, decision-making, self-monitoring, and goal setting (Shogren, Wehmeyer, and Palmer 2017; Wehmeyer, Agran and Hughes 1998; Wehmeyer et al. 2012). An approach to self-management is found in the Self-Determined Learning Model of Instruction (SDLMI) (Wehmeyer et al. 2000) that was initially designed to teach students how to personalize their learning process through setting goals, making choices, developing plans, and tracking progress. Susan Palmer and Michael Wehmeyer (2003) outline a series of steps to guide learners through the SDLMI process that teaches individuals to strategize how they will set and achieve their goals. The initial step in SDLMI requires the learner to identify a possible solution to a specific problem. This step is followed by asking the individual to consider possible barriers to solving the problem and, finally, how those barriers may be overcome. In this way SDLMI requires the individual to engage in critical thinking to strategically resolve a problem.

While the SDLMI process charges the learner with the bulk of the strategic planning activities, Palmer and Wehmeyer (2003) emphasize the importance of continual mentor support. The following "Taking Action" list based on their model exemplifies their view of how a learner may act upon a goal that they have previously set (Learner Action Items) using prompts from the mentor (Mentor Question for Learner).

Taking Action

- Mentor Question for Learner: What do you need to learn?
- Learner Action Items:
  - Make a list of your strengths and weaknesses.
  - Prioritize your weaknesses in terms of what needs to be improved first.
  - Set short- and long-term goals for learning new information skills.
- Mentor Question for Learner: What do you currently know about the topics/skills that you need to improve?
- Learner Action Items:
  - Write down what you understand about the topic/skill.
  - Make a list of questions you have about the topic/skill.
  - Determine how you can learn more about the topic/skill.
- Mentor Question for Learner: What do you need to change in order to learn the topic/skill?

- Learner Action Items:
  - Discuss your personal beliefs or self-talk that deter you from progressing.
  - Identify your personal or professional circumstances that create barriers for your learning.
  - Review your schedule and how you manage your time. Suggest ways you can improve your time management.
- Mentor Question for Learner: What choices can you make to be successful?
- Learner Action Items:
  - Set short-term and long-term goals for your professional development.
  - Discuss how you will remove barriers to accomplishing these goals.
  - Set follow-up meetings with your mentor to discuss your progress toward meeting your goals. (SDLMI, Phase 1, adapted from Palmer and Wehmeyer 2003, 116)

Given that instructors' personal, academic, and professional profiles may greatly vary, the supervisor should be prepared to adjust to the unique scenarios of each debriefing meeting (Sharpe and Faye 2009). In language education programs, it is common that faculty members are from diverse ethnic and cultural backgrounds. These differences and the demographic match between instructor and supervisor (or between instructors and students in language courses) may affect how the evaluation process is carried out as well as the final outcomes (Gershenson, Holt, and Papageorge 2016). The following section highlights major cultural themes in goal-setting literature.

CULTURAL DIFFERENCES AND GOAL SETTING

Goal setting across cultures has many commonalities, such as the fact that goals must be specific and challenging in order to render high-performance outcomes. Other universal goal-setting trends across cultures include the influence of extrinsic and intrinsic motivators in goal choice and commitment (Chang et al. 2004; Grouzet et al. 2005). While there are several aspects of the goal-setting process that override cultural differences, cultural values and practices have an important bearing on the interpersonal relationships and interactions that take place during this process (Erez 2010; Latham and Pinder 2005; Locke and Latham 2002). This next section outlines some key cultural differences that influence the goal-setting process.

Goal Choice

Due to one's cultural influence on how one perceives themself within society, cultural values have an undeniable influence on the types of goals that individuals choose as well as on their motivation (Elliot et al. 2001; Heine et al. 2001). Cultural differences in goal choice have been explained from the perspective of individual versus collective cultural practices (Chen and Miller 2011; Taras, Kirkman, and Steel 2010). Given that individualistic cultures value forging one's way in society and gaining personal independence, people within this type of culture often find appealing goals that are difficult or those that (upon achievement) would set them apart from others in their peer group (Locke and Latham 2002). Conversely, collective cultural values promote "fitting in" and being part of a cohesive group. Therefore, individuals from collectivist cultures often find attractive goals that are moderate and that maintain a status quo (Aaker and Lee 2001; Kurman 2001).

Motivation and Commitment

Motivation in collectivist and individualist cultures has been explained in terms of preventative and promotional goals (Schwartz 1990). In this dichotomy, preventative goals are those that allow individuals to maintain the status quo set by strong cultural norms. Collectivist cultures may prefer preventative goals as they do not entail a high risk of not meeting the goal and losing face among peers and supervisors (Heine et al. 1999). On the other hand, individualistic cultures are those that have looser cultural norms and tolerate more individuality (Gelfand et al. 2011). People from individualist cultures tend to value promotional goals or those that entail a higher risk of failure but, if achieved, provide greater recognition.

These differences should especially be kept in mind when an instructor's goal requires the instructor to work collaboratively with others on a project. Instructors should be advised that when groups of individuals from diverse cultural backgrounds are required to work toward a common goal, it is imperative that differences in motivation for achieving that goal be acknowledged. For example, individuals from a collective culture may be motivated by a financial goal that seeks to help others in the community, while a financial goal set in a more individualist culture may have more personal motivations (DeShon and Gillespie 2005; Hofstede 1980, 2001; Keister and Zhang 2009). For this reason, goals set for collaborative instructor projects should recognize that project member's motivations may differ when striving to attain the goal; therefore, the goals set need to be specific and clear in order to minimize differences in the interpretation of the goal at hand (Erez and Nouri 2010).

In sum, as was the case in giving feedback during the debriefing process, in the goal-setting sessions, supervisors need to work within an ecological framework and take into account the cultural background of the instructor in order for the negotiation dialogue to be a productive one and for instructor goals to be set that are reasonable and attainable.

CASE STUDY OF GOAL SETTING IN FORMATIVE ASSESSMENT

This case study provides -*emic* (insider) perspectives on the goal-setting process between instructors and supervisors.

Methodology

This section provides information on the participants, instruments, and procedures of this case study.

Participants. The instructors who participated in this study are the same as those profiled in the chapter 7 case study. They are a group of nine new online instructors from varying levels of teaching appointments (e.g., graduate students, adjunct faculty, instructors, lecturers).

Instruments. The instruments used to collect data from this case study were a version of the OLIMR described in chapter 6 but customized to evaluate appropriate skills for these instructors in King Ramírez's university context and in the OLIMR evaluation summary document in appendix C-3.

Procedures. During the pre-semester orientation, new online instructors were given a modified version of the Online Language Instructor Modular Rubric (OLIMR) discussed in chapter 6 and presented in appendix C-2 of this volume. They were asked to review the rubric throughout the semester and contact the supervisor if they had questions or comments. Mid-semester, the supervisor met with the new online instructors to explain how the formative assessment process works, how to complete the OLIMR self-assessment using the rubric and self-reflections, and how to set up a one-hour meeting to debrief the instructor's OLIMR self-assessment and discuss the online instructor's experiences.

The debriefing session loosely followed the Vásquez and Reppen (2007) model but was modified to address the role of the online instructor. The following model was developed by King Ramírez during her time as a program director:

- Instructors are invited to talk about their online teaching experience: How was your experience teaching online for the first time? What differences did you notice between teaching online and teaching F2F?
- Instructors are asked about their experience with the mentorship program. How many times did you meet with your mentor? How did your mentor help guide you?
- Instructors are asked about their experience completing the OLIMR rubric and the assessment process. For example, the instructors are asked if there were parts of the rubric that were difficult to understand or repetitive. They are also asked to give their overall impressions of the rubric as an assessment and describe differences between the OLIMR process and previous assessments that they had received.
- The supervisor and the instructor review their OLIMR evaluations of the instructor's performance. Special attention is paid to differences between the supervisor and instructor's evaluation of the instructor using the OLIMR rubric and reflection.
- The instructor is invited to talk about their responses to the open-ended reflection questions. Based on the debriefing conversation, the supervisor points out the instructor's strengths as well as areas for growth.
- The supervisor presents the instructor with the OLIMR evaluation summary document (see appendix C-3). This document provides an overview of the evaluation highlights and a space for the instructor to set a goal for the following semester.
- The following semester, the instructors work with their mentor to revisit the goals they set. Instructors work on these goals throughout the semester and report on their progress at the next OLIMR-Supervisor debriefing meeting.

Results

Sample instructor reflections on professional development opportunities and teaching and grading are included below.

Professional development opportunities. The most common feedback that the instructors provide regarding the OLIMR evaluation process focuses on the professional development portion. As many of the online faculty do not hold tenured or tenure-track positions, it is possible that they have never formally been asked about the continuing education aspect of their careers. In her reflection of the evaluation process, a graduate student commented that she was pleased with her overall evaluation but would like to seek more professional development opportunities: "I felt the rubric covered extensive areas of self-evaluation. As I worked through the rubric, I felt satisfied by my performance in most areas. It also served as a good source to reassess which areas I would like to continue to improve on. That for me is particularly important because I would like to continue to gain strategies and experience as an online instructor" (Graduate Student 2). One of the online instructors made a similar observation regarding the usefulness of the rubric as a reflection tool. However, he noted that as an instructor who teaches four classes per semester, he has difficulty finding time to participate in professional development activities during the semester.

> Esta rúbrica primeramente me hizo reflexionar sobre todo lo vivido durante el semestre. Además de esto, la rúbrica también me informó sobre la importancia de hacer desarrollo personal. Fue algo que me hubiera gustado hacer más, pero infelizmente con clases de niveles y modalidades diferentes lo hizo difícil este semestre. Sin embargo, ya tengo en mi lista algunos libros de pedagogía que me gustaría leer en el verano. (Instructor 3)

> [First of all, this rubric made me reflect on everything I've gone through during the semester. Aside from that, the rubric also informed me about the importance of personal development. That's something that I would have liked to do more of but, unfortunately, that was hard to do this semester since I was teaching classes of various levels and modalities. However, I already have in my list some pedagogy books that I would like to read in the summer.]

Despite circumstances that might make professional development difficult during the semester, the online instructors showed interest in seeking out professional development activities. Those who had not actively participated in professional development during the past year set that as their goal: "I would like to look for more opportunities to improve my professional development. My goal is to look for workshops that are offered virtually during the summer and I want to attend to the ACTFL Conference in November if possible" (Adjunct Faculty 2). While more established instructors may seek professional development opportunities at well-recognized, national conferences, this may not be feasible for graduate students and adjunct faculty. Instructor B noted her interest in completing online trainings to increase her knowledge in the field of online education: "My goal would be to attend a minimum of 2 online teaching workshops in order to stay up to date with best teaching practices and new technology available for online teaching for second language acquisition" (Graduate Student 2).

Instructor roles and responsibilities. The online instructors found that their roles and responsibilities were different in an online environment as compared to their F2F courses. In the online format, the majority of the instructors' time was spent developing course content and assessing students' acquisition of that content. Faculty often commented that the most difficult part of the teaching for the online Spanish program was keeping up with the grading. In order to help the new instructors to budget their time, the supervisor offered a grading strategies workshop. At the end of the semester, Graduate Student 3 noted that she still struggled with completing her grading in a timely manner: "Going forward, I will make efforts to decrease the amount of time I spend grading by: focusing on the grammar topics emphasized in each assignment, not marking every error, and setting a timer" (Graduate Student 3). Instructor F also set a grading-related goal. While she had effectively provided written feedback and used the required program rubrics throughout the semester, she was interested in implementing the oral feedback recordings that other instructors had mentioned during a training session: "If I am to be a successful online Spanish instructor, I feel that I need to add some new teaching strategies by implementing other nonrequired teaching tools in my class. I also want to incorporate oral feedback to my students" (Adjunct Faculty 1). The goals set by the instructors indicated an awareness of their need to develop specific skills related to online teaching. The instructors stated their belief that they could become better online instructors by attending workshops and other professional development activities.

CONCLUSIONS

Instructors who participated in this study were given the opportunity to set their own professional goals after the debriefing session with their supervisor. The goals they set were directly related to the areas for improvement identified during that session. The next step in this process would be to engage the participants in a structured plan to move forward with their set goal.

Research has shown that failure to incorporate structured activities related to the goal results in decreased motivation and a lack of further action (Locke, Cartledge, and Koeppel 1968). Mentors may help instructors to commit to the goal-setting process by using time lines and frequent check-ins to keep the learners engaged and productive (Locke and Latham 1990). In order for the goal-setting activity to be successful, the supervisor must incorporate professional development activities in workshops and meetings throughout the following year.

PUTTING IT ALL TOGETHER

To ensure continuous improvement of the goal-setting process, the CTE literature and the results of the case study just described call for the following action items:

- Invite instructors to reflect on areas of growth discussed in the debriefing session.
- Require instructors to write a specific goal on their evaluation summary and sign the document (see appendix C-3).
- At the beginning of the next term, ask the instructors to bring the goals to the first meeting and share them with their peers, mentors, and supervisors.
- Have the instructors write specific steps with a corresponding time line for meeting short- and long-term goals.
- Assign mentors to work with the instructors on goal follow-up each month.
- Include the progress made on the goal-setting activity in the next formative evaluation.

The preceding chapters (7, 8, and 9) have explored professional development for online language instructors at the micro level (i.e., self-assessment, peer mentoring, goal setting), which complements the meso-level training they receive in departmental workshops, seminars, courses, and so on. (Gruba et al. 2016). Chapter 10 provides an overview of the topics reviewed in this volume and provides suggestions for the normalization of a critical approach to CTE in online environments.

10

An Ecological Approach to the Normalization of a Critical CTE

In the context of the COVID-19 crisis and the civil unrest and social justice issues that the United States is confronting, it is imperative that we use a critical lens and an ecological approach to understand how we can improve the training and assessment of online language instructors and help them integrate technologies that facilitate the development of more inclusive worldviews in their teaching. Such an ecological approach takes into consideration the experiences, roles, and responsibilities of online faculty when creating training programs for them and when assessing their ability to reach appropriate standards that measure their technological, pedagogical, and evaluative competencies within a particular pedagogical context as well as their ability to self-evaluate, engage in self-directed learning, and seek out professional development opportunities. An ecological approach to the training and assessment of online language instructors would also make sure that instructors understand their relationship to and connectedness with members of their departmental culture and members of the target cultures with whom they will communicate after their training programs have ended.

Our first chapter opens this avenue of discussion by pointing out the essential differences between teaching in physical versus digital spaces and by bringing to our attention the need for equitable and contextualized evaluations of students and language teachers from diverse backgrounds who have been asked to participate in online pedagogical spaces, perhaps for the first time. In chapters 2 and 3 we describe current CTE training models and proposed solutions to the challenges CTE programs face, suggesting that departments foster the development of critical cultural awareness in educators and students and implement a seismic paradigmatic shift in the way we conceptualize education in order to create a departmental culture of inclusion and respect among all members. In addition, in chapters 4 through 9 we identify essential online instructor skills required to teach effectively in digital spaces and proposed processes for equitably evaluating their attainment of those skills through contextualized assessment processes and mentoring in an ecologically based framework.

In the introduction to this volume, we agree with Kwang Hee Hong (2010) that the integration of technology into the language curriculum is "the ultimate goal of CALL teacher education" (53). However, as discussed in chapter 1, faculty resistance to this integration may delay or curb this integration process. As we note in chapter 3, in order to decrease this resistance, administrators must make cognitive, emotional, and functional investments to meet instructors' needs and thus facilitate faculty acceptance of the paradigm shift to digital pedagogical platforms. A new departmental culture that demonstrates respect for faculty's proven pedagogical success in physical spaces and at the same time opens doors and avenues of support for them to be successful instructors in digital spaces will not only be able to help them integrate CALL technologies in their curricula but will be able to *normalize* that integration as well as the teaching of language in online environments within that new unit culture.

THE ISSUE OF NORMALIZATION

The idea of normalization began to gain traction in discussions within CALL research circles after Stephen Bax's (2003) characterization of this process. Drawing on Everett Rogers's (1995) ideas on the ways in which innovations become diffused in society, Bax defines the normalization of CALL as "the stage when the technology becomes invisible, embedded in everyday practice and hence 'normalised'" (23). However, this view is criticized by Phil Hubbard and Mike Levy (2006a), who propose that while this "invisibility" may be somewhat valid when talking about classroom activities in institutions with sufficient technological resources, technology cannot be invisible in the areas of curriculum development/design and CALL research. Here we use the term "normalization" of CALL in a much broader sense, that is, to refer to a state in which the ideal of the integration of technology into language teaching is adopted by a departmental culture as a core value and effective actions are taken to turn that integration into a normal, sustainable practice. In the context of these concluding remarks to the volume, we focus on the normalization of CALL and its integration into the practice of online language instruction, the normalization of a Critical CALL, and the normalization of a critical approach to CTE training and instructor assessment.

The Normalization of CALL and Online Language Teaching

Several CALL scholars have identified several factors that either promote or hinder the normalization of CALL technologies. For instance, Andrea Chambers and Bax (2006) used an *-emic* approach to the study of these factors by including interviews with teachers and other stakeholders, class observations, informal conversations, and field notes. From their data analysis, Chambers and Bax (2006) identify syllabus integration—that is, "the need to integrate CALL into the syllabus in such a way that teachers are expected, as often as the facilities allow, to use computers in their teaching" (477)—as a crucial factor for the normalization of CALL. However, Chambers and Bax also note the need for the administration to provide CALL instructors with

> sympathetic support, both technical and pedagogical; they need the opportunity for sympathetic development, probably in collaborative mode; they need computing facilities to be accessible and organized in ways conducive to the easy integration of computer activities with non-computer activities; they need the software to be authorable as far as possible so that teachers can fit the software to their students' particular needs. Since time has been identified above as a significant factor impeding teachers in their use of new technologies, this factor must also be borne in mind by administrators and managers in their planning. (477)

In addition, Barbara Lafford's (2015b) survey of CALL scholars (reported in Lafford 2019) found that the following factors helped to promote the integration and normalization of CALL technologies in the language curriculum: access and transparent usage of technology, ease of use of technology, CALL training for language teachers, collaboration among teachers, administrative support, and the appropriate use of resources for labs or mobile technologies.

On the other hand, CALL researchers have also identified several factors that hinder the integration and normalization of technologies into language programs. For instance, Chambers and Bax's (2006) data show that the following factors impeded CALL normalization: logistics; stakeholders' conceptions; knowledge and abilities; syllabus and software integration; and training, development, and support. In addition, Lafford's (2015b) survey of CALL scholars found that inhibiting factors to CALL normalization include lack of technological training and access to technology by students and teachers and lack of technical and administrative support (Lafford 2019).

Greg Kessler and Hubbard (2017) note that the greatest challenge to the normalization of CALL technologies is appropriate teacher preparation: "To achieve adequate teacher preparation, faculty in a teacher preparation program need to have the necessary CALL knowledge and experience to reach normalization" (287). Chapter 3 of this volume discusses in detail the factors that hinder the normalization of online language teaching (e.g., lack of understanding of the affordances of CALL technologies to teach online, faculty resistance to reinventing themselves as pedagogues and changing their pedagogical practices, insufficient online teaching expertise among teacher trainers, lack of reliable infrastructure and technical support, lack of technological expertise among language faculty and resulting technophobia, inequitable instructor assessment practices, a lack of teacher voice in the creation and modification of instructor training and assessment rubrics, and an institutional culture that does not adequately reward the instructor effort required to teach online). To meet these challenges, we propose using Anthony Muhammad and Luis Cruz's (2019) investment framework in which administrators and supervisors make the cognitive, emotional, and functional investments necessary to facilitate faculty's competent transition to digital teaching spaces. Thus, the key to the normalization of CALL and online teaching practices in a department is to provide language faculty with sufficient and appropriate online instructor training, assessment, and support.

The normalization of online language instructor training and assessment can be facilitated by establishing a reiterative training and evaluation life cycle (Tobin, Mandernach, and Taylor 2015), discussed throughout this volume. If a department's culture holds as a core value the integration of faculty training, the professional development of core competencies evidenced in instructor behaviors, and the assessment of those competencies as points along a reiterative cyclic continuum of practice, then all of these processes will become part of a normalized professional development routine for online educators. After its first iteration, the cycle is sustained through ongoing instructor mentoring and self-directed learning.

In addition to the issue of lack of teacher training as a factor hindering the normalization of CALL technologies into the language curriculum, Lafford (2019) adds two other items to the list of impeding factors, that is, "the possible lack of instructor awareness about student and global technology use and the lack of a critical approach to CALL on the part of students and instructors" (135). Just as Lafford (2019) calls for the creation and normalization of a Critical CALL approach to teaching with technology or online (discussed in chapter 3), we propose the implementation of a Critical CTE approach to the training and assessment of online language instructors.

The Normalization of Critical CALL, CTE, and Instructor Assessment

Language departments wishing to take a critical approach to CALL must take measures to promote the acquisition of critical cultural awareness (CCA) by instructors and language students. As noted earlier, this construct was defined by Michael Byram (1997) as the "ability to evaluate critically and on the basis of explicit criteria, perspectives, practices and products in one's own and other cultures and countries" (63). The three practical steps that Lafford (2019) proposes for implementing the normalization of a Critical CALL—the awareness of access, training, and use issues; the infusion of CCA and social justice themes into curriculum design; and the creation of appropriate assessments for Critical CALL—can also be integrated into the creation of a Critical CTE.

First, in their CTE training, teachers need to be encouraged to seek out information on and try to remedy any difficulties their students may have in accessing technology and getting trained to use the technology as well as information on the actual technology their students own and know how to use. Second, as part of their CCA, online language instructors need to be cognizant of how lack of access to and experience with technology (resulting from a "digital divide" separating those with access to technology from those that lack that access) may affect students in their classes, especially those from marginalized and multicultural communities or those living with disabilities. In addition to warning readers about the stereotyping that can accompany the use of the term "digital divide" (chapter 4), Mark Warschauer (2002b) broadens the original definition of digital divide beyond the inequity of access issue to encompass "differences in knowledge and skills in using computers, or in attitudes toward using them" as well as "issues of content, language, education, literacy, or community and social resources." CTE training that prepares online language instructors to be aware of their students' access to mobile and wireless technologies, skill levels, and attitudes toward technology can help teachers make intelligent choices in selecting task-based activities that can be completed using smartphones and tablets instead of requiring laptops or desktop computers.

In addition, CTE training in CCA must provide opportunities for teachers to understand (through their study of social justice and identity issues) how language programs must meet the needs of diverse faculty, students, and communities who have been marginalized in their society. Finally, CTE training must include awareness of the need to create appropriate assessments and feedback strategies for language teachers teaching online that take into account the instructors' cultural backgrounds, their role and responsibilities in the online system, and their experience teaching languages in digital spaces.

ACTION PLAN FOR CREATING AND SUSTAINING A CRITICAL CTE APPROACH

One of the most critical factors needed to normalize and sustain Critical CTE is the need for a departmental culture that identifies this approach as a core value. This value can be demonstrated by an action plan that includes (1) the establishment of a contextualized and reiterative training/evaluation life cycle with (2) professional development opportunities that are informed by CCA and (3) a demonstrated awareness of instructor professional growth as being supported by three essential, complementary elements—institutional support, professional development training opportunities, and self-development.

Rena Palloff and Keith Pratt (2011, 115) propose a "Best System" for the professional development of excellent online instructors that can be adapted to include critical awareness and training and assessment practices that reflect it. A modified version of their professional development system is pictured graphically by the triangle in figure 10.1. The three major elements of this model include departmental professional development training opportunities for the online language teacher (e.g., via formal training and assessment, mentoring), institutional support (e.g., sufficient infrastructure and cognitive, emotional, and functional investments in CTE training and assessment), and self-development (e.g., self-evaluation, reflection, self-directed learning through the use of personal learning environments and personal learning networks).

In order for departments to normalize and sustain a Critical CTE approach, more attention needs to be paid to expanding what is understood by the "self-development" element in the framework. In a Critical CTE, the concept of self-development must go beyond what individuals need to do to enhance and improve the way they teach, but it also should include the way they work on their own attitudes and prejudices to understand how they view the world and their role in it.

Thus, a Critical CTE would include pointing online language instructors to resources that they can use to help them maximize their human potential and their identities as *homo loquens, homo analyticus, homo socius, homo faber, homo ludens,* and *homo fabulans* (Blake and Guillén 2020). In addition, a Critical CTE would provide online language instructors with opportunities to develop a knowledge of their students' access to and use of technologies as well as an understanding of and an empathy for marginalized linguistic and cultural groups and their sociocultural context. This understanding would then be translated into suggested action strategies for instructors to use with their online students to work (virtually or in person) with these communities to meet the societal challenges they face.

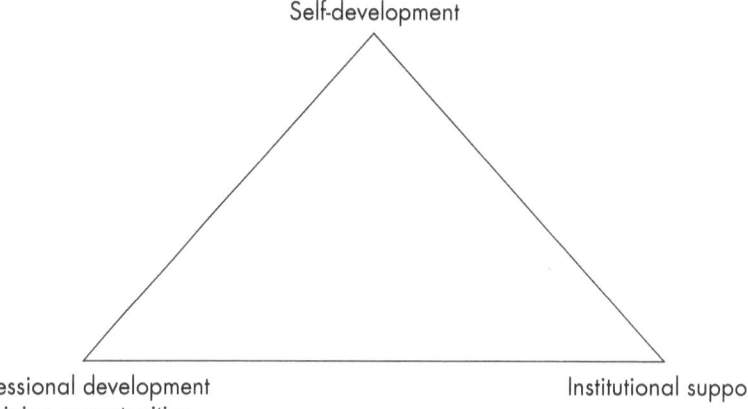

FIGURE 10.1 Modified Version of Palloff and Pratt's (2011, 115) Model for "Best System" for Professional Development of Online Instructors

In addition, a Critical CTE would also provide online language instructors the opportunity to think critically and work collaboratively to make good decisions and propose appropriate solutions to real-world problems (e.g., case studies on social justice issues), maintain respectful online communication (e.g., netiquette), and create and participate in CoPs and CoIs and personal reflections to find their professional and personal purpose and strategize how they can make a positive impact on their local and global communities. Once they develop these personal skills, they can transfer these abilities to meet future workplace challenges and help their online students to engender those same self-development skills (King Ramírez and Lafford 2018).

In order for Critical CTE to become established in language departments, more research needs to be carried out on the best ways to infuse CCA into various elements in the training/assessment cycle.

FUTURE RESEARCH IN CRITICAL CTE TRAINING AND ASSESSMENT

One of the best rationales for conducting Critical CALL research is articulated by Lourdes Ortega (2017): "Once we acknowledge that the majority of the world is multilingual, but inequitably multilingual, and that much of the world is also technologized, but inequitably so, it becomes not only our business, but also our professional responsibility to generate research about language learning and digital literacies for language learning that addresses these problems" (288). To extend this critical lens to CTE research, we propose a brief sample of possible lines of investigation to build a body of knowledge of best practices for the normalization of a critical approach to online language instructor training and assessment. The research questions are organized by elements in Thomas Tobin and colleagues' (2015) Online Teaching/Evaluation Life Cycle:

- Faculty Training and Professional Development
    - *To identify the most effective training and professional development activities that would lead to the development of CCA*: Which professional development training activities most often lead directly to instructor's integration of certain technologies into their language curricula to develop CCA? What characteristics of these training activities are perceived to be the most effective in getting the instructor to implement these activities?
    - *To assess the effectiveness of online instructor training and professional development activities in fostering CCA and intercultural sensitivity*: How effective are certain training and professional development activities in increasing instructors' CCA or intercultural sensitivity (as measured by, for example, Milton Bennett's [1986, 1993] Developmental Model of Intercultural Sensitivity or Guo-Ming Chen and William Starosta's [2000] Intercultural Sensitivity Scale)? How does the level of an instructor's intercultural sensitivity relate to their willingness and ability to effectively integrate CCA into their student language learning curricula?
    - *To address CCA issues related to access and CTE training*:
        —What factors help to create/ameliorate inequities in access and digital literacy training for instructors and students from diverse backgrounds?
        —What are the most effective ways to integrate CCA into CTE training in order to help instructors recognize social justice issues affecting individuals (students, instructors, and community members) from various cultural and socioeconomic backgrounds (e.g., awareness of access issues among students and teachers as well as a recognition of strengths of student and instructor diversity)? What are the most effective ways to get faculty to integrate this training into their pedagogical practice?
    - *To assess the effect of institutional support for online language instructor training*: What institutional factors foster or hinder the development

of digital literacy skills in online language instructors? What institutional solutions can foster these skills in both online instructors and students?
- Core Competencies and Instructional Behaviors
    - *Use of technical, pedagogical, and evaluation skills to further the development of CCA*: Which technological tools are most effective for instructors to use to motivate students to explore CCA issues (e.g., social media platforms, social justice blogs)? What types of instructor-created tasks related to CCA topics facilitate and energize student discussions and presentations? What are the most effective ways for language instructors to teach learners to discern the validity and authenticity of sources of information on CCA topics on the internet? In what ways does self-reflection on the development of one's CCA abilities lead to a change in instructor or learner behavior?
    - *Use of collaborative CoPs and CoIs to facilitate instructor and student knowledge and understanding of international and marginalized cultures*: Which social media or discussion platforms are most effective for instructors to create an environment that fosters critical discussions of issues facing international communities and marginalized cultures in the United States and abroad? What are the characteristics of successful collaborative practice within CoPs and CoIs for the development of L2 abilities, intercultural communicative competence (ICC), and types of interaction within project-based activities, wikis, blogs, and virtual exchanges based on domestic and international service learning?
    - *Use of digital stories from instructors, students, community members to gain insight into groups of people from various cultural backgrounds*: What insights can digital stories provide into the kind of power and positionality issues (Vollmer Rivera 2018) that come into play in the formation of identities of individuals from marginalized groups who teach or learn languages online? How can digital stories from community members help instructors and students understand the challenges faced by marginalized communities?
    - *Use of teleconferencing for the acquisition of the L2 and ICC*: How do virtual exchanges between instructors, students, and members of international and marginalized communities on critical topics dispel or strengthen stereotypical thinking patterns among the participants?
    - *Use of digital film annotations for the acquisition of ICC*: Does the inclusion of digital annotations in film affect student achievement

of critical intercultural learning outcomes? And if so, in what ways? (Ocando Finol 2019)
- *Use of translanguaging (using more than one language or semiotic system to communicate) on social media sites to increase understanding of power and positionality*: How is translanguaging used to manage issues of power and positionality in virtual exchanges between various combinations of native and nonnative speaker interlocutors? (Teske 2018; Vollmer Rivera 2018)

- Assessment and Evaluation Guidelines
  - *Use of modular rubrics for instructor evaluation*: In what ways does the use of flexible, modular rubrics increase the efficacy and equity of online language instructor assessments?
  - *Use of e-portfolios in order to gain a deeper understanding of instructor progress toward attaining core competencies*: Does the use of e-portfolios by online language instructors (containing evidence of meeting departmental standards, self-reflections, and background instructor information) lead to more effective and equitable instructor assessments than traditional assessment procedures?
  - *Use of mentoring to facilitate instructor professional development*: How is the effectiveness of formative assessment through mentoring perceived by peer mentors and instructors? What elements of the mentoring program are demonstrated to be most/least effective in developing instructor skills and abilities (including CCA)?
  - *Use of a critical pedagogical approach to the assessment of online faculty from marginalized background*:
    —Are pre- and in-service online faculty from marginalized groups being evaluated fairly, taking into account prior research findings on how teachers of color or international faculty may be evaluated by students and administrators?
    —Do CTE training programs and current or future work venues expect language instructors from marginalized groups or lower socioeconomic status backgrounds to attain the same teacher and student technological standards as other trainees if they and their students lack extensive prior experience with technology and are lacking in access to current and reliable technologies and technical support? What are the most effective strategies for facilitating their attainment of these standards?
  - *Use of feedback tailored to instructor's cultural expectations*: Are there preferred ways for supervisors to give feedback on CALL skills or ideas for goal setting to teachers from different cultural backgrounds

(e.g., heritage speakers, international teaching assistants, instructors from individualist versus collectivist cultures) so that the feedback is understood, respected, and incorporated into their future teaching?
- *Assessment of the effectiveness of instructor curricular design and student assessment procedures*: What types of technology-based course materials and task-based activities are most effective at facilitating students' attainment of CCA and social justice objectives? What types of alternative (equitable) student assessments can be facilitated by CALL?

LOOKING AHEAD

This volume takes an ecological approach to CTE training and assessment that can help inform supervisors and administrators in their planning of appropriate professional development and evaluation procedures for online language instructors. In this case, an ecological approach to instructor training and assessment thoughtfully considers the instructor's needs within a larger social and experiential context and encourages administrators to adjust departmental training and assessment practices to meet those needs. For instance, this approach gathers information on the background experiences of instructors (experience teaching languages with technology and online) and their cultural expectations for receiving feedback from supervisors on the quality of their teaching. This information then informs the creation of specific training and mentoring sessions that can be flexibly tailored to meet the current needs and expectations of a diverse group of online language faculty.

This ecological approach also informs the cognitive, emotional, and functional investments that administrators must make in the training and assessment of online language instructors in order to ensure the sustainability of a quality online language program and the development of their faculty, not only as scholars but as beings who possess CCA and are ready to realize their human potential and inform themselves to speak out against injustice and take action to work with international and marginalized communities in addressing the challenges they face. In doing so, we can take up the challenge to fight complacency implied by the prescient words of Dr. Martin Luther King Jr.: "We will have to repent in this generation not merely for the hateful words and actions of the bad people but for the appalling silence of the good people" (1963).

APPENDIX A

Checklists for Online Language Instructor Training and Assessment

Appendix A contains checklists related to essential elements of CTE training for online language instructors, strategies for meeting the challenges related to that training, and core competencies/skills needed by online language faculty.

A-1: CHECKLIST OF ESSENTIAL ELEMENTS OF CTE TRAINING PROGRAMS FOR ONLINE LANGUAGE INSTRUCTORS

This CTE training checklist was informed by research carried out by CTE scholars discussed in chapters 2 and 4 of this volume.

Institution: _____
Purpose/Focus of training: _____
Scope of training (breadth-first or depth-first): _____
Target audience for training: _____
Type of courses trainees will be teaching (blended/online): _____
Mode of training (F2F/blended/online): _____
Duration of training: _____
Trainer: _____

CTE Training Elements	Elements Needed by This Training Course for Target Audience/Institution (Y/N)
Audience for CTE Training	
Training is appropriate for the audience (prior experience with technology, control they have over the curriculum, institutional role)	

CTE Training Elements	Elements Needed by This Training Course for Target Audience/Institution (Y/N)
Review of roles and responsibilities of individuals in CTE programs	
Curriculum Design	
Development of curricular design abilities	
Training in how to carry out a needs analysis	
Understanding of breadth-first or depth-first training	
Situated learning	
Use of technology to teach technology	
Project-based learning	
Reflective learning	
Collaborative learning/socialization/telecollaboration (virtual exchange)	
Communities of practice and communities of inquiry	
Netiquette rules in home and target culture and lexical items for virtual environments	
Self-directed learning and use of "critical friend" for feedback	
In-service mentoring and mentoring oversight	
Integration of technology standards/goals into teacher education	
Provision of models of CALL syllabi for different audiences and purposes	
Technology Training	
Select appropriate technology skills for training from Core Competencies/Skills Checklist Needed by Online Language Faculty	
Pedagogy Training	
Select appropriate pedagogy skills for training from Core Competencies/Skills Checklist Needed by Online Language Faculty	

CTE Training Elements	Elements Needed by This Training Course for Target Audience/Institution (Y/N)
Evaluation Training	
Select appropriate evaluation skills for training from Core Competencies/Skills Checklist Needed by Online Language Faculty	
Professional Development Training	
Select appropriate professional development skills for training from Core Competencies/Skills Checklist Needed by Online Language Faculty	

A-2: CHECKLIST OF STRATEGIES FOR MEETING CHALLENGES OF CTE ONLINE TRAINING PROGRAMS

This CTE training strategies checklist was informed by research carried out by CTE scholars discussed in chapter 3 of this volume.

Institution: _____
Purpose of training: _____
Target audience for training: _____
Setting and mode of training (F2F/blended/online): _____
Type of courses trainees will be teaching (blended/online): _____
Date of training: _____
Duration of training: _____
Trainer: _____

Training Challenges Addressed	Training Investment Strategies	Strategies Needed for This Training (Y/N)
Cognitive Investment Strategies		
C-1. Faculty do not understand the role of technology and how it can be used effectively in their pedagogical context.	Invite all stakeholders to discuss a vision of technology integration, provide critical information on resources to help accomplish this, and ask for their ideas and their leadership to realize this vision.	

Training Challenges Addressed	Training Investment Strategies	Strategies Needed for This Training (Y/N)
C-2. Faculty may not understand their role and responsibilities vis-à-vis those of other stakeholders in their online system for language instruction.	Review roles and responsibilities of stakeholders (e.g., students, course developers, site coordinators, tutors, proctors, student support services, management/administration, teachers, researchers, trainers).	
C-3. Faculty trainers may have naive beliefs that there is no need for technology training for digital natives.	Provide faculty with sources of research on challenging the assumption that digital natives need little to no CTE training.	
	Carry out a needs analysis in order to tailor training to meet the needs of faculty with different skill levels.	
C-4. Faculty may not understand what skills they need to acquire to succeed as language instructors in online pedagogical environments.	Make sure faculty are aware of the technological, pedagogical, and evaluative skills they need to acquire to be successful online language instructors.	
E-1. Faculty feel overwhelmed by time availability and time management issues.	Encourage faculty to consider thoughtful integration of some assignments that can be graded in an efficient manner (e.g., automatically corrected lexical and grammatical activities, holistic grading of essay drafts).	
	Provide faculty with information on resources on best practices regarding the efficient creation and evaluation of online interaction (e.g., professional development training, CoPs with more experienced online faculty).	
	Assign trained no-cost graders (e.g., undergraduate preservice language teacher candidates needing internship credit) with a high level of target-language proficiency to help ease instructor's workload in grading student assignments.	

Training Challenges Addressed	Training Investment Strategies	Strategies Needed for This Training (Y/N)
	Encourage learners and instructors to realize the value of working through the challenges of synchronous communication across distances.	
E-2. Faculty feel underappreciated due to a lack of rewards for their time and effort they spend integrating technologies into their language curriculum and maintaining effective communication with their online students.	Provide language faculty with incentives for time spent on technology integration in the form of heightened employment prospects (for preservice teachers) and release time, recognition, and financial compensation (for in-service teachers).	
E-3. Faculty resent institutional pressure for them to reinvent themselves as pedagogues and change their pedagogical practice to teach in digital spaces. • Faculty asked to teach online do not feel respected and valued for their prior pedagogical knowledge and experience in nondigital spaces. • Faculty perceive institutional pressure to have them teach in digital spaces as a face-threatening experience that challenges their perceptions of their autonomy and control over their teaching, their roles, and their identities.	Demonstrate that faculty's pedagogical success as experienced WL professionals in nondigital spaces is valued and acknowledged.	
	Enhance faculty agency by soliciting their collective advice, collaborative problem-solving, and input into the creation of the online training itself, the assessment process, and the rubrics that will be used to evaluate faculty's implementation of the training in their own pedagogical practice.	
	Prepare faculty to accept their new roles and identities in a new digital environment by building their confidence and encouraging them to seek out advice from more experienced online faculty mentors.	
	Encourage faculty to reinvent themselves and their pedagogical practice so they can serve as role models for other online faculty to help students succeed via student-centered learning in new digital environments.	

Training Challenges Addressed	Training Investment Strategies	Strategies Needed for This Training (Y/N)
E-4. Administrative unit's lack of critical cultural awareness to recognize and address issues of technology access, training, and usage among marginalized social groups and to include in the language curricula social justice issues to meet the needs of marginalized students, faculty, and communities.	Adopt a Critical CALL approach to CTE training that includes explorations of topics of inequitable access to technology and training among marginalized groups (e.g., communities of color, people living with disabilities) and social justice issues.	
Functional Investment Strategies		
F-1. In-service faculty believe that they have received insufficient and inadequate online training for them to meet their workplace needs.	Keep the training audience in mind; provide frequent and ongoing hands-on training focusing both on breadth-first and depth-first approaches for faculty at different levels of expertise that respects their time and types of preferred learning experiences.	
	Start CALL technology training early and integrate it into existing methodology and other educational program courses that teacher candidates take as they progress through the program.	
	Provide training that respects faculty time and types of preferred learning experiences.	
	Conduct research into the effectiveness of CTE training for meeting current technological needs of in-service teachers in the workplace in order to inform future training for pre- and in-service teachers.	
F-2. Faculty voice concerns over a lack of sufficient infrastructure, lack of access to current and reliable equipment and applications, and lack of technical support.	To keep up with the rapid pace of technological change, update unit hardware and software, the identification of online skills needed by language faculty, and training materials.	

Training Challenges Addressed	Training Investment Strategies	Strategies Needed for This Training (Y/N)
	Include information on 24/7 technology support for faculty and students in the CTE training.	
F-3. A focus on technology over pedagogy in CTE training courses can lead to tools being presented without discussing the possibilities and appropriate uses of those tools in specific pedagogical contexts.	CTE training must involve a discussion of the affordances and constraints of tools in online teaching contexts and how to implement technological tools effectively to help students meet their learning objectives.	
F-4. Lack of CALL expertise on the part of teacher trainers and language program directors who believe a CALL specialist should be hired to train them.	Hire a CALL/online specialist to serve as a point person to train language faculty using an approach that prioritizes pedagogy over technology and is grounded in relevant theoretical frameworks and empirical CALL research.	
	CALL specialists should use the CTE training they provide in situated online environments as a model for training faculty to acquire relevant skills to use in those same digital contexts.	
	CALL specialists should work with departmental administrators and supervisors to set up virtual field experiences and virtual practicums for preservice teachers to build their confidence before they take responsibility for an online class.	
F-5. As a result of these functional challenges, faculty can develop a discomfort with technology (technophobia) that diminishes their willingness to integrate technology into their pedagogical practice.	Prepare faculty for changes in technologies and for developing basic information and communication technologies competence, specific technical competence of the software, dealing with constraints and possibilities of the medium and affordances and constraints of their institutional environment.	

Training Challenges Addressed	Training Investment Strategies	Strategies Needed for This Training (Y/N)
	Prepare teachers for interactive materials (natural language processing and gaming).	
	Prepare teachers for a social future and participation (with teacher cognitive, social, and teaching presence) in post-course discussion lists, CoPs and CoIs, and MOOCs; involve them in project-based collaborative tasks (e.g., wikis) and encourage them to develop their creativity and own personal style in these spaces; and give them target-language lexicon for working in digital spaces and target culture netiquette norms.	
F-6. Discomfort may also arise when language teachers (students) do not feel connected to language teacher trainers (faculty) when using technology to communicate and interact in digital spaces.	Leading by example, teacher trainers need to instill in language teachers the need to establish cognitive, social, and teaching presence in virtual teaching environments and help students overcome their online anxiety.	
F-7. Faculty have noted insufficient follow-up (resources or ongoing mentoring) to their initial training.	Provide faculty with a list of CALL/online resources for self-directed learning.	
	Provide faculty with opportunities for mentoring for pre- and in-service teachers and provide mentoring oversight.	

Return on Investment: Faculty Accountability

FA-1. A consistent, theoretically and empirically grounded method of holding faculty accountable for their technological, pedagogical, and evaluative training may be lacking in academic units.	In recognition of the fact that CTE faculty development is an ongoing need, assign a mentor to monitor and assess faculty integration of technological, pedagogical, and evaluative skills into their language curricula during and after their training using formative and summative assessments.	

Training Challenges Addressed	Training Investment Strategies	Strategies Needed for This Training (Y/N)
FA-2. Faculty need to be assessed fairly on their integration of technology into their pedagogical practice, according to their individual circumstances.	Use modular rubrics that fairly assess faculty expertise in online language teaching according to their level of pedagogical, technological, and evaluation skills; their roles; their cultural expectations for types of feedback; and the affordances and constraints of their workplace environment.	
FA-3. The conclusions of faculty self-assessments may vary widely from those of supervisor assessments, even when the same rubric is used.	Invite instructor input into the creation of the faculty assessment rubrics and have them participate in norming session so that there is agreement on the manner in which the rubrics are to be applied.	
FA-4. The quality and usefulness of training programs, the assessment process, and rubrics need to be evaluated by all stakeholders, and those results should inform future iterations of training and assessment processes and instruments.	All stakeholders provide feedback on the unit's CTE training and assessment process and rubrics; administrators and trainers must incorporate that feedback into improving the quality of their training programs.	
FA-5. Traditional institutional culture may not recognize and appreciate the value of digital teaching spaces and the time and expertise it takes to integrate technology successfully into a language curriculum and to maintain a quality online language program.	Change institutional cultures to value and reward technological integration into the language curriculum using a student-centered, constructivist approach within a normalized Critical CALL cultural and ecological framework.	
	Establish an Online Teaching-Evaluation Life Cycle as part of this new culture.	

A-3: CHECKLIST FOR CORE COMPETENCIES/SKILLS NEEDED BY ONLINE LANGUAGE FACULTY

This skills checklist was informed by research carried out by CALL scholars discussed in chapter 4 of this volume.

Institution: _____
Instructor: _____
Language taught: _____
Faculty role: ___ Full-Time Instructor ___ Teaching Assistant
___ Adjunct
Background teaching with technology: _____ yrs. _____ levels
Background teaching online: _____ yrs. _____ levels
Access to technology: ___ Sufficient ___ Insufficient for workplace needs
Curricular control: ___ Yes ___ No
Date: _____
Supervisor: _____

Type of Skill	Skill needed at this time	NA (skill not applicable to role) or NE (skill not expected at this time)
Technological Skills		
Develop CALL literacies to meet teacher technology standards.		
Develop Technological Pedagogical Content Knowledge (TPACK).		
Acquire basic technological skills meeting or exceeding technology standards for students defined by the unit and make sure students meet those standards.		
Use and modify language management system features and technologies required for the course; identify and understand their affordances and constraints within the unit's pedagogical context.		
Make unit aware of technological infrastructure insufficiencies or course-related issues that hinder pedagogical progress.		

Type of Skill	Skill needed at this time	NA (skill not applicable to role) or NE (skill not expected at this time)
Be aware of 24/7 technical support resources available to faculty and students.		
Integrate technology coherently into pedagogical approaches.		
Choose suitable technology and software to match online tasks and facilitate online language learning.		
Develop critical semiotic awareness to use, troubleshoot, adapt, and create technology applications for online tasks.		
Apply technology appropriately in record keeping and feedback.		
Reflect on the pedagogical effectiveness of their use of technology in the course and student engagement with it.		
Leverage students' interest in personal uses of technology (e.g., Twitter, Instagram, Snapchat, Facebook, augmented reality, gaming, multimedia resources, podcasts, internet) to provide authentic input and interactional opportunities to engage students for language learning.		
Demonstrate an understanding of where to find CALL resources to catch and maintain students' interest.		
Strive to expand their own skill and knowledge base to evaluate, adopt, and adapt emerging technologies in their program and throughout their careers.		
Pedagogical Skills		
Apply language learning theories to online language teaching by grounding pedagogy in knowledge of CALL history, language learning theories, and CALL empirical research.		
Prioritize pedagogy over technology.		
Curriculum Design		
Apply curriculum design frameworks to create theoretically and empirically grounded curriculum design.		
Integrate relevant linguistic, cultural, technological, and professional standards into the language curriculum to set course goals and objectives.		

Type of Skill	Skill needed at this time	NA (skill not applicable to role) or NE (skill not expected at this time)
Conduct a needs analysis to determine students' linguistic, cultural, technological, and professional needs to set course objectives.		
Use digital learning materials that provide authentic input to students.		
Implement focus on form and task-based instruction		
Follow Universal Design for Learning or Quality Matters standards for course design (course overview and introduction, learning objectives [competencies], assessment and measurement, instructional materials, learning activities and learner interaction, course technology, learner support, accessibility and usability).		
Focus on Student-Centered Learning		
Focus on student-centered learning in which learning is seen as a process and student agency is promoted in order to create a supportive learning environment that meets individual students' needs.		
Use clear communication to clarify instructions and course expectations.		
Provide quality and timely written or oral feedback for individuals or the class as a whole.		
Encourage peer feedback among students.		
Vary the course structure to cater to various student learning needs, learning styles, access to technology, and disabilities.		
Make sure that internet sources and Web pages used meet the compliance standards of the American Disabilities Act (1990/2008) and follow Web Content Accessibility Guidelines.		
Promote student efficacy by encouraging self-directed, self-regulated, individualized, and personalized learning.		
Develop creativity and personal style in using, adapting, and creating technological applications and culturally appropriate materials to meet student needs.		

Type of Skill	Skill needed at this time	NA (skill not applicable to role) or NE (skill not expected at this time)
Encourage learners to be creative in telling their stories and to co-construct their own understanding, class resources, and the learning environment, and to co-create new learning and knowledge.		
Foster real-life problem-solving, critical thinking, and reflective skills among students.		
Integrate critical cultural awareness into critical CALL pedagogical practices.		
Foster Interaction, Collaboration, and Socialization		
Interaction		
Facilitate student oral and written interaction and stimulate active student participation in discussion boards or various communication tools (e.g., social media platforms), in pair and group discussions for different interaction purposes.		
Facilitate high-quality student interactions with different interlocutors (including target-language community members) and multiple opportunities for negotiation of meaning and cultural understanding to develop their communicative, intercultural communicative, and technological competencies.		
Provide students information on target-language lexicon and behaviors (netiquette) appropriate for target culture online interaction.		
Collaboration		
Use technology to facilitate and maintain effective student-instructor communication and collaboration among stakeholders to work together on a project, solve a problem, advocate for language and culture learning, or address social justice issues that affect target culture communities.		
Promote, plan, and manage student collaboration, design appropriate activities, moderate appropriately, choose appropriate environments and tools, and get students to negotiate ground rules for collaboration.		

Type of Skill	Skill needed at this time	NA (skill not applicable to role) or NE (skill not expected at this time)
Promote reciprocity and cooperation among students		
Encourage student collaborative tasks (e.g., wikis, telecollaboration) and project-based activities.		
Socialization		
Develop socioaffective regulation to effectively and creatively facilitate online socialization and to establish good rapport and a sense of community among interlocutors.		
Be aware of and address the anxiety issues of online language students.		
Develop teacher cognitive, social, and teaching presence in online interactions to mediate interaction and foster socialization.		
Foster the creation of online learning communities (CoPs and CoIs) via socialization.		
Evaluation Skills		
Carry out thoughtful self-assessment and self-reflection on performance and pedagogical choices.		
Require that learners measure their own linguistic, cultural, and professional competencies within the context of the ACTFL World Readiness Standards and the NACE and P21 career-readiness standards (e.g., critical thinking, collaboration, adaptability, intercultural competence) so that students can be prepared to transfer these skills to their own professional contexts. Facilitates students' acquisition of transferable skills.		
Critically review the online teaching performance of others via peer mentor evaluations.		
Carry out appropriate, systematic, and reliable assessments of student performance with a variety of formative and summative assessments and a standardized grading system.		
Evaluate materials for suitability and effectiveness.		
Evaluate tasks for suitability and effectiveness.		

Type of Skill	Skill needed at this time	NA (skill not applicable to role) or NE (skill not expected at this time)
Evaluate CTE courses/trainings for suitability and effectiveness.		
Evaluate assessment process and rubrics for suitability and effectiveness.		
Use results of evaluations to improve teaching, tasks, materials selection, courses, training, assessment process and rubrics, and procedures.		
Professional Development and Professionalism		
Seek out and participate in professional development opportunities at the departmental level and beyond and use professional development resources to improve teaching.		
Create effective personal learning environments and personal learning networks to facilitate ongoing self-directed professional development.		
Seek to work with a mentor to receive personal feedback and set goals for improvement.		
Establish effective communication with people to whom they report or supervise.		
Model professional behavior for students.		

APPENDIX B

Rubrics for Evaluation of Online Language Instructor Training and Assessment

This appendix contains assessment instruments for stakeholders (instructors/trainees, supervisors/trainers, and departmental administrators) to evaluate the online language instructor training program, the online instructor assessment process, and the OLIMR rubric itself.

B-1: STAKEHOLDERS' EVALUATION OF THE ONLINE LANGUAGE INSTRUCTOR TRAINING PROGRAM

As noted in chapter 3, supervisors and administrators can show respect for faculty members by asking them to provide feedback on the online training program they undergo. By soliciting faculty advice and input into the ongoing modifications of faculty online training, instructor agency is enhanced and instructors are given partial ownership of the training process. The instruments below allow for instructor formative, summative, and retrospective assessment of the online language instructor training sessions and program. Incorporating teacher voices (Egbert et al. 2009) into the assessment of the effectiveness of the online language instructor training sessions and programs facilitates the updating of the training program to remain relevant to trainees about to enter the language teaching profession. Instructors' feedback on their training can be captured with instruments using questions similar to the ones provided below. As discussed in chapter 3, this type of administrative emotional investment (Muhammad and Cruz 2019) can help to mitigate faculty resistance to online teaching and to facilitate faculty taking a leadership role in the process of transitioning to digital pedagogical spaces. Questions on these training assessment instruments are partially inspired by those used by Greg Kessler (2006), Paula Winke and Senta Goertler (2008), and Scott Windeatt (2017).

Instructor's Formative Evaluation of Online Language Instructor Training

The following questionnaire on the quality of individual training sessions on various topics can be given to trainees during their training period. This type of formative assessment allows supervisors and departmental administrators to adjust and continuously improve their training as it is being implemented throughout the semester or academic year. The questions are the same for each training to provide feedback that can facilitate the comparison of training sessions and trainers.

Rubric for Instructor Formative Evaluation of Training
Purpose/focus/topic of training: _____
Type of courses trainee is teaching (blended/online):_____
Mode of training (F2F/blended/online): _____
Dates and duration of training: _____
Trainer/s:_____

Using the following scale, indicate your level of agreement with the statements below regarding the training unit to teach with technology/online in which you have recently participated:

SA = strongly agree; A = agree; N/A = neither agree or disagree; D = disagree; SD = strongly disagree

Statement	SA	A	N/A	D	SD
The instructions given by the trainer were clear.					
There was adequate time to practice the skills that were demonstrated by the trainer.					
I feel confident that I can apply the skills I learned to my teaching.					

Please feel free to comment further on any of these points here:
_____
_____
_____

Please provide thoughtful, extended answers to the following questions:

- Was the information delivered by the trainer clear? If not, what areas could be made clearer to trainees?
- Did you have sufficient opportunity to practice the skills taught? Do you need more time to practice one or more of these skills before applying them to your teaching? Please explain.
- Do you now feel confident about your ability to apply that knowledge to your teaching? Why/why not? What kind of further training would help you apply this knowledge/new skill?
- Will this training be useful to you in your teaching? Was this training session helpful? In what way?
- What could be done differently to improve this training?

Instructor Summative Post-Training Evaluation of Online Language Instructor Training

The following questionnaire on the quality of the online language instructor training programs can be given to trainees at the end of a given training or degree program. This provides supervisors and departmental administrators with feedback on the instructors' overall assessment of their training program, which can be used to improve elements of the program the next time it is offered. The questions are the same for each training program to provide feedback that can facilitate the comparison of institutional training programs and trainers over time.

Rubric for Instructor Summative Evaluation of Training
Mode of training just completed (F2F/blended/online): _____
Format of training (course, workshops, mentoring): _____
Dates and duration of training: _____
Trainer/s:_____
Type of courses trainee will be teaching (F2F/blended/online): _____

Using the following scale, indicate your level of agreement with the following statements regarding the training you received to teach with technology/online:

SA = strongly agree; A = agree; N/A = neither agree nor disagree; D = disagree; SD = strongly disagree

Statement	SA	A	N/A	D	SD
The instructions given by the trainer(s) were clear throughout the training program.					
There was adequate time to practice the skills that were demonstrated by the trainer(s).					
I feel confident that I can apply the skills I learned to my teaching.					

Please feel free to comment further on any of these points here:

_____
_____
_____

Please provide thoughtful, extended answers to the following questions:

- How many courses that you took in your degree program involved substantial training (more than 20 percent of the time) for teaching online?
- Other than formal coursework, what other kinds of training to teach online were offered by your degree program/institution (e.g., workshops, demonstrations, talks, mentoring)? Did you participate in any of those training opportunities? Please explain.
- Was the information delivered by the trainer(s) clear throughout the training programs you took in your degree program to teach with technology/online? If not, what areas could be made clearer to trainees?
- Did you have sufficient opportunity to practice the skills you were taught to teach with technology/online? Do you need more time to practice one or more of these skills before applying them to your teaching? Please explain.
- Do you now feel confident about your ability to apply knowledge from your training to teach with technology/online? Why / why not? What kind of further training would help you apply this knowledge or hone new skills? Please explain.
- Do you believe that your degree program prepared you well for teaching with technology/online in your future career as a language teacher? What were the most positive aspects of the training? Please explain.

- What could be done differently to improve the training you took on teaching with technology/online? Please explain.
- Was the training you received helpful to your understanding of the advantages and challenges of teaching with technology/online? In what ways? Please explain.
- Do you believe that in your degree program sufficient time was devoted to training language instructors to teach with technology/online? Please explain.
- Do you believe you would have benefited from more instruction in your degree program regarding teaching with technology/online? Please explain.

Instructor Retrospective Evaluation of Online Language Instructor Training

The following list of sample questions can be used to create a summative delayed (retrospective) evaluation instrument for graduates of a given language teaching program. The purpose of the questionnaire (modified to fit the needs of the institution) is to provide the degree program with an understanding of the long-term effectiveness of the online instructor training they gave their graduates to teach online.

This questionnaire can be given to trainees after they have started working as a language teacher for at least a year after the original training period has ended. The answers to these questions facilitate the improvement of an institution's online training program and allows for a comparison of the efficacy of specific online training programs and trainers over time.

The list of questions below are meant to illustrate the thematic areas to be assessed in a retrospective evaluation of a training program. First, in order to understand the current teaching context of the instructors answering this retrospective questionnaire, they answer questions on their background teaching history and current teaching situation as well as the role of online teaching in their current workplace. Then instructors are asked to evaluate (retrospectively) how well their online language instructor training prepared them for their current teaching responsibilities.

These open-ended questions could be asked of individual in-service language instructors in writing or in oral interviews or they could serve as the basis for questions given to a (virtual or in-person) focus group of degree program graduates a year or two after they graduate when they are in the field working as language teachers. Some of these themes could also be converted into Likert-scale questions to gather data quickly and efficiently from program graduates to assess the effectiveness of the training they received in their degree program to teach online.

Rubric for Instructor Retrospective Evaluation of Training
Background Teaching History and Current Teaching Situation:

- For how many years have you taught a second/foreign language?
- What types of courses do you currently teach (F2F, blended, online)?
- What is the highest degree you hold (BA, MA, PhD, EDD)?
- What languages do you currently teach?
- In what type of institution do you currently teach languages (high school/community college/university)?

Please provide thoughtful, extended answers to the following questions:

- Is online language teaching encouraged or required at your current workplace? Please explain.
- What advantages of online teaching have you noted for you and your language students? Please explain.
- What challenges do you face teaching online at your current workplace? Please explain.
- Are language teachers at your current institution required to teach online? Please explain.
- Does your institution offer incentives to teach or develop courses online? If so, please explain.
- Would you have offered to teach online without incentives? Please explain.
- What is the most promising aspect of teaching languages online? Please explain.
- What is the most difficult aspect? Please explain.

Information on Online Language Instructor Training Received

Institution of original training:
Degree program:
Dates of your participation in your degree program (Month: _____ 20__ to Month: _____ 20__)
Modes of delivery of original online training (F2F/blended/online):
Dates of original training sessions to teach online (approximate semesters/years in which you received this kind of training during your degree

program; please indicate if this training was integrated throughout your training program): _____

- How many courses that you took in your degree program involved substantial training (more than 20 percent of the time) for teaching online?
- Other than formal coursework, what other kinds of training to teach online were offered by your degree program/institution (e.g., workshops, demonstrations, talks, mentoring)? Did you participate in any of those training opportunities? Please explain.
- How many years have you taught languages online since your original training in your degree program?

Please provide thoughtful, extended answers to the following questions:

- Considering the demands of your current teaching position and your experience teaching online at your current institution, in retrospect do you believe that your original online training program adequately prepared you to meet those demands? Please explain.
  - In what ways did it prepare you well?
  - What could your original online training in your degree program have done to prepare you better for the demands of your current position? Please explain.
  - In your degree program, what would an ideal training to teach online look like? Please explain.
- In retrospect, was there a sufficient amount of time invested in training future teachers in your degree program to teach online? Please explain.
- Did your degree program offer a mentoring program, and did you participate in it to receive assistance from a teacher more experienced with teaching online? Please explain.
- Was there enough supervisor/administrator support for trainees during the training process? Please explain.
- Was the online teaching training you received provided by your department/unit or by the university at large, or both? Please explain.
- Since graduating from your degree program, have you taken further training in teaching online? Please explain.
- What format did this supplemental training take (a full course or workshops at conferences or educational institutions)? Please explain.
- How did the quality of this supplemental training compare to that you received in your degree program? Please explain.

- Do you currently feel confident using technology to teach languages online? Please explain.
  - If not, what further training do you need and in what areas? Please explain.
- Do you stay current with CALL literature, belong to professional organizations that hold conferences that feature sessions on teaching online (e.g., CALICO, EuroCALL, TESOL, ACTFL, IALL), and regularly attend conferences and workshops on teaching online? Please explain.
- What resources do you consult if you want to do some self-directed learning in CALL or teaching languages online? Please explain.
- Do you currently belong to online language teaching communities that serve as a source of support or mentoring? Please explain.
- Do you currently mentor language teachers learning to teach online? Please explain.
- Do you have any other comments that would be useful for your degree program's institution to understand about the online training you received?

Supervisor Assessment of Online Language Instructor Training Program

To infuse the training/assessment cycle (Tobin, Mandernach, and Taylor 2015) for online language instructors with helpful information to improve the training element in this reiterative evaluation system, supervisors need to make periodic assessments of the effectiveness of those programs.

To gauge the efficacy of these training programs, supervisors can study the results of the questionnaires filled out by instructors for their formative, summative, and retrospective evaluations of their training programs (above). Supervisors can also carry out their own evaluations of the training program using questionnaires, interviews, and focus groups with all language supervisors and online language instructors that can incorporate versions of the reflection questions below.

If the training was created and delivered by the departmental supervisors, as part of their own self-evaluations, these faculty trainers can also make observations on how they perceive the effectiveness of various elements of the training programs they offer, what training challenges they faced, and how they overcame them. If the online instructor training was provided outside the language department (e.g., university-wide general online training), supervisors should be given the opportunity to advise departmental administrators concerning the strengths and weaknesses of the training programs and the need for further training of departmental online language instructors.

In addition, results of evaluations of online instructor training from faculty trainees and from supervisors' training evaluations at the micro level of evaluation can form part of the body of information sent to departmental administrators for their meso-level annual evaluations or evaluations for promotion and tenure for tenured/tenure-track faculty supervisors (see Gruba et al. 2016 for more extensive definitions of micro, meso, and macro levels of program evaluation).

Rubric for Supervisor Evaluation of Online Language Instructor Training

The supervisor evaluation on the online language instructor training consists of a summary of the instructor formative, summative, and retrospective evaluations of their training (see questions just below) as well as supervisors' own reflective assessment of that training.

- Data from Instructor Formative Evaluations: What strengths and weaknesses of the training program for online language instructors were identified by trainees throughout their training? Was instructor feedback on strengths and weakness of the training program from formative evaluations used to adjust the training throughout the semester? What aspects were changed? What aspects still need to be changed? Please explain.
- Data from Instructor Summative Post-Training Evaluations: What strengths and weaknesses of the training program for online language instructors were identified by faculty at the end of their training? Was instructor feedback from the summative evaluations used to adjust the training for the next time it was offered? What aspects were changed? What aspects still need to be changed? Please explain.
- Data from Instructor Retrospective Evaluations: What strengths of the training program for online language instructors were identified by in-service language teachers who graduated from your degree program? According to those in-service teachers, what could have been done better to prepare them for the demands of their current positions regarding teaching with technology/online?

Please provide thoughtful, extended answers to the following questions:

- What university unit created the online instructor training taken by your department's faculty? If your department created the training program, what type of faculty were involved in the creation of this

training and what were their roles (e.g., instructors, [online] language program directors, faculty supervisors)?
- What do you perceive as strengths of the online instructor training program? What aspects need improvement?
- Based on your observation of the instructors' course sites and their interaction with online students,
  - what parts of their training programs were applied successfully by faculty trainees when teaching their online language courses?
  - what part of their training was not applied successfully to their teaching, and to what do you attribute this lack of implementation of knowledge/skills taught in the training sessions?
- What steps can you (as supervisor) take to improve the training for online language instructors in your unit?
- What other training and support needs to be given to online instructors by supervisors?
- Was instructor feedback used to adjust the training for the next time it was offered? What aspects were changed? What aspects still need to be changed? Please explain.
- What type of administrative support is needed to improve training programs for online language instructors?
- What specific action plan needs to be set in motion to accomplish this improvement?

Departmental Administrator Assessment of the Online Language Instructor Training Program

Departmental administrators normally carry out summative assessments to know how effective their unit's training programs have been for future language instructors who will be teaching with technology or online. In order to gauge this, they can study the results of the questionnaires filled out by instructors in their formative, summative, and retrospective written evaluations of their training programs and by supervisors who offer the training programs. Departmental administrators can also evaluate the online instructor training program through the use of questionnaires, interviews, and focus groups with supervisors and online language instructors that incorporate versions of the training assessment questions asked of instructors and supervisors.

Administrative evaluations of online language instructor training programs may occur when the department/unit decides to carry out a meso (departmental)-level evaluation for quality control purposes or when the entire language program undergoes macro (institutional)-level evaluation, such as an Academic Program Review by their university's accreditation office or an outside evaluation by a regional accreditation association (e.g., North Central Association of Colleges and Schools). In the process of these accreditation evaluations, units provide a self-assessment of program strengths and weaknesses and invite outside evaluators to come to campus to evaluate the strengths and points for improvement in their programs. The feedback received from these outside evaluations can help administrators carry out continuous improvements in the way they train language instructors to teach online.

More information on language program assessments may be found in Davis and McKay (2018), Gruba et al. (2016), and Healey et al. (2011) (see discussion in chapter 5). A comprehensive assessment instrument for evaluating language programs that integrate technology into their curriculum can be found in Healey et al. (2011, 206–17).

Rubric for Departmental Administrator Evaluation of Online Language Instructor Training

Although the data from instructor formative, summative, and retrospective evaluations of the training were addressed by the supervisors in their training program evaluation (see questions just below), departmental administrators may ask to see primary sources of data that informed those evaluations when writing up their own reflective assessments of the training program for online language instructors.

- Data from Instructor Formative Evaluations: What strengths and weaknesses of the training program for online language instructors were identified by trainees throughout their training? Was instructor feedback on strengths and weaknesses of the training program from formative evaluations used to adjust the training throughout the semester? What aspects were changed? What aspects still need to be changed? Please explain.
- Data from Instructor Summative Evaluations: What strengths and weaknesses of the training program for online language instructors were identified by faculty at the end of their training? Was instructor feedback from the summative evaluations used to adjust the training for the next time it was offered? What aspects were changed? What aspects still need to be changed? Please explain.
- Data from Instructor Retrospective Evaluations: What strengths of the training program for online language instructors were identified

by in-service language teachers who graduated from your degree program? According to those in-service teachers, what could have been done better to prepare them for the demands of their current positions regarding teaching languages online?
- Data from Supervisor Evaluations: What strengths of the online language instructor training program were noted by the supervisor? What aspects still need to be improved? Was instructor feedback used to adjust the training for the next time it was offered? What aspects were changed? What aspects still need to be changed? Please explain. What parts of the training programs were applied successfully or not applied to the instructor's online teaching practices? What factors influenced the successful application of knowledge and skills taught in the training program to instructor pedagogical practice? According to this report, what administrative support and resources are needed to improve the training program for online language instructors?

Please provide thoughtful, extended answers to the following questions:

- Was the training program for online instructors provided by your department or by your college or institution?
    - If the online training was from outside your department, please comment on its quality and its ability to prepare your faculty for teaching their subjects online (strengths, deficiencies).
    - If the training was offered outside your department, what ability do you have to effect changes in that training program? What administrators and resources can you call upon to help make those changes?
- If the online training was offered by your department, please answer the following questions:
    - What are the strengths of your department's online training program?
    - What steps need to be taken to improve the quality of the training program for online language instructors?
    - What other training and support needs to be given to online instructors by supervisors?
    - What administrative support and resources can you offer to facilitate these improvements?
    - What specific action plan needs to be set in motion to accomplish these training improvements?

B-2: STAKEHOLDERS' EVALUATION OF THE ONLINE LANGUAGE INSTRUCTOR ASSESSMENT PROCESS

This section proposes rubrics for the evaluation of the online language instructor assessment process by various stakeholders—the instructors, supervisors, and departmental administrators.

Online Language Instructor Evaluation of the Assessment Process

In order for faculty to feel as though they have a voice in the process used to assess them, efforts must be made to gather information on their view of the procedures used to evaluate their performance. The presence of teacher voice (Egbert et al. 2009) in decision-making reflects the emotional investments (Muhammad and Cruz 2019) administrators must make to facilitate faculty's transition to online teaching environments. Questions similar to the ones provided below can help facilitate the implementation of this investment and develop faculty self-efficacy.

Rubric for Online Language Instructor Evaluation
of the Assessment Process
Please provide thoughtful, extended answers to the following questions:

- How has this assessment process differed from those of your past evaluations?
- What aspects of the current assessment process have been helpful to your professional development as an online teacher (e.g., having input into the creation of the training and the instructor assessment rubric, applying the rubric to your self-assessment, answering reflection questions on the quality of your teaching, participating in post-observation debriefing and goal setting meetings with your mentor, participating in the entire mentoring process itself)?
- What challenges have arisen in the online instructor assessment process and how were those addressed?
- What aspects of this assessment process would you like to change? Please explain the reason for these changes.

Supervisor Evaluation of the Assessment Process

Supervisors need to provide ongoing feedback on the effectiveness of the assessment process that evaluates online language instructors (e.g., ongoing mentoring feedback, post-observation debriefing interviews when self-assessments are compared with mentor assessments, and goal setting). To carry out this assessment, supervisors can rely on online instructor feedback and can also evaluate the online instructor assessment processes through the use of questionnaires, interviews, and focus groups with evaluators and online instructors. The following reflection questions can be used by supervisors to evaluate the online instructor assessment process.

Rubric for Supervisor Evaluation of the Assessment Process
Please provide thoughtful, extended answers to the following questions:

- What are the unique aspects of this online instructor assessment program that distinguishes it from other programs?
- What aspects of this assessment process have helped instructors improve their performance?
- What challenges have arisen in the online instructor assessment process and how were those addressed?
- What aspects of the assessment process still need to be changed? Please explain the need for these changes.
- What changes to the assessment process have been made by those in charge of that process as a result of faculty and evaluator feedback?
- What type of administrative support or resources are needed to effect these changes?

Departmental Administrator Evaluation of the Assessment Process

Departmental administrators need to understand the efficacy of their instructor assessment processes so that necessary changes can be made to improve these evaluation procedures. To carry out this process assessment, administrators can rely on instructors' and supervisors' written reports or may decide to evaluate the processes themselves through the use of questionnaires, interviews, and focus groups with evaluators and online instructors.

Rubric for Departmental Administrator Evaluation
of the Assessment Process
Please provide thoughtful, extended answers to the following questions:

- What are the unique aspects of this online instructor assessment program that distinguishes it from other programs?
- What aspects of the assessment process have helped instructors improve their performance?
- What challenges have arisen in the online instructor assessment process and how were those addressed?
- What aspects of the assessment process still need to be changed? Please explain the need for these changes.
- What changes to the assessment process have been made by those in charge of that process as a result of faculty and evaluator feedback?
- What type of administrative support or resources are you willing to provide to effect these changes?

B-3: STAKEHOLDERS' EVALUATION OF THE ONLINE LANGUAGE INSTRUCTOR MODULAR RUBRIC

The following section proposes rubrics for the evaluation of the Online Language Instructor Modular Rubric (OLIMR) by various stakeholders—the instructors, supervisors, and departmental administrators.

Online Instructor Evaluation of the OLIMR Rubric

As noted in chapter 3, respect for faculty members asked to teach online can be shown by enhancing their agency in the assessment. For instance, administrators can solicit their faculty's collective advice, collaborative problem-solving, and input into the creation of the rubrics that will be used to evaluate the integration and implementation of their training into their own pedagogical practice. Faculty continuous feedback on the effectiveness of the instructor evaluation rubric can be captured with an instrument using questions similar to the ones provided below. This type of administrative emotional investment (Muhammad and Cruz 2019) can help to mitigate faculty resistance to online teaching and to facilitate their taking a leadership role in the process of transitioning to digital pedagogical spaces.

Rubric for Online Language Instructor
Evaluation of the OLIMR Rubric
Please provide thoughtful, extended answers to the following questions about the effectiveness of the OLIMR rubric:

- How well did this rubric help you assess and reflect on your online instruction (your strengths and areas in which you need to improve)?
- What are the strengths of this rubric?
- Which parts of the rubric were confusing or difficult to complete?
- Are the evaluation metrics fair? Do they capture well what you actually do in the course?
- If not, in order to conduct fair evaluations of instructors, what would you change about the rubric?
  - What assessment elements should be added to the rubric?
  - What assessment elements should be modified? In what way?
  - What assessment elements should be omitted?
- Are there areas for which you would like to be recognized that were not represented in this instructor assessment rubric?

Supervisor Evaluation of the OLIMR Rubric

To ensure that instructor evaluation instruments continue to provide relevant and helpful information on the quality of teaching in the department, input from supervisors on the efficacy and appropriateness of those instruments must be gathered periodically. In addition, these stakeholders should have access to instructor written evaluations of those instruments (see above) and can also seek further feedback on those rubrics from evaluators and online instructors through the use of interviews and focus groups. That information can then be used to ensure that the OLIMR evaluation instrument adequately captures the strengths of the online instructor's performance as well as areas in which they need to improve to meet the departmental standards reflected in the OLIMR rubric.

The sample reflection questions below can facilitate the process of gathering assessments of the instructor evaluation rubric from supervisors.

Rubric for Supervisor Evaluation of the OLIMR Rubric
Please provide thoughtful, extended answers to the following questions about the effectiveness of the OLIMR rubric:

- How well did the rubric evaluate the strengths of the instructor?

- How well did the rubric evaluate the areas in which the online instructor needs to improve?
- How well does the rubric capture what you saw in the online course and in teacher performance?
- What are the strengths of the rubric?
- Which parts of the rubric were confusing or difficult to complete for instructors?
- Does the rubric allow for a fair evaluation of instructors?
  - If not, in order to conduct fair evaluations of instructors, what would you change about the rubric?
    —What assessment elements should be added to the rubric?
    —What assessment elements should be modified? In what way?
    —What assessment elements should be omitted?
- Have faculty in charge of creating and maintaining the rubric used instructor and peer mentor feedback as well as their own evaluation of the effectiveness of the OLIMR rubric to make improvements to the rubric over time? In what ways? What still needs to be changed?
- What kind of departmental support and resources would facilitate the updating of the OLIMR rubric to meet faculty and departmental needs?

Departmental Administrator Evaluation of the OLIMR Rubric

As part of macro-level program assessment (e.g., for institutional assessment offices, accreditation), departmental administrators are often asked to provide evidence of the quality of their faculty's teaching. However, the departmental administrators should have confidence that the rubrics being used for faculty assessment are appropriate and capture essential information on the quality of faculty teaching performance.

If the departmental administrators are not the supervisors of the online faculty members, they need to rely on summative reports on the rubric's effectiveness carried out by people who supervise and evaluate faculty on an annual basis. In addition, departmental administrators should have access to instructor written evaluations of those instruments and can also seek further feedback on those rubrics from evaluators and online instructors through the use of interviews and focus groups, in which they can incorporate versions of the reflection questions below. That information can then be used to make sure that the evaluation instrument adequately captures the strengths of the online instructor's performance as well as areas in which they need to improve to meet the departmental standards expressed in the OLIMR rubric.

Administrators of departments that teach many languages, or in which languages form only a component (e.g., humanities departments/units), may also want to explore the efficacy and appropriateness of the instruments used to capture the quality of instruction taking place across the various language groups or subunits of their department. In order to facilitate that process, administrators must be given the opportunity to evaluate the assessment tools used across the board in their units for their effectiveness in capturing online faculty strengths and areas in need of improvement.

Rubric for Departmental Administrator Evaluation of the OLIMR Rubric

Please provide thoughtful, extended answers to the following questions about the effectiveness of the OLIMR rubric:

- Does the instructor assessment rubric appropriately evaluate the fit between instructor behaviors and characteristics and departmental/unit objectives?
- How well did the rubric evaluate the strengths of the instructor?
- How well did the rubric evaluate the instructor's areas in need of improvement?
- How well did the rubric capture what evaluators saw in the online course and teacher performance?
- What are the strengths of the rubric?
- Does the rubric allow for a fair evaluation of instructors?
    - If not, in order to conduct fair evaluations of instructors, what would you change about the rubric?
        —What assessment elements should be added to the rubric?
        —What assessment elements should be modified? In what way?
        —What assessment elements should be omitted?
- Have faculty in charge of creating and maintaining the rubric used instructor and peer mentor feedback as well as their own evaluation of the effectiveness of the OLIMR rubric to make improvements to the rubric over time? In what ways? What still needs to be changed?
- What kind of departmental support and resources could you offer to facilitate the updating of the OLIMR rubric to meet faculty and departmental needs?

APPENDIX C

Online Language Instructor Performance Rubrics

Appendix C contains rubrics to assess online language instructor performance that will be carried out by students, peer mentors/supervisors, departmental administrators, and the instructors themselves.

C-1: Online Language Instructor Student Evaluation Rubric

This student evaluation rubric was informed by research carried out by CTE scholars discussed in chapter 6 of this volume and by several extant student rubrics (Arizona State University 2019a, 2019b, 2019c; Quality Matters 2018).

Online Language Instructor Student Evaluation Rubric

Course:
Instructor:
Semester:
Date of evaluation:

Instructions:
Using the following scale, indicate your level of agreement with the following statements regarding the quality of instruction you received in your online course:

SA = strongly agree; A = agree; N/A= neither agree nor disagree;
D = disagree; SD = strongly disagree

	SA	A	N/A	D	SD
Course Introduction & Overview					

A. **Introduction to Course**
- The learning objectives of the course were clearly stated.[a]
- Minimum technology requirements for the course were clearly stated (e.g., laptop needed, headset).[a]
- Computer skills expected of the learner were clearly stated.[a]
- Expectations for prerequisite courses, knowledge, or competencies were clearly stated.[a]

	SA	A	N/A	D	SD

B. Information on Policies and Resources
- The course provided information on how to find various course components in the course site (e.g., course materials, links to upload assignments, discussion board).
- The course site provided clear information on institutional policies with which the student had to comply (e.g., academic integrity).[a]
- The course site provided clear information on university resources for student success (e.g., academic student support services, accessibility policies and support services).[a]
- The course site provided clear information on course policies with which the student had to comply (e.g., participation, late assignments).[a]
- The course site provided clear information on how to use the online course technologies.
- The course site provided clear information on technical support available to students.
- The course site provided clear guidelines for online interactions (netiquette) (e.g., e-mail, discussion boards).[a]
- The course used a standardized grading system (e.g., rubric, grading scale, grading contract).
- The course grading policies were clearly stated at the beginning of the course and followed throughout the course.[a]
- Course rubrics used to evaluate students were provided to them before they turned in their assignments.

Instructor Presence

- The instructor provided an online introductory video bio about himself/herself at the beginning of the course.[a]
- The instructor maintained regular contact with the online students.
- The instructor encouraged students to contact him/her with questions or concerns they had.
- The instructor responded to online student inquiries within the time frame outlined in the course policies.
- The instructor used a variety of different mediums to interact with students and be visibly present in this online course (e.g., posted announcements in the learning management system [LMS], was active in class discussions, answered student inquiries on discussion boards).
- The instructor gave video/audio feedback to the online class via weekly recaps.

	SA	A	N/A	D	SD
Classroom Community					
• The instructor created a positive online learning environment for students to build a sense of community.					
• The instructor required learners to introduce themselves to other online class members.					
• The instructor provided opportunities for online students to interact with each other and encouraged them to do so (e.g., discussion boards, video conferencing, social media, partnered activities, peer reviews).					
• The instructor managed and facilitated online discussions well (e.g., making sure netiquette rules are observed).					
• The instructor gave clear instructions about how to complete each online assignment (e.g., pair/group conversations, written work, creation of digital products).					
• The instructor clearly stated student expectations for online interaction assignments during pair or group work (e.g., no students should dominate the discussion, contributions by each student should be encouraged).					
Feedback and Assessment					
• The instructor gave feedback on assignments within the time period established in the syllabus.[b]					
• The instructor gave helpful feedback on assignments.[b]					
• The instructor informed students about their grades on a regular basis.[b]					
• Evaluation of student work was based on previously established criteria.[b]					
Course Organization					
• The online course was easy to navigate to find various course elements (e.g., discussion board, course content, instructor feedback on assignments, grades).[c]					
• The online course materials were well organized in a standard format, such as folders, modules, etc.					
• It was easy to find and access my current grades throughout the course.					
Materials, Activities, and Assignments					
• The course provided a variety of online course materials, activities, and assignments (e.g., videos, readings, internet multimedia resources).[a]					
• The online course presentations contributed to student learning.[c]					

	SA	A	N/A	D	SD

- The technological tools/applications used in the course engaged the students (e.g., discussion board, social media, teleconferencing tools [e.g., Zoom]).[a]
- The course provided a variety of online course materials, activities, and assignments (e.g., videos, readings, internet multimedia resources).[a]
- The online course presentations contributed to student learning.[c]
- The technological tools/applications used in the course engaged the students (e.g., discussion board, social media, teleconferencing tools [e.g., Zoom]).[a]
- The class activities and assignments were clearly related to the learning objectives.[a]
- The instructor assigned work that required online students to use internet resources to listen to and read authentic texts (created by native speakers of the target language for other native speakers of that language).
- The instructor assigned online language tasks that resembled real-world conversations (e.g., decision-making, problem solving).
- The instructor encouraged student creativity to use and create online resources (e.g., creating digital stories, wikis, projects).

The Student Experience & Digital Accessibility

- What device or devices did you use to access your course? Choose all that apply: ___ desktop computer ___ laptop computer ___ smartphone ___ tablet ___ other

- Did your institution/language department provide instructional videos to help you with the technology in this online course? ___ No ___ Yes

If yes, were these instructional videos on technology helpful with your online coursework? Please explain.

- What other types of technologies or learning tools would have been useful to you to carry out the work for this course (e.g., other topics that needed to be covered, videos that gave clearer instructions)?

- What were the strengths of this course?
- What were the strengths of the instructor?
- What suggestions would you offer to make this instructor more effective?

---

[a] Quality Matters (2018)
[b] Arizona State University (2019b)
[c] Arizona State University (2019a)
[d] Arizona State University (2019c)

C-2: ONLINE LANGUAGE INSTRUCTOR MODULAR RUBRIC

This OLIMR rubric was informed by research carried out by CTE scholars discussed in chapters 1–7 of this volume.

Online Language Instructor Modular Rubric (OLIMR)		
Instructor name:		
Course number and title:		
What are your responsibilities in this course? (please check all that apply)	Designer	Instructor
Have you taught this online course before? If so, indicate how many semesters.	Yes	No
Do you currently have adequate technological resources to teach online? Please explain.		
Have you completed any online instructor trainings? If so, when/where?		
Background teaching target language: _____ yrs. _____ levels (upper/lower division) Background teaching online: _____ yrs. _____ levels (upper/lower division)		
Evidence: Read the prompts and provide examples or evidence (screenshots or other documentation) from your online course that support your categories. Indicate where this evidence can be found in your online course pages or professional documents.		
Evaluation Categories Developing: No evidence or little evidence of meeting the expectation/standard Performing: Evidence that meets minimum expectation/standard Excelling: Evidence that exceeds expectation/standard		

I. COURSE DESIGN

A. Navigation

1. Instructor follows ADA (Americans with Disabilities Act), university requirements, or both for online course design.
   Evaluation Category: Developing   Performing   Excelling
   Evidence:
2. Instructor organizes course around folders that contain clearly marked content elements (e.g., unit objectives, assignments, instructions, and due dates).
   Evaluation Category: Developing   Performing   Excelling
   Evidence:
3. Instructor creates consistency throughout the course by using a common format (e.g., organizes learning units by weeks, chapters, or themes).
   Evaluation Category: Developing   Performing   Excelling
   Evidence:
4. Instructor considers best practices for Universal Design for Learning.
   Evaluation Category: Developing   Performing   Excelling
   Evidence:

B. Learning Objectives

1. Instructor bases course objectives on best practices and standards (e.g., the ACTFL World Readiness Standards for Learning Languages, career-readiness standards, National Association of Colleges and Employers [NACE], Partnership for the Twenty-First Century [P21]).
   Evaluation Category: Developing   Performing   Excelling
   Evidence:
2. Instructor creates learning objectives that are measurable and observable.
   Evaluation Category: Developing   Performing   Excelling
   Evidence:
3. Instructor creates learning objectives that are level appropriate.
   Evaluation Category: Developing   Performing   Excelling
   Evidence:
4. Instructor writes learning objectives in a way that learners can understand what is expected of them.
   Evaluation Category: Developing   Performing   Excelling
   Evidence:

C. Course Materials (e.g., textbooks, videos, podcasts, articles)

1. Instructor uses course materials that directly facilitate the acquisition of course objectives.
   Evaluation Category: Developing   Performing   Excelling
   Evidence:
2. Instructor uses course materials that are current and adapted for online learning.
   Evaluation Category: Developing   Performing   Excelling
   Evidence:
3. Instructor uses a variety of pedagogical material in the course (e.g., PowerPoint presentations, videos, podcasts, Web pages, discussion boards, social media).
   Evaluation Category: Developing   Performing   Excelling
   Evidence:

4. Instructor uses digital learning materials that provide authentic input to students (e.g., current newspaper articles, videos, podcasts, web pages, blog and social media posts from the target culture)
   Evaluation Category: Developing   Performing   Excelling
   Evidence:

D. Course Activities

1. Instructor incorporates task-based instruction that reflects real-world activities (e.g., problem solving, project-based learning).
   Evaluation Category: Developing   Performing   Excelling
   Evidence:
2. Instructor varies the course activities (e.g., essays, exams, presentations, group work) to meet the needs of learners with diverse learning styles.
   Evaluation Category: Developing   Performing   Excelling
   Evidence:
3. Instructor provides activities that require oral or written asynchronous online interactions in the target language.
   Evaluation Category: Developing   Performing   Excelling
   Evidence:
4. Instructor provides activities that require oral or written synchronous online interactions in the target language.
   Evaluation Category: Developing   Performing   Excelling
   Evidence:

II. ONLINE WORLD LANGUAGE TEACHING

A. Instructor-Learner Communication

1. Instructor posts weekly overview videos that help students to navigate upcoming course assignments.
   Evaluation Category: Developing   Performing   Excelling
   Evidence:
2. Instructor maintains regular communication with students via personal e-mails, course announcements, and virtual office hours.
   Evaluation Category: Developing   Performing   Excelling
   Evidence:
3. Instructor responds to students' e-mails within a twenty-four-hour time frame.
   Evaluation Category: Developing   Performing   Excelling
   Evidence:
4. Instructor regularly works with online mentor to clarify questions about course content and policies.
   Evaluation Category: Developing   Performing   Excelling
   Evidence:

B. Instructor Clarification of Course Content

1. Instructor clarifies common questions/mistakes for each learning unit/module.
   Evaluation Category: Developing   Performing   Excelling
   Evidence:

2. Instructor directs students to the proper resource to resolve issues related to the learning management system (LMS) platform, course content, and courseware.
   Evaluation Category: Developing Performing Excelling
   Evidence:
3. Instructor regularly creates content videos regarding grammar and other course learning objectives.
   Evaluation Category: Developing Performing Excelling
   Evidence:

C. Development of Communicative Competence

1. Oral Interpretive Mode: Instructor provides level-appropriate oral input in the target language so that learners understand, interpret, and analyze what they hear or view on a variety of topics.
   Evaluation Category: Developing Performing Excelling
   Evidence:
2. Written Interpretive Mode: Instructor provides level-appropriate written input in the target language so that learners understand, interpret, and analyze what they read on a variety of topics.
   Evaluation Category: Developing Performing Excelling
   Evidence:
3. Oral Presentational Mode: Instructor provides opportunities for learners to use their target language speaking skills to present information, concepts, and ideas to inform, explain, persuade, and narrate on a variety of topics using appropriate media and adapting to various audiences of listeners, readers, or viewers.
   Evaluation Category: Developing Performing Excelling
   Evidence:
4. Written Presentational Mode: Instructor provides opportunities for learners to use their target language writing skills to present information, concepts, and ideas to inform, explain, persuade, and narrate on a variety of topics using appropriate media and adapting to various audiences of listeners, readers, or viewers.
   Evaluation Category: Developing Performing Excelling
   Evidence:
5. Interpersonal Mode (oral/signed): Instructor provides opportunities for learners to converse and collaborate with others in the target language in order to interact and negotiate meaning in spoken or signed conversations to share information, reactions, feelings, and opinions (e.g., virtual meetings, gaming, project-based learning).
   Evaluation Category: Developing Performing Excelling
   Evidence:
6. Interpersonal Mode (written): Instructor provides opportunities for learners to collaborate with others in the target language in order to interact and negotiate meaning in written conversations to share information, reactions, feelings, and opinions (e.g., chats, discussion boards, blog posts and reactions, gaming, project-based learning).
   Evaluation Category: Developing Performing Excelling
   Evidence:

D. Making Connections and Comparisons across Languages and Cultural Products, Practices, and Perspectives

1. Making Connections: Instructor provides opportunities for learners to build, reinforce, and expand their knowledge of other disciplines while using the language to develop critical thinking and to solve problems creatively.
   Evaluation Category: Developing   Performing   Excelling
   Evidence:
2. Acquiring Information and Diverse Perspectives: Instructor provides opportunities for learners to access and evaluate information and diverse perspectives that are available through the language and its cultures.
   Evaluation Category: Developing   Performing   Excelling
   Evidence:
3. Cultural Comparisons: Instructor provides opportunities for learners to recognize, investigate, explain, and reflect on the concept of culture through comparisons of their native and target cultures (e.g., comparisons of cultural perspectives that underlie how world news and events are portrayed in different cultural and linguistic contexts).
   Evaluation Category: Developing   Performing   Excelling
   Evidence:
4. Language Comparisons: Instructor provides opportunities for learners to investigate, explain, and reflect on the nature of language through comparisons of their native and target languages.
   Evaluation Category: Developing   Performing   Excelling
   Evidence:

5. Cultural Products (relating cultural products to perspectives): Instructor provides opportunities for learners to investigate, explain, and reflect on how target culture products (e.g., clothing, food, art, music, architecture, literature) reflect target cultural perspectives.
   Evaluation Category: Developing   Performing   Excelling
   Evidence:
6. Cultural Practices (relating cultural practices to perspectives): Instructor provides opportunities for learners to investigate, explain, and reflect on how target culture practices reflect target cultural perspectives.
   Evaluation Category: Developing   Performing   Excelling
   Evidence:
7. Culture (relating cultural products and practices to perspectives): Instructor provides opportunities for learners to investigate, explain, and reflect on racism, classism, and other discriminatory attitudes in digital media sources.
   Evaluation Category: Developing   Performing   Excelling
   Evidence:

E. Understanding Use of Media Forms by Target Culture(s)

1. Instructor provides opportunities for learners to preview, discuss, and analyze authentic, current media forms developed by the target culture(s).
   Evaluation Category: Developing   Performing   Excelling
   Evidence:

2. Instructor provides opportunities to compare/contrast how digital media is consumed across different cultures.
   Evaluation Category: Developing   Performing   Excelling
   Evidence:
3. Instructor provides opportunities for learners to recognize, discuss, and analyze how the target language is used in digital media in the target culture.
   Evaluation Category: Developing   Performing   Excelling
   Evidence:

F. Integration of Critical Cultural Awareness

1. Instructor provides opportunities for learners to recognize, discuss, analyze the target culture/communities' access to and use of digital media (e.g., access to and use of internet, technology, tools).
   Evaluation Category: Developing   Performing   Excelling
   Evidence:
2. Instructor provides opportunities for learners to recognize, discuss, analyze factors related to digital access and usage across different cultures.
   Evaluation Category: Developing   Performing   Excelling
   Evidence:
3. Instructor provides opportunities for learners to recognize, discuss, and analyze factors that contribute to the social justice challenges faced by marginalized communities across different cultures and to brainstorm solutions to meet those challenges.
   Evaluation Category: Developing   Performing   Excelling
   Evidence:

G. Community Building

1. Instructor provides learners with an understanding of netiquette and appropriate online behavior.
   Evaluation Category: Developing   Performing   Excelling
   Evidence:
2. School Communities of Practice: Instructor is "present" throughout the course and offers opportunities for learners to interact with him/her (i.e., virtual office hours, learner conferences).
   Evaluation Category: Developing   Performing   Excelling
   Evidence:
3. School Communities of Practice: Instructor facilitates opportunities for learners to interact and collaborate with other learners in the course (e.g., collaborative projects, online discussions).
   Evaluation Category: Developing   Performing   Excelling
   Evidence:
4. Local and Global Communities of Practice: Instructor provides opportunities for learners to use the language beyond the classroom to interact and collaborate in their community and the globalized world (e.g., telecollaboration, virtual exchanges).
   Evaluation Category: Developing   Performing   Excelling
   Evidence:
5. Lifelong Learning: Instructor provides opportunities for learners to set goals and reflect on their progress in using languages for enjoyment, enrichment, and advancement.
   Evaluation Category: Developing   Performing   Excelling
   Evidence:

III. FEEDBACK AND ASSESSMENT

A. Feedback

1. Instructor provides timely quality feedback for the entire class when general issues, questions, and concerns arise.
   Evaluation Category: Developing   Performing   Excelling
   Evidence:
2. Instructor provides quality written or oral individual feedback (e.g., feedback using specific examples from learners' work, suggestions for improvement referencing assignment rubrics) when issues, questions, and concerns arise.
   Evaluation Category: Developing   Performing   Excelling
   Evidence:
3. Instructor encourages students to provide peer feedback to each other (e.g., required responses to classmates' work, collaborative projects, shared virtual documents).
   Evaluation Category: Developing   Performing   Excelling
   Evidence:

B. Assessment

1. Instructor demonstrates ability to evaluate learner outcomes systematically and reliably using appropriate rubrics.
   Evaluation Category: Developing   Performing   Excelling
   Evidence:
2. Instructor requires that learners measure their own linguistic, cultural, and professional competencies within the context of the ACTFL World Readiness Standards and the NACE and P21 career-readiness standards (e.g., critical thinking, collaboration, adaptability, intercultural competence).
   Evaluation Category: Developing   Performing   Excelling
   Evidence:
3. Instructor uses a standardized grading system (e.g., rubric, grading scale, grading contract).
   Evaluation Category: Developing   Performing   Excelling
   Evidence:
4. Instructor completes assessments in a timely manner.
   Evaluation Category: Developing   Performing   Excelling
   Evidence:
5. Instructor uses the LMS to post assessment materials (grades, rubrics, feedback) for learners.
   Evaluation Category: Developing   Performing   Excelling
   Evidence:

IV. TECHNOLOGY IN ONLINE LANGUAGE TEACHING

1. Instructor uses interactive software/technologies that facilitate online language learning.
   Evaluation Category: Developing   Performing   Excelling
   Evidence:
2. Instructor can make modifications to the course LMS (e.g., course widgets, online gradebook, digital content).
   Evaluation Category: Developing   Performing   Excelling
   Evidence:

3. Instructor has explored/implemented nonrequired learning tools that enhance their teaching and/or the learners' online experiences.
   Evaluation Category: Developing   Performing   Excelling
   Evidence:
4. Instructor can troubleshoot digital media related to the course (e.g., online textbook, LMS site, Web pages).
   Evaluation Category: Developing   Performing   Excelling
   Evidence:
5. Instructor applies technology appropriately in record-keeping and feedback.
   Evaluation Category: Developing   Performing   Excelling
   Evidence:

V. PROFESSIONAL DEVELOPMENT

A. Program Policies and Standards

1. Instructor provides accommodations for learners with disabilities and other identified issues.
   Evaluation Category: Developing   Performing   Excelling
   Evidence:
2. Instructor communicates learner/course problems to the program director or supervisor in a prompt fashion.
   Evaluation Category: Developing   Performing   Excelling
   Evidence:
3. Instructor attends and actively participates in departmental and program faculty meetings.
   Evaluation Category: Developing   Performing   Excelling
   Evidence:
4. Instructor can independently locate and complete course administration forms related to drop/add, learner evaluations, etc.
   Evaluation Category: Developing   Performing   Excelling
   Evidence:

B. Workshops and Trainings

1. Instructor regularly participates in departmental professional development workshops.
   Evaluation Category: Developing   Performing   Excelling
   Evidence:
2. Instructor regularly participates in college/university professional development workshops.
   Evaluation Category: Developing   Performing   Excelling
   Evidence:
3. Instructor regularly seeks opportunities outside of the university for professional development (e.g., workshops at professional meetings, conferences).
   Evaluation Category: Developing   Performing   Excelling
   Evidence:

C. Instructor's Ability to Evaluate Online Language Teaching

1. Instructor demonstrates ability to self-reflect on the implementation of best practices for digital learning/teaching.
   Evaluation Category: Developing   Performing   Excelling
   Evidence:

2. Instructor demonstrates ability to critically review the online teaching performance of other instructors.
   Evaluation Category: Developing Performing Excelling
   Evidence:
3. Instructor demonstrates ability to mentor peers who teach online.
   Evaluation Category: Developing Performing Excelling
   Evidence:

VI. SELF-REFLECTION QUESTIONS
(answered by instructor being evaluated)

Please provide thoughtful, extended (first-person "I…") answers to the following questions:

1. In which areas of online instruction do you excel? Give concrete examples tied to specific standards in this rubric.
2. In which areas would you like to improve as an instructor? Refer to specific standards in this rubric.
3. What kind of training or administrative support do you need to improve your teaching?
4. Describe a challenge that you faced with an online learner and how you resolved it.
5. What types of technology/assignments would you like to implement in your online course and how would they further student learning or assessment?
6. How well did this rubric help you reflect on your online instruction?
7. Are there areas for which you would like to be recognized that were not represented in the evaluation rubric?

C-3: SUMMARY OF ONLINE LANGUAGE INSTRUCTOR EVALUATION USING THE OLIMR RUBRIC

The points covered here refer to metrics described in the OLIMR rubric. The following is an example of how a program supervisor can highlight specific evaluation points to provide a concise summative evaluation that may be used in instructors' professional portfolios.

Instructor-Learner Communication			
Evaluation Point	Developing	Performing	Excelling
✓ Maintains regular communication with students via personal e-mails, course announcements, and virtual office hours			
✓ Regularly works with online mentor to clarify questions about course content and policies			
✓ Clarifies common questions/mistakes for each learning unit/module			
Comments:			

Development of Communicative and Cultural Competence

Evaluation Point	Developing	Performing	Excelling
✓ Facilitates learners' development of communicative competence in the target language			
✓ Requires learners to make connections and comparisons across languages and cultural products, practices, and perspectives			
✓ Requires learners to analyze factors that challenge marginalized communities and brainstorm solutions			

Comments:

Feedback and Assessment

Evaluation Point	Developing	Performing	Excelling
✓ Gives feedback with specific examples from students' own work			
✓ Regularly uses the university online program rubrics			
✓ Posts feedback and grades in a timely manner (within two weeks of the assignment due date)			

Comments:

Technology in Online Language Teaching

Evaluation Point	Developing	Performing	Excelling
✓ Uses interactive software/technologies that facilitates online language learning			
✓ Applies technology appropriately in record-keeping and feedback			

Comments:

Professional Development and Professionalism

Evaluation Point	Developing	Performing	Excelling
✓ Communicates learner/course problems to the program director or supervisor in a prompt fashion			
✓ Attends and actively participates in faculty meetings and professional development activities			
✓ Demonstrates ability to reflect on teaching and professional development activities			

Comments:

Online Teaching Goal (set by instructor):

Sign below to indicate that this summary has been reviewed and discussed by both the evaluator and instructor.

Instructor Name   Signature/Date

Evaluator Name   Signature/Date

C-4: SUPERVISOR/DEPARTMENTAL ADMINISTRATOR ASSESSMENT OF INSTRUCTORS: REFLECTION QUESTIONS

The following reflection questions were informed by research carried out by CTE scholars discussed in chapter 6 of this volume.

- Does the online instructor's performance meet departmental teaching standards as identified in the OLIMR rubric?
- Did the instructor meet your institution's expectations for professionalism?
- Did the instructor's performance help advance program, departmental, and institutional missions and goals?

- In what areas did the instructor excel?
- In what areas does the instructor need to improve?
- What kind of further training does the instructor need to improve his/her performance?
- In what ways does your evaluation of the instructor's performance agree with the results of student evaluations, instructor self-evaluations, and peer mentor/supervisor evaluations?
- In what ways does your evaluation of the instructor's performance disagree with the results of student evaluations, instructor self-evaluations, and peer mentor/supervisor evaluations? To what do you attribute this discrepancy of opinion?
- What kind of additional administrator support or technological infrastructure is needed / can you provide to facilitate this instructor's improved performance?

C-5: ONLINE LANGUAGE INSTRUCTOR SELF-ASSESSMENT

As noted in chapter 7, self-assessment by online language instructors is a crucial part of their professional development process. By measuring their attainment of departmental standards for teaching languages online, instructors can identify their strengths and areas for improvement.

In the assessment process we have proposed in chapters 7–9, online instructors use both the OLIMR and self-reflection questions to evaluate their own performance. Having both instructors and mentors use the same OLIMR rubric to assess the instructor's performance allows for consistency in the way instructor evaluations are carried out, especially when norming sessions are instituted that allow instructors and mentors to understand how that rubric should be applied.

Being able to use the OLIMR rubric for self-assessments with statements in the third person (e.g., "Instructor facilitates opportunities for learners to interact and collaborate with other learners in the course [e.g., collaborative projects, online discussions]") allows for objectivity and prepares the instructor to use the rubric to assess the performance of others when they become mentors in the future.

After instructors perform this self-assessment, they then meet with their mentors in the post-observation briefing to receive feedback on their performance and compare their OLIMR-based assessment with that carried out by their mentors, and they set goals with their mentors to improve their teaching.

The reflection questions just below can be used by online language instructors as part of this self-evaluation process.

Rubric for Online Language Instructor Self-Evaluation:
Reflection Questions
Please provide thoughtful, extended (first-person "I...") answers to the following questions:

- In which areas of online instruction do you excel? Give concrete examples tied to specific standards in this rubric.
- In which areas would you like to improve as an instructor? Refer to specific standards in this rubric.
- What kind of training, administrative support do you need in order to improve your teaching?
- Describe a challenge that you faced with an online learner and how you resolved it.
- What types of technology/assignments would you like to implement in your online course and how would they further student learning?
- How well did this rubric help you to reflect on your teaching?
- Are there areas for which you would like to be recognized that were not represented in the evaluation rubric?

GLOSSARY

blended teaching: A combination of face-to-face (F2F) and online language teaching.

CALL teacher education (CTE): This term refers to the training of language teachers to teach with technology or to teach completely online in a pedagogically sound manner.

cognitive investment strategies: Strategies used by supervisors to clearly explain to faculty why a certain change is necessary (e.g., technological integration or teaching in online digital formats) (Muhammad and Cruz 2019).

community of inquiry (CoI): A term coined by D. Randy Garrison, Terry Anderson, and Walter Archer (2001) to refer to a framework specifically designed to understand text-based online learning in a CoP. It focuses on three types of teacher presence (cognitive, social, and teaching) that are necessary for successful online interaction.

community of practice (CoP): Jean Lave and Etienne Wenger (1991) coined the term "community of practice" as a mechanism for facilitating learning by belonging (Wenger 1998). Wenger, Richard McDermott, and William Snyder (2002) define CoPs as "groups of people who share a concern, a set of problems or a passion about a topic, and who deepen their knowledge and expertise in this area by interacting on an ongoing basis" (4).

computer-assisted language learning (CALL): Carol Chapelle (2006) defines the field as "the strand of applied linguistics concerned with teaching and learning of second-languages through computer technology" (vii). Although the term originally focused on the use of computers to facilitate language learning, in this volume we use the term more inclusively to also refer to technology-assisted language learning, which would include smartphones, tablets, and so on, as well as computers and laptops.

computer-mediated communication (CMC): Communication that takes place in computer-mediated formats such as e-mail, chat, instant messaging, video conferencing, online forums, and social media.

COVID-19: Coronavirus identified in 2019 that started a global pandemic in early 2020, which caused many educational institutions to move their courses online.

Critical CALL: The application of the tenets of critical pedagogy to CALL.
Critical CTE: The application of the tenets of critical pedagogy to CTE.
critical cultural awareness (CCA): This term is defined by Michael Byram (1997) as the "ability to evaluate critically and on the basis of explicit criteria, perspectives, practices and products in one's own and other cultures and countries" (63).
critical pedagogy: Henry Giroux (2010) defines critical pedagogy as an "educational movement, guided by passion and principle, to help students develop consciousness of freedom, recognize authoritarian tendencies, and connect knowledge to power and the ability to take constructive action."
departmental administrator (DA): An individual in charge of the entire academic unit (department chair, unit head, school director) who carries out meso- and macro-level program evaluations.
ecological approach to CALL/CTE: The study of the uses of technologies for language learning understood within the particular rhetorical and physical environments in which they were implemented (Van Lier 2004).
emotional investment strategies: Strategies that supervisors and administrators use to recognize and respond to their instructors' emotions and life experiences so that faculty feel valued and believe that their concerns are understood (Muhammad and Cruz 2019).
face-to-face (F2F) teaching: Instruction takes place in a physical classroom.
formative assessments: Assessments that provide feedback "to improve the ongoing teaching and learning process (formative evaluation)" (Tobin, Mandernach, and Taylor 2015, 76).
functional investment strategies: Strategies that build capacity among members of an organization (e.g., training language instructors to teach with technology and to teach completely online; Muhammad and Cruz 2019).
investment strategies: Anthony Muhammad and Luis Cruz (2019) propose cognitive, emotional, and functional strategies to facilitate educators' acceptance of changes in an educational institution.
language program director: An individual in charge of administering a language program.
language program evaluation: A process of assessing a program in which information is gathered "to improve and assist an organization in ways that enable people to perform their work more effectively" (Gruba et al. 2016, 11).
macro-level assessment: Evaluations of the administrative unit/department for internal and external accreditation, normally carried out by the institution/university or an outside accreditation association (Gruba et al. 2016).

meso-level assessment: Summative evaluations of instructors, training programs, and assessments, normally carried out by the departmental administrator for instructor annual reviews and promotion/tenure processes as well as for gathering information on the quality of instructor training and assessment in the unit (Gruba et al. 2016).

micro-level assessment: Formative assessments of instructors carried out by peer mentors and formative and summative assessments taking place at the instructor-supervisor level (Gruba et al. 2016).

mobile-assisted language learning (MALL): Learning languages with the aid of mobile devices such as smartphones and tablets.

normalization of CALL: A state in which the ideal of the integration of technology into language teaching is adopted by a departmental culture as a core value and effective actions are taken to turn that integration into a normal, sustainable practice.

online language instructor: An individual who teaches languages online (e.g., tenured/tenure-track faculty, lecturers, instructors, teaching assistants, adjunct faculty).

Online Language Instructor Modular Rubric (OLIMR): The OLIMR is used mostly by instructors and supervisors for micro-level assessments of the quality of an instructor's teaching.

online language program director: An individual in charge of administering an online language program. If this position does not exist per se, this term refers to the faculty member who is supervising the online language instructor.

online language teaching: Internet-based teaching in which the entire course is delivered online in digital spaces.

peer mentor: A more experienced faculty member who enters into a mentoring relationship with a more inexperienced instructor to provide formative assessments of the instructor's progress in their ability to teach languages online.

personal learning environment (PLE): The milieu in which online faculty immerse themselves, which they have created by exploring, collecting, and curating the knowledge they acquire about specific topics (Hanson-Smith 2016).

personal learning network (PLN): CoPs that can be formed with individuals with similar educational interests so that mutual learning can take place (Hanson-Smith 2016).

summative assessments: Assessments that "gauge instructors' overall effectiveness or skill in an online classroom in order to inform their subsequent teaching experience (summative evaluation)" (Tobin, Mandernach, and Taylor 2015, 76).

supervisor: An individual who directly supervises the work of the online language instructor and carries out micro-level evaluations of that instructor (e.g., language program director, online language program director, faculty supervisor).

REFERENCES

Aaker, Jennifer L., and Angela Y. Lee. 2001. "'I' Seek Pleasures and 'We' Avoid Pains: The Role of Self-Regulatory Goals in Information Processing and Persuasion." *Journal of Consumer Research* 28, no. 1: 33–49.

Abedi, Jamal. 2004. "The No Child Left Behind Act and English Language Learners: Assessment and Accountability Issues." *Educational Researcher* 33, no. 1: 4–14.

Alexander, Bryan. 2015. "Digital Storytelling." In *Teaching Online: A Guide to Theory, Research, and Practice,* edited by Claire Howell Major, 224–25. Baltimore: Johns Hopkins University Press.

———. 2020. "How the Coronavirus Will Change Faculty Life Forever." *Chronicle of Higher Education,* May 11, 2020. Accessed April 15, 2020. https://www.chronicle.com/article/how-the-coronavirus-will-change-faculty-life-forever/.

Alexander, Patricia. 2018. "Reframing Black or Ethnic Minority Teachers as Role Models." PhD diss., Goldsmiths, University of London.

Allen, Belinda, Alan Crosky, Emma Yench, Louise Lutze-Mann, Peter Blennerhassett, Rebecca Lebard, Pall Thordarson, and Krystyna Wilk. 2010. "A Model for Transformation: A Trans-Disciplinary Approach to Disseminating Good Practice in Blended Learning in Science Faculty." In *Curriculum, Technology & Transformation for Unknown Future. Proceedings of Ascilite Sydney,* edited by Caroline Steel, Mike Keppell, Philippa Gerbic, and Simon Housego, 36–48. Brisbane, Australia: University of Queensland E-Space. Accessed May 1, 2020. https://pdfs.semanticscholar.org/8a00/60de776f95d06326d8fc7165584f8ee13e96.pdf.

Allen, I. Elaine, and Jeff Seaman. 2011. *Online Report Card: Tracking Online Education in the United States.* Wellesley, MA: Babson College, Babson Survey Research Group.

Allen, Tammy D., Lillian T. Eby, and Elizabeth Lentz. 2006. "Mentorship Behaviors and Mentorship Quality Associated with Formal Mentoring Programs: Closing the Gap between Research and Practice." *Journal of Applied Psychology* 91, no. 3: 567–78.

Allwright, Dick. 2003. "Exploratory Practice: Rethinking Practitioner Research in Language Teaching." *Language Teaching Research* 71, no. 2: 113–41.

Ambrose, Maureen L., and Carol T. Kulik. 1999. "Old Friends, New Faces: Motivation Research in the 1990s." *Journal of Management* 25, no. 3: 231–92.

American Council for the Teaching of Foreign Languages (ACTFL). 2012. "ACTFL Proficiency Guidelines." https://www.actfl.org/resources/actfl-proficiency-guidelines-2012.

———. 2015. "World-Readiness Standards for Learning Languages" (summary document). https://www.actfl.org/resources/world-readiness-standards-learning-languages.

———. 2017. "NCSSFL-ACTFL Can-Do Statements." https://www.actfl.org/publications/guidelines-and-manuals/ncssfl-actfl-can-do-statements.

———. 2019. "Critical and Social Justice Approaches (CSJA)." Alexandria, VA: ACTFL. Accessed September 11, 2020. https://www.actfl.org/connect/special-interest-groups/critical-and-social-justice-approaches.

American Council for the Teaching of Foreign Languages / Council for the Accreditation of Educator Preparation (ACTFL/CAEP). 2013. *ACTFL/CAEP Program Standards for the Preparation of Foreign Language Teachers.* Updated 2015. Accessed March 1, 2020. https://www.actfl.org/sites/default/files/caep/ACTFLCAEPStandards2013_v2015.pdf.

Americans with Disabilities Act. 1990/2008. "American Disabilities Act of 1990, as amended." https://www.ada.gov/pubs/adastatute08.htm.

Anderson, Lorin W., and David R. Krathwohl, eds. 2001. *A Taxonomy for Learning, Teaching, and Assessing: A Revision of Bloom's Taxonomy of Educational Objectives.* Boston: Allyn and Bacon.

Anderson, Monica, and Andrew Perrin. 2018. "Nearly One in Five Teens Can't Always Finish Their Homework Because of the Digital Divide." Pew Research Center, October 26. http://www.pewresearch.org/fact-tank/2018/10/26/nearly-one-in-five-teens-cant-always-finish-their-homework-because-of-the-digital-divide/.

Andrade, Heidi, and Anna Valtcheva. 2009. "Promoting Learning and Achievement through Self-Assessment." *Theory into Practice* 48, no. 1: 12–19.

Arizona State University. 2019a. "Course Instructor Rubric for Student Evaluations: Languages and Cultures." Course materials.

———. 2019b. "Course Instructor Rubric for Student Evaluations: School of International Languages and Cultures." Course materials.

———. 2019c. "Program Rubric for Online Content and Instruction: ASUONLINE." Course materials.

Armstrong, Patricia. 2019. "Bloom's Taxonomy." Center for Teaching, Vanderbilt University. Accessed March 15, 2020. https://cft.vanderbilt.edu/guides-sub-pages/blooms-taxonomy/.

Arnold, Nike. 2017. "Technology and Second Language Teacher Professional Development." In *Language, Education and Technology, Encyclopedia of Language and Education,* vol. 9, edited by Steven Thorne and Stephen May, 1–13. New York: Springer.

Arnold, Nike, and Lara Ducate. 2015. "Contextualized Views of Practices and Competencies in CALL Teacher Education Research." *Language Learning & Technology* 19, no. 1: 1–9.

Arnold, Nike, Lara Ducate, and Lara Lomicka. 2007. "Virtual Communities of Practice in Teacher Education." In *Preparing and Developing Technology-Proficient L2 Teachers,* edited by Margaret Ann Kassen, Roberta Z. Lavine, Kathryn Murphy-Judy, and Martine Peters, 103–32. San Marcos, TX: CALICO.

Arnold, Nike, Lara Ducate, Lara Lomicka, and Gillian Lord. 2005. "Using Computer-Mediated Communication to Establish Social and Supportive Environments in Teacher Education." *CALICO Journal* 22, no. 3: 537–66.

Association of American Colleges & Universities (AACU). n.d. "Intercultural Knowledge and Competence Value Rubric." Accessed March 1, 2019. https://www.aacu.org/sites/default/files/files/VALUE/InterculturalKnowledge.pdf.

Aylett, Robert, and Kenneth Gregory, eds. 2012. *Evaluating Teacher Quality in Higher Education.* Abingdon, UK: Routledge.

Bair, David E., and Mary A. Bair. 2011. "Paradoxes of Online Teaching." *International Journal for the Scholarship of Teaching and Learning* 5, no. 2, art. 10. https://doi.org/10.20429/ijsotl.2011.050210.

Bandura, Albert. 1986. "The Explanatory and Predictive Scope of Self-Efficacy Theory." *Journal of Social and Clinical Psychology* 4, no. 3: 359–73.

———. 1997. *Self-Efficacy: The Exercise of Control.* New York: Freeman.

Bandura, Albert, and Edwin A. Locke. 2003. "Negative Self-Efficacy and Goal Effects Revisited." *Journal of Applied Psychology* 88, no. 1: 87–99.
Barkhuizen, Gary, ed. 2016. *Reflections on Language Teacher Identity Research*. New York: Taylor & Francis.
Barnett, Ronald. 1992. *Improving Higher Education: Total Quality Care*. London: Open University Press.
Başöz, Tutku, and Feryal Çubukçu. 2014. "Pre-Service EFL Teachers' Attitudes towards Computer Assisted Language Learning (CALL)." *Procedia: Behavioral and Social Sciences* 116: 531–35.
Bass, Bernard M. 1981. *Stogdill's Handbook of Leadership: A Survey of Theory and Research*, rev. and exp. ed. New York: Free Press.
Bauer-Ramazani, Christine. 2006. "Training CALL Teachers Online." *Teacher Education in CALL*, edited by Philip Hubbard and Mike Levy, 183–200. Amsterdam: John Benjamins.
———. 2017. "Teacher Training with CALL Online (Distance): A Project- and Standards-Based Approach." In *Language Teacher Education and Technology: Approaches and Practices*, edited by Jeong-Bae Son and Scott Windeatt, 129–52. New York: Bloomsbury.
Bavelas, Janet B., and Eric S. Lee. 1978. "Effects of Goal Level on Performance: A Trade-Off of Quantity and Quality." *Canadian Journal of Psychology/Revue canadienne de psychologie* 32, no. 4: 219–40.
Bax, Stephen. 2003. "CALL- Past, Present and Future." *System* 31, no. 1: 13–28.
Beaven, Tita, Martina Emke, Pauline Ernest, Aline Germain-Rutherford, Regine Hampel, Joseph Hopkins, Mateusz-Milan Stanojevic, and Ursula Stickler. 2010. "Needs and Challenges for Online Language Teachers—The ECML Project DOTS." *Teaching English with Technology—Developing Online Teaching Skills*, Special Issue 10, no. 2: 5–20.
Bejarano, Yael, Tamar Levine, Elite Olshtain, and Judy Steiner. 1997. "The Skilled Use of Interaction Strategies: Creating a Framework for Improved Small-Group Communicative Interaction in the Language Classroom." *System* 25, no. 2: 203–14.
Bell, Amani, and Rosina Mladenovic. 2008. "The Benefits of Peer Observation of Teaching for Tutor Development." *Higher Education* 55, no. 6: 735–52.
Bell, Maureen. 2001. "Supported Reflective Practice: A Program of Peer Observation and Feedback for Academic Teaching Development." *International Journal for Academic Development* 6, no. 1: 29–39.
Belz, Julie A., and Andreas Müller-Hartmann. 2003. "Negotiating German-American Telecollaboration along the Institutional Fault Line." *Modern Language Journal* 87, no. 1: 71–89.
Bennett, Liz. 2014. "Learning from the Early Adopters: Developing the Digital Practitioner." *Research in Learning Technology* 22 (July). https://doi.org/10.3402/rlt.v22.21453.
Bennett, Milton J. 1986. "A Developmental Approach to Training for Intercultural Sensitivity." *International Journal of Intercultural Relations* 10, no. 2: 179–96.
———. 1993. "Towards Ethnorelativism: A Developmental Model of Intercultural Sensitivity (revised)." In *Education for the Intercultural Experience*, edited by R. Michael Paige, 21–71. Yarmouth, ME: Intercultural Press.
———. 2004. "Becoming Interculturally Competent." *Toward Multiculturalism: A Reader in Multicultural Education*. 2nd ed., edited by Jaime S. Wurzel, 62–77. Yarmouth, ME: Intercultural Press.
Bennett, Shirley, and Debra Marsh. 2002. "Are We Expecting Online Tutors to Run Before They Can Walk?" *Innovations in Education and Teaching International* 39, no. 1: 14–20.

Benwell, Bethan, and Elizabeth Stokoe. 2006. *Discourse and Identity*. Edinburgh: Edinburgh University Press.

Berber-McNeill, Rebecca. 2015. "Identifying and Developing Online Language Teaching Skills: A Case Study." Master's thesis, Arizona State University, Tempe.

Berchini, Christina. 2015. "Why Are All the Teachers White?" *Education Week*, April 28, 2015. http://www.edweek.org/tm/articles/2015/04/28/why-are-all-the-teachers-white.html.

Bierema, Laura L., and Sharan B. Merriam. 2002. "E-mentoring: Using Computer Mediated Communication to Enhance the Mentoring Process." *Innovative Higher Education* 26, no. 3: 211–27.

Black, Paul, and Dylan Wiliam. 1998. "Assessment and Classroom Learning." *Assessment in Education: Principles, Policy & Practice* 5, no. 1: 7–74.

———. 2005. *Inside the Black Box: Raising Standards through Classroom Assessment*. London: Granada Learning.

Blake, Robert. 2013. *Brave New Digital Classroom: Technology and Foreign Language Learning*. 2nd ed. Washington, DC: Georgetown University Press.

Blake, Robert, and Gabriel Guillén. 2020. *Brave New Digital Classroom: Technology and Foreign Language Learning*. 3rd ed. Washington, DC: Georgetown University Press.

Blau, Gary. 1993. "Operationalizing Direction and Level of Effort and Testing Their Relationships to Individual Job Performance." *Organizational Behavior and Human Decision Processes* 55, no. 1: 152–70.

Block, David. 2003. *The Social Turn in Second Language Acquisition*. Washington, DC: Georgetown University Press.

Bosch, Ferrán L., and Amalia Creus. 2013. "Prácticas reales en entornos no presenciales: La agencia virtual de comunicación como herramienta de aprendizaje profesionalizador." *Historia y Comunicación Social* 12: 199–211.

Boud, David, and Nancy Falchikov. 1989. "Quantitative Studies of Student Self-Assessment in Higher Education: A Critical Analysis of Findings." *Higher Education* 18, no. 5: 529–49.

Branch, Robert Maribe, and Theodore J. Kopcha. 2014. "Instructional Design Models." In *Handbook of Research on Educational Communications and Technology*, edited by J. Michael Spector, M. David Merrill, Jen Elen, and M. J. Bishop, 77–87. New York: Springer.

Brandl, Klaus. 2002. "Integrating Internet-Based Reading Materials into the Foreign Language Curriculum: From Teacher to Student-Centered Approaches." *Language Learning & Technology* 6, no. 3: 87–107.

Britzman, Deborah P. 1991. "Decentering Discourses in Teacher Education: Or, the Unleashing of Unpopular Things." *Journal of Education* 173, no. 3: 60–80.

Brockett, Ralph G., and Roger Hiemstra. 1991. "A Conceptual Framework for Understanding Self-Direction in Adult Learning." In *Self-Direction in Adult Learning: Perspectives on Theory, Research, and Practice*, 18–33. New York: Routledge.

Brown, Angela H., Ronald M. Cervero, and Juanita Johnson-Bailey. 2000. "Making the Invisible Visible: Race, Gender, and Teaching in Adult Education." *Adult Education Quarterly* 50, no. 4: 273–88.

Brown, John Seely, Allan Collins, and Paul Duguid. 1989. "Situated Cognition and the Culture of Learning." *Educational Researcher* 18, no. 1: 32–42.

Bruner, J. 1966. *Toward a Theory of Instruction*. Cambridge, MA: Harvard University Press.

Bucholtz, Mary, and Kira Hall. 2005. "Identity and Interaction: A Sociocultural Linguistic Approach." *Discourse Studies* 7, no. 4–5: 585–614.

Burgoon, Judee K., and Jerold L. Hale. 1987. "Validation and Measurement of the Fundamental Themes of Relational Communication." *Communications Monographs* 54, no. 1: 19–41.

Burton, D., and C. Weiss. 2008. "The Fundamental Goal Concept: The Path to Process and Performance Success." In *Advances in Sport Psychology. Human Kinetics.* 3rd ed., edited by Thelma S. Horn, 339–75. Champaign, IL: Human Kinetics.

Bustamante, Carolina, and Aleidine J. Moeller. 2013. "The Convergence of Content, Pedagogy and Technology in Online Professional Development for Teachers of German: An Intrinsic Case Study." *CALICO Journal* 30, no. 1: 82–104.

Butterworth, Christina, Jo Henderson, and Caroline Minshell. 2008. "Increase Your Status with Mentoring." *Occupational Health & Wellbeing* 60, no. 37: 29–37.

Button, Scott B., John E. Mathieu, and Dennis M. Zajac. 1996. "Goal Orientation in Organizational Research: A Conceptual and Empirical Foundation." *Organizational Behavior and Human Decision Processes* 67, no. 1: 26–48.

Byram, Michael. 1997. *Teaching and Assessing Intercultural Communicative Competence.* Bristol, UK: Multilingual Matters.

———. 2012. "Language Awareness and (Critical) Cultural Awareness—Relationships, Comparisons, Contrasts." *Language Awareness* 21, no. 102: 5–13.

Caffarella, Rosemary S. 2002. *Planning Programs for Adult Learners: A Practical Guide.* San Francisco, CA: Jossey-Bass.

Canale, Michael, and Merrill Swain. 1980. "Theoretical Bases of Communicative Approaches to Second Language Teaching and Testing." *Applied Linguistics* 1, no. 1: 1–47.

Candy, Philip C. 1991. *Self-Direction for Lifelong Learning. A Comprehensive Guide to Theory and Practice.* San Francisco: Jossey-Bass.

Cappella, Joseph N. 1985. "The Management of Conversations." In *Handbook of Interpersonal Communication,* edited by Mark L. Knapp and Gerald R. Miller, 393–438. Beverly Hills, CA: Sage.

Center for Applied Language Studies (CASLS). 2020. "Lingua Folio Online." Accessed June 1, 2020. https://linguafolio.uoregon.edu/.

Center for Applied Language Studies (CASLS) and Professionals in Education Advancing Research and Language Learning (PEARLL). 2020. "Catalyst: Professional E-Portfolios for Language Educators." Accessed March 1, 2020. https://casls.uoregon.edu/classroom-resources/catalyst-professional-eportfolio/.

Centra, John A. 1976. *Faculty Development Practices in US Colleges and Universities.* Princeton, NJ: Educational Testing Service.

———. 1993. *Reflective Faculty Evaluation: Enhancing Teaching and Determining Faculty Effectiveness. The Jossey-Bass Higher and Adult Education Series.* San Francisco: Jossey-Bass.

Chamberlin, Carla R. 2000. "Nonverbal Behaviors and Initial Impressions of Trustworthiness in Teacher-Supervisor Relationships." *Communication Education* 49, no. 4: 352–64.

Chambers, Andrea, and Stephen Bax. 2006. "Making CALL Work: Towards Normalization." *System* 34, no. 4: 465–79.

Chametzky, Barry. 2019. "The Online World Languages Anxiety Scale (OWLAS)." *Creative Education* 10, no. 1 (January): 59–77. https://www.scirp.org/journal/PaperInformation.aspx?PaperID=89910.

Chang, Chi-Cheng, Kuo-Hung Tseng, and Shi-Jer Lou. 2012. "A Comparative Analysis of the Consistency and Difference among Teacher-Assessment, Student Self-Assessment and Peer-Assessment in a Web-Based Portfolio Assessment Environment for High School Students." *Computers & Education* 58, no. 1: 303–20.

Chang, Lin Chiat, Robert M. Arkin, Frederick T. Leong, Darius K. S. Chan, and Kwok Leung. 2004. "Subjective Overachievement in American and Chinese College Students." *Journal of Cross-Cultural Psychology* 35, no. 2: 152–73.

Chao, Chin-chi. 2006. "How WebQuests Send Technology to the Background: Scaffolding EFL Teacher Professional Development in CALL." In *Teacher Education in CALL*, edited by Phil Hubbard and Mike Levy, 221–34. Amsterdam: John Benjamins.

Chapelle, Carol A. 2001. *Computer Applications in Second Language Acquisition: Foundations for Teaching, Testing and Research*. Cambridge: Cambridge University Press.

———. 2005. "Interactionist SLA Theory in CALL Research." In *CALL Research Perspectives*, edited by Joy L. Egbert and Gina Mikel Petrie, 53–64. Mahwah, NJ: Erlbaum.

———. 2006. "Foreword." In *Teacher Education in CALL*, edited by Philip Hubbard and Mike Levy, vii–viii. Philadelphia: John Benjamins.

Chapelle, Carol A., Mary K. Enright, and Joan Jamieson. 2008. "Does an Argument-Based Approach to Validity Make a Difference?" *Educational Measurement: Issues and Practice* 29, no. 1: 3–13.

Chapelle, Carol A., and Volker Hegelheimer. 2004. "The Language Teacher in the 21st Century." In *New Perspectives on CALL for Second Language Classrooms*, edited by Sandra Fotos and Charles M. Browne, 297–313. Mahwah, NJ: Lawrence Erlbaum.

Chatham-Carpenter, April, and Alexandria Spadaro. 2019. "Growing Pains: Faculty Challenges and Triumphs in Moving a Communication Program Online." *Journal of Educators Online* 16, no. 2. https://www.thejeo.com/archive/2019_16_2~2/chatham_carpenter_spadaro.

Chaudhuri, Sanghamitra, and Rajashi Ghosh. 2012. "Reverse Mentoring: A Social Exchange Tool for Keeping the Boomers Engaged and Millennials Committed." *Human Resource Development Review* 11, no. 1: 55–76. https://doi.org/10.1177%2F1534484311417562.

Chen, Guo-Ming, and William J. Starosta. 2000. "The Development and Validation of the Intercultural Sensitivity Scale." *Human Communication* 3: 1–15.

Chen, Ming-Jer, and Danny Miller. 2011. "The Relational Perspective as a Business Mindset: Managerial Implications for East and West." *Academy of Management Perspectives* 25, no. 3: 6–18.

Cherng, Hua-Yu Sebastian, and Peter F. Halpin. 2016. "The Importance of Minority Teachers: Student Perceptions of Minority versus White Teachers." *Educational Researcher* 45, no. 7: 407–20.

Chickering, Arthur W., and Zelda F. Gamson. 1987. "Seven Principles for Good Practice in Undergraduate Education." *AAHE Bulletin* 3: 7.

Clark, Christine, and Paul Gorski. 2001. "Multicultural Education and the Digital Divide: Focus on Race, Language, Socioeconomic Class, Sex, and Disability." *Multicultural Perspectives* 3, no. 3: 39–44.

Cohen, Peter A. 1981. "Student Ratings of Instruction and Student Achievement: A Meta-Analysis of Multisection Validity Studies." *Review of Educational Research* 51, no. 3: 281–309.

Comas-Quinn, Anna. 2011. "Learning to Teach Online or Learning to Become an Online Teacher: An Exploration of Teacher Experiences in a Blended Learning Course." *ReCall* 23 (Special Issue 3): 218–32.

Compton, Lily K. L. 2009. "Preparing Language Teachers to Teach Language Online: A Look at Skills, Roles and Responsibilities." *Computer Assisted Language Learning* 22, no. 1: 73–99.

Compton, Lily, and Niki Davis. 2010. "The Impact of and Key Elements for a Successful Virtual Early Field Experience." *Contemporary Issues in Technology and Teacher Education* 10, no. 3: 309–37. https://citejournal.org/wp-content/uploads/2016/04/v10i3general1.pdf.

Conover, Georgia Davis, and Jacob C. Miller. 2014. "Teaching Human Geography through Places in the Media: An Exploration of Critical Geographic Pedagogy Online." *Journal of Geography* 113, no. 2: 85–96.

Cope, William, and Mary Kalantzis. 2015. "The Things You Do to Know: An Introduction to the Pedagogy of Multiliteracies." In *A Pedagogy of Multiliteracies: Learning by Design*, edited by Bill Cope and Mary Kalantzis, 1–36. London: Palgrave.

Council of Europe. 2001. *Common European Framework of Reference for Languages: Learning, Teaching, Assessment.* Cambridge: Cambridge University Press.

Cowan, Pamela, P. S. Neil, and E. Winter. 2013. "A Connectivist Perspective of the Transition from Face-to-Face to Online Teaching in Higher Education." *International Journal of Emerging Technologies in Learning* 8, no. 1: 10–19. https://www.online-journals.org/index.php/i-jet/article/download/2346/2518.

Crant, J. Michael. 1996. "The Proactive Personality Scale as a Predictor of Entrepreneurial Intentions." *Journal of Small Business Management* 34, no. 3: 42–49.

Cummins, Patricia W. 2007. "LinguaFolio and Electronic Language Portfolios in Teacher Training." In *Preparing and Developing Technology-Proficient L2 Teachers*, edited by Margaret Ann Kassen, Roberta Z. Lavine, Kathryn Murphy-Judy, and Martine Peters, 321–44. San Marcos, TX: CALICO.

Cunningham, Bryan. 2007. "All the Right Features: Towards an 'Architecture' for Mentoring Trainee Teachers in UK Further Education Colleges." *Journal of Education for Teaching* 33, no. 1: 83–97.

Cutrim Schmid, Euline, and Shona Whyte. 2012. "Interactive Whiteboards in State School Settings: Teacher Responses to Socio-Constructivist Hegemonies." *Language Learning & Technology* 16, no. 2: 65–86.

Dailey-Hebert, Amber, B. Jean Mandernach, Emily Donnelli-Sallee, and Virgil Rusty Norris. 2014. "Expectations, Motivations, and Barriers to Professional Development: Perspectives from Adjunct Instructor Teaching Online." *Journal of Faculty Development* 28, no. 1: 67–82.

Daniels, Jessie. 2015. "'My Brain Database Doesn't See Skin Color' Color-Blind Racism in the Technology Industry and in Theorizing the Web." *American Behavioral Scientist* 59, no. 11: 1377–93.

Dasborough, Marie, Paul Harvey, and Mark J. Martinko. 2011. "An Introduction to Attributional Influences in Organizations." *Group & Organization Management* 36, no. 4: 419–26.

Davies, Bronwyn, and Rom Harré. 1990. "Positioning: The Discursive Production of Selves." *Journal for the Theory of Social Behaviour* 20, no. 1: 43–63.

Davies, Graham. 2012. ICT4LT Web site. In *Information and Communications Technology for Language Teachers* (ICT4LT). Edited by Graham Davies. Slough, Thames Valley University [Online]. http://www.ict4lt.org/en/en_home.htm.

Davis, John McE., and Todd H. McKay, eds. 2018. *A Guide to Useful Evaluation of Language Programs.* Washington, DC: Georgetown University Press.

Debski, Robert. 2006. "Theory and Practice in Teaching Project-Oriented CALL." In *Teacher Education in CALL*, edited by Phil Hubbard and Mike Levy, 99–116. Amsterdam: John Benjamins.

DeShon, Richard P., and Jennifer Z. Gillespie. 2005. "A Motivated Action Theory Account of Goal Orientation." *Journal of Applied Psychology* 90, no. 6: 1096–127.

Desjardins, François, and Martine Peters. 2007. "Single-Course Approach versus a Program Approach to Develop Technological Competencies in Preservice Language Teachers." In *Preparing and Developing Technology-Proficient L2 Teachers*, edited by Margaret Ann Kassen, Roberta Z. Lavine, Kathryn Murphy-Judy, and Martine Peters, 3–22. San Marcos, TX: CALICO.

Dewar, Jacqueline M., and Curtis D. Bennett. 2014. "Understanding SoTL and Its Potential Benefits." In *Doing the Scholarship of Teaching and Learning in Mathematics*, edited by Jacqueline M. Dewar and Curtis D. Bennett, 3–12. Washington, DC: Mathematical Association of America.

Dewey, John. 1938/1988. "Experience in Education." In *John Dewey: The Later Works, 1925–1953*, vol. 13, *1938–1939*, edited by Jo Ann Boydston and Barbara Levine, 1–62. Carbondale: Southern Illinois University Press.

Dickens, Charles. 1859/1999. *A Tale of Two Cities*. Mineola, NY: Dover Thrift Editions.

Dieterich, Raoul, Tanja Endrass, Norbert Kathmann, and Anna Weinberg. 2019. "Unpredictability Impairs Goal-Directed Target Processing and Performance." *Biological Psychology* 142: 29–36.

Donnarumma, David, and Sarah Hamilton. 2018. "Face-to-Face Teacher to Online Course Developer." In *Assessment Across Online Language Education*, edited by Stephanie Link and Jinrong Li, 138–64. Sheffield, England: Equinox.

Downey, Douglas B., and Shana Pribesh. 2004. "When Race Matters: Teachers' Evaluations of Students' Classroom Behavior." *Sociology of Education* 77, no. 4: 267–82.

Downing, Jillian J., and Janet E. Dyment. 2013. "Teacher Educators' Readiness, Preparation, and Perceptions of Preparing Preservice Teachers in a Fully Online Environment: An Exploratory Study." *Teacher Educator* 48, no. 2: 96–109.

Drake, Jackson M. 1984. "Improving Teacher Performance through Evaluation and Supervision." Paper presented at the 68th Annual Meeting of the National Association of Secondary School Principals, Las Vegas, Nevada, February.

Drewelow, Isabelle. 2013. "Exploring Graduate Teaching Assistants' Perspectives on Their Roles in a Foreign Language Hybrid Course." *System* 41, no. 4: 1006–22.

Duensing, Annette, Ursula Stickler, Carolyn Batstone, and Barbara Heins. 2006. "Face-to-Face and Online Interactions—Is a Task a Task?" *Journal of Learning Design* 1, no. 2: 35–45.

Easton, Susan S. 2003. "Clarifying the Instructor's Role in Online Distance Learning." *Communication Education* 52, no. 2: 87–105.

EdSurge. 2014. "How Teachers Are Learning: Professional Development Remix." Accessed March 15, 2020. https://www.edsurge.com/research/guides/how-teachers-are-learning-professional-development-remix.

Egbert, Joy. 2006. "Learning in Context." In *Teacher Education in CALL*, edited by Phil Hubbard and Mike Levy, 27–40. Amsterdam: John Benjamins.

Egbert, Joy, Leslie Huff, Levi McNeil, Cara Preuss, Joanne Sellen. 2009. "Pedagogy, Process, and Classroom Context: Integrating Teacher Voice and Experience into Research on Technology-Enhanced Language Learning." *Modern Language Journal* 93, no. s1: 754–68.

Egbert, Joy, Trena M. Paulus, and Yoko Nakamichi. 2002. "The Impact of CALL Instruction on Classroom Computer Use: A Foundation for Rethinking Technology in Teacher Education." *Language Learning & Technology* 6, no. 3: 108–26.

Eib, B. J., and Pamela Miller. 2006. "Faculty Development as Community Building." *International Review of Research in Open and Distance Learning* 7, no. 2: 1–15.

Elliot, Andrew J., Valary I. Chirkov, Youngmee Kim, and Kennon M. Sheldon. 2001. "A Cross-Cultural Analysis of Avoidance (Relative to Approach) Personal Goals." *Psychological Science* 12, no. 6: 505–10.

Ellis, Rod, Helen Basturkmen, and Shawn Loewen. 2002. "Doing Focus-on-Form." *System* 30, no. 4: 419–32.

Ellis, Roger. 1993. *Quality Assurance for University Teaching*. Bristol, PA: Taylor & Francis.

Ellyson, Steve L., and John F. Dovidio. 1985. "Power, Dominance, and Nonverbal Behavior: Basic Concepts and Issues." In *Power, Dominance, and Nonverbal Behavior*, edited by Steve L. Ellyson and John F. Dovidio, 1–27. New York: Springer.

Elvers, Greg C., Donald J. Polzella, and Ken Graetz. 2003. "Procrastination in Online Courses: Performance and Attitudinal Differences." *Teaching of Psychology* 30, no. 2: 159–62.

Emdin, Christopher. 2016. *For White Folks Who Teach in the Hood . . . and the Rest of Y'all Too: Reality Pedagogy and Urban Education*. Boston: Beacon.

Engin, Marion, and Kara McKeown. 2012. "Cultural Influences on Motivational Issues in Students and Their Goals for Studying at University." *Learning and Teaching in Higher Education: Gulf Perspectives* 9, no. 1: 1–15.

Erez, Miriam. 2010. "Culture and Job Design." *Journal of Organizational Behavior* 31, no. 2/3: 389–400.

Erez, Miriam, and Rikki Nouri. 2010. "Creativity: The Influence of Cultural, Social, and Work Contexts." *Management and Organization Review* 6, no. 3: 351–70.

Ernest, Pauline, Montse Guitert Catasús, Regine Hampel, Sarah Heisner, Joseph Hopkins, Linda Murphy, and Ursula Stickler. 2013. "Online Teacher Development: Collaborating in a Virtual Learning Environment." *Computer Assisted Language Learning* 26, no. 4: 311–33.

Ernest, Pauline, and Joseph Hopkins. 2006. "Coordination and Teacher Development in an Online Learning Environment." *CALICO Journal* 23, no. 3: 551–68.

Eskenazi, Maxine, and Jonathan Brown. 2006. "Teaching the Creation of Software That Uses Speech Recognition." In *Teacher Education in CALL*, edited by Phil Hubbard and Mike Levy, 135–51. Amsterdam: John Benjamins.

Falchikov, Nancy, and David Boud. 1989. "Student Self-Assessment in Higher Education: A Meta-Analysis." *Review of Educational Research* 59, no. 4: 395–430.

Faubert, Violaine. 2009. *School Evaluation: Current Practices in OECD Countries and a Literature Review*. OECD Education Working Papers, No. 42. Paris: OECD Publishing. https://doi.org/10.1787/218816547156.

Fischer, Karin. 2020. "An Admissions Bet Goes Bust: For Colleges That Gambled on Foreign Enrollment, Now What?" *Chronicle of Higher Education*, March 6, 2020, 17–25.

Fisher, Sandra L., and J. Kevin Ford. 1998. "Differential Effects of Learner Effort and Goal Orientation on Two Learning Outcomes." *Personnel Psychology* 51, no. 2: 397–420.

Fox, Shaul, and Yossi Dinur. 1988. "Validity of Self-Assessment: A Field Evaluation." *Personnel Psychology* 41, no. 3: 581–92.

Fox, Susannah. 2011. "Americans Living with Disability and Their Technological Profile." Pew Research Center: Internet and Technology, January 21. https://www.pewinternet.org/2011/01/21/americans-living-with-disability-and-their-technology-profile/.

Frink, Dwight D., and Gerald R. Ferris. 1998. "Accountability, Impression Management, and Goal Setting in the Performance Evaluation Process." *Human Relations* 51, no. 10: 1259–283.

Fuchs, Carolin. 2006. "Exploring German Preservice Teachers' Electronic and Professional Literacy Skills." *ReCALL* 18, no. 2: 174–92.

Fullan, Michael. 2005. *Leadership & Sustainability: System Thinkers in Action.* Thousand Oaks, CO: Corwin.

Gabriel, Martha A., and Kandra J. Kaufield. 2008. "Reciprocal Mentorship: An Effective Support for Online Instructors." *Mentoring & Tutoring: Partnership in Learning* 16, no. 3: 311–27.

Galbraith, Jay R. 1977. *Organization Design.* Boston: Addison Wesley.

———. 2012. "The Evolution of Enterprise Organization Designs." *Journal of Organization Design* 1, no. 2: 1–13.

Gardner, Lee. 2020. "Covid-19 Has Forced Higher Ed to Pivot to Online Learning. Here Are 7 Takeaways So Far." *Chronicle of Higher Education*, March 20, 2020. https://www.chronicle.com/article/covid-19-has-forced-higher-ed-to-pivot-to-online-learning-here-are-7-takeaways-so-far/.

Gardner, William L., and Mark J. Martinko. 1988. "Impression Management in Organizations." *Journal of Management* 14, no. 2: 321–38.

Garrison, D. Randy. 1997. "Self-Directed Learning: Toward a Comprehensive Model." *Adult Education Quarterly* 48, no. 1: 18–33.

Garrison, D. Randy, Terry Anderson, and Walter Archer. 2000. "Critical Inquiry in a Text-Based Environment: Computer Conferencing in Higher Education." *The Internet and Higher Education* 2, nos. 2–3: 87–105. Accessed May 1, 2020. http://cde.athabascau.ca/coi_site/documents/Garrison_Anderson_Archer_Critical_Inquiry_model.pdf.

———. 2001. "Critical Thinking, Cognitive Presence, and Computer Conferencing in Distance Education." *American Journal of Distance Education* 15, no. 1: 7–23.

Gay, Geneva. 2018. *Culturally Responsive Teaching: Theory, Research, and Practice.* New York: Teachers College Press.

Gelfand, Michele J., Jana L. Raver, Lisa Nishii, Lisa M. Leslie, Janetta Lun, Beng Chong Lim, and Lili Duan. 2011. "Differences between Tight and Loose Cultures: A 33-Nation Study." *Science* 332, no. 6033: 1100–1104.

Germain-Rutherford, Aline, and Pauline Ernest. 2015. "European Language Teachers and ICT: Experiences, Expectations, and Training Needs." In *Developing Online Language Teaching: Research-Based Pedagogies and Reflective Practices*, edited by Regine Hampel and Ursula Stickler, 12–27. New York: Palgrave Macmillan.

Gershenson, Seth, Stephen B. Holt, and Nicholas W. Papageorge. 2016. "Who Believes in Me? The Effect of Student–Teacher Demographic Match on Teacher Expectations." *Economics of Education Review* 52: 209–24.

Girons, Alba, and Nicholas Swinehart. 2020. *Teaching Languages in Blended Synchronous Learning Classrooms: Practical Guide.* Washington, DC: Georgetown University Press.

Giroux, Henry A. 2010. "Lessons from Paulo Freire." *Chronicle of Higher Education.* October 17. https://www.chronicle.com/article/lessons-from-paulo-freire/.

———. 2011. *On Critical Pedagogy.* New York: Continuum.

Gleason, Jesse, and Elena Schmitt. 2018. "Evaluating Teacher Tech Literacies Using an Argument-Based Approach." In *Assessment Across Online Language Education*, edited by Stephanie Link and Jinrong Li, 116–37. Bristol, CT: Equinox.

Glynn, Cassandra, Pamela Wesely, and Beth Wassell. 2018. *Words and Actions: Teaching Languages through the Lens of Social Justice.* 2nd ed. Alexandria, VA: ACTFL.

Goertler, Senta, and Paula Winke, eds. 2008. *Opening Doors through Distance Language Education: Principles, Perspectives, and Practices.* San Marcos, TX: CALICO.

Goffman, Erving. 1959. *The Presentation of Self in Everyday Life*. Garden City, NY: Doubleday.
Goldstein, Gary S., and Victor A. Benassi. 2006. "Students and Instructors' Beliefs about Excellent Lecturers and Discussion Leaders." *Research in Higher Education* 47, no. 6: 685–707.
Gollwitzer, Peter M., Heinz Heckhausen, and Heike Ratajczak. 1990. "From Weighing to Willing: Approaching a Change Decision through Pre- or Postdecisional Mentation." *Organizational Behavior and Human Decision Processes* 45, no. 1: 41–65.
González-Lloret, Marta. 2016. *A Practical Guide to Integrating Technology into Task-Based Language Teaching*. Washington, DC: Georgetown University Press.
Gordon, Stephen P. 2003. *Professional Development for School Improvement: Empowering Learning Communities*. London: Pearson.
Graham, Charles, Kursat Cagiltay, Byung-Ro Lim, Joni Craner, and Thomas M. Duffy. 2001. "Seven Principles of Effective Teaching: A Practical Lens for Evaluating Online Courses." *The Technology Source* 30, no. 5: 50.
Graves, Kathleen. 2009. "The Curriculum of Second Language Teacher Education." In *The Cambridge Guide to Second Language Teacher Education*, edited by Anne Burns and Jack C. Richards, 115–24. New York: Cambridge University Press.
Greene, Cara Nicole. 2013. "Computer Assisted Language Learning (CALL) for the Inclusive Classroom." PhD diss., Dublin City University, School of Computing, Dublin, Ireland.
Grgurovic, Maya, and Carol Chapelle. 2007. "Effectiveness of CALL: A Meta-Analysis and Research Synthesis." Paper presented at the Annual Meeting of the Computer Assisted Language Instruction Consortium, San Marcos, Texas. May 2007.
Grimm, Emily Dolci, Trent Kaufman, and Dave Doty. 2014. "Rethinking Classroom Observation." *Educational Leadership* 71, no. 8: 24–29.
Grosbois, Muriel. 2011. "CMC-Based Projects and L2 Learning: Confirming the Importance of Nativisation." *ReCALL* 23, no. 3: 294–310. doi:10.1017/S095834401100019X.
Grouzet, Frederick M. E., Tim Kasser, Aaron Ahuvia, José Miguel Fernández Dols, Youngmee Kim, Sing Lau, Richard M. Ryan, Shaun Saunders, Peter Schmuck, and Kennon M. Sheldon. 2005. "The Structure of Goal Contents across 15 Cultures." *Journal of Personality and Social Psychology* 89, no. 5: 800–816.
Gruba, Paul. 2004. "Computer Assisted Language Learning (CALL)." In *Handbook of Applied Linguistics*, edited by Alan Davies and Catherine Elder, 623–48. Oxford: Blackwell.
———. 2007. "Decoding Visual Elements in Digitized Foreign Newscasts." In *ICT: Providing Choices for Learners and Learning. Proceedings ASCILITE*, Singapore, December 2–5, 2007. https://www.ascilite.org/conferences/singapore07/procs/gruba.pdf.
Gruba, Paul, Mónica S. Cárdenas-Claros, Ruslan Suvorov, and Catherine Rick. 2016. *Blended Language Program Evaluation*. New York: Palgrave Macmillan.
Gruba, Paul, and Don Hinkelman. 2012. *Blending Technologies in Second Language Classrooms*. Basingstoke, UK: Palgrave Macmillan.
Guasch, Teresa, Ibis Alvarez, and Anna Espasa. 2010. "University Teacher Competencies in a Virtual Teaching/Learning Environment: Analysis of a Teacher Training Experience." *Teaching and Teacher Education* 26, no. 2: 199–206.
Guichon, Nicolas. 2009. "Training Future Language Teachers to Develop Online Tutors' Competence through Reflective Analysis." *ReCALL* 21, no. 2: 166–85.
Guichon, Nicolas, and Mirjam Hauck. 2011. "Editorial: Teacher Education Research in CALL and CMC: More in Demand than Ever." *ReCall* 23, no. 3: 187–99.
Hafner, Christoph A., Alice Chik, and Rodney H. Jones. 2015. "Digital Literacies and Language Learning." *Language Learning & Technology* 19, no. 3:1–7.

Hall, Tracey E., Anne Meyer, and David H. Rose, eds. 2012. *Universal Design for Learning in the Classroom: Practical Applications.* New York: Guilford.

Hampel, Regine. 2009. "Training Teachers for the Multimedia Age: Developing Teacher Expertise to Enhance Online Learner Interaction and Collaboration." *Innovation in Language Learning and Teaching* 3, no. 1: 35–50.

Hampel, Regine, and Ursula Stickler. 2005. "New Skills for New Classrooms: Training Tutors to Teach Languages Online." *Computer Assisted Language Learning* 18, no. 4: 311–26.

———. 2015. *Developing Online Language Teaching: Research-Based Pedagogies and Reflective Practices.* New York: Palgrave Macmillan.

Hamre, Bridget K., and Robert C. Pianta. 2005. "Can Instructional and Emotional Support in the First-Grade Classroom Make a Difference for Children at Risk of School Failure?" *Child Development* 76, no. 5: 949–67.

Hannon, John, and Brian D'Netto. 2007. "Cultural Diversity Online: Student Engagement with Learning Technologies." *International Journal of Educational Management* 21, no. 5: 418–32.

Hanson-Smith, Elizabeth. 2006. "Communities of Practice for Pre- and In-Service Teacher Education." In *Teacher Education in CALL*, edited by Philip Hubbard and Mike Levy, 301–16. Philadelphia: John Benjamins.

———. 2016. "Teacher Education and Technology." In *The Routledge Handbook of Language Learning and Technology*, edited by Fiona Farr and Liam Murray, 269–88. New York: Routledge.

Harper, Dennis O. 1985. *Computer Education for Developing Nations.* Eugene: University of Oregon.

Harris, Ben M., and Martha N. Ovando. 1992. "Collaborative Supervision and the Developmental Evaluation of Teaching." *Journal of School Administrators Association of New York State* 23, no. 1: 12–18.

Harrison, Chris. 2009. "Assessing the Impact of Assessment for Learning 10 Years On." *Curriculum Management*, November: 4–10.

Hart, Sandra G., and Lowell E. Staveland. 1988. "Development of NASA-TLX (Task Load Index): Results of Empirical and Theoretical Research." *Advances in Psychology* 52: 139–83.

Hartley, Kendall, and Lisa D. Bendixen. 2001. "Educational Research in the Internet Age: Examining the Role of Individual Characteristics." *Educational Researcher* 30, no. 9: 22–26.

Headlam-Wells, Jenny, Julian Gosland, and Jane Craig. 2006. "Beyond the Organisation: The Design and Management of E-Mentoring Systems." *International Journal of Information Management* 26, no. 5: 372–85.

Healey, Deborah, Elizabeth Hanson-Smith, Philip Hubbard, Sophie Ioannou-Georgiou, Greg Kessler, and Paige Ware. 2011. *TESOL Technology Standards: Description, Implementation, Integration.* Alexandria, VA: TESOL, Inc.

Healey, Deborah, Volker Hegelheimer, Phil Hubbard, Sophie Ioannou-Georgiou, Greg Kessler, and Paige Ware. 2008. *TESOL Technology Standards Framework.* Alexandria, VA: TESOL.

Healey, Deborah, and Norman Johnson. 2009. "A Place to Start in Selecting Software." *CAELL Journal* 8. Originally published 1997/98, updated 2009. https://www.deborahhealey.com/cj_software_selection.html.

Hegelheimer, Volker. 2006. "When the Technology Course Is Required." In *Teacher Education in CALL*, edited by Phil Hubbard and Mike Levy, 117–33. Amsterdam: John Benjamins.

Heine, Steven J., Shinobu Kitayama, Darrin R. Lehman, Toshitake Takata, Eugene Ide, Cecilia Leung, and Hisaya Matsumoto. 2001. "Divergent Consequences of Success and Failure in Japan and North America: An Investigation of Self-Improving Motivations and Malleable Selves." *Journal of Personality and Social Psychology* 81, no. 4: 599–615.

Heine, Steven J., Darrin R. Lehman, Hazel Rose Markus, and Shinobu Kitayama. 1999. "Is There a Universal Need for Positive Self-Regard?" *Psychological Review* 106, no. 4: 766–94.

Helm, Francesca. 2015. "Critical CALL." In *Proceedings of the 2015 EuroCALL Conference*, edited by Francesca Helm, Linda Bradley, Marta Guarda, and Sylvie Thouesny, 1–6. Research-publishing.net. https://doi.org/10.14705/rpnet.2015.000300.

Herman, Jennifer Heather. 2012. "Faculty Development Programs: The Frequency and Variety of Professional Development Programs Available to Online Instructors." *Journal of Asynchronous Learning Networks* 16, no. 5: 87–106.

Herman, Jennifer, Ellen Osmundson, and David Silver. 2010. *Capturing Quality in Formative Assessment Practice: Measurement Challenges*. Report No. 770. Los Angeles: University of California, National Center for Research on Evaluation, Standards, and Student Testing.

Hickey, Daniel T. 1997. "Motivation and Contemporary Socio-Contructivist Institutional Perspectives." *Educational Psychologist* 32, no. 3: 175–93.

Hill, Janette R., and Michael J. Hannafin. 2001. "Teaching and Learning in Digital Environments: The Resurgence of Resource-Based Learning." *Educational Technology Research and Development* 49, no. 3: 37–52.

Hofstede, Geert. 1980. "Culture and Organizations." *International Studies of Management & Organization* 10, no. 4: 15–41.

———. 2001. *Culture's Consequences: Comparing Values, Behaviors, Institutions and Organizations across Nations*. Thousand Oaks, CA: Sage.

Holland, Barbara A., and Sherril B. Gelman. 1998. "The State of the 'Engaged Campus': What Have We Learned about Building and Sustaining University-Community Partnerships?" *AAHE Bulletin* 51: 3–6.

Hollenbeck, John R., Charles R. Williams, and Howard J. Klein. 1989. "An Empirical Examination of the Antecedents of Commitment to Difficult Goals." *Journal of Applied Psychology* 74, no. 18: 105–19.

Hong, Kwang Hee. 2010. "CALL Teacher Education as an Impetus for L2 Teachers in Integrating Technology." *ReCALL* 22, no. 1: 53–69.

hooks, bell. 1994. *Teaching to Transgress*. New York: Routledge.

Horwitz, Elaine K., Michael B. Horwitz, and Joann Cope. 1986. "Foreign Language Classroom Anxiety." *Modern Language Journal* 70, no. 2: 125–32.

Hoven, Deborah. 2007. "The Affordances of Technology for Student Teachers to Shape Their Teacher Education Experience." In *Preparing and Developing Technology-Proficient L2 Teachers*, edited by Margaret Ann Kassen, Roberta Z. Lavine, Kathryn Murphy-Judy, and Martine Peters, 133–63. San Marcos, TX: CALICO.

Hubbard, Phil. 2008. "CALL and the Future of Language Teacher Education." *CALICO Journal* 25, no. 2: 175–88.

———, ed. 2009. *Computer Assisted Language Learning: Critical Concepts, Volumes I-IV*. New York: Routledge.

———. 2020. "An Invitation to CALL Course." Linguistics Department, Stanford University. Accessed March 1, 2020. https://web.stanford.edu/~efs/callcourse/CALL1.htm.

Hubbard, Phil, and Mike Levy. 2006a. "The Scope of CALL Education." In *Teacher Education in CALL*, edited by Phil Hubbard and Mike Levy, 3–20. Amsterdam: John Benjamins.

———, eds. 2006b. *Teacher Education in CALL*. Amsterdam: John Benjamins.
Hughes, Arthur. 2003. *Testing for Language Teachers*. Stuttgart, Germany: Ernst Klett Sprachen.
Hurd, Stella. 2007. "Anxiety and Non-Anxiety in a Distance Language Learning Environment: The Distance Factor as a Modifying Influence." *System* 35, no. 4: 487–508.
International Society for Technology in Education (ISTE). 2000. *National Education Technology Standards for Teachers*. Eugene, OR: ISTE.
———. 2007. *National Education Technology Standards for Students*. 2nd ed. Eugene, OR: ISTE.
———. 2020. "ISTE Standards for Educators." Accessed March 1, 2020. https://www.iste.org/standards/for-educators.
International Technology Education Association (ITEA). 2003. *Advancing Excellence in Technological Literacy: Student Assessment, Professional Development and Program Standards*. Reston, VA: ITEA.
Ioannou-Georgiou, Sophie, and P. Michaelides. 2001. "MOOtivating English Language Learners in Pastures: New Gateway to the Future." Paper presented at 35th TESOL Conference. St. Louis, Missouri, February–March 2001.
Irani, Tracy, and Ricky Telg. 2001. "Going the Distance: Developing a Model Distance Education Faculty Training Program." *Syllabus* 15, no. 1: 14–16.
———. 2002. "Building It So They Will Come: Assessing Universities' Distance Education Faculty Training and Development Programs." *Journal of Distance Education* 17, no. 1: 36–46.
Jamieson, Joan, Carol Chapelle, and Sherry Preiss. 2005. "CALL Evaluation by Developers, a Teacher, and Students." *CALICO Journal* 23, no. 1: 93–138.
Jaschik, Scott, and Doug Lederman. 2019. *2019 Inside Survey of Faculty Attitudes on Technology: A Study by Inside Higher Ed and Gallup*. Washington, DC: Inside Higher Education.
Jennings, Jack, and Diane Stark Rentner. 2006. "Ten Big Effects of the No Child Left Behind Act on Public Schools." *Phi Delta Kappan* 88, no. 2: 110–13.
Jones, Christopher M., and Bonnie L. Youngs. 2006. "Teacher Preparation for Online Language Instruction." In *Teacher Education in CALL*, edited by Phil Hubbard and Mike Levy, 267–82. Amsterdam: John Benjamins.
Jones, Edward E., and Thane S. Pittman. 1982. "Toward a General Theory of Strategic Self-Presentation." *Psychological Perspectives on the Self* 1, no. 1: 231–62.
June, Audrey Williams. 2020. "The Classroom Goes Digital: Are Colleges Ready to Move Online?" *Chronicle of Higher Education*. March 20, 2020, 11.
Kane, Michael T. 2006. "Validation." In *Educational Measurement*, 4th ed., edited by Robert L. Brennan, 17–64. Westport, CT: Praeger.
———. 2012. "Validating Score Interpretations and Uses." Messick Lecture. Language Testing Research Colloquium, Cambridge, April 2010. *Language Testing* 29, no. 1: 3–17.
Kanfer, Ruth. 1990. "Motivation Theory and Industrial and Organizational Psychology." In *Handbook of Industrial and Organizational Psychology*, edited by Marvin D. Dunnette and Leaetta M. Hough, 75–170. Palo Alto, CA: Consulting Psychologists Press.
———. 1992. "Work Motivation: New Directions in Theory and Research." *International Review of Industrial and Organizational Psychology* 7: 1–53.
Kanfer, Ruth, and Phillip L. Ackerman. 1989. "Motivation and Cognitive Abilities: An Integrative/Aptitude-Treatment Interaction Approach to Skill Acquisition." *Journal of Applied Psychology* 74, no. 4: 657–90.
Kassen, Margaret Ann, Roberta Z. Lavine, Kathryn Murphy-Judy, and Martine Peters, eds. 2007. *Preparing and Developing Technology-Proficient L2 Teachers*. San Marcos, TX: CALICO.

Kasworm, Carol E., and Carroll A. Londoner. 2000. "Adult Learning and Technology." In *Handbook of Adult and Continuing Education*, edited by Arthur L. Wilson and Elisabeth Hayes, 224–41. San Francisco: Jossey-Bass.

Katzell, Raymond A., and Donna E. Thompson. 1990. "Work Motivation: Theory and Practice." *American Psychologist* 45, no. 2: 144–53.

Kebritchi, Mansureh, Angie Lipschuetz, and Lilia Santiague. 2017. "Issues and Challenges for Teaching Successful Online Courses in Higher Education: A Literature Review." *Journal of Educational Technology Systems* 46, no. 1: 4–29.

Keister, Lisa A., and Yanlong Zhang. 2009. "8 Organizations and Management in China." *Academy of Management Annals* 3, no. 1: 377–420.

Kelly, Michael, Michael Grenfell, Rebecca Allan, Christine Kriza, and William McEvoy. 2004. *European Profile for Language Teacher Education: A Frame of Reference. Final Report. A Report to the European Commission Directorate General for Education and Culture*. Brussels, Belgium: European Commission.

Kember, David, Winnie Jenkins, and Kwok Chi Ng. 2004. "Adult Students' Perceptions of Good Teaching as a Function of Their Conceptions of Learning—Part 2. Implications for the Evaluation of Teaching." *Studies in Continuing Education* 26, no. 1: 81–97.

Kentnor, Hope E. 2015. "Distance Education and the Evolution of Online Learning in the United States." *Curriculum and Teaching Dialogue* 17, no. 1: 21–34.

Kersten, Thomas A., and Marla S. Israel. 2005. "Teacher Evaluation: Principals' Insights and Suggestions for Improvement." *Planning and Changing* 36: 47–67.

Kessler, Greg. 2006. "Assessing CALL Teacher Training: What Are We Doing and What Could We Do Better?" In *Teacher Education in CALL*, edited by Philip Hubbard and Mike Levy, 23–44. Philadelphia, PA: John Benjamins.

———. 2007. "Formal and Informal CALL Preparation and Teacher Attitude toward Technology." *Computer Assisted Language Learning* 20, no. 2: 173–88. https://doi.org/10.1080/09588220701331394.

———. 2016. "Technology Standards for Language Teacher Preparation." In *The Routledge Handbook of Language Learning and Technology*, edited by Fiona Farr and Liam Murray, 57–70. New York: Routledge.

Kessler, Greg, and Phil Hubbard. 2017. "Language Teacher Education and Technology." In *The Handbook of Technology and Second Language Teaching and Learning*, edited by Carol A. Chapelle and Shannon Sauro, 278–92. Hoboken, NJ: Wiley.

Killion, Cheryl M., Susan Gallagher-Lepak, and Janet Reilly. 2015. "Are Virtual Classrooms Colorblind?" *Journal of Professional Nursing* 31, no. 5: 407–15. https://doi.org/10.1016/j.profnurs.2015.03.006.

Kim, Kyong-Jee, and Curtis J. Bonk. 2002. "Cross-Cultural Comparisons of Online Collaboration." *Journal of Computer-Mediated Communication* 8, no. 1. https://doi.org/10.1111/j.1083-6101.2002.tb00163.x.

King, Martin Luther, Jr. 1963. "A Letter from a Birmingham Jail." April 16. African Studies Center, University of Pennsylvania. https://www.africa.upenn.edu/Articles_Gen/Letter_Birmingham.html.

King de Ramírez, Carmen. 2019. "Global Citizenship Education through Collaborative Online International Learning in the Borderlands: A Case of the Arizona–Sonora Megaregion." *Journal of Studies in International Education*, November, 1–17.

———. 2020. "The Implications of Academic Culture in Collaborative Online International Learning (COIL): Differences between Mexican and U.S. Students' Perspectives." *Foreign Language Annals*, no. 53: 438–57.

King Ramírez, Carmen, and Barbara Lafford, eds. 2018. *Transferable Skills for the 21st Century: Preparing Students for the Workplace through World Languages for Specific Purposes*. Provo, UT: Sabio.

Klassen, Robert M., Lindsey L. Krawchuk, and Sukaina Rajani. 2008. "Academic Procrastination of Undergraduates: Low Self-Efficacy to Self-Regulate Predicts Higher Levels of Procrastination." *Contemporary Educational Psychology* 33, no. 4: 915–31.

Klenowski, Val. 1995. "Student Self-Evaluation Processes in Student-Centered Teaching and Learning Contexts of Australia and England." *Assessment in Education: Principles, Policy & Practice* 2, no. 2: 145–63.

Knapper, Christopher. 2010. "Changing Teaching Practice: Barriers and Strategies." In *Taking Stock. Research on Teaching and Learning in Higher Education*, edited by Julia Christensen Hughes and Joy Mighty, 229–42. Montreal: McGill-Queen's University Press.

Knowles, Malcolm S. 1975. *Self-Directed Learning: A Guide for Learners and Teachers*. Englewood Cliffs, NJ: Cambridge Adult Education.

———. 1980. "What Is Andragogy." In *The Modern Practice of Adult Education, from Pedagogy to Andragogy*, 40–62. Englewood Cliffs, NJ: Cambridge Adult Education.

Knutson, Sonja. 2003. "Experiential Learning in Second-Language Classrooms." *TESL Canada Journal/ Revue/TESL du Canada* 20, no. 2: 52–64.

Kochan, Frances K., and Susan B. Trimble. 2000. "From Mentoring to Co-Mentoring: Establishing Collaborative Relationships." *Theory into Practice* 39, no. 1: 20–28.

Kolaitis, Marinna, Mary Ann Mahoney, Howard Pomann, and Philip Hubbard. 2006. "Training Ourselves to Train Our Students for CALL." In *Teacher Education in CALL*, edited by Phil Hubbard and Mike Levy, 317–32. Amsterdam: John Benjamins.

Kolb, David A. 1984. *Experiential Learning: Experience as the Source of Learning and Development*. Englewood Cliffs, NJ: Prentice-Hall.

Kouzes, James M., and Barry Z. Posner. 2003. *Credibility: How Leaders Gain and Lose It, Why People Demand It*. San Francisco: Jossey-Bass.

Kramsch, Claire. 1999. "Thirdness: The Intercultural Stance." In *Language, Culture and Identity*, edited by Torben Vestergaard, 41–58. Aalborg, Denmark: Aalborg University Press.

———. 2009. "Third Culture and Language Education." In *Contemporary Applied Linguistics. Vol. 1, Language Teaching and Learning*, edited by Vivian Cook and Li Wei, 233–54. London: Continuum.

———. 2013. "Forward." In *Brave New Digital Classroom: Technology and Foreign Language Learning*, 2nd ed., edited by Robert Blake, xi–xiii. Washington, DC: Georgetown University Press.

Kruger, Justin, Nicholas Epley, Jason Parker, and Zhi-Wen Ng. 2005. "Egocentrism over E-mail: Can We Communicate as Well as We Think?" *Journal of Personality and Social Psychology* 89, no. 6: 925–36.

Kuhn, Thomas S. 1962. *The Structure of Scientific Revolutions*. Cambridge: Cambridge University Press.

Kurman, Jenny. 2001. "Self-Regulation Strategies in Achievement Settings: Culture and Gender Differences." *Journal of Cross-Cultural Psychology* 32, no. 4: 491–503.

Lackey, Karen. 2011. "Faculty Development: An Analysis of Current and Effective Training Strategies for Preparing Faculty to Teach Online." *Online Journal of Distance Learning Administration* 14, no. 5. https://www.westga.edu/~distance/ojdla/winter144/lackey144.html.

Lafford, Barbara. 2009. "Toward an Ecological CALL: Update to Garrett (1991) Trends and Issues." *Modern Language Journal* 93, no. s1: 673–96.

———. 2015a. "Implications of LSP Curricular Design for Mainstream World Language Classes." *CASLS InterCom*, April 27. http://caslsintercom.uoregon.edu/content/19318.

———. 2015b. "The Normalization of CALL: Reflections and Implications for Language Learning and Teacher Education." Plenary address, AZCALL conference, February 21, Tempe, AZ.

———. 2017. "The Evolution of Future Spanish Graduate Programs to Meet Diverse Student Needs." *Hispania* 100, no. 5: 195–201.

———. 2019. "Revisiting the Normalization of CALL: A Critical Pedagogical Approach." *Céfiro: A Journal of the Céfiro Graduate Student Organization* 15: 134–64.

Lafford, Barbara, Ann Abbott, and Darcy Lear. 2014. "Spanish in the Professions and in the Community." *Journal of Spanish Language Teaching* 1, no. 2: 171–86.

Lafford, Barbara, and Carmen King de Ramírez. 2018. "Afterword: The Development of Transferable Skills in WLSP and World Languages Classrooms." In *Transferable Skills for the 21st Century: Preparing Students for the Workplace through World Languages for Specific Purposes*, edited by Carmen King Ramirez and Barbara A. Lafford, 317–52. Provo, UT: Sabio.

Lafford, Barbara, Carmen King de Ramírez, and James Wermers. 2018. "Issues and Challenges of the Assessment of Online Language Teacher Performance." In *Assessment across Online Language Education*, edited by Stephanie Link and Jinrong Li, 93–115. Sheffield, England: Equinox.

Lai, Chun, and Guofang Li. 2011. "Technology and Task-Based Language Teaching: A Critical Review." *CALICO Journal* 28, no. 2, 498–521.

Lai, Chun, Yong Zhao, and Ning Li. 2008. "Designing a Distance Foreign Language Learning Environment." In *Opening Doors through Distance Language Education: Principles, Perspectives, and Practices*, edited by Senta Goertler and Paula Winke, 85–108. San Marcos, TX: CALICO.

Lai, Horng-Ji. 2011. "The Influence of Adult Learners' Self-Directed Learning Readiness and Network Literacy on Online Learning Effectiveness: A Study of Civil Servants in Taiwan." *Journal of Educational Technology & Society* 14, no. 2: 98–106.

Lam, Wing, Xu Huang, and Ed Snape. 2007. "Feedback-Seeking Behavior and Leader-Member Exchange: Do Supervisor-Attributed Motives Matter?" *Academy of Management Journal* 50, no. 2: 348–63.

Lamy, Marie-Noëlle, and Regine Hampel. 2007. *Online Communication for Language Learning and Teaching*. New York: Palgrave.

Lankshear, Colin, and M. Michele Knobel. 2008. "Introduction: Digital Literacies—Concepts, Policies and Practices." In *Digital Literacies: Concepts, Policies and Practices*, edited by Colin Lankshear and Michel Knobel, 1–16. New York: Peter Lang.

Lantolf, James P. 2000. *Sociocultural Theory and Second Language Learning*. Oxford: Oxford University Press.

Lao, Teresa, and Carmen Gonzales. 2005. "Understanding Online Learning through a Qualitative Description of Professors and Students' Experiences." *Journal of Technology and Teacher Education* 13, no. 3: 459–74.

Latham, Gary P., and Craig C. Pinder. 2005. "Work Motivation Theory and Research at the Dawn of the Twenty-First Century." *Annual Review of Psychology* 56: 485–516.

Latham, Gary P., and Lise M. Saari. 1979. "Importance of Supportive Relationships in Goal Setting." *Journal of Applied Psychology* 64, no. 2: 151–56.

Latham, Gary P., Terence R. Mitchell, and Dennis L. Dossett. 1978. "Importance of Participative Goal Setting and Anticipated Rewards on Goal Difficulty and Job Performance." *Journal of Applied Psychology* 63, no. 2: 163–71.

Lave, Jean, and Etienne Wenger. 1991. *Situated Learning: Legitimate Peripheral Participation*. Cambridge: Cambridge University Press.

Leary, Mark R., and Robin M. Kowalski. 1990. "Impression Management: A Literature Review and Two-Component Model." *Psychological Bulletin* 107, no. 1: 34–47.

Lee, June. 2001. "Instructional Support for Distance Education and Faculty Motivation, Commitment, Satisfaction." *British Journal of Educational Technology* 32, no. 2: 153–60.

Leeman, Jennifer, and Lisa Rabin. 2007. "Critical Perspectives for the Literature Classroom." *Hispania* 90, no. 2: 304–15.

Levy, Mike, and Glenn Stockwell. 2006. *CALL Dimensions: Options and Issues in Computer-Assisted Language Learning*. Mahwah, NJ: Erlbaum.

Levy, Mike, Yuping Wang, and Nian-Shing Chen. 2009. "Developing the Skills and Techniques for Online Language Teaching: A Focus on the Process." *Innovation in Learning and Teaching* 3, no. 1: 17–34.

Lewis, Tim. 2006. "When Teaching Is Learning: A Personal Account of Learning to Teach Online." *CALICO Journal* 23, no. 3: 581–99.

Lewis, Tim, and Robert O'Dowd. 2016a. *Online Intercultural Exchange: Policy, Pedagogy, Practice*. New York: Routledge.

———. 2016b. "Online Intercultural Exchange and Foreign Language Learning: A Systematic Review." In *Online Intercultural Exchange: Policy, Pedagogy, Practice*, edited by Robert O'Dowd and Tim Lewis, 21–66. New York: Routledge.

Lightbown, Patsy M., and Nina Spada. 2006. *How Languages Are Learned*. 3rd ed. Oxford: Oxford University Press.

Livingston, Gretchen. 2011. "Latinos and Digital Technology, 2010." Pew Research Center: Hispanic Trends. Accessed February 1, 2020. http://www.pewhispanic.org/2011/02/09/latinos-and-digital-technology-2010/.

Locke, Edwin A. 1968. "Toward a Theory of Task Motivation and Incentives." *Organizational Behavior and Human Performance* 3, no. 2: 157–89.

Locke, Edwin A., and Judith F. Bryan. 1969. "The Directing Function of Goals in Task Performance." *Organizational Behavior and Human Performance* 4, no. 1: 35–42.

Locke, Edwin A., Norman Cartledge, and Jeffrey Koeppel. 1968. "Motivational Effects of Knowledge of Results: A Goal-Setting Phenomenon?" *Psychological Bulletin* 70, no. 6 (Pt. 1): 474–85.

Locke, Edwin A., and Gary P. Latham. 1990. *A Theory of Goal Setting & Task Performance*. Upper Saddle River, NJ: Prentice-Hall.

———. 2002. "Building a Practically Useful Theory of Goal Setting and Task Motivation: A 35-Year Odyssey." *American Psychologist* 57, no. 9: 705–17.

Locke, Edwin A., Karyll N. Shaw, Lise M. Saari, and Gary P. Latham. 1981. "Goal Setting and Task Performance: 1969–1980." *Psychological Bulletin* 90, no. 1: 125–52.

Long, Michael H. 1985. "A Role for Instruction in Second Language Acquisition: Task-Based Language Training." In *Modelling and Assessing Second Language Acquisition*, edited by Kenneth Hyltenstam and Manfred Pienemann, 77–99. Clevedon, Avon: Multilingual Matters.

Looney, Janet. 2011. "Integrating Formative and Summative Assessment: Progress toward a Seamless System?" *OECD Education Working Papers*, No. 58. Paris: OECD Publishing. https://doi.org/10.1787/5kghx3kbl734-en.

Lord, Gillian. 2014. *Language Program Direction: Theory and Practice.* New York: Pearson.
Lucas, Susan. 2015. "Being Present." In *Teaching Online: A Guide to Theory, Research, and Practice,* edited by Claire Howell Major, 186–87. Baltimore: Johns Hopkins University Press.
Lyman, Robert D. 1984. "The Effect of Private and Public Goal Setting on Classroom On-Task Behavior of Emotionally Disturbed Children." *Behavior Therapy* 15, no. 4: 395–402.
Magnan, Sally, Dianna Murphy, and Narek Sahakyan. 2014. *Goals of Collegiate Learners and the Standards for Foreign Language Learning. Modern Language Journal* 98, no. s1:1–293.
Major, Claire Howell. 2015. *Teaching Online: A Guide to Theory, Research, and Practice.* Baltimore: Johns Hopkins University Press.
Marginson, Simon. 2006. "Dynamics of National and Global Competition in Higher Education." *Higher Education* 52, no. 1: 1–39.
Marincovich, Michele, Jack Prostko, and Frederic Stout. 1998. *The Professional Development of Graduate Teaching Assistants.* Bolton, MA: Anker.
Martin, Florence, Kiran Budhrani, Swapna Kumar, and Albert Ritzhaupt. 2019. "Award-Winning Faculty Online Teaching Practices: Roles and Competencies." *Online Learning* 23, no. 1: 184–205.
Martin, Sidney, and Ibis M. Álvarez Valdivia. 2017. "Students' Feedback Beliefs and Anxiety in Online Foreign Language Oral Tasks." *International Journal of Educational Technology in Higher Education* 14, no. 1: 18. https://educationaltechnologyjournal.springeropen.com/articles/10.1186/s41239-017-0056-z.
Martínez-Arboleda, Antonio. 2013. "Discovering Spanish Voices Abroad in a Digital World." In *Case Studies of Openness in the Language Classroom,* edited by Ana Beaven, Anna Comas-Quinn, and Barbara Sawhill, 176–88. Voillans France: Research-Publishing.net.
Marzano, Robert J., Timothy Waters, and Brian A. McNulty. 2005. *School Leadership That Works: From Research to Results.* Alexandria, VA: Association for Supervision and Curriculum Development.
Matthews, Gail. 2007. "The Impact of Commitment, Accountability, and Written Goals on Goal Achievement." Paper presented at the 87th Annual Convention of the Western Psychological Association, Vancouver, BC, Canada, May 2007.
McCann, Thomas M., and Larry R. Johannessen. 2004. "Why Do New Teachers Cry?" *The Clearing House: A Journal of Educational Strategies, Issues and Ideas* 77, no. 4: 138–45.
McCann, Thomas M., Larry R. Johannessen, and Emily Liebenberg. 2010. "Mentoring Matters." *English Journal* 99, no. 6: 86–88.
McCanney, Helena. January 2018. "Focus on Reverse Mentoring." CRANNÓG Collaborative Knowledge Exchange for Learning Impact. January. https://www.teachingandlearning.ie/wp-content/uploads/Crannog_Reverse-Mentoring.pdf.
McDonald, Betty, and David Boud. 2003. "The Impact of Self-Assessment on Achievement: The Effects of Self-Assessment Training on Performance in External Examinations." *Assessment in Education: Principles, Policy & Practice* 10, no. 2: 209–20.
McDonald, Morva A. 2005. "The Integration of Social Justice in Teacher Education: Dimensions of Prospective Teachers' Opportunities to Learn." *Journal of Teacher Education* 56, no. 5: 418–35.
McGee, Patricia, Deborah Windes, and Maria Torres. 2017. "Experienced Online Instructors: Beliefs and Preferred Supports Regarding Online Teaching." *Journal of Computing in Higher Education* 29, no. 2: 331–52.
McGreal, Thomas L. 1983. *Successful Teacher Evaluation.* Alexandria, VA: Association for Supervision and Curriculum Development.

McKeachie, Wilbert James. 1961. *Motivation, Teaching Methods, and College Learning*. Ann Arbor: University of Michigan.

McMurtrie, Beth. 2020. "Teaching in a Crisis: Coronavirus Pushed Professors Online. Can They Keep Up?" *Chronicle of Higher Education*, April 3, 2020, 14–20.

Mehrabian, Albert. 1971. *Silent Messages*. Belmont, CA: Wadsworth.

Mena Marcos, Juan José, Emilio Sánchez, and Harm Tillema. 2008. "Teachers Reflecting on Their Work: Articulating What Is Said about What Is Done." *Teachers and Teaching: Theory and Practice* 14, no. 2: 95–114.

Menges, Robert J. 1985. "Career-Span Faculty Evaluation." *College Teaching* 33: 181–84.

Merriam, Sharan B. 1998. *Qualitative Research and Case Study Applications in Education. Revised and Expanded from "Case Study Research in Education."* San Francisco: Jossey-Bass.

Meskill, Carla J., and Natasha Anthony. 2007. "Learning to Orchestrate Online Instructional Conversations: A Case of Faculty Development for Foreign Language Educators." *Journal of Computer Assisted Language Learning* 20, no. 1: 5–19.

———. 2015. *Teaching Languages Online*. 2nd ed. Tonawanda, NY: Multilingual Matters.

Meskill, Carla, Natasha Anthony, Shannon Hilliker-VanStander, Chi-Hua Tseng, and Jieun You. 2006. "Expert-Novice Teacher Mentoring in Language Learning Technology." In *Teacher Education in CALL*, edited by Phil Hubbard and Mike Levy, 283–99. Amsterdam: John Benjamins.

Meunier, Lydie E. 1998. "Personality and Motivational Factors in Computer-Mediated Foreign Language Communication (CMFLC)." In *New Ways of Learning and Teaching: Focus on Technology and Foreign Language Education*, edited by Judith Muyskens, 145–97. Boston: Heinle and Heinle.

Mezirow, Jack. 1991. *Transformative Dimensions of Adult Learning*. San Francisco: Jossey-Bass.

Michieka, Martha. 2010. "Holistic or Analytic Scoring? Issues in Grading ESL Writing." *TNTESOL* 3: 75–83.

Milheim, William D., and Barbara L. Martin. 1991. "Theoretical Bases for the Use of Learner Control: Three Different Perspectives." *Journal of Computer-Based Instruction* 8, no. 3: 99–105.

Mishan, Freda. 2005. *Designing Authenticity into Language Learning Materials*. Bristol, UK: Intellect.

Mishra, Punyashloke, and Mathew J. Koehler. 2006. "Technological Pedagogical Content Knowledge: A Framework for Teacher Knowledge." *Teachers College Record* 108, no. 6: 1017–54.

Mitchell, Lorianne D., Jennifer D. Parlamis, and Sarah A. Claiborne. 2015. "Overcoming Faculty Avoidance of Online Education: From Resistance to Support to Active Participation." *Journal of Management Education* 39, no. 3: 350–71.

Modern Language Association. 2007. "Foreign Languages and Higher Education: New Structures for a Changed World." https://www.mla.org/Resources/Research/Surveys-Reports-and-Other-Documents/Teaching-Enrollments-and-Programs/Foreign-Languages-and-Higher-Education-New-Structures-for-a-Changed-World.

Mojica-Díaz, Clara, and Lourdes Sánchez-López. 2016. *El mundo hispanohablante contemporáneo: Historia, política, sociedades y culturas*. New York: Routledge.

Montelongo, Ricardo. 2019. "Less Than/More Than: Issues Associated with High-Impact Online Teaching and Learning." *Administrative Issues Journal: Connecting Education, Practice, and Research* 9, no. 1: 68–79.

Montelongo, Ricardo, and Paul William Eaton. 2019. "Strategies and Reflections on Teaching Diversity in Digital Learning Space(s)." In *Care and Culturally Responsive Pedagogy in*

Online Settings, edited by Lydia Kyei-Blankson and Joseph Blankson, 41–62. Hershey, PA: IGI Global.

Moore, Francis X. 1995. "Section 504 and the Americans with Disabilities Act: Accommodating the Learning Disabled Student in the Foreign Language Curriculum." *ADFL Bulletin* 26, no. 2: 59–62.

Moore, Janet C. 2005. *The Sloan Consortium Quality Framework and the Five Pillars*. Needham, MA: Sloan Consortium.

Moore, Michael, and Greg Kearsley. 1996. *Distance Education: A Systems View*. Belmont: Wadsworth.

Morris, Sean Michael. 2018. "Online Learning Shouldn't Be 'Less Than.'" *Inside Higher Ed*, April 4. https://www.insidehighered.com/digital-learning/views/2018/04/04/are-we-giving-online-students-education-all-nuance-and-complexity.

Morrison, Elizabeth Wolfe, Ya-Ru Chen, and Susan Reilly Salgado. 2004. "Cultural Differences in Newcomer Feedback Seeking: A Comparison of the United States and Hong Kong." *Applied Psychology* 53, no. 1: 1–22.

Muhammad, Anthony, and Luis F. Cruz. 2019. *Time for Change: Essential Skills for Transformational School and District Leaders*. Bloomington, IN: Solution Tree.

Murphy, Linda. 2015. "Online Language Teaching: The Learner's Perspective." In *Developing Online Language Teaching: Research-Based Pedagogies and Reflective Practices*, edited by Regine Hampel and Ursula Stickler, 45–62. New York: Palgrave Macmillan.

Murphy-Judy, Kathryn, and Bonnie Youngs. 2006. "Technology Standards for Teacher Education, Credentialing and Certification." In *Teacher Education in CALL*, edited by Phil Hubbard and Mike Levy, 45–60. Amsterdam: John Benjamins.

Nakamura, Lisa, and Peter Chow-White, eds. 2012. *Race after the Internet*. New York: Routledge.

Nasser, Fadia, and Barbara Fresko. 2002. "Faculty Views of Student Evaluation of College Teaching." *Assessment & Evaluation in Higher Education* 27, no. 2: 187–98.

National Association of Colleges and Employers (NACE). 2017. "Career Readiness Competencies: Employer Survey Results." Accessed March 1, 2020. https://www.naceweb.org/career-readiness/competencies/career-readiness-competencies-employer-survey-results/.

National Center for Education Statistics (NCES). 2018. *Digest of Education Statistics: 2018*. https://nces.ed.gov/programs/digest/d18/.

National Survey of Student Engagement (NSSE) Institute. 2019. "Faculty Survey of Student Engagement." Accessed May 15, 2020. https://fsse.indiana.edu/.

Nemiro, Jill. 2004. *Creativity in Virtual Teams: Key Components for Success*. Vol. 6. Hoboken, NJ: Wiley.

Neumann, Daniel K. 2009. "The Effect of Emoticons on Social Connectivity in Online Learning." PhD diss., Capella University, Minneapolis, Minnesota.

New London Group. 1996. "A Pedagogy of Multiliteracies: Designing Social Futures." *Harvard Educational Review* 66, no. 1: 60–92.

Nugent, Kristen, and Theresa Catalano. 2015. "Critical Cultural Awareness in the Foreign Language Classroom." *NECTFL Review* 75: 15–30.

Ocando Finol, María Virginia. 2019. "Film Annotation for the L2 Classroom: A Tech-Mediated Model for Intercultural Learning." PhD diss., Arizona State University, Tempe.

O'Donoghue, Kieran. 2015. "Research and Knowledge Building on Social Supervision." In *Proceedings from Social Work Supervision: Challenges and Advantages*, 13–21. Singapore: Office of the Director of Social Welfare, Ministry of Social and Family Development.

Accessed April 30, 2020. https://www.msf.gov.sg/ODGSW/documents/Publications_from_ODSW_Social_Work_Supervsion.pdf.

O'Dowd, Robert. 2015a. "Supporting In-Service Language Educators in Learning to Telecollaborate." *Language Learning & Technology* 19, no. 1: 64–83.

———. 2015b. "Twenty Years on and Still Reinventing the Wheel: A Critical Review of Telecollaborative Exchange in FL Education." Plenary address, Eurocall conference, August 26, 2015, Padova, Italy. https://www.youtube.com/watch?v=BwCsUAytOB8&t=3308s.

———. 2018. "Moving from Intercultural Contact to Intercultural Learning in Virtual Exchange." Keynote address, Sixth International Conference on the Development and Assessment of Intercultural Competence, January 25, 2018, Tucson, Arizona. https://www.youtube.com/watch?v=hOpsl8NktQw&t=658s.

Olesova, Larissa, and Christine Foster Meloni. 2006. "Designing and Implementing Collaborative Internet Projects in Siberia." In *Teacher Education in CALL*, edited by Phil Hubbard and Mike Levy, 237–49. Amsterdam: John Benjamins.

Open University. n.d. "Teaching and Research." Accessed April 15, 2020. https://www.open.ac.uk/about/main/teaching-and-research.

Organization for Economic Cooperation Development (OECD), Steering Group on Corporate Governance. 2001. *Behind the Corporate Veil: Using Corporate Entities for Illicit Purposes*. Paris, France: OECD Publications.

Ortega, Lourdes. 2017. "New CALL-SLA Interfaces for the 21st Century: Towards Equitable Multilingualism." *CALICO Journal* 34, no. 3: 285–316.

———. 2018. "Studying Multilingualism for Social Justice: A Response to Difficult Times." Paper presented given at SUNY Stony Brook MIC Distinguished Lecture Series, October 17. https://www.youtube.com/watch?v=W717j1ATLf8.

Ory, John C., and Katherine Ryan. 2001. "How Do Student Ratings Measure Up to a New Validity Framework?" *New Directions for Institutional Research* 109: 27–44.

Oskoz, Ana, and Idoia Elola. 2016. "Digital Stories: Bringing Multimodal Texts to the Spanish Writing Classroom." *ReCALL* 28, no. 3: 326–42.

Ovando, Martha N. 1995. "Enhancing Teaching and Learning through Collaborative Supervision." *People in Education* 3, no. 2: 145–55.

———. 2005. "Building Instructional Leaders' Capacity to Deliver Constructive Feedback to Teachers." *Journal of Personnel Evaluation in Education* 18, no. 3: 171–83.

Paas, Fred G. W. C., Jeroen J. G. Van Merriënboer, and Jos J. Adam. 1994. "Measurement of Cognitive Load in Instructional Research." *Perceptual and Motor Skills* 79, no. 1: 419–30. https://doi.org/10.2466%2Fpms.1994.79.1.419.

Pakaslahti, Laura, and Liisa Keltikangas-Jarvinen. 2000. "Comparison of Peer, Teacher and Self-Assessments on Adolescent Direct and Indirect Aggression." *Educational Psychology* 20, no. 2: 177–90.

Palloff, Rena M., and Keith Pratt. 2009. *Assessing the Online Learner: Resources and Strategies for Faculty*. San Francisco: Jossey-Bass.

———. 2011. *The Excellent Online Instructor: Strategies for Professional Development*. Hoboken, NJ: Wiley.

Palmer, Susan B., and Michael L. Wehmeyer. 2003. "Promoting Self-Determination in Early Elementary School: Teaching Self-Regulated Problem-Solving and Goal-Setting Skills." *Remedial and Special Education* 24, no. 2: 115–26.

Pan, Cheng-Chang Sam, and Kelvin Thompson. 2009. "Exploring Dynamics between Instructional Designers and Higher Education Faculty: An Ethnographic Case Study." *Journal of Educational Technology Development and Exchange (JETDE)* 2, no. 1: 33–52.

Partnership for 21st Century Learning (P21). 2019. "Framework for 21st Century Learning." http://static.battelleforkids.org/documents/p21/P21_Framework_Brief.pdf.

Pearson. n.d. "MyLab and Mastering." Accessed April 15, 2020. https://www.pearsonmylabandmastering.com/northamerica/mylanguagelabs/.

Pennie, Iris. 2001. "Managing Quality in Higher Education: An International Perspective on Institutional Assessment and Change." *Quality Assurance in Education* 9, no. 2: 116–17.

Pennington, Martha C. 1996. *The Power of CALL*. Houston: Athelstan.

Perrin, Andrew. 2017. "Digital Gap between Rural and Non-rural America Persists." Pew Research Center. May 19. https://www.pewresearch.org/fact-tank/2019/05/31/digital-gap-between-rural-and-nonrural-america-persists/.

Perry, Edward H., and Michelle L. Pilati. 2011. "Online Learning." *New Directions for Teaching and Learning* 128: 95–104.

Peters, Martine. 2006. "Developing Computer Competencies for Pre-service Language Teachers: Is One Course Enough?" In *Teacher Education in CALL*, edited by Philip Hubbard and Mike Levy, 153–66. Philadelphia, PA: John Benjamins.

Peterson, Kenneth D. 2000. *Teacher Evaluation: A Comprehensive Guide to New Directions and Practices*. Thousand Oaks, CA: Corwin.

Petrides, Lisa A. 2002. "Web-Based Technologies for Distributed (or Distance) Learning: Creating Learning-Centered Educational Experiences in the Higher Education Classroom." *International Journal of Instructional Media* 29, no. 1: 69–77.

Pew Research Center. 2018. "Social Media Fact Sheet." Accessed February 1, 2019. http://www.pewinternet.org/fact-sheet/social-media/.

———. 2019. "Digital Divide." Accessed February 1, 2019. http://www.pewresearch.org/topics/digital-divide/.

Piaget, Jean. 1971. *Psychology and Epistemology: Towards a Theory of Knowledge*. New York: Grossman.

Pica, Teresa, and Catherine Doughty. 1985. "The Role of Group Work in Classroom Second Language Acquisition." *Studies in Second Language Acquisition* 7, no. 2: 233–48.

Pichette, François. 2009. "Second Language Anxiety and Distance Language Learning." *Foreign Language Annals* 42, no. 1: 77–93. https://doi.org/10.1111/j.1944-9720.2009.01009.x.

Pieper, Shannon K. 2004. "The Mentoring Cycle: A Six-Phase Process for Success." *Healthcare Executive* 19, no. 6: 16–28.

Pilling-Cormick, Jane. 1997. "Transformative and Self-Directed Learning in Practice." *New Directions for Adult and Continuing Education* 74: 69–77.

Pinder, Craig C. 2014. *Work Motivation in Organizational Behavior*. New York: Psychology Press.

Pintrich, Paul R. 2004. "A Conceptual Framework for Assessing Motivation and Self-Regulated Learning in College Students." *Educational Psychology Review* 16, no. 4: 385–407.

Planar, Dolors, and Soledad Moya. 2016. "The Effectiveness of Instructor Personalized and Formative Feedback Provided by Instructor in an Online Setting: Some Unresolved Issues." *Electronic Journal of E-Learning* 14, no. 3: 196–203.

Porter, Lyman W., and Edward E. Lawler. 1968. *Managerial Attitudes and Performance*. Homewood, IL: Irwin-Dorsey.

Prensky. Marc. 2001. "Digital Natives, Digital Immigrants." *On the Horizon* 9, no. 5:1–6.
Price, Linda, and Adrian Kirkwood. 2014. "Using Technology for Teaching and Learning in Higher Education: A Critical Review of the Role of Evidence in Informing Practice." *Higher Education Research & Development* 33, no. 3: 549–64.
Prosser, Michael, and Keith Trigwell. 1999. *Understanding Learning and Teaching: The Experience in Higher Education*. London: McGraw-Hill Education.
Purcell, Kevin. 2004. "Making E-Mentoring More Effective." *American Journal of Health-System Pharmacy* 61, no. 3: 284–86.
Pyszczynski, Tom, Jeff Greenberg, Sheldon Solomon, Jamie Arndt, and Jeff Schimel. 2004. "Why Do People Need Self-Esteem? A Theoretical and Empirical Review." *Psychological Bulletin* 130, no. 3: 435–68.
Quality Matters. 2018. "Specific Review Standards from the QM Higher Education Rubric, Sixth Edition." Maryland Online, Inc. Accessed May 22, 2020. https://www.qualitymatters.org/sites/default/files/PDFs/StandardsfromtheQMHigherEducationRubric.pdf.
Quinney, Kayla L., Sara D. Smith, and Quinn Galbraith. 2010. "Bridging the Gap: Self-Directed Staff Technology Training." *Information Technology and Libraries* 29, no. 4: 205–13.
Ramsden, Paul. 1995. *Recognizing and Rewarding Good Teaching in Australian Higher Education: A Project Commissioned by the Committee for the Advancement of University Teaching*. Canberra: Australian Government Publishing Service.
———. 2003. *Learning to Teach in Higher Education*. Abingdon, UK: Routledge.
Redmond, Petrea. 2011. "From Face-to-Face Teaching to Online Teaching: Pedagogical Transitions." In *Proceedings of Ascilite 2011*, 1050–60. Brisbane, Australia: University of Queensland E-Space. https://eprints.usq.edu.au/20400/2/Redmond_ascilite_2011_PV.pdf.
Reinders, Hayo. 2009. "Technology and Second Language Teacher Education." In *The Cambridge Guide to Second Language Teacher Education*, edited by Anne Burns and Jack C. Richards, 230–38. New York: Cambridge University Press.
Reinhardt, Jonathon. 2020. "Social Media for Virtual Exchange: Exploring Relationships between Tools and Practices." Paper presented at the virtual L2DL Symposium: Critical Transnational Dialogue and Virtual Exchange, October 2020.
Rickard, Angela, Françoise Blin, and Christine Appel. 2006. "Training for Trainers: Challenges, Outcomes, and Principles of In-Service Training across the Irish Education System." In *Teacher Education in CALL*, edited by Philip Hubbard and Mike Levy, 203–18. Philadelphia, PA: John Benjamins.
Robb, Thomas N. 2006. "Helping Teachers to Help Themselves." In *Teacher Education in CALL*, edited by Philip Hubbard and Mike Levy, 335–48. Amsterdam: John Benjamins.
Rockoff, Jonah E., and Cecilia Speroni. 2010. "Subjective and Objective Evaluations of Teacher Effectiveness." *American Economic Review* 100, no. 2: 261–66.
Rodesiler, Luke, and Lauren Tripp. 2012. "It's All about Personal Connections: Pre-Service English Teachers' Experiences Engaging in Networked Learning." In *Virtual Professional Development and Informal Learning via Social Networks*, edited by Vanessa P. Dennen and Jennifer B. Myers, 185–202. Hershey, PA: IGI Global.
Rogers, Everett. 1995. *Diffusion of Innovations*. 4th ed. New York: Free Press.
Ross, John A. 2006. "The Reliability, Validity, and Utility of Self-Assessment." *Practical Assessment, Research, and Evaluation* 11, no. 10: 1–13.
Ross, John A., and Catherine D. Bruce. 2007. "Teacher Self-Assessment: A Mechanism for Facilitating Professional Growth." *Teaching and Teacher Education* 23, no. 2: 146–59.

Ross, John A., Anne Hogaboam-Gray, and Carol Rolheiser. 2002. "Student Self-Evaluation in Grade 5–6 Mathematics Effects on Problem-Solving Achievement." *Educational Assessment* 8, no. 1: 43–59.

Ross, John A., and Michelle Starling. 2005. "Effects of Self-Evaluation Training on Achievement and Self-Efficacy in a Computer-Supported Learning Environment." Paper presented at the Annual Meeting of the American Educational Research Association, Montreal, Canada, April 2005. https://legacy.oise.utoronto.ca/research/field-centres/ross/Ross-Starling%20AERA%202005.pdf.

Ross, Steven. 1998. "Self-Assessment in Second Language Testing: A Meta-Analysis and Analysis of Experiential Factors." *Language Testing* 15, no. 1: 1–20.

Sadler, D. Royce. 1989. "Formative Assessment and the Design of Instructional Systems." *Instructional Science* 18, no. 2: 119–44.

Salo, Age, Krista Uibu, Aino Ugaste, and Helena Rasku-Puttonen. 2019. "The Challenge for School-Based Teacher Educators: Establishing Teaching and Supervision Goals." *Teacher Development* 23, no. 5: 609–26.

Samani, Ebrahim, Roselan Baki, and Abu Bakar Razali. 2014. "Pre-Service Teachers' Uses of and Barriers from Adopting Computer-Assisted Language Learning (CALL) Programs." *Advances in Language and Literary Studies* 5, no. 4: 176–83.

Scandura, Terri A., and Betti A. Hamilton. 2002. "Enhancing Performance through Mentoring." In *Psychological Management of Individual Performance*, edited by Sabine Sonnentag, 293–308. Hoboken, NJ: Wiley.

Schneider, Carol, George O. Klemp, and Susan Kastendiek. 1981. *The Balancing Act: Competencies of Effective Teachers and Mentors in Degree Programs for Adults*. Chicago: Center for Continuing Education, University of Chicago.

Schön, Donald A. 1983. *The Reflective Practitioner: How Professionals Think in Action*. New York: Basic Books.

———. 1987. *Educating the Reflective Practitioner*. San Francisco: Jossey-Bass.

Schwartz, Barry, Abraham Tesser, and Evan Powell. 1982. "Dominance Cues in Nonverbal Behavior." *Social Psychology Quarterly* 45, no. 2: 114–20.

Schwartz, Shalom H. 1990. "Individualism-Collectivism: Critique and Proposed Refinements." *Journal of Cross-Cultural Psychology* 21, no. 2: 139–57.

Scott, Donald E., and Shelleyann Scott. 2016. "Leadership for Quality University Teaching: How Bottom-Up Academic Insights Can Inform Top-Down Leadership." *Educational Management Administration & Leadership* 44, no. 3: 511–31.

Scott, Shelleyann, and Kathryn Dixon. 2008. "The Changing Nature of Higher Education in the 21st Century: Developments and Trends." In *The Globalized University Trends and Challenges in Teaching and Learning*, edited by Shelleyann Scott and Kathryn Dixon, 1–17. San Francisco: Black Swan.

Scott, Shelleyann, and Tomayess Issa. 2006. "Lessons Learned from Using Students' Feedback to Inform Academic Teaching Practice." In *15th Annual Teaching Learning Forum. Experience of Learning*. https://clt.curtin.edu.au/events/conferences/tlf/tlf2006/refereed/scott-s.html.

Scott, William. 2002. "Education and Sustainable Development: Challenges, Responsibilities, and Frames of Mind." *Trumpeter* 18, no. 1. http://trumpeter.athabascau.ca/index.php/trumpet/article/download/123/134?inline=1.

Scriven, Michael. 1967. *The Methodology of Evaluation*. New York: Rand McNally.

Sebba, Judy. 2006. "Policy and Practice in Assessment for Learning: The Experience of Selected OECD Countries." In *Assessment and Learning*, edited by John Gardner, 185–96. London: Sage.

Selber, Stuart. 2004. *Multiliteracies for a Digital Age*. Carbondale: Southern Illinois University Press.

Sergiovanni, Thomas J., and Robert J. Starratt. 2001. "Supervision as Professional Development and Renewal." In *Supervision: A Redefinition*, 7th ed., edited by Robert J. Starratt and Thomas Sergiovanni, 309–32. San Francisco: McGraw-Hill.

Shackelford, Jo L., and Marge Maxwell. 2012. "Sense of Community in Graduate Online Education: Contribution of Learner to Learner Interaction." *International Review of Research in Open and Distributed Learning* 13, no. 4: 228–49.

Sharpe, Donald, and Cathy Faye. 2009. "A Second Look at Debriefing Practices: Madness in Our Method?" *Ethics & Behavior* 19, no. 5: 432–47.

Shogren, Karrie A., Michael L. Wehmeyer, and Susan B. Palmer. 2017. "Causal Agency Theory." In *Development of Self-Determination through the Life-Course*, edited by Michael L. Wehmeyer, Karrie A. Shogren, Todd D. Little, and Shane J. Lopez, 55–67. Dordrecht, NL: Springer.

Shor, Ira. 2012. *Empowering Education: Critical Teaching for Social Change*. Chicago: University of Chicago Press.

———. 2014. *When Students Have Power: Negotiating Authority in a Critical Pedagogy*. Chicago: University of Chicago Press.

Shulman, Lee S. 1986. "Those Who Understand: Knowledge Growth in Teaching." *Educational Research* 15, no. 2: 4–14.

Single, Peg Boyle, and Richard M. Single. 2005. "E-mentoring for Social Equity: Review of Research to Inform Program Development." *Mentoring & Tutoring: Partnership in Learning* 13, no. 2: 301–20.

Skehan, Peter. 1998. *A Cognitive Approach to Language Learning*. Oxford: Oxford University Press.

Slaouti, Diane, and Gary Motteram. 2006. "Reconstructing Practice: Language Teacher Education and ICT." In *Teacher Education in CALL*, edited by Philip Hubbard and Mike Levy, 81–98. Amsterdam: John Benjamins.

Smith, Aaron. 2014. "African Americans and Technology Use: A Demographic Portrait." Pew Research Center: Internet and Technology. Accessed February 1, 2019. http://www.pewinternet.org/2014/01/06/african-americans-and-technology-use/.

Smith, Karl A., Sheri D. Sheppard, David W. Johnson, and Roger T. Johnson. 2005. "Pedagogies of Engagement: Classroom-Based Practices." *Journal of Engineering Education* 94, no. 1: 87–101.

Son, Jeong-Bae, and Scott Windeatt. 2017a. *Language Teacher Education and Technology: Approaches and Practices*. New York: Bloomsbury.

———. 2017b. "Teacher Training in Computer-Assisted Language Learning: Voices of Teacher Educators." In *Language Teacher Education and Technology: Approaches and Practices*, edited by Jeong-Bae Son and Scott Windeatt, 1–17. New York: Bloomsbury.

Song, Liyan, and Janette R. Hill. 2007. "A Conceptual Model for Understanding Self-Directed Learning in Online Environments." *Journal of Interactive Online Learning* 6, no. 1: 27–42.

Sorenson, D. Lynn, and Christian Reiner. 2003. "Charting the Uncharted Seas of Online Student Ratings of Instruction." *New Directions for Teaching and Learning* 96: 1–24.

Spiegel, John, and Pavel Machotka. 1974. *Messages of the Body*. New York: Free Press.
Spitzberg, Brian H., and William R. Cupach. 1984. *Interpersonal Communication Competence*. Vol. 4. Thousand Oaks, CA: Sage.
Sproat, Ethan, Dana Lynn Driscoll, and Allen Brizee. 2012. "Elements of Rhetorical Situations." Online Writing Lab. OWL at Purdue University. Accessed April 12, 2015. https://owl.purdue.edu/owl/general_writing/academic_writing/rhetorical_situation/elements_of_rhetorical_situations.html.
Stanojevic, Mateusz-Milan. 2015. "Developing Online Teaching Skills: The DOTS Project." In *Developing Online Language Teaching*, edited by Regine Hampel and Ursula Stickler, 150–62. New York: Springer.
Steeples, Christine, and Christopher Jones, eds. 2012. *Networked Learning: Perspectives and Issues*. Berlin: Springer Science & Business Media.
Stickler, Ursula, and Regine Hampel. 2015. "Transforming Teaching: New Skills for Online Language Learning Spaces." In *Developing Online Language Teaching: Research-Based Pedagogies and Reflective Practices*, edited by Regine Hampel and Ursula Stickler, 63–77. New York: Palgrave Macmillan.
Stockwell, Glenn. 2009. "Teacher Education in CALL: Teaching Teachers to Educate Themselves." *International Journal of Innovation in Language Learning and Teaching* 3, no. 1: 99–112.
Strambi, Antonella, and Eric Bouvet. 2003. "Flexibility and Interaction at a Distance: A Mixed-Mode Environment for Language Learning." *Language Learning & Technology* 7, no. 3: 81–102.
Strauss, Valerie. 2015. "Why We Should Diversity the Overwhelmingly White U.S. Teaching Force—And How." *Washington Post*, May 21, 2015. https://www.washingtonpost.com/news/answer-sheet/wp/2015/05/21/why-we-should-diversify-the-overwhelming-white-u-s-teaching-force-and-how/.
Stronge, James H. 2006. "Teacher Evaluation and School Improvement: Improving the Educational Landscape." In *Evaluating Teaching: A Guide to Current Thinking and Best Practice*, 2nd ed., edited by James H. Stronge, 1–23. Thousand Oaks, CA: Corwin Press.
Sully De Luque, Mary F., and Steven M. Sommer. 2000. "The Impact of Culture on Feedback-Seeking Behavior: An Integrated Model and Propositions." *Academy of Management Review* 25, no. 4: 829–49.
Sun, Susan Yue Hua. 2011. "Online Language Teaching: The Pedagogical Challenges." *Knowledge Management & E-Learning: An International Journal* 3, no. 3: 428–47.
Tai, Shu-Ju Diana. 2015. "From TPACK-in-Action Workshops to Classrooms: ALL Competency Developed and Integrated." *Language Learning & Technology* 19, no. 1: 139–64.
Taras, Maddalena. 2005. "Assessment–Summative and Formative–Some Theoretical Reflections." *British Journal of Educational Studies* 53, no. 4: 466–78.
———. 2008. "Summative and Formative Assessment: Perceptions and Realities." *Active Learning in Higher Education* 9, no. 2: 172–92.
Taras, Vas, Bradley L. Kirkman, and Piers Steel. 2010. "Examining the Impact of Culture's Consequences: A Three-Decade, Multilevel, Meta-Analytic Review of Hofstede's Cultural Value Dimensions." *Journal of Applied Psychology* 95, no. 3: 405–39.
Taubman, Peter Maas. 2010. *Teaching by Numbers: Deconstructing the Discourse of Standards and Accountability in Education*. London: Routledge.
Teaching Tolerance. 2016. "Social Justice Standards: The Teaching Tolerance Anti-Bias Framework." Southern Poverty Law Center. Accessed February 20, 2019. https://www.tolerance

.org/professional-development/social-justice-standards-the-teaching-tolerance-antibias-framework.

Terantino, J., and Edoh Agbehonou. 2012. "Comparing Faculty Perceptions of an Online Development Course: Addressing Faculty Needs for Online Teaching." *Journal of Distance Learning Administration* 15, no. 2: 112–23.

Terborg, James R. 1976. "The Motivational Components of Goal Setting." *Journal of Applied Psychology* 61, no. 5: 613–21.

Teske, Kaitlyn. 2018. "Language Learners' Translanguaging Practices and Development of Performative Competence in Digital Affinity Spaces." PhD diss., Arizona State University, Tempe, Arizona.

TESOL International Association. 2010. "Standards for the Recognition of Initial TESOL Programs in P-12 ESL Teacher Education." Alexandria, VA: TESOL International Association. https://www.tesol.org/docs/default-source/advocacy/the-revised-tesol-ncate-standards-for-the-recognition-of-initial-tesol-programs-in-p-12-esl-teacher-education-(2010-pdf).pdf.

Tesone, Dana V., and Peter Ricci. 2005. "Job Competency Expectations for Hospitality and Tourism Employees: Perceptions of Educational Preparation." *Journal of Human Resources in Hospitality & Tourism* 4, no. 2: 53–64.

Theoharis, George, and Joanne O'Toole. 2011. "Leading Inclusive ELL: Social Justice Leadership for English Language Learners." *Educational Administration Quarterly* 47, no. 4: 646–88.

Thorne, Steve L., and Bryan Smith. 2011. "Second Language Development Theories and Technology-Mediated Language Learning." *CALICO Journal* 28, no. 2: 268–77.

Tobin, Martin J. 2004. "Mentoring: Seven Roles and Some Specifics." *American Journal of Respiratory and Critical Care Medicine* 170, no. 2: 114–17.

Tobin, Thomas J., B. Jean Mandernach, and Ann H. Taylor. 2015. *Evaluating Online Language Teaching: Implementing Best Practices*. San Francisco: Jossey-Bass.

Tochon, François V., and Nathan Jeffrey Black. 2007. "Narrative Analysis of Electronic Portfolios: Preservice Teachers' Struggles in Researching Pedagogically Appropriate Technology Integration." In *Preparing and Developing Technology-Proficient L2 Teachers*, edited by Margaret Ann Kassen, Roberta Z. Lavine, Kathryn Murphy-Judy, and Martine Peters, 295–320. San Marcos, TX: CALICO.

Torres, Julio, and Ellen J. Serafini. 2015. "The Utility of Needs Analysis for Nondomain Expert Instructors in Designing Task-Based Spanish for the Professions Curricula." *Foreign Language Annals* 48, no. 3: 447–72.

Torsani, Simone. 2015. "Linguistics, Procedure and Technique in CALL Teacher Education." *Jalt CALL Journal* 11, no. 2: 155–64.

———. 2016. *CALL Teacher Education: Language Teachers and Technology Integration*. Boston: Sense Publishers.

Turoff, Murray. 2006. "The Changing Role of Faculty and Online Education." *Journal of Asynchronous Learning Networks* 10, no. 4: 129–38.

Ubell, Robert. 2017. "Why Faculty Still Don't Want to Teach Online." *OLC Insights* (blog). Online Learning Consortium. January 10, 2017. Accessed March 15, 2020. https://onlinelearningconsortium.org/faculty-still-dont-want-teach-online/.

United Nations Educational, Scientific, and Cultural Organization (UNESCO). 2008a. *ICT Competency Standards for Teachers: Competency Standards Modules*. Paris: UNESCO.

———. 2008b. *ICT Competency Standards for Teachers: Implementation Guidelines*. Paris: UNESCO.

———. 2008c. *ICT Competency Standards for Teachers: Policy Framework*. Paris: UNESCO.

US Department of Education. 2001. "No Child Left Behind. Elementary and Secondary Education Act." Accessed June 1, 2020. https://www2.ed.gov/nclb/landing.jhtml.

US Department of Education, Office of Educational Technology. n.d. "Funding Digital Learning," Accessed March 18, 2020. https://tech.ed.gov/funding/.

Van De Vliert, Evert, Kan Shi, Karin Sanders, Yongli Wang, and Xu Huang. 2004. "Chinese and Dutch Interpretations of Supervisory Feedback." *Journal of Cross-Cultural Psychology* 35, no. 4: 417–35.

Van Dyck, Cathy, Michael Frese, Markus Baer, and Sabine Sonnentag. 2005. "Organizational Error Management Culture and Its Impact on Performance: A Two-Study Replication." *Journal of Applied Psychology* 90, no. 6: 1228–40.

van Lier, Leo. 2004. *The Ecology and Semiotics of Language Learning*. New York: Klewer Academic.

Van Manen, Max. 1977. "Linking Ways of Knowing with Ways of Being Practical." *Curriculum Inquiry* 6, no. 3: 205–28.

———. 1991. *The Tact of Teaching. The Meaning of Pedagogical Thoughtfulness*. Albany: State University of New York Press.

Van Olphen, Marcela. 2007. "Digital Portfolios: Balancing the Academic and Professional Needs of World Language Teacher Candidates." In *Preparing and Developing Technology-Proficient L2 Teachers*, edited by Margaret Ann Kassen, Roberta Z. Lavine, Kathryn Murphy-Judy, and Martine Peters, 265–94. San Marcos, TX: CALICO.

Vásquez, Camilla. 2004. "'Very Carefully Managed': Advice and Suggestions in Post-Observation Meetings." *Linguistics and Education* 15, no. 1–2: 33–58.

Vásquez, Camilla, and Randi Reppen. 2007. "Transforming Practice: Changing Patterns of Participation in Post-Observation Meetings." *Language Awareness* 16, no. 3: 153–72.

Venables, Louise, and Stephen H. Fairclough. 2009. "The Influence of Performance Feedback on Goal-Setting and Mental Effort Regulation." *Motivation and Emotion* 33, no. 1: 63–74.

Vitale, Anne T. 2010. "Faculty Development and Mentorship Using Selected Online Asynchronous Teaching Strategies." *Journal of Continuing Education in Nursing* 41, no. 12: 549–56.

Vollmer Rivera, Alexis. 2018. "Fostering Social Change through Community Engagement: A Critical Insight into Identity and Strategic Knowledge during Domestic Professional Internships in Spanish for Specific Purposes." PhD diss., Arizona State University.

Vonderwell, Selma, and Sandra Turner. 2005. "Active Learning and Preservice Teachers' Experiences in an Online Course: A Case Study." *Journal of Technology and Teacher Education* 13, no. 1: 65–84.

Vygotsky, Lev S. 1962. *Thought and Language*. Cambridge, MA: MIT Press.

———. 1978. *Mind and Society: The Development of Higher Mental Processes*. Cambridge, MA: Harvard University Press.

W3C Web Accessibility Initiative (WAI). 2019. "Web Content Accessibility Guidelines (WCAG)," WCAG 2.1. Web Accessibility Initiative. Accessed February 15, 2019. https://www.w3.org/WAI/standards-guidelines/wcag/.

Warschauer, Mark. 1996. "Motivational Aspects of Using Computers for Writing and Communication." In *Telecommunication in Foreign Language Learning: Proceedings of the Hawai'i*

Conference, edited by Mark Warschauer, 29–46. Honolulu: University of Hawai'i, Second Language Teaching and Curriculum Center.

———. 2002a. "A Developmental Perspective on Technology in Language Education." *TESOL Quarterly* 36, no. 3: 453–75.

———. 2002b. "Reconceptualizing the Digital Divide." *First Monday* 7, no. 7 (July 1). https://journals.uic.edu/ojs/index.php/fm/article/view/967/888.

Watanabe, Yukiko, John M. Norris, and Marta González-Lloret. 2009. "Identifying and Responding to Evaluation Needs in College Foreign Language Programs." In *Toward Useful Program Evaluation in College Foreign Language Education,* edited by John M. Norris, J. McE. Davis, Castle Sinicrope, and Yukiko Watanabe, 5–58. Honolulu: University of Hawai'i, National Foreign Language Resource Center.

Webb, Alan, Scott A. Jeffrey, and Axel Schulz. 2010. "Factors Affecting Goal Difficulty and Performance When Employees Select Their Own Performance Goals: Evidence from the Field." *Journal of Management Accounting Research* 22, no. 1: 209–32.

Wehmeyer, Michael L., Martin Agran, and Carolyn Hughes. 1998. *Teaching Self-Determination to Students with Disabilities: Basic Skills for Successful Transition.* Baltimore: Brookes.

Wehmeyer, Michael L., Susan B. Palmer, Martin Agran, Dennis E. Mithaug, and James E. Martin. 2000. "Promoting Causal Agency: The Self-Determined Learning Model of Instruction." *Exceptional Children* 66, no. 4: 439–53.

Wehmeyer, Michael L., Karrie A. Shogren, Susan B. Palmer, Kendra L. Williams-Diehm, Todd D. Little, and Aaron Boulton. 2012. "The Impact of the Self-Determined Learning Model of Instruction on Student Self-Determination." *Exceptional Children* 78, no. 2: 135–53.

Weimer, Maryellen. 2002. *Learner-Centered Teaching: Five Key Changes to Practice.* Hoboken, NJ: Wiley.

Weinberg, Robert, Deanna Morrison, Megan Loftin, Thelma Horn, Elizabeth Goodwin, Emily Wright, and Carly Block. 2019. "Writing Down Goals: Does It Actually Improve Performance?" *Sport Psychologist* 33, no. 1: 35–41.

Weiner, Bernard. 2008. "Reflections on the History of Attribution Theory and Research: People, Personalities, Publications, Problems." *Social Psychology* 39, no. 3: 151–56.

Wenger, Etienne. 1998. *Communities of Practice: Learning, Meaning, and Identity.* Cambridge, UK: Cambridge University Press.

Wenger, Etienne, Richard McDermott, and William M. Snyder. 2002. *Cultivating Communities of Practice: A Guide to Managing Knowledge.* Boston: Harvard Business School Press.

Westbrook, Timothy Paul. 2014. "Global Contexts for Learning: Exploring the Relationship between Low-Context Online Learning and High-Context Learners." *Christian Higher Education* 13, no. 4: 281–94.

Williams, Jane R., and Michael A. Johnson. 2000. "Self-Supervisor Agreement: The Influence of Feedback Seeking on the Relationship between Self and Supervisor Ratings of Performance 1." *Journal of Applied Social Psychology* 30, no. 2: 275–92.

Williams, Teresa, Melissa Layne, and Phil Ice. 2014. "Online Faculty Perceptions on Effective Faculty Mentoring: A Qualitative Study." *Online Journal of Distance Learning Administration* 17, no. 2. https://www.westga.edu/~distance/ojdla/summer172/Williams_Layne_Ice172.html.

Windeatt, Scott. 2017. "Training Teachers to Create and Use Materials for Computer-Assisted Language Learning." In *Language Teacher Education and Technology: Approaches and Practices,* edited by Jeong-Bae Son and Scott Windeatt, 910–1109. New York: Bloomsbury.

Windes, Deborah L., and Faye L. Lesht. 2014. "The Effects of Online Teaching Experience and Institution Type on Faculty Perceptions of Teaching Online." *Online Journal of Distance Learning Administration* 17, no. 1. https://www.westga.edu/~distance/ojdla/spring171/windes_lesht171.html.

Winke, Paula, and Senta Goertler. 2008. "The Effectiveness of Technology-Enhanced Foreign Language Teaching." In *Opening Doors through Distance Language Education: Principles, Perspectives, and Practices*, edited by Senta Goertler and Paula Winke, 233–60. San Marcos, TX: CALICO.

Wisconsin Center for Education Research. n.d. "Aris: Create Location-Based Games and Stories." Field Day Learning Games, University of Wisconsin. Accessed October 30, 2019. https://fielddaylab.org/make/aris/.

Wolcott, Linda L. 1997. "Tenure, Promotion, and Distance Education: Examining the Culture of Faculty Rewards." *American Journal of Distance Education* 11, no. 2: 3–18.

Wolcott, Linda L., and Kristen S. Betts. 1999. "What's in It for Me? Incentives for Faculty Participation in Distance Education." *Journal of Distance Education* 14, no. 2: 34–49.

Wolf, Patricia D. 2006. "Best Practices in the Training of Faculty to Teach Online." *Journal of Computing in Higher Education* 17, no. 2: 47.

Wong, Andrew Lap-sang. 2007. "Cross-Cultural Delivery of e-Learning Programs: Perspectives from Hong Kong." *International Review of Research in Open and Distance Learning* 8, no. 3: 1–16.

Wong, Lillian, and Phil Benson. 2006. "In-Service CALL Education: What Happens after the Course Is Over?" In *Teacher Education in CALL*, edited by Philip Hubbard and Mike Levy, 251–66. Amsterdam: John Benjamins.

Wong, Lillian L. C., and David Nunan. 2011. "The Learning Styles and Strategies of Effective Language Learners." *System* 39: 144–63.

Wood, David, Jerome S. Bruner, and Gail Ross. 1976. "The Role of Tutoring in Problem Solving." *Journal of Child Psychology and Psychiatry* 17, no. 2: 89–100.

Wylie, E. Caroline, Laura Goe, Dawn Marie Leusner, Christine J. Lyon, Cynthia Tocic, E. Caroline Wylie, Donna Cleland et al. 2008. "Tight but Loose: Scaling Up Teacher Professional Development in Diverse Contexts." *ETS Research Report Series*, no. 1: i–141.

Xiao, Junhong. 2012. "Successful and Unsuccessful Distance Language Learners: An 'Affective' Perspective." *Open Learning: The Journal of Open, Distance and E- Learning* 27, no. 2:121–36. https://doi.org/10.1080/02680513.2012.678611.

Yuzer, Volkan T., Belgin Aydin, and S. Ipek Kuru Gonen. 2009. "Learners' Perceptions toward Online Learning: An Application for a Synchronous E-Class." *Journal of Educational Technology* 6, no. 2: 30–40.

Zeichner, Kenneth, and Daniel Liston. 1987. "Teaching Student Teachers to Reflect." *Harvard Educational Review* 57, no. 1: 23–49.

Zeichner, Kenneth M., and B. Robert Tabachnick. 1982. "The Belief Systems of University Supervisors in an Elementary Student-Teaching Program." *British Journal of Teacher Education* 8, no. 1: 34–54.

Zhang, Xiuyuan, and Gang Cui. 2010. "Learning Beliefs of Distance Foreign Language Learners in China: A Survey Study." *System* 38, no. 1: 30–40. https://doi.org/10.1016/j.system.2009.12.003.

Zhao, Yong. 2003. "Recent Developments in Technology and Language Learning: A Literature Review and Meta-Analysis." *CALICO Journal* 21, no. 1: 7–28.

Zhao, Yong, and Gary A. Cziko. 2001. "Teacher Adoption of Technology: A Perceptual Control Theory Perspective." *Journal of Technology and Teacher Education* 9, no. 1: 5–30.

Zimmerman, Barry J. 2000. "Attaining Self-Regulation: A Social Cognitive Perspective." In *Handbook of Self-Regulation*, edited by Monique Boekaerts, Paul R. Pintrich, and Moshe Zeider, 13–39. San Diego: Academic.

INDEX

Figures and tables are indicated by f and t following the page number.

ACTFL (American Council for the Teaching of Foreign Languages), 56–57; World Readiness Standards, 79, 87
adjunct faculty: assessment of, 117; as audience for CTE training, 25; goal setting for, 182, 184–85; mentorship relationships and, 162; OLIMR and, 133; self-evaluation practices and, 144, 146
administrators: assessment of instructors by, 17, 92–95, 110, 116–17, 131–32, 224–32, 247–48; cognitive investment strategies and, 47–49; core competencies for online language instruction and, 76, 89; critical CTE and, 188–90, 196–97; critical pedagogy and, 19; emotional investment strategies and, 51, 53–54, 56, 165; faculty accountability strategies and, 65, 67–68, 70; faculty resistance to online learning and, 13, 188; functional investment strategies and, 58–61, 65; mentorship programs and, 167–69; normalization of CTE training and, 188–90; self-evaluation practices for, 140–41
Allwright, Dick, 140
Álvarez Valdivia, Ibis, 86
American Council for the Teaching of Foreign Languages (ACTFL), 56–57; World Readiness Standards, 79, 87
Americans with Disabilities Act of 1990, 55, 81
Anderson, Terry, 29, 63
Anthony, Natasha, 42
anxiety in online interactions, 46, 63–64, 85–86
Appel, Christine, 38

Archer, Walter, 29, 63
Arizona State University, 128
Arnold, Nike, 29, 30
assessment of instructors, 93–186; audience considerations for, 126–27; context of, 122–23; debriefing stages and strategies, 171–74, 173t; by departmental administrators, 131–32, 224–26, 228–29, 231–32, 247–48; ecological approach to, 124–27; formative assessments, 124–26, 216–17; goal setting and, 174–85; high-stakes assessments, 126; implementation ideas for, 118–19, 135; importance of, 121–22; initiatives for increased faculty assessment, 123–24; institutional evaluations, 129–32; instruments for, 121–35; language program assessment, 93–96; low-stakes assessments, 126; mentorship and, 129–30, 151–69; OLIMR for, 132–35, 237–47; online competencies and skills, 98–118; self-evaluation practices, 137–50; student evaluations, 127–29, 233–37; summative assessments, 124–26, 217–19; by supervisors, 130–31, 222–24, 228, 230–31, 247–48
Association of American Colleges and Universities, 118
asynchronous online faculty development, 59
audience: in assessment of instructors, 124, 126–27; course design and, 35, 37; for CTE training, 22–23, 25–26, 39; evaluation skills and, 88
autonomy of instructors, 13, 52–53, 158
Aydin, Belgin, 86

Baki, Roselan, 37
Başöz, Tutku, 37
Bauer-Ramazani, Christine, 28, 36, 38, 51, 72
Bax, Stephen, 188, 189
Beaven, Tita, 37, 59, 61
Belz, Julie A., 29, 41
Bennett, Liz, 97
Bennett, Milton, 118
Bennett, Shirley, 102
Benson, Phil, 38, 68
Berber-McNeill, Rebecca, 40
Blake, Robert, 3, 4
Blin, Françoise, 38
Bloom's Taxonomy, 178
Brown, John Seeley, 27
Brown, Jonathan, 36
Bruce, Catherine, 130
Bruner, Jerome, 152
Budhrani, Kiran, 15
Byram, Michael, 55, 191

Caffarella, Rosemary S., 16
CALL (computer-assisted language learning): expansion of, 2, 21–22; functional investment strategies and, 61; integration of technologies for online language teaching, 4–5, 78; need to embrace, 3–4; normalization of, 189–93, 197; technologies for, 4, 39, 42, 75, 111, 115, 188–90. *See also* CTE (CALL teacher eduction)
Candy, Philip, 158
CASLS (Center for Applied Language Studies), 141
Catalano, Theresa, 82
CCA (critical cultural awareness), 50, 54–56, 82–83, 90, 118–19, 187, 191–97
Center for Applied Language Studies (CASLS), 141
Chambers, Andrea, 189
Chametzky, Barry, 85–86
Chao, Chin-chi, 38
Chapelle, Carol, 88, 95, 108, 111
Chen, Guo-Ming, 118
Chen, Nian-Shing, 38
Chik, Alice, 72

CK (content knowledge), 73–74, 74f, 141
cognitively based challenges and investment strategies, 47–50
COIL (Collaborative Online International Learning), 83
collaboration: in assessment frameworks for instructors, 112–15, 125; core competencies for instructors, 75–76, 84, 90, 211–12; course design and, 38; CTE training and assessment and, 22–23, 29–30; functional investment strategies and, 61; normalization of CTE and, 189
Collaborative Online International Learning (COIL), 83
Collins, Allan, 27
Comas-Quinn, Anna, 43, 53
communicative competence, 31, 61, 100–102, 104–7, 160
communities of practice, 29–30, 153
community building: in assessment frameworks for instructors, 107–9, 115; collaboration and, 84; core competencies and, 84–85; importance of, 14; in mentorship relationships, 153; platforms for, 4–5; reflective learning and, 29–30
Compton, Lily: assessment framework for online instructors, 98, 100, 105–10, 106f, 114–15, 133; on core competencies for instructors, 75, 77, 79–80, 87; CTE training framework, 30, 32–35; on evaluation skills, 87; on pedagogical skills, 79–80
computer-assisted language learning. *See* CALL
content knowledge (CK), 73–74, 74f, 141
Cope, Joann, 85
Cope, William, 71
core competencies for online language instructors, 71–92; assessment of instructors, 98–118; checklist for, 208–13; collaboration skills, 84, 211–12; communicative competence, 31, 61, 100–102, 104–7, 160; course design, 79–80, 209–10; development of, 71–73; evaluation skills, 87–89, 212–13; implementation ideas, 90–92; integration of technology skills, 73–89,

74f, 75t; interaction skills, 83–84, 211; operational competence, 111, 113, 139; pedagogical skills, 78–83, 209; professional development and professionalism, 89, 213; socialization skills, 84–87, 212; student-centered learning, 80–83, 210–11; technological skills, 77–78, 208–9
Council of Europe, 26
course design: audience and, 35, 37; collaboration and, 38; core competencies for instructors and, 79–80; in-service training and, 37–39; preservice training and, 36–37
COVID-19 pandemic, 9, 17, 86, 187
creativity: in assessment frameworks for instructors, 101–2, 104, 106–7, 109, 115; core competencies for instructors, 76, 81, 90; CTE training frameworks and, 31; functional investment strategies and, 63; pedagogical skills and, 81
critical CTE: action plan for creating and sustaining, 192–93; ecological approach to, 187–97; future research needs, 193–97; normalization of, 191
critical cultural awareness (CCA), 50, 54–56, 82–83, 90, 118–19, 187, 191–97
Cruz, Luis F., 6, 45–46, 47, 50, 58, 65, 70, 190
CTE (CALL teacher education): alternative modes of, 41–43; audience considerations, 25–26; breadth-first vs. depth-first approach, 26–27; challenges of, 45–70, 201–7; checklists for, 199–213; cognitive challenges and investment strategies, 47–50, 201–4; collaborative learning and, 29–30; communities of practice and, 29–30; Compton's framework for, 32–35; critical CTE approaches, 187–97; ecological view of, 5–6; effectiveness of, 39–41; elements of, 23–30, 199–201; emotional challenges and investment strategies, 50–57; faculty accountability challenges and strategies, 65–70, 69f, 206–7; formal modes for, 36–41; frameworks for, 30–35; functional challenges and investment strategies, 58–65, 204–6; Hampel and Stickler's framework for, 31–32; in-service training and course design, 37–39; mentorship for, 43; need for, 2; needs analysis of, 26; normalization of, 187–93; online training and assessment, 21–44; overview and theoretical base of, 21–23; preservice training and course design, 36–37; project-based learning development, 28; reflective learning and, 28–29; self-directed, 41–43; situated learning and, 27; strategies for, 45–70; teacher technology standards integrated into, 30; using technology to teach technology, 28. See also assessment of instructors; critical CTE
Çubukçu, Feryal, 37
Cui, Gang, 86
cultural issues: in assessment frameworks for instructors, 118, 122; collectivist cultures, 174, 181, 197; CTE training and, 24; departmental cultures, 5, 53, 68–69, 172, 188; ecological shift from physical to digital spaces, 10; emotional investment strategies and, 55–57; faculty accountability strategies and, 67–68; goal setting and, 180–82; institutional cultures, 65, 67; language instruction and, 2; mentorship relationships and, 154; normalization of CTE and, 191, 195–96; pedagogical skills and, 79, 82–83; post-observation debriefing and, 172, 174; self-evaluation practices and, 143; student-centered learning and, 82–83. See also critical cultural awareness

Dailey-Hebert, Amber, 59
Davies, Graham, 75
Davis, John, 95
Davis, Niki, 34
debriefing stages and strategies, 171–74, 173t
Debski, Robert, 28
departmental administrators: assessment of instructors by, 110, 118, 121, 131–32, 224–32, 247–48; emotional investment

departmental administrators (*continued*)
    strategies and, 54; functional investment strategies and, 61. *See also* administrators
Desjardins, François, 34
Developmental Model of Intercultural Sensitivity, 118
Dewey, John, 139, 156
Dixon, Kathryn, 124
Donnarumma, David, 97
DOTS (Developing Online Teaching Skills) project, 26, 38
Drewelow, Isabelle, 53
Ducate, Lara, 29
Duensing, Annette, 23
Duguid, Paul, 27

Easton, Susan, 23
ecological approach: in assessment frameworks for instructors, 117, 119, 124–27, 134–35; core competencies for instructors and, 90; to critical CTE, 187–97; in CTE training and assessment, 5–7, 23, 25; emotional investment strategies and, 55–56; faculty accountability strategies and, 66; goal setting and, 171, 174, 176, 182; mentorship relationship and, 151; pedagogical skills and, 82; self-evaluation practices and, 137
Egbert, Joy, 27, 33, 36, 37
Eib, B. J., 153
Ellis, Rod, 80
Ellis, Roger, 123
emotionally based challenges and investment strategies, 50–57
Enright, Mary K., 95
Ernest, Pauline, 30, 38, 103, 130
Eskenazi, Maxine, 36
European Centre for Modern Languages, 26
evaluation skills, 66, 87–89, 108, 212–13
experiential learning, 28, 73, 139
expertise: in assessment frameworks for instructors, 102, 105–6, 114–16; collaborative learning and, 29–30; CTE training effectiveness and, 40; faculty accountability strategies and, 67; functional investment strategies and, 58;

mentorship relationship and, 43, 153, 161; self-evaluation practices and, 138

faculty: accountability challenges and strategies, 65–70; asynchronous online faculty development, 59; development of, 65, 69, 69f, 152–53; resistance to online classes and training, 13, 16, 45, 50–57, 69f, 98, 188, 190; self-evaluation practices, 66, 87, 131. *See also* adjunct faculty; assessment of instructors
Faculty Survey of Student Engagement, 3
Fairclough, Stephen, 172
feedback: in assessment frameworks for instructors, 93, 96, 98, 112, 114, 119, 123–24, 127, 129–30, 132–35; constructive, 127, 131, 135, 171, 173; CTE course design and, 39, 41; cultural issues related to, 7, 196–97; faculty accountability strategies and, 66–67; functional investment strategies and, 61; goal setting and, 182; in-service training and, 39; mentorship relationship and, 152, 159, 163, 165–67; in online spaces, 12–13; pedagogical skills and, 81; positive, 104, 172–73; in post-observation debriefing, 171–74; self-evaluation practices and, 140, 142–44, 148; socialization skills and, 85–86; student-centered learning and, 81; technological skills and, 78
Foreign Language Classroom Anxiety Scale, 85
formative assessments: in assessment frameworks for instructors, 124–26; mentorship relationship and, 151–69; self-evaluation practices and, 137–50
functionally based challenges and investment strategies, 6, 46, 58–65, 169, 188

Gallup survey of faculty attitudes toward technology (2019), 10
Garrison, D. Randy, 29, 63
gender issues in online language education, 18–19, 128. *See also* critical cultural awareness
Germain-Rutherford, Aline, 30

Giroux, Henry, 18
Gleason, Jesse, 71–72
goal setting in assessment process, 174–86; in assessment frameworks for instructors, 96; case study, 182–85; choice and, 175–76, 181; commitment to, 177–78, 181–82; cultural differences in, 180–82; effort and, 176–77; implementation ideas, 186; motivation and, 181–82; strategy for, 178–80
Goertler, Senta, 40, 49
Gonen, S. Ipek Kuru, 86
Graves, Kathleen, 76
Grosbois, Muriel, 29
Gruba, Paul, 95, 96
Guichon, Nicolas, 29, 33, 41, 75, 85, 140
Guillén, Gabriel, 4

Hafner, Christoph, 72
Hamilton, Sarah, 97
Hampel, Regine: assessment framework for online instructors, 98, 100–105, 101*f*, 104*f*, 107–8, 115, 133; on core competencies for instructors, 75, 86; CTE training framework, 23–24, 30, 31–32, 34–35, 40, 42; on functional investment strategies, 63; on mentorships, 152; on self-evaluation practices, 141
Hanson-Smith, Elizabeth, 29, 42, 50–51, 64, 76
Hauck, Mirjam, 33, 41, 75
Healey, Deborah: assessment framework for online instructors, 98, 110–18, 133; on core competencies for instructors, 75, 88; CTE training framework, 26, 28, 29, 30, 40; on faculty resistance to online classes, 45; on functional investment strategies, 58
Hegelheimer, Volker, 33, 36, 111
high-stakes assessments, 126
Hinkelman, Don, 96
Hong, Kwang Hee, 4–5, 188
hooks, bell, 18
Hopkins, Joseph, 130
Horwitz, Elaine, 85
Horwitz, Michael B., 85

Hoven, Deborah, 26
Hubbard, Phil, 21, 25, 34, 36–40, 42, 62, 74, 76, 188, 190
Hurd, Stella, 85, 86

Information and Communication Technologies Competency Standards for Teachers (UNESCO), 110
in-service training and course design, 37–39
Inside Higher Ed, 10, 13
institutional cultures, 65, 67
institutional evaluations, 129–32
interaction skills, 83–84, 211
intercultural sensitivity, 118, 194. *See also* critical cultural awareness; cultural issues
International Technology Education Association (ISTE), 71, 110

Jamieson, Joan, 88, 95
Johnson, Norman, 88
Jones, Christopher M., 38
Jones, Rodney, 72
June, Audrey Williams, 3

Kalantzis, Mary, 71
Kane, Michael, 95
Kearsley, Greg, 25, 33
Kessler, Greg, 33, 40, 41, 48, 52, 61, 62, 76, 111, 190
King Ramírez, Carmen, 24, 53, 62, 143–50, 161–68, 182–85
Knobel, Michele, 72
Knowles, Malcolm, 156
Knutson, Sonja, 139–40
Koehler, Mathew, 73
Kolaitis, Marinna, 42, 153
Kolb, David, 139
Kramsch, Claire, 3
Kuhn, Thomas, 1
Kumar, Swapna, 15

Lafford, Barbara, 5, 24, 53, 55–56, 62, 66, 82, 98, 189–90
Lai, Chun, 76, 80
Lankshear, Colin, 72
Lave, Jean, 27, 29

Levy, Mike, 5, 21, 25, 36, 38, 74, 76, 188
Lewis, Tim, 41, 140
Li, Guofang, 80
Li, Ning, 76
Livingston, Gretchen, 55
Lomicka, Lara, 29
low-stakes assessments, 126

MALL (mobile-assisted language learning), 4, 37, 55, 62, 78, 138
Mandernach, B. Jean, 17, 69–70, 71, 124, 130–32, 137–38
marginalized students, 54–55. *See also* critical cultural awareness
Marsh, Debra, 102
Martin, Florence, 15
Martin, Sidney, 86
Marzano, Robert, 64
massive open online courses (MOOCs), 15, 63
McDermott, Richard, 29
McDonald, Morva, 56
McKay, Todd, 95
McNulty, Brian, 64
Meloni, Christine Foster, 38
Menges, Robert, 129
mentorship: assessment of instructors by peer mentors, 129–30; case study, 161–68; challenges and opportunities in, 157–59; for CTE online training and assessment, 43; in formative assessment process, 151–69; implementation ideas, 168–69; online mentorship relationships, 153–56; positive mentor-instructor relationship, 159–60; self-evaluation facilitated by, 156–57, 157*f*
Meskill, Carla, 30, 42, 152
Miller, Pamela, 153
Mishra, Punyashloke, 73
mobile-assisted language learning (MALL), 4, 37, 55, 62, 78, 138
Modern Language Association, 67
Modern Language Journal, 5
Montelongo, Ricardo, 18
MOOCs (massive open online courses), 15, 63
Moore, Michael, 25, 33

More DOTS project, 26
motivation: assessment frameworks for instructors and, 110; core competencies for instructors and, 84; CTE training and, 45, 63; goal setting and, 177, 181; post-observation debriefing and, 173
Motteram, Gary, 28, 29, 140
Muhammad, Anthony, 6, 45–46, 47, 50, 58, 65, 70, 190
Müller-Hartmann, Andreas, 29, 41
Murphy-Judy, Kathryn, 76
Murphy, Linda, 85

Nakamichi, Yoko, 27, 33
National Center for Education Statistics, 10
National Educational Technology Standards (ISTE), 110
Nemiro, Jill, 154
New London Group, 71
No Child Left Behind campaign, 121
normalization of CTE, 5, 7, 57, 187–93
Nugent, Kristen, 82

Ocando Finol, María, 57
O'Dowd, Robert, 57
Olesova, Larissa, 38
OLIMR (Online Language Instructor Modular Rubric): assessment of instructors via, 132–35, 237–47; criteria determination for, 134–35; departmental administrator evaluations of, 231–32; instructions for application of, 133–34; self-evaluation practices in, 143–50, 248–49; stakeholder evaluations of, 229–32; supervisor evaluations of, 230–31
online language instruction: anxiety in online interactions, 46, 63–64, 85–86; challenges of, 9–20; core competencies for, 71–92, 208–13; critical pedagogy for, 18–19; ecological shift from physical to digital spaces, 3, 10–14; evaluation of instructors, 16–18, 233–49; performance rubrics, 233–49; training for, 14–16. *See also* assessment of instructors; CALL (computer-assisted language learning); CTE online training and assessment

Online Language Instructor Modular Rubric (OLIMR). *See* OLIMR (Online Language Instructor Modular Rubric)
online socialization, 101–4, 107, 109, 114
Open University, 31, 85, 100–101
operational competence, 111, 113, 139
Ortega, Lourdes, 193
O'Toole, Joanne, 56

Palloff, Rena: assessment framework for online instructors, 98, 99–100, 109; on critical CTE approach, 192; CTE training framework, 14, 15–16, 25–26; on self-evaluation practices, 137, 138, 140–41
Palmer, Susan, 179
Paulus, Trena, 27, 33
PCK (pedagogical content knowledge), 73–74, 74f
PEARLL (Professionals in Education Advancing Research and Language Learning), 141
pedagogical approaches and skills: in assessment frameworks for instructors, 98, 105, 108–9, 112, 114–15, 117, 125–26; core competencies for instructors, 75–83; critical pedagogy, 2, 6, 18, 23; CTE training and, 26, 33, 35, 40; emotional investment strategies and, 53–54; faculty accountability strategies and, 65–70; functional investment strategies and, 58, 60–61; online class challenges, 11; self-evaluation practices and, 143–44
pedagogical content knowledge (PCK), 73–74
pedagogical knowledge (PK), 30, 52, 73–75, 111–12
peer mentors: assessment frameworks for instructors and, 97, 118, 124, 129–32; functional investment strategies and, 64. *See also* mentorship
Perrin, Andrew, 55
Peters, Martine, 27, 33, 34, 36
Pew Research Center, 55
Pichette, François, 86
Pieper, Shannon K., 155

PK (pedagogical knowledge), 30, 52, 73–75, 111–12
post-observation debriefing, 171–74, 173t
Pratt, Keith: assessment framework for online instructors, 98, 99–100, 109; on critical CTE approach, 192; CTE training framework, 14, 15–16, 25–26; on self-evaluation practices, 137, 138, 140–41
Preiss, Sherry, 88
preservice training and course design, 36–37
professional development and professionalism: assessment frameworks for instructors and, 124, 133–35; cognitive investment strategies and, 47–48; core competencies for instructors and, 77, 89, 91, 213; CTE training and, 28–29, 43; functional investment strategies and, 64; goal setting in assessment process and, 183–84; mentorship and, 153, 157, 169; normalization of CTE and, 190, 192–94, 196; post-observation debriefing and, 171, 173; self-evaluation practices and, 145
Professionals in Education Advancing Research and Language Learning (PEARLL), 141
project-based learning, 28

Quality Matters standards, 80, 127, 128, 133

race and online language education pedagogy, 18–19. *See also* critical cultural awareness
Razali, Abu Bakar, 37
reflective learning, 25, 28–29, 35, 41, 140
Reppen, Randi, 183
Ricci, Peter, 153
Rickard, Angela, 38
Ritzhaupt, Albert, 15
Rogers, Everett, 188
Ross, Gail, 152
Ross, John, 130, 142

Samani, Ebrahim, 37
SCEs (student course evaluations), 127–29, 233–37

Schmitt, Elena, 71–72
Schön, Donald, 140
Scott, Shelleyann, 124
SDL (self-directed learning). *See* self-directed learning (SDL)
Self-Determined Learning Model of Instruction (SDLMI), 179–80
self-directed learning (SDL): CTE training and, 21, 32, 35, 41–43, 44, 46; functional investment strategies and, 58, 64; mentorships and, 158–59; normalization of critical CTE and, 187, 190, 192
self-evaluation practices, 137–50; checklists for, 137–39; implementation ideas, 150; mentorship relationship and, 156–57, 157*f*; in OLIMR evaluation process, 143–50, 248–49; with professional learning network, 142–43
Shor, Ira, 18
Shulman, Lee, 73
situated learning, 22, 25, 27–28, 80, 140
Slaouti, Diane, 28, 29, 140
Sloan Consortium, 152
Smith, Aaron, 55
Smith, Bryan, 4
Snyder, William, 29
socialization skills: in assessment frameworks for instructors, 97–98, 106–7, 109, 114–15, 212; core competencies for instructors, 77, 79, 84–87; language learning and, 5; online socialization and, 101–4, 107, 109, 114
social justice issues, 54, 56, 83–84, 119, 187, 193–94
Son, Jeong-Bae, 38, 39
Starosta, William J., 118
Stickler, Ursula: assessment framework for online instructors, 98, 100–105, 101*f*, 104*f*, 107–8, 115, 133; on core competencies for instructors, 75; CTE training framework, 23, 24, 30, 31–32, 34–35, 40, 42; on mentorships, 152; on self-evaluation practices, 141
Stockwell, Glenn, 5, 42
student-centered learning, 80–83
student course evaluations (SCEs), 127–29, 233–37

summative assessments: in assessment frameworks for instructors, 93, 98, 124–26, 128–29, 131; core competencies for instructors and, 88, 91; CTE training and, 65, 70; goal setting and, 171, 174; self-evaluation practices and, 142, 150
Sun, Susan Yue Hua, 23, 75, 108–9
supervisors: assessment frameworks for instructors and, 97, 118, 129–35, 222–24, 228, 230–31, 247–48; core competencies for instructors and, 91–92; CTE training and, 47–48; emotional investment strategies and, 51, 53–54; faculty accountability strategies and, 66; functional investment strategies and, 59–61; goal setting and, 174–83, 185–86; involvement in cognitive investment strategies, 48; mentorships and, 151, 153, 155–56, 159–61, 165, 167–68; normalization of critical CTE and, 190, 196–97; post-observation debriefings and, 171–74, 173*t*; self-evaluation practices and, 142–43, 145, 148, 150

Tai, Shu-Ju Diana, 73
TAs (teaching assistants). *See* teaching assistants (TAs)
Taylor, Ann, 17, 69–70, 71, 124, 130–32, 137–38
TCK (technological content knowledge), 73–74, 74*f*
teaching assistants (TAs): assessment frameworks for instructors and, 117, 126, 133; CTE training and, 22, 25, 36–37; emotional investment strategies and, 53; functional investment strategies and, 64; normalization of critical CTE and, 197
teaching styles, 12, 97, 102, 117, 125–26, 140. *See also* pedagogical approaches and skills
Teaching Tolerance initiative, 56
technological content knowledge (TCK), 73–74, 74*f*
technological knowledge (TK), 73–74, 74*f*, 98, 139
technological pedagogical content knowledge (TPACK), 73–76, 74*f*, 90

technological pedagogical knowledge (TPK), 73–74, 75t
technological skills: in assessment frameworks for instructors, 101, 103–4, 107–8, 114; core competencies for instructors, 77–78; emotional investment strategies and, 56–57; functional investment strategies and, 61, 62; integration of technology, 21, 26, 44–47, 52, 59, 66, 70, 73–78, 95, 188; mentorships and, 153; standards for, 76–77, 110–11, 114; training for, 27, 33–34, 36, 40, 49
TESOL Technology Standards, 94, 110–18, 138–39, 140
Tesone, Dana, 153
Theoharis, George, 56
Thorne, Steve, 4
time management issues, 50–51, 164
TK (technological knowledge), 73–74, 74f, 98, 139
Tobin, Martin, 129–30
Tobin, Thomas, 17, 69–70, 71, 98, 124, 130–32, 137–38, 194
Torsani, Simone, 28, 29, 37, 38, 76, 140
TPACK (technological pedagogical content knowledge), 73–76, 74f, 90
TPK (technological pedagogical knowledge), 73–74, 74f
training. *See* CTE (CALL teacher education)
tutors, 25, 31–35, 48, 105, 152

Ubell, Robert, 13

UN Education, Scientific, and Cultural Organization (UNESCO), 110
Universal Design for Learning, 80

Van Manen, Max, 156
Vásquez, Camilla, 183
Venables, Louise, 172
virtual environments, 23–24, 38, 58, 154
Vygotsky, Lev, 152

Wang, Yuping, 38
Warschauer, Mark, 4, 72, 82, 191
Waters, Timothy, 64
Web Content Accessibility Guidelines, 55, 81
Wehmeyer, Michael, 179
Wenger, Etienne, 27, 29
Wermers, James, 24, 53, 62, 66
Windeatt, Scott, 38, 39, 40
Winke, Paula, 40, 49
Wong, Lillian, 38, 68
Wood, David, 152
Wylie, E. Caroline, 126

Xiao, Junhong, 86

Youngs, Bonnie, 38, 76
Yuzer, Volkan, 86

Zhang, Xiuyuan, 86
Zhao, Yong, 76, 110–11
Zone of Proximal Development (ZPD), 22, 152

ABOUT THE AUTHORS

CARMEN KING RAMÍREZ is an associate professor of Spanish at the University of Arizona. She is the founding director of the University of Arizona online Spanish program. Dr. King Ramírez has developed course curricula, trained instructors, and taught for online language programs at the University of Arizona, Arizona State University, and la Universidad de Sonora. Her research interests include online teacher training and assessment, international education, Spanish in the United States, and languages for specific purposes. Dr. King Ramírez has published in various peer refereed journals and academic volumes and coedited the volume *Transferable Skills for the 21st Century: Preparing Students for the Workplace through World Languages for Specific Purposes* (2018) with Barbara A. Lafford. Her publications pertaining to online education include an article in the *Hispania* (2018) centenary edition, a coauthored chapter with Barbara A. Lafford and James E. Wermers in the volume *Assessment across Online Language Education* (2018; Stephanie Link and Jinrong Li, coeditors), and an article on collaborative online international learning in the *Journal of Studies in International Education* (2019).

BARBARA A. LAFFORD is professor emerita of Spanish from Arizona State University. For close to four decades she trained and supervised teaching assistants and language instructors who taught courses in face-to-face, hybrid, and online formats. Her research areas include Spanish sociolinguistics, second language acquisition, Spanish applied linguistics, computer-assisted language learning, and languages for specific purposes. Professor Lafford has served as associate editor for the applied linguistics section of *Hispania* (1996–2002), chair of the board for CALICO (the Computer-Assisted Language Instruction Consortium) in 2006–7, and as editor for the Monograph/Focus Issue Series of the *Modern Language Journal* (*MLJ*) from 2005 to 2014, in which she published a 2009 volume dedicated to CALL issues. In addition, she and her two coauthors (Peter A. Lafford and Julie Sykes) received the CALICO research award in 2007 for the most outstanding article published in that journal during that calendar year ("Entre dicho y hecho....: An Assessment of the Application of Second Language Acquisition and Related

Research to the Creation of Spanish CALL Materials for Lexical Acquisition"). In 2018 her coauthored article (with Carmen King de Ramírez and James Wermers) appeared in the volume *Assessment across Online Language Education* (Stephanie Link and Jinrong Li, coeditors). Professor Lafford also has coedited two successful volumes on Spanish second language acquisition and teaching for Georgetown University Press with Rafael Salaberry (*Spanish Second Language Acquisition: State of the Science*, 2003; *The Art of Teaching Spanish: Second Language Acquisition from Research to Praxis*, 2006) and has coedited the book *Transferable Skills for the 21st Century: Preparing Students for the Workplace through World Languages for Specific Purposes* (2018) with Carmen King Ramírez.

JAMES E. WERMERS is a clinical assistant professor of humanities in the Languages and Cultures unit in the College of Integrative Sciences and Arts, a faculty fellow in the Center for the Study of Race and Democracy, and a faculty affiliate in the Arizona Center for Medieval and Renaissance Studies at Arizona State University. He publishes on Shakespeare, pedagogy, and issues of race and democracy (often all at once); teaches courses in composition, film, gender studies, literature, philosophy, and religious studies; and develops and leads innovative and engaging community programs like Words on Wheels. In 2018 his coauthored article (with Carmen King de Ramírez and Barbara A. Lafford) appeared in the volume *Assessment across Online Language Education* (Stephanie Link and Jinrong Li, coeditors).

www.ingramcontent.com/pod-product-compliance
Lightning Source LLC
Chambersburg PA
CBHW030524230426
43665CB00010B/759